Server-Side Flash™:
Scripts, Databases, and
Dynamic Development

Server-Side Flash™: Scripts, Databases, and Dynamic Development

William B. Sanders and Mark Winstanley

Hungry Minds™

Best-Selling Books • Digital Downloads • e-Books • Answer Networks • e-Newsletters • Branded Web Sites • e-Learning

New York, NY ✦ Cleveland, OH ✦ Indianapolis, IN

Server-Side Flash™: Scripts, Databases, and Dynamic Development

Published by
Hungry Minds, Inc.
909 Third Avenue
New York, NY 10022
www.hungryminds.com

Library of Congress Control Number: 2001089312

ISBN: 0-7645-3598-6

Printed in the United States of America

10 9 8 7 6 5 4 3 2 1

1B/SQ/QW/QR/IN

Distributed in the United States by Hungry Minds, Inc.

Distributed by CDG Books Canada Inc. for Canada; by Transworld Publishers Limited in the United Kingdom; by IDG Norge Books for Norway; by IDG Sweden Books for Sweden; by IDG Books Australia Publishing Corporation Pty. Ltd. for Australia and New Zealand; by TransQuest Publishers Pte Ltd. for Singapore, Malaysia, Thailand, Indonesia, and Hong Kong; by Gotop Information Inc. for Taiwan; by ICG Muse, Inc. for Japan; by Intersoft for South Africa; by Eyrolles for France; by International Thomson Publishing for Germany, Austria, and Switzerland; by Distribuidora Cuspide for Argentina; by LR International for Brazil; by Galileo Libros for Chile; by Ediciones ZETA S.C.R. Ltda. for Peru; by WS Computer Publishing Corporation, Inc., for the Philippines; by Contemporanea de Ediciones for Venezuela; by Express Computer Distributors for the Caribbean and West Indies; by Micronesia Media Distributor, Inc. for Micronesia; by Chips Computadoras S.A. de C.V. for Mexico; by Editorial Norma de Panama S.A. for Panama; by American Bookshops for Finland.

For general information on Hungry Minds' products and services please contact our Customer Care department within the U.S. at 800-762-2974, outside the U.S. at 317-572-3993 or fax 317-572-4002.

For sales inquiries and reseller information, including discounts, premium and bulk quantity sales, and foreign-language translations, please contact our Customer Care department at 800-434-3422, fax 317-572-4002 or write to Hungry Minds, Inc., Attn: Customer Care Department, 10475 Crosspoint Boulevard, Indianapolis, IN 46256.

For information on licensing foreign or domestic rights, please contact our Sub-Rights Customer Care department at 212-884-5000.

For information on using Hungry Minds' products and services in the classroom or for ordering examination copies, please contact our Educational Sales department at 800-434-2086 or fax 317-572-4005.

For press review copies, author interviews, or other publicity information, please contact our Public Relations department at 317-572-3168 or fax 317-572-4168.

For authorization to photocopy items for corporate, personal, or educational use, please contact Copyright Clearance Center, 222 Rosewood Drive, Danvers, MA 01923, or fax 978-750-4470.

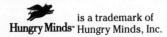 is a trademark of Hungry Minds, Inc.

About the Authors

William B. Sanders has published two previous books on Flash 5 and has been an avid devotee of Flash since Flash 3. Having written a total of 35 computer books on a range of topics from assembly language programming to hypertext scripts, Bill's diverse background helped provide the wide range of connections with Flash 5 on the server-side found in this book. Bill is a professor in the University of Hartford's innovative program in Interactive Information Technology. He lives in a rural setting in Connecticut with his wife, Delia, and dog, Bogee.

Mark Winstanley is the author and editor of many books focusing on Flash. He is an accomplished computer programmer and musician who consults for clients such as Virgin Records and Time Warner. Mark is president and cofounder of MultiMeteor, Inc., which hosts the FlashCore.com worldwide community, Web site, and developer training, as well as the Los Angeles Macromedia Flash Users Group. Currently living and working in Los Angeles, he is always achieving new ways of bringing convergence and technological integration to the forefront of development and sharing his knowledge with the Web development community at large.

Credits

Acquisitions Editors
Michael L. Roney and Carol Sheehan

Senior Project Editor
Jodi Jensen

Development Editor
Heather Stith

Technical Editors
Joel Lee and Jonathan Danylko
JTL Networks, Inc.

Copy Editor
Heather Stith

Editorial Manager
Colleen Totz

Project Coordinator
Nancee Reeves

Graphics and Production Specialists
Heather Pope, Brian Torwelle,
Jeremey Unger

Quality Control Technician
Laura Albert, Carl Pierce, Charles
Spencer

Permissions Editor
Laura Moss

Media Development Specialist
Angela Denny

Media Development Coordinator
Marisa E. Pearman

Cover Image
Deborah Reincrio

Special Help
Jeremy Zucker, Jean Rogers,
William A. Barton

Proofreading and Indexing
TECHBOOKS Production Services, Inc.

Preface

Flash 5 is well known as a powerful and dynamic front end for the Web. However, Flash is also a great interface for server-side applications. Unlike forms in HTML that require different code for different browsers, Flash 5 is stable across browsers. This stability means that viewers of any Flash movie see the same thing no matter what browser they're using, and the developer has to write only one version of a movie.

This book shows you exactly how to work with server-side applications with everything from CGI to PHP. And it shows you how to create XML documents and read the documents using Flash 5's new ActionScript XML objects. You also learn how to create and use Generator objects in Flash. On top of that, we tried to include all the little undocumented secrets in Flash that even some of the pros don't know about, such as using cookies with Flash and printing what you want from Flash.

For some readers, this book may be your first venture into the server-side world of the Internet and the Web. To make the transition as enriching and pleasing as possible, we provide tutorials for using Active Server Pages (VBScript), Perl/CGI, PHP, and XML. Likewise, the Structured Query Languages of both SQL and MySQL are introduced so that you can pull data out of a Microsoft Access or MySQL file. Even if you know nothing about the server-side world of the Web, you can use this book to create and launch your own server-side applications that are fully integrated with Flash 5.

To further ease your transition from client-side to server-side scripts, we've made arrangements with hosting services for readers to have free trial access to a real-world server while learning the material. In this way, you can use any version of Windows or Macintosh OS while your server scripts reside on an NT or Linux server. So, even if you have never worked with any type of server-side applications, CGI, PHP, and ASP will be much easier to master because you won't have to format your system to be both client and server. The section "Using the Free Trial Hosting Services" at the end of this Preface gives you more details. In addition, you can find steps for accessing these free services in both the "What's on the CD-ROM?" appendix and on the CD bound into the back of the book.

Who Should Read This Book?

This book is designed for the Flash Web developer and/or designer who wants to take the next step and enter the server-side world of the Web using Flash 5. To many Flash developers, the server side of the Web seems shrouded in mystery and complexity, and we want to open up this exciting new world where Flash 5 can be employed. Readers should be familiar with both Flash 5 and Flash 5 ActionScript. You don't need to be an expert in Flash or ActionScript, but you should have some experience using both.

Most of the Flash 5 movies and scripts we use as examples are straightforward and designed to show you how to connect Flash with a server-side application. The tutorials in Perl, ASP, PHP, and XML are designed to give you a practical running start in each of these languages, and this book serves as an introduction to these advanced topics as they relate to Flash. The several little projects in the book are meant to help you through this transition, and two larger projects in gaming and e-commerce at the end of the book show how you can use Flash 5 and ActionScript with practical applications.

What Hardware and Software Do You Need?

This book was designed around Flash 5, so the recommended hardware and software is what's required for Flash. All of the server-side scripts are intended for placement on remote servers. You can configure certain systems to act as both host and client, but such configurations are wholly dependent on the type of system you have and what type of server-side software you want to include on your own system. If you use your own system as client and server, you will need more than the recommended amounts of memory and disk space. We have included software for an Apache server, MySQL, and PHP on the disk with this book for those of you who want to transfer them to your own system.

For the purpose of learning how to use the different types of server-side software, we use both JTLNet.com (Apache server) and HosTek.com (NT Server). These two companies are offering 30 days of free Web hosting for readers of this book. (See "Using the Free Trial Hosting Services" section at the end of this Preface.) You also can download a free, 30-day trial of the Macromedia Generator Server from www.macromedia.com. So by buying this book, you have access to server resources for just about everything covered in these pages.

Windows

Macromedia recommends the following minimum requirements for running Flash 5 on a Windows system:

- ✦ Intel Pentium processor; 133 MHz or equivalent (200 MHz recommended) processor
- ✦ Windows 95/98, ME, Windows 2000, NT 4.0 or later
- ✦ 32MB of available RAM (64MB recommended)
- ✦ 40MB of available disk space
- ✦ Color monitor capable of 800 × 600 resolution
- ✦ CD-ROM drive

Macintosh

Macromedia recommends the following minimum requirements for running Flash 5 on a Macintosh:

- ✦ Power Macintosh PowerPC (G3 or higher recommended)
- ✦ MacOS 8.5 or later
- ✦ 32MB of available RAM
- ✦ 40MB of available disk space
- ✦ Color monitor capable of 800 × 600 resolution
- ✦ CD-ROM drive

Note   These are the minimum requirements. As with all graphics-based design tools, more capability is definitely better for using Flash 5, especially in terms of memory and processor speed.

How This Book Is Organized

This book is divided into four parts.

Part I: A Walk on the Server Side

Part I begins with an overview of moving information between Flash and the Internet. The first chapter explains what you need to know about the ways in which Flash 5 and ActionScript move data and variables into and out of a Flash movie on the Web. After you understand the fundamentals of moving data into and out of Flash, the second chapter jumps right in with information about using CGI (Common Gateway Interface) and the server-side programming language Perl.

Chapters 3 and 4 introduce two middleware languages: ASP and PHP. Most of the work in ASP is handled by VBScript, a language that is a close cousin of Microsoft Visual Basic. Chapter 3 also shows you how to work with Structured Query Language (SQL, pronounced *sequel*) to read data from and write data to database files such as those generated by Microsoft Access. Chapter 4 provides an introduction to an exciting new server-side language called PHP. This language is very similar to ActionScript and works on Apache servers. Chapter 4 also introduces you to a database language called MySQL (pronounced *my S-Q -L*) and helps you understand the relationship between PHP, MySQL, and Flash. By the end of Part I, you'll be able to write server-side scripts in Perl, VBScript, and PHP and work with both SQL and MySQL databases.

Part II: Back End Objects and Printing

In the second part, the book explores the world of XML, printing, and Macromedia Generator. The introduction of a set of XML objects in Flash 5 ActionScript produced a great deal of excitement, but many Flash users were not sure what XML documents were or how to use XML objects within Flash. Chapter 5 attempts to fill this void by introducing XML and DTD (document type definitions) and explaining how to use Flash to read data from a well-formed XML file.

Printing in Flash is another ignored area where data in Flash must be sent outside of one's computer to a printer. Chapter 6 shows all of the tricks and techniques for getting what's in Flash 5 to a printer and on paper.

The final chapter in Part II covers a much ignored, but very powerful, Flash 5 feature: Generator. Chapter 7 explores the data-formatting techniques for the various Generator objects. This chapter includes clear explanations and examples of how to use the many different charts, lists, tickers, and plots that you can create in Flash and dynamically change by using the Generator Server. Chapter 7 also explains how to set up and use the server.

Part III: The Dynamics of Gaming

Part III includes two chapters about the most dynamic aspects of game development with Flash. Chapter 8 gets into all the little (and not so little) techniques and tricks that game developers use in Flash 5. The chapter explains object manipulation and the most efficient ways to deal with tracking multiple objects in Flash 5. These concepts are essential to understand — whether you are working with Flash in general or working with all the pieces that go into a game. Chapter 9 expands on the dynamic elements discussed in Chapter 8 as it walks you through the development of a more complex game.

Part IV: The Two Sides of an eBusiness

The book finishes up with Flash 5 movies and server-side scripts that are involved in the process of setting up and administering an eBusiness site on the Web. Chapter 10 shows you all the steps needed in Flash 5 to create the client side of the eBusiness. The business has bouncing drop-down menus from which the customer can select products or services in an online Web design shop. The data for the transaction is recorded and then sent off to a PHP script for processing. The site includes all the crucial elements of a good eBusiness site, including a contact form that automatically sends the viewer an e-mail, in addition to a conventional e-mail button. The site even features a floating Cart Recorder so that the customer can see how much he or she has spent as items are added to the shopping cart.

Chapter 11 shows you how to create an eBusiness administrative tool and write PHP scripts that record the data from the eBusiness front end in a MySQL database and retrieve them in the Flash data-administration utility. You can use both of the eBusiness movies to do everything except take money to the bank!

Conventions Used in This Book

We use the following conventions throughout this book.

Windows and Macintosh conventions

Because *Server-Side Flash: Scripts, Databases, and Dynamic Development* is a cross-platform book, it gives instructions for both Windows and Macintosh users when keystrokes for a particular task differ. Throughout this book, the Windows keystrokes are given first, followed by the Macintosh keystrokes.

Key combinations

When you are instructed to press two or more keys simultaneously, each key in the combination is separated by a plus sign, as shown in the following example:

Ctrl+Alt+T (Cmd+Option+T)

The first key combination tells you that if you're working in Windows, you should press the Ctrl, Alt, and T keys all at the same time. If you're working on a Mac, you should press the Cmd, Option, and T keys together. (In pressing the three keys, you can first hold down one or two of the keys and then add the final key. You don't have to press all three at exactly the same moment.) Release all the keys at the same time.

Mouse instructions

When you're instructed to *click* an item, move the mouse pointer to the specified item and click the mouse button once. Windows users use the left mouse button unless otherwise instructed. *Double-click* means to click the mouse button twice in rapid succession.

When you're instructed to select an item, you may click it once as previously described. If you are selecting text or multiple objects, click the mouse button once, hold it down, and then move the mouse to a new location. The color of the selected item or items inverts to indicate the selection. To clear the selection, click once anywhere on the Web page.

Menu commands

When you're instructed to select a command from a menu, you see the menu and the command separated by an arrow symbol. For example, when you're asked to choose the Open command from the File menu, you see the notation File ⇨ Open. Some menus use submenus, in which case you see an arrow for each submenu: Modify ⇨ Transform ⇨ Edit Center.

Typographical conventions

We use *italic* type to indicate new terms and for emphasis. We use **boldface** type to indicate text that you need to type directly from the computer keyboard.

Code

A special typeface indicates ActionScript or other code, as demonstrated in the following example of PHP code:

```
for($counter=0;$counter<$cusNum;$counter++) {
    $row=mysql_fetch_row($result);
}
```

This special code font is also used within paragraphs to make elements such as XML tags (`</name>`) stand out from the regular text.

Italic type in this special font is used in code syntax definitions to indicate that you must substitute an actual parameter in place of the italicized word(s):

```
loadVariablesNum( url , levelnumber);
```

Navigating This Book

This book is highly modular. You can read most of the chapters without reading earlier chapters. Chapters 7 and 8 (Generator objects and the Generator Server), 9 and 10 (game project), and 11 and 12 (eBusiness project) should be read as modules by reading the first of the pair before the second. However, the rest of the book is a set of independent chapters focusing on different server-side and back-end applications. For example, you might want to read the chapter on ASP (Chapter 3) and then the chapter on printing (Chapter 6). Reading Chapter 1 first may help you get an overview of how Flash 5 works when communicating over the Internet. Otherwise, you can read the book in just about any order you find most useful.

Icons appear in the text to indicate important or especially helpful items. Here's a list of the icons and their functions:

Tips provide you with extra knowledge that separates the novice from the pro.

Notes provide additional or critical information and technical data on the current topic.

Cross-Reference icons indicate places where you can find more information on a particular topic.

The Caution icon is your warning of a potential problem or pitfall.

The On the CD-ROM icon indicates that the accompanying CD-ROM contains a related file in the given folder. See the "What's on the CD-ROM?" appendix for more information about using the CD.

Using the Free Trial Hosting Services

We realized very early in the writing phase of this book that learning to use server-side applications would be much easier for readers if we used common server resources. Using common resources also meant that readers wouldn't have to wade through separate explanations of the different versions of Windows and the Macintosh operating systems to get to the version they needed. We wanted to include both Windows NT servers for ASP and Apache servers for PHP, and we knew that we had to find hosting services that anyone could use. After locating the best hosting services we could find—JTLNet.com (Linux based) and HosTek.com (NT Server)— we arranged for the purchasers of this book to have 30 days of Web hosting at no charge.

In the book, we explain how to use each hosting service for setting up your server-side scripts and databases. When learning to use ASP (Chapter 3), use the HosTek service with the NT Server; when learning to use PHP (Chapter 4), use JTLNet, which has an Apache server. Either service readily handles Perl and CGI (Chapter 2). After your one-month trial is over, you may elect to continue the service with one or the other (or both) providers. Both offer hosting programs for under $10 per month, and they both provide outstanding customer support—that's why we selected them. If you don't have your own hosting service that offers the kind of server-side support you need (for example, Perl, PHP, ASP, MySQL), we believe you will find great value in either of these two services. To get the most out of the free trials, we suggest that you use them sequentially rather than set them both up at the same time. To initiate your free trial hosting service, see the information provided in the "What's on the CD-ROM?" appendix or on the CD-ROM bound into the back of this book.

If you decide not to transfer any domains to the hosting services but to use them instead as test environments, be sure to remember the unique information given to you when you sign up. For example, in most cases in this book when you need to enter a URL to your Web server, you see this in the sample code:

```
http://www.yourdomain.com
```

If you haven't transferred an actual domain name to your Web-hosting test environment, you won't be entering an address that starts with www. Instead, you must type the unique URL provided to you when you sign up with either JTLNet or HosTek. Here's an example of a unique URL from JTLNet:

```
http://thebes.jtlnet.com/~youraccount/pagename.html
```

When signing up with one of the free Web-hosting services, you might be given an IP address to use instead of a domain. However, using the IP address works the same way. For example, instead of the domain name you would enter your IP address such as

```
http:// 216.15.158.57/pagename.asp
```

Specific information on how to access your account is provided when you sign up for the hosting service.

Further Information

You can find more help for specific problems and questions by investigating several Web sites. Macromedia's own Flash Web site is a good place to start:

    www.flash.com

We also recommend visiting the following server-side support sites:

    www.php.net

    www.mysql.com

    www.apache.org

    www.tcp-ip.com (Active Server Pages & VBScript)

    www.msdn.microsoft.com/scripting/ (Select VBScript)

    www.cpan.org (Comprehensive Perl Archive Network)

    www.w3.org/XML/ (A real treasure trove for XML)

    www.macromedia.com (Path: Home ➪ Products ➪ Generator)

You can contact the authors through their respective sites:

    www.sandlight.com (Bill)

    www.flashcore.com (Mark)

Acknowledgments

We were most fortunate to work with the great people who assisted us in this book in one way or another. Gayle Pietras and Meredith Searcy at Macromedia provided product information and logistical support for Generator and the Generator servers. Other technical advice from Macromedia was supplied by Eric Wittman, Brad Bechtel, Matt Wobensmith, Mike William, and Jeremy Clark. The technical editing by Joel Lee and Jonathan Danylko was first rate and always helpful. Maria Tepora at Flashnique.com and Nate Yarrington at Entertainovision.com provided graphics used in some of the example files. Many of the color combinations relied on Leslie Cabarga's books *The Designer's Guide to Color Combinations* (North Light Books, 1999) and *The Designer's Guide to Global Color Combinations* (North Light Books, expected November 2001).

We were able to arrange the trial hosting services for our readers because of the assistance of Brian Anderson at HosTek and Joel Lee at JTLNet. Steve Misovich and Lou Boudreau were part of a PHP group that was very helpful, and David Demers provided insight into ASP. Chris Maden gave invaluable help on the right way to use XML. George Brophy and Dave Kelley at the University of Hartford provided support in setting up an NT Server, and John Gray, Chair of the University of Hartford's Interactive Information Technology program, provided much-needed general support. Hungry Minds editors Mike Roney, Carol Sheehan, Chris Johnson, Jodi Jensen, and Heather Stith kept the book on track during the editorial process, and Margot Maley Hutchison at Waterside Productions is responsible for the connections that made the book possible.

Contents at a Glance

Contents

Part II: Back End Objects and Printing   217

Chapter 5: Reading XML Documents with Flash 5 219

Chapter 6: Printing Directly from Flash 247

Chapter 7: Data Format for Generator Objects 273

Part III: The Dynamics of Gaming   323

Chapter 8: Dynamic Game Development: The Essentials 325

Chapter 9: Advanced Gaming Concepts 353

A Walk on the Server Side

◆ ◆ ◆ ◆

◆ ◆ ◆ ◆

The Essentials: URL Encoding and Basic Server Integration

Flash 5 is now the tool of choice for dynamic, integrated Web sites. To truly interact with the user and create a customized, dynamic experience, Flash needs to retrieve dynamic data from a Web server and be able to decipher, operate on, or return that data for storage or more operations on the Web server. In this chapter, you'll learn the basics of data transfer over the Internet between browsers and Web servers and the unique new ways Flash 5 has introduced to send, receive, and deal with this data.

Using URL Encoding to Transfer Data

Data as it relates to the Internet is basically just lists of variables. These variables could be lists of items in your virtual shopping cart, information regarding the highest score in a game, or even personal data that is stored in a cookie on your own computer (usually without your knowledge) by almost every Web site today. These variables need to be sent back and forth between Web browsers and servers in a standard format that allows for communication over great distances.

For example, you may be ordering some wine from an e-commerce site in France while you sit comfortably on the beaches of Hawaii. To ensure that the data detailing your order makes it all the way to France and a confirmation of your order comes back to you, a standard syntax has been developed to transmit data. That standard is called *URL encoding,* and it has worked well since the humble beginnings of the Internet. Because Flash is basically a plug-in that sits inside a Web browser, Flash also uses URL encoding to interact with Web servers on the Internet.

URL encoding is a process by which lists of multiple variables being sent between servers and browsers are encoded as a single chunk of continuous data. Individual characters within the data chunk that might be confusing to the browser or server interpreting them are converted into a new special character or sequence of special characters.

Browsers and servers like to send and receive data in well-defined pieces and don't want to have to decide if the space between some data represents the space between someone's first and last name, an error, or the beginning of a new piece of data. Web computers look for *reserved characters,* such as ampersands and percent signs, within the data chunk to clearly designate when a variable begins and ends and when a variable includes a special character. A variable value that contains such a character could cause problems for the server if the value is not URL-encoded.

URL encoding follows these basic rules:

- ✦ Multiple variable name and value pairs are chained together with ampersands (&).

- ✦ Each variable's name is separated from its value by an equals sign (=), just like in Flash.

- ✦ Spaces anywhere within the variable's name or value are usually represented by a plus sign (+).

- ✦ Any characters other than letters and spaces (such as hyphens or pound signs or exclamation points) are represented by their URL-encoded replacements that start with a percent sign (%) followed by the hexadecimal equivalent of that character's ASCII value. For example, a hyphen is converted to %2D in URL encoding.

Note   The great thing about the Internet and programs like Flash that are being used to build the Internet these days is that you don't have to worry about what those ASCII codes are or what the word *hexadecimal* means. You just have to be able to recognize URL encoding when you see it and understand that even when you can't see the data, it's still traveling across the Web in the URL-encoded format.

To get a feel for how URL encoding works, suppose you defined these two variables in Flash ActionScript:

```
address="7095 Hollywood Blvd";
city="Van Nuys";
```

This code would need to be translated into URL encoding by Flash before being sent across the Internet. All the spaces between the words in the string variables would be turned into plus signs (+), and an ampersand (&) would be used to designate the beginning of a new variable:

```
address=7095+Hollywood+Blvd&city=Van+Nuys
```

To understand how URL encoding handles special or reserved characters in variable values, consider this definition in Flash ActionScript:

```
authors="Winstanley&Sanders";
```

If this variable were to be passed across the Internet using URL encoding, it would appear this way:

```
authors=Winstanley%26Sanders
```

Remember that in the specific syntax of URL encoding, an ampersand (&) is used to designate the point where one variable ends and another begins when multiple variables are transmitted. If the ampersand in the variable's value as defined in Flash wasn't translated to its URL-encoded value of %26 before being sent across the Internet, the Web server receiving the data would think that a new variable named Sanders was about to be defined.

URL encoding syntax

If you've ever visited a Web site and suddenly looked up at the link in your browser's address line and noticed that it's turned into a long, cryptic string of text, you've seen URL encoding in action.

Take a look at this example:

```
http://www.flashcore.com/index.htm?name=mark&title=co%2Dauthor
```

Most developers recognize the first part of the address as being a standard Internet URL, but everything after the question mark looks somewhat cryptic. This example is set up to go to FlashCore.com and pass two variables named name and title to the Web page index.htm, which usually would be a PHP, ASP, or CGI page ready to read and make use of those variables. The URL includes the variables by presenting them in a URL-encoded format and attaching them to the end of the domain name with a question mark (?) followed by what's known as a query string. We'll define what a query string is and does later in this chapter; first we need to break down the exact syntax of URL encoding.

In the example, two variables are disguised in the query string following the URL. The first variable is labeled name with an actual value of mark, and the second variable is labeled title with an actual value of co-author. Notice that each variable label is followed by an equals sign (=) and then the variable's value. The hyphen in the middle of co-author is replaced with its URL-encoded value of %2D.

Note Again, the beauty in using Flash is that when Flash has to send data out over the Internet, it does the URL encoding and combining for you! The reverse applies for when Flash receives data. If the data contains URL-encoded characters, Flash recognizes these and transforms them back into the actual characters needed. Flash also splits up any incoming variable/value pairs denoted by ampersands into individual variables. Nice job, Macromedia!

Don't worry about having to write URL encoding in Flash, it will happen by itself. Server scripts, on the other hand, usually need a little bit of help. As you'll see in Chapter 2 with CGI and Perl, Perl needs a few lines of code to decipher those URL-encoded variables before it can operate on them correctly. Variables also need to be formatted as URL-encoded when returned from a server script, and this functionality often has to be manually coded into the script.

URL encoding in real time

In order to let you see URL-encoding for just about any character combination you can think of, Flash includes an ActionScript command named escape that will take any string specified and convert it to URL-encoded format.

On the CD-ROM If you view the source for url_encoder.fla on the CD-ROM and click the two text boxes, you'll notice that they're a movie clip with the repetitive onClipEvent command set to keep taking the input text field and converting it to URL encoding for display in the output text field.

To see URL encoding in real-time action, locate the file url_encoder.fla on the CD-ROM and open it within Flash. Preview the file within Flash or within your browser. Start typing in the box that prompts you to enter text. The URL-encoded equivalent of whatever you type will be shown in the box below it. Try experimenting with typing in lots of different words and special characters like exclamation points. Notice that pressing the spacebar yields a result of %20, which is acceptable even though (as mentioned previously) spaces are usually converted to plus signs in URL encoding when they leave Flash for travel on the Internet.

Note This escape ActionScript command is not necessary for transferring data across the Internet from Flash. It exists for convenience and to create neat little displays like the one in the url_encoder.fla file. As you'll see later in the chapter, Flash does the URL encoding for you without any special commands.

Now that you've seen how the characters within an individual variable are displayed in URL encoding, take a look at what a chain of URL-encoded variables looks like when strung together:

1. Create a new Flash file.

2. Create a button on the stage or drag one to the stage from the Standard library by choosing Window ⇨ Common Libraries ⇨ Buttons.

3. Make sure that the ActionScript window is open and in expert mode. Then select the button you just created by clicking it once.

4. Add the following code to the button:

```
on (release) {
    name="mark";
    title="co-author";
    getURL ("http://www.flashcore.com/index.htm", "_blank",
"GET");
}
```

5. Preview the movie in your Web browser by pressing F12 and then clicking the button in the Flash movie.

You should see a new browser window pop up with FlashCore.com in it. You may not see an actual Web page, but what you want to look at is the URL field in your browser. Take a look at the entire URL; notice that it's the same as the example in the previous section:

```
http://www.flashcore.com/index.htm?name=mark&title=co%2Dauthor
```

In Flash, you defined the two variables `name` and `title` and then issued the `getURL` statement to launch the page in a `_blank` or new window. The last argument in the `getURL` statement is the word `GET`. This word specifies that any variables you just defined are to be sent out of Flash along with the standard URL and attached to the end of it in a query string. Don't worry, the mysteries of the query string will be unveiled shortly, but for now just notice that you didn't have to do anything out of the ordinary when defining the variables in the Flash ActionScript to have them sent out in a URL-encoded format. You simply defined your variables and then issued the `getURL` statement and specified with `GET` that variables were to be sent; Flash took over from there, figuring out all the URL encoding for you. Try adding some extra variable names and values in the ActionScript after `title` and preview the results again. The URL in the pop-up Web browser will become longer and longer as you add more variables.

Methods of sending variables with URL encoding

You may think that URL encoding itself is the method by which Flash sends out variables, but there are two distinct methods of sending variables using URL encoding: `GET` and `POST`. The following sections provide a general overview of these two methods.

More details on sending variables out of Flash are available later in this chapter under the heading "Sending variables to the server."

The GET method and its query string

A *query string* is nothing but a long string of URL-encoded data following a URL. That string of URL-encoded data is separated from the domain name or Web page name with a question mark (?), hence the name query string. The presence of a query string indicates that the GET method is being used to send the variables. Using the GET method simply means that a query string is present that follows a URL and contains all the data variables that are being transmitted someplace. (If we were in charge of naming methods, we would just call it the QUERY STRING method.) So whenever you see a query string amended to the end of a URL while you're out surfing the Web, you know that whoever sent that data sent it by using the GET method, either from Flash, from an HTML form page, or directly from a scripting language like JavaScript or PHP.

The POST method of transmission

Sending your data using the POST method is a more secure way to send data over the Internet; POST is the preferred method for transmitting sensitive data and can be used in almost all circumstances. The POST method does not use a query string; therefore, a casual observer has no way of seeing the data, even in the browser cache. Instead of using a query string, POST packs the data into an invisible header that is sent along with the URL. The only drawback is that depending on what server-scripting language you choose to handle your data, unpacking those variables and shuttling them around is sometimes more difficult than variables in the GET method. Flash offers the option of using the POST method in both its getURL and loadVariables ActionScript commands.

Loading External Variables into Flash

Variables that are loaded from an external text file or dynamically generated from a server script are the best way to make the Flash experience truly dynamic and interactive. Using external variables is an easy way for you or your client to make quick and easy changes to both numeric and text data without having to open Flash and re-export a new SWF file.

As we've mentioned, the URL-encoded format for variables is the standard used across the Internet, and Macromedia logically chose this format as the required format for any external variables to be loaded into the Flash environment. In this section, you'll discover how to format and load variables from external text files, where to put these variables, and how to check for them to arrive before attempting to operate on them.

Formatting variables in text files

The easiest way to begin loading variables into Flash is to type them into a plain old text file using a text editor and then issue the loadVariables command in Flash to reference the name of this file. (A common PC text editor to use is Notepad; a common Mac text editor is SimpleText.) The loadVariables command directs Flash to look in the referenced text file and try and make some sense of what it finds inside. (Complete and detailed information on the loadVariables command is available later in this chapter.)

If Flash finds nice sets of variables in a URL-encoded format, it will take note of what they are and transfer their values back to Flash. If Flash can't make any sense of what it finds inside, it will just ignore the entire text file. On the one hand, improper formatting keeps your variables out of Flash, but on the other hand, Flash proceeds with its business and doesn't display any loud warning messages. Flash is forgiving and likes to maintain transparency and fluidity in the user experience.

On the CD-ROM You need to copy the files `first_variables.fla` and `first_variables.txt` from the CD-ROM to your hard drive because you'll be modifying them quite extensively. Make sure that you put them both in the same directory. It may be a good idea at this time to transfer all the files for this chapter to a new directory on your hard drive where you'll have an easy time modifying them and saving changes.

Copy the files `first_variables.fla` and `first_variables.txt` from the CD-ROM to a directory on your hard drive. Open the file `first_variables.fla` that is now on your hard drive. You'll see one green button and a rather large text field. With the Text Options panel open, click the text field and notice that it has been assigned to display the value of a variable named `output` should one ever come into existence.

Choose File ➪ Publish Preview ➪ Default to preview in your Web browser. Click the green button. Suddenly the big empty text field is filled with lots of text! Figure 1-1 illustrates what you should see. This text is all contained within the file `first_variables.txt` and is loaded into Flash through the `loadVariables` statement attached to the green button.

While you still have the preview of the Flash movie visible, open the `first_variables.txt` file from your hard drive in your text editor to examine how the URL-encoded formatting in the text file is translated into Flash. Begin by comparing what you see in the text file with what you see in the Flash movie. The first line of code visible in the text file is

```
&output=This is the text contained in the variable named
'output'.
```

Notice the ampersand and then the variable name `output` and the equal sign (=) following it in the text file. These items do not appear in the text field assigned to `output` that is in the Flash movie or anywhere in the code of the Flash movie because the `output` variable is defined in the text file. Flash looks at the text file and sees `output` properly defined and assigns everything following it as the value for `output`.

Lots of lines of raw text in the text file are separated by spaces, carriage returns, and punctuation, which is not strictly formatted URL-encoded text. We're cheating a little here. Thankfully we can, because Flash is forgiving. The key to formatting your text file variables for loading into Flash is the proper use of ampersands: Begin and end every variable declaration with an ampersand. The ampersands act like big brick walls, marking off the area where a variable's value begins and ends.

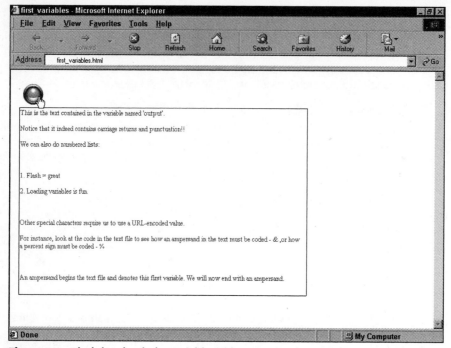

Figure 1-1: Flash has loaded a variable with a very long string of text as its value from an external text file.

Caution   Although the ampersand at the very beginning or end of the entire text file is not always necessary, you should always include them. When these ampersands are not included, some browsers have trouble interpreting the data stream or skip the last variable in a series. Ampersands between multiple variable declarations are always necessary.

Take a look at the bottom lines of text in the text file. A big comment in there says, "HEY LOOK." Two lines before those words appear, however, is an ampersand that acts as the brick wall denoting the end of the variable `output`. When Flash reaches that second ampersand, it ignores anything it sees afterwards until it finds another ampersand and then a variable name with an equal sign.

Although spaces between the ampersand, variable name, and equal sign are not allowed when you declare your variables in the external text file, you can freely use spaces, most punctuation, carriage returns, and even equal signs inside your variable values. In situations not relating to Flash (such as a traditional Web browser query string), this kind of formatting would be unacceptable.

URL encoding reserved characters

The only characters you can't use in variable names and values in a text file without confusing Flash are ampersands (&), percent signs (%), and plus signs (+). Flash and the URL encoding format reserve the use of ampersands for figuring out where variables begin and end, percent signs for recognizing URL-encoded characters, and plus signs for spaces in variable names and values. In order to use these characters, you must enter their URL-encoded equivalents into the text file:

✦ To display an ampersand, enter **%26** into the text file.

✦ To display a percent sign, enter **%25** into the text file.

✦ To display a plus sign, enter **%2B** into the text file.

For an example of how reserved characters are coded in text files, look at this line from the `first_variables.txt` file:

```
For instance, look at the code in the text file to see how an
ampersand in the text must be coded - %26 or how a percent sign
must be coded - %25.
```

The resulting display in the Flash movie is as follows:

```
For instance, look at the code in the text file to see how an
ampersand in the text must be coded - & or how a percent sign
must be coded - %.
```

Flash is set up to recognize URL-encoded values inside text files, so you can freely drop them in when necessary. If you ever have trouble displaying certain characters or symbols when loading from text files, replace that character in the text file with its URL-encoded equivalent. You can use the Flash file `url_encoder.fla` to help you in your quest for cryptic hexadecimal values.

Carriage returns

You may have noticed that the gaps between lines of text in the Flash movie are much larger than the gaps between lines in the text file. That difference occurs because the text file contains an actual carriage return instead of the URL-encoded equivalent of `%0D`. If you want the convenience of typing blocks of text in a text file just like you would a word processor, you could change the line spacing of the `output` text field in Flash by selecting it and using the Text Paragraph palette and the line spacing parameter.

To get normally spaced carriage returns to appear in Flash without changing the text field formatting, you would type all your lines of text in the external text file in sequence without any carriage returns. Then, wherever you want Flash to show a new line, you would insert `%0D` into the text file. The following example shows how a line from such a text file might look:

```
&output=Here is line one%0Dhere is line two%0Dhere is line
three&
```

Flash would load this file in and display the following in its output text field:

```
Here is line one
Here is line two
Here is line three
```

The carriage returns would display true to form in Flash, but looking at that continuous line of data with the multiple %0D codes in the text file can get confusing very fast, especially if a dynamic text file system is being created for a client. By changing the text field formatting on the Flash stage instead of using %0D in the external text file, you'll have a text file that is easy to decipher but will, unfortunately, have a Flash display with improper spacing between the lines. You'll have to decide which is more important when planning your Flash projects.

Numbers and multiple variables

Numeric values in a text file to be loaded into Flash require no special formatting. For example, if you wanted to make the output variable equal to a value 392.7, the code in the text file would look like the following:

```
&output=392.7&
```

Formatting multiple variables and values can be slightly more complicated. Flash will automatically recognize and bring back as many variables and values as you can cram into a text file, but exactly how you cram those variables in the text file affects the ease with which you can make changes to the file later.

Imagine if you wanted to create a record for a person's contact info in a text file. The standard URL-encoded continuous string format for this information would look something like this:

```
name=Bob+Jones&address=1840+Grant+St%2E&city=Philadelphia&state
=PA&zipcode=19120&age=27
```

This nicely formatted list text file accomplishes the same feat and is much easier to read:

```
&name=Bob Jones&
&address=1840 Grant St.&
&city=Philadelphia&
&state=PA&
&zipcode=19120&
&age=27&
```

Notice the beginning and ending ampersands, which denote the breaks between the variables. Writing the text file in this format makes it easy to see what you're looking at, and most people can be taught to recognize and make changes to these types of files. This format is not strict URL encoding, but it works and is much cleaner to edit than it would be if the variables were in the standard URL-encoded format. A good general rule might be this: If you ever anticipate modifying multiple variables in an external text file by hand, use the list formatting method. If you're using a server scripting language to write your text files for you (as in Chapter 2), you can use a snapshot of a query string (which is in the standard URL-encoded format) instead. Flash is happy either way.

Arrays

If you want to put an array in the text file that you want to pull into Flash, you can format the array using commas to denote the separation between each element in it. For example, if you defined an array in Flash named `carColors` and the elements consisted of the colors red, white, blue, and green, you'd normally define this array in ActionScript with this line of code:

```
carColors=new Array("red","white","blue","green");
```

To define this array in an external text file to be loaded into Flash, you would just leave out all the quotes:

```
&carColors=red,white,blue,green&
```

Unfortunately, though, if you loaded this line into Flash, Flash wouldn't immediately recognize it as an array; Flash would look at `carColors` as one single variable with the string literal value of `red,white,blue,green`. Flash needs some extra help to get it to recognize `carColors` as an array. This extra help comes in the form of the ActionScript command `split`, which is covered later in this chapter along with a more detailed explanation of arrays under the heading "Displaying and outputting arrays."

For now, just keep in mind that if you plan on dealing with a set of data as an array, it should appear in the text file as one variable name followed by all the values separated by commas (,). Although you can use any separator you'd like, we recommend sticking with commas because Flash uses this format when it sends out an array, as covered later in this chapter under the heading "Sending variables to the server."

Using the loadVariables command

Up until this point, we've been concentrating solely on the differences in formatting between a data/text file and its final output in Flash. This section explains how the variables go from external files into Flash. To get the whole process of loading (and sending) variables to begin in Flash, you need to use the `loadVariables` command. You can attach this command to a frame or button or use it as a clip action within the Flash 5 `onClipEvent` statement.

This command comes in two styles with this basic syntax:

```
loadVariablesNum ( url, level, method );
```

or

```
loadVariables ( url, target, method );
```

Both styles of the `loadVariables` command call for three parameters: `url`, `target`, and `method`; `method` is the only optional parameter.

The url parameter

The `url` parameter designates the URL of the text file that contains the variables. The URL must be enclosed in quotes when you are naming the file directly, although you could designate the filename with another variable or expression, in which case you would use quotes only as necessary.

Caution   Flash contains a security feature that prohibits loading variables from a file not on the same Web server as your SWF Flash movie. When you use the `loadVariables` command, the specified URL must exist on the current Web server if the files are online. You can specify just a path, such as `/textfiles/loadmein.txt`, but you cannot specify an `http://` style URL that is not in the same domain as the Flash movie executing the `loadVariables` command. Macromedia has included this security feature to prevent people from hijacking scripts and text file data from other people's domains.

The URL that you're calling for can be a direct reference starting with `http://`, or you can specify a path directly from the directory where the Flash movie is located. Always keep in mind this Flash security feature concerning URLs. The exception to the rule is that if you're testing the Flash movie on your local machine or running it from a projector, you can load text files safely from anywhere on your machine and from anywhere on the Web. However, if the Flash movie has been uploaded to a Web server and you're viewing it in your browser, any text files that Flash movie calls for must be on the same Web server and in the same domain as the Flash movie.

The level and target parameters

The `level` or `target` parameter specifies where the variables will be placed when they arrive. The `loadVariablesNum` syntax with its `level` parameter automatically signals Flash that it is looking for the number of a level in Flash where the variables will be placed. Do not put this level number in quotations.

Specifying 0 as the `level` parameter makes Flash load whatever variables it finds in the text file into Level 0, which is basically equivalent to the main timeline (unless the movie issuing the command is on another level). Loading into Level 0 will make your variables accessible from anywhere within Flash by preceding the variable name with `_root`. This chapter provides more information about this topic under the heading "Accessing variables within Flash."

When the destination of your variables is the timeline of a movie clip somewhere in your Flash movie, the plain old `loadVariables` syntax is used with the `target` parameter. Here you specify the path name to a movie clip where you want your variables to end up. The path must be enclosed in quotation marks. For example, if you want to load your variables into a movie clip named `lion` that is nested inside a movie clip named `zoo` that is sitting on the main timeline, you could execute the following action from anywhere within Flash:

```
loadVariables ( "sometextfile.txt", "_root.zoo.lion");
```

If the movie clip that originates any type of `loadVariables` statement (whether by button or frame action) is deeply nested within many movie clips, you can use the self-reference `this` if you're not sure of the path and would like the variables to be loaded into the same movie clip that called for them. You do not use quotes in this case because `this` is an ActionScript object referencing whatever timeline or movie clip is issuing it. For example, if a frame action inside a movie clip that is nested 10 clips deep needs to load variables into itself, the easy way to code it is as follows:

```
loadVariables ( "sometextfile.txt", this);
```

Using the self-reference object `this` saves you the trouble of having to type in a long path to a movie clip when you're at the right spot to begin with!

The method parameter

Notice that the preceding examples make no reference to the `method` parameter in the code. The `method` parameter is necessary only if you're also going to be sending variables as well as or instead of just receiving them. The two methods available are `POST` and `GET`. Whichever one you choose must be enclosed in quotation marks. More information about sending variables from Flash is in this chapter under the heading "Sending variables to the server."

The loadVariables statement logic

If you don't already have the CD-ROM file `first_variables.fla` open from a previous example, please open it now in the Flash authoring environment. After you've previewed the movie using Control, Test Movie and clicked the green button, return to the Flash authoring environment. Make sure the ActionScript panel is open and set to Normal mode. Click the green button on the stage and examine the code attached it:

```
on (release) {
    output = "";
    loadVariablesNum ("first_variables.txt", 0);
}
```

The first line of code inside the `on(release)` button statement just resets the `output` variable's field to be empty and is here only for aesthetics. The next line of code uses `loadVariablesNum` to load any variables from the text file named `first_variables`.

txt into Level 0. Because the only variable inside this text file is named output and there's a text field on the stage assigned a variable name to match, the following actions occur as soon as you click the green button:

1. Flash resets the output field to be empty.

2. Flash executes the loadVariablesNum statement and looks for a file named first_variables.txt in the same directory as the Flash movie (because no http:// reference is made).

3. If Flash locates this file, it begins to read and parse the text file looking for any properly formatted variables it can pull back into Flash.

4. Flash finds the variable output properly defined in the text file and immediately places that variable name and value into Level 0.

5. The value of the variable output is immediately displayed in the text field because the field has been previously assigned the variable reference output.

Caution   This set of actions happens quite quickly on your personal computer. But when the files all reside on the Internet, there can be some serious delays in the response time of the server. Imagine if you issued a loadVariables command in Frame 1 of a Flash movie and then tried to do something with those variables only a few frames later, but the server took 5 or 10 seconds to provide the text file. The variables wouldn't arrive in time for your operations! This extremely common predicament is covered thoroughly later in this chapter in "Checking for the arrival of variables."

With the green button still selected and the code still showing in the ActionScript panel, highlight the line of code containing the loadVariables statement. In the parameters section of the ActionScript panel, notice the choices in the drop-down menu labeled Location. Try switching between the setting for Level and Target. Notice as you do this that Flash toggles the line of code between the two syntaxes of the loadVariables command: loadVariables and loadVariablesNum.

Flash also automatically adds quotation marks where needed in the target or level parameter area of the code line. Try selecting POST or GET from the Variables drop-down menu. Flash takes care of properly adding the correct method to the statement and attempts to send variables to the specified URL using the method selected.

Tip   The Normal mode of the ActionScript panel is great for quickly determining correct syntax and parameter choices.

Loading multiple variables

The project in this section uses all the code, commands, and techniques presented thus far. In this project, we will create some quick mock Web site sections that load text and numerical data from an external text file and format them for use in Flash. The theme of this Web site is that of a jewelry store. Maria Tepora of www.flashnique. com provided the graphics and artwork for this example.

This project uses the `jewelrysite.fla` file found on the CD-ROM. Open this file in Flash and then save it to your local hard drive. In that same directory on your local hard drive, create and save an empty text file named `jewelrydata.txt` using your favorite text editor.

The Flash file `jewelrysite.fla` on the CD-ROM contains some graphics and four buttons on the right side labeled About Us, Product, Special, and Contact Us. No ActionScripting has been added yet. The following steps lead you through the process of adding the capability to load in data from a text file to this Web site:

1. To prepare the text file and fill it with data that you want to load, open the `jewelrydata.txt` file you created in your text editor.

2. Add four variables named `aboutus`, `products`, `specials`, and `contactus`. Each variable has some text as its value that corresponds to the data you want to appear when a user clicks one of the four buttons on the right side of the Flash movie. Enter the following code into your text file:

```
&aboutus=de Legacy Jewelers was founded in 2001 and is a
completely fictitious company for the purpose of displaying
the loading of multiple variables&

&products=We carry a large assortment of diamond rings,
earrings, necklaces, and fashion jewelry&

&specials=This week's special includes a diamond bracelet for
$399.00 and a gold necklace for $450.00&

&contactus=de Legacy Jewelers is open 24 hours a day, 365
days per year and can be reached anytime at:
1-800-123-4567&
```

3. Save these changes to the text file `jewelrydata.txt` and make sure that file is in the same directory on your hard drive as `jewelrysite.fla`. (If you encounter any problems along the course of this example, the text file is also on the CD-ROM.)

4. With the `jewelrysite.fla` file open in Flash, you must first create a text field where all the data about the jewelry store is going to be displayed. Use the Text tool to create a dynamic text field on the stage that fills in the area in the center of the stage to the left of the buttons. Figure 1-2 shows the approximate placement of this text field.

5. Select this text field, and under the Text Options panel, make sure that Dynamic Text is selected from the first drop-down menu and Multiline is selected from the second drop down menu. Check only the Word Wrap check box and make sure the others are unchecked on the right side of the panel.

6. In the Variable field of the Text Options panel, type in **displayfield** to associate this field with the Flash variable `displayfield`.

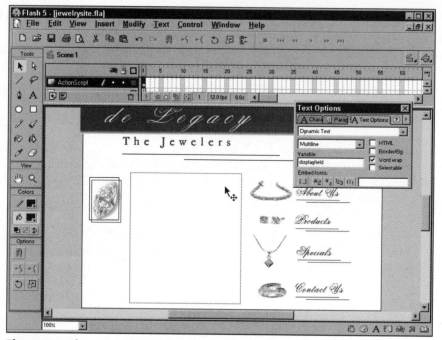

Figure 1-2: The approximate placement of the dynamic text field on the stage of jewelrysite.fla.

7. With the dynamic text field still selected, open the Character panel and choose Times New Roman in black at a point size of 22. Choose Bold and Italic as well. In the Paragraph panel, choose Center alignment.

8. Add the following ActionScript to Frame 1 of the ActionScript layer on the main timeline:

```
loadVariablesNum ("jewelrydata.txt", 0);
```

This ActionScript will cause Flash to load in all the variables you defined in the text file the instant that the movie begins and to make them accessible on the main timeline. Keep in mind that if you were to upload this to the Web, you'd have to add ActionScript to make up for the delay in getting the variables, which is covered in this chapter under the heading "Checking for the arrival of variables." Because the file involved in this example is on your local hard drive, there will be no delay, and you can proceed.

9. Add the following ActionScript to the About Us button:

```
on(press){
    displayfield=aboutus;
}
```

This code will make the dynamic text field that you created display the text that was loaded in from the text file jewelrydata.txt for the variable aboutus.

10. Add the same ActionScript to the remaining three buttons, replacing the variable reference `aboutus` with the variable names `products`, `specials`, and `contactus` for the respective buttons.

11. Test the movie in your browser using F12. As you click each button, you should see the text that you saved in the file jewelrydata.txt appearing in the dynamic text field. Figure 1-3 shows the information displayed when you click Contact Us. (If you encounter any problems, the completed file is available on the CD-ROM as `jewelrysite_completed.fla`.)

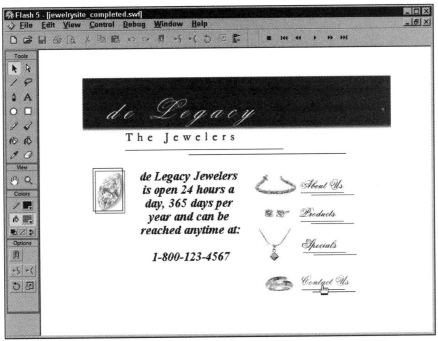

Figure 1-3: Flash displays one of the variables it loaded from a text file when a user clicks the appropriate button.

Flash has successfully pulled in a series of variables you defined in an external text file and shown only the appropriate one in the `displayfield` text field when each button was clicked. Try opening the text file and changing the values for the variables and previewing the Flash movie again. You'll see that Flash reflects all your changes and pulls in the new updated data. By assigning individual variables to the dynamic text field, you've operated on this data. The next section delves deeper into operating on external data after you've requested it with the `loadVariables` ActionScript statement.

Browser caching of text files and SWF movies

Please read this section thoroughly; it contains information that will ensure the dynamic capabilities of your Flash movies. Don't worry; we just need to discuss the role that the Web browser plays when Flash is loading in text files via the loadVariables statement.

Flash Player details

The Flash Player is basically a plug-in that sits inside a Web browser, so anytime Flash wants to make contact with the outside world, it needs to talk through the browser. When Flash loads a text file with the loadVariables command or loads in another SWF file via the loadMovie command, it has to ask the Web browser to get the file and pass it on to Flash. This process happens transparently and without much hoopla until you realize that Web browsers have a habit of caching and storing their files!

Browser cache storage area

Just about every Web browser has a cache (storage area) where it stores files so that it doesn't have to constantly waste time calling out across the Web to get files that it might need to use again in the near future. Because Web browsers aren't all that smart, they usually can't figure out which files they will need again, so they just store all of them! This storage is great for faster Web surfing because when your browser encounters a file reference in an HTML page, it first checks the cache storage area (located on your hard drive) to see whether it has the file handy, instead of downloading it again and wasting time. Browsers cache just about any file type, including GIFs, JPEGs, HTML pages, SWF files, and text files.

Caching is bad for dynamic text files that you'd like to load into Flash. Updating your text files doesn't do much good if everyone who's looking at your Flash movie is seeing outdated information. They see outdated information because their browsers are pulling the text file from their local cache instead of pulling the new, updated text file from your Web server. The same problem occurs with Flash SWF files that you've made changes to!

Tip

Most browsers let you view the area where cached files are temporarily stored. In Internet Explorer, choose Tools ➪ Internet Options, click the General tab, click the Settings button, and then click the View Files button. Most browsers also let the user designate a megabyte limit for storage of files, and they delete the oldest files stored in memory as new ones are stored. These limitations keep the browser cache from eating up too much hard drive space; 50MB is usually the average.

A Web browser's cache references a file only by its name, type, and the Web site it originated from. So if a file named flashdata.txt has been stored in a user's browser cache from your Web site, and that user goes back to your Web page and a Flash movie executes a loadVariables statement that calls for flashdata.txt, that user is going to get data from the flashdata.txt file stored on his or her local hard drive instead of the new, updated file from your Web site. This situation has caused many headaches in the world of Flash.

Solution to the evil browser cache

The way around this dilemma is to make Flash always ask for the same file but with a different name. Huh? The way to do this is to append a query string to the end of the text file's name each time Flash executes a call for outside data. For example, a button script might read as follows:

```
on (release) {
    loadVariablesNum ("flashdata.txt?x=55", 0);
}
```

This script makes the browser store the entire filename `flashdata.txt?x=55` in its cache, even though Flash will just be reading the file `flashdata.txt`. Don't worry about the variable name x or even the value 55; these things don't matter. This trick just ensures that Flash receives the latest version of `flashdata.txt` from the server if the user's Web browser already has already cached it.

Wait a minute though, the trick isn't complete yet! Once the user's browser has both the filenames `flashdata.txt` and `flashdata.txt?x=55` in its cache, you can't use `?x=55` at the end of the filename again, because the browser will now have that in its cache, too. The solution is to dynamically attach a query string variable to the end of the filename of each and every external file you plan to update often. The correct script consists of two statements: one to set a dynamic number and the `loadVariables` statement that attaches that random number in a query string to the end of the filename.

```
rn = Math.round(Math.random()*1000000);
loadVariablesNum ("flashdata.txt?reload="+rn, 0);
```

The first line of code sets a variable named `rn` (for random number) equal to a random number between one and a million. The second line of code is just the `loadVariablesNum` statement, but it appends a query string with a variable named `reload` and then adds the random number defined in `rn` to the end of the filename. When using this technique, be sure that everything other than the value you're attaching remains inside the quotation marks along with your filename.

If these two lines of ActionScript were in the first frame of your Flash movie, and a user came back three times to visit your site and then looked in his or her browser cache, that user would see something like the following:

```
flashdata.txt?reload=456192
flashdata.txt?reload=889056
flashdata.txt?reload=155607
```

When you set that random number and then attach it to the filename, you ensure that there's only a one in a million chance that a user will not receive the latest and greatest text file information you've posted to your Web site. Of course, this solution also means that users' browser caches are filled with extra files every time they visit your site. But most people don't look in their browser caches, and browser caches automatically delete excess files anyway, so don't worry about it. This solution is also the only way to fix this problem, so feel free to use it often.

Note Even though you specify a variable name in the query string following the text file's name, you're not putting any extra variables into the text file. This code is merely a trick to fool the browser cache. You can use any variable name you'd like instead of reload, as well as any range of random numbers. We just thought "one in a million" looked like good odds!

The same solution works great for loading in SWF files via the loadMovie command. If you've constructed a Flash file that you use as a shell to load in other SWF files that are often changed, you can use this code:

```
rn = Math.round(Math.random()*1000000);
loadMovieNum ("contentMovie.swf?reload="+rn, 1);
```

In this example, the filename contentMovie.swf is the name of the movie you're loading into Flash. This trick is indispensable in making sure that anyone viewing your Flash movies always sees the latest and greatest content provided by you!

Hiding all your files from the cache

The browser cache solutions we've discussed so far ensure that the viewers of your Flash movies get to see the most current content, even if it means that extra files are present in their browser cache. If you want to make sure that someone viewing your Flash movie can't pull the files from their browser cache, you have two solutions. The first solution keeps the browser from caching any files that are referenced in the current Web page, but it doesn't work in all cases so your mileage may vary. The standard meta tags to prevent a browser from caching content are as follows:

```
<META HTPP-EQUIV ="pragma" content="nocache">,
<META HTPP-EQUIV ="expires" content="Thu, 1 January 1900
00:00:00 PST">
```

If you add these two tags to your HTML code, it will, in some cases, prevent the user's browser from caching any files contained in the HTML page. Unfortunately, it doesn't always work. We've presented it here just so you're aware of it.

A much better way to hide your content from the end users is to make sure that your Flash SWF files are difficult, if not impossible, to find in the browser cache. You may wonder what purpose it would serve for someone to take your Flash movies out of their browser cache and put them on their hard drive or their own Web site. For one, they could easily put your content on their Web site. By using loadMovie with some clever masking and timeline control techniques, they can easily make it look like *their* Flash movies. In addition, every time you load a text file filled with data into Flash and it appears in a browser cache, it's vulnerable to the same interception.

The solution here is deceptively simple and involves nothing more than renaming your Flash movies and dynamic text files to have extensions other than swf or txt at the end of the filename. You can choose a typical extension like gif, jpeg, mp3, or even make up extensions like thz and nmb. This solution works because a movie or a text file loaded into Flash will load correctly as long as the contents of the file are readable by Flash, regardless of the file extension. For example if you have an SWF movie named `bounce.swf` and a dynamic text file named `colors.txt`, you could rename them to `bounce.gif` and `colors.jpeg` and place them in the same directory as the master Flash movie that is referencing them via ActionScript. The ActionScript in the master Flash movie would then read:

```
loadMovieNum ("bounce.gif", 1);
loadVariablesNum ("colors.jpeg", 0);
```

After executing this ActionScript, the Flash movie now named `bounce.gif` (originally named `bounce.swf`) would be loaded into Level 1. Additionally, the text file `colors.jpeg` (originally named `colors.txt`) containing data that you want to load into Flash would be loaded into Level 0, and the data would be available on the main timeline. This is a great way to disguise your Flash and dynamic text files that will appear in the browser cache of someone viewing your Web pages. If a user opens his or her browser cache after visiting your site, the user wouldn't see any Flash files or text files, only GIF and JPEG files. If you have static graphics on your Web pages that have names and extensions similar to the disguised files, it's very difficult for users to distinguish any of the files in their browser cache as being Flash or Flash-related.

This ActionScript works only when Flash movies or text files are loaded into a Flash movie that already exists on a Web page (or in a projector file). You can't rename the original file referenced in the HTML code in the `<OBJECT>` and `<EMBED>` tags to anything other than SWF. This first file must maintain the `swf` extension in order for the Flash browser plug-in to load it correctly. The great thing is that this first Flash file can be completely empty and contain nothing more than a `loadMovie` action referencing your disguised files that contain the bulk of the content for your Flash site!

Caution   All your ActionScript code is vulnerable to dissection and discovery, even if you've checked Protect From Import in the Flash export dialog box. The reason your code is vulnerable is because a program called the Action Script Viewer, available at www.buraks.com, enables a person to vacuum the ActionScript code out of any Flash movie and use it for their own purposes. Renaming your files to `gif` or `mp3` extensions can keep the casual viewer from finding them in their cache and realizing they're Flash movies. But anyone who uses a program like Action Script Viewer will see the name of every file that you're referencing in your code and follow the trail to eventually find your movies. For most people, protecting code is more trouble than it's worth. You should still, however, be aware of the risks.

Operating on Loaded Data

Now that you know how to load variables into Flash, you need to know what to do with them once they show up. This section deals with some fundamentals concerning variables in Flash and also helps to dispel some myths and misunderstandings concerning how variables are dealt with and accessed in Flash.

Accessing variables within Flash

Because you're reading this book, we assume that you're familiar with the concept of a variable and how to set one, change one, and even concatenate a few of them together. What many developers don't realize is that Flash has some unique ways of dealing with its variables.

Directory assistance

Variables in Flash are stored either in the main timeline of a Flash movie or within an individual movie clip's timeline. Timelines are the only places that Flash can set and retrieve a variable. This section provides some general definitions of the paths that need to precede variables when you want to access or operate on them in Flash.

Levels of the Flash Player

As mentioned previously in this chapter, the Flash Player is a plug-in that sits in a Web browser. When an HTML page embeds this plug-in, it usually makes reference to an initial SWF file that is loaded into Level 0 of the player, and this movie begins playing. Each Flash Player plug-in can hold 16,000 Flash movie SWF files at one time (theoretically), with one SWF file each on levels that are numbered 0 thru 15,999. The first movie loaded in by the HTML page occupies Level 0, and this movie sets the frame rate and background color for any movies loaded into levels 1 through 15,999.

So anytime you're using the `loadMovieNum` command in your Flash travels, keep in mind that you're not loading any SWF files into each other, they're being stacked into the Flash Player plug-in. When you need to access a movie on another level (from anywhere in Flash), the correct path syntax is an underscore (_) followed by the level name:

```
_level25.gotoAndPlay("myframe");
```

When you need to address a submovie clip in an SWF file on another level (from anywhere in Flash), you use this syntax:

```
_level4.zoo.cage.tiger.claws=8;
```

When called from anywhere in Flash, that statement will make the variable named `claws`, which is inside the movie clip `tiger`, which is nested somewhere in an SWF file that has been loaded into `_level4`, and has a value of 8.

The _root path

Many developers think that the path syntax `_root` is the same as `_level0` or the default Flash movie timeline, but it isn't. Every SWF file has a main timeline, and this timeline is what `_root` references. For example, if you are in the habit of referencing `_level0` whenever you'd like to access the main timeline, what happens when an SWF file you make is loaded into Level 4? In this case, you would use the `_root` syntax to access the main timeline of the SWF file you're in, regardless of whether the file is in Level 0 or Level 13,952.

All movie clips and variables flow down in a tree-like structure from the `_root`, which is an SWF file's main timeline. In a Web site directory on your FTP server, you'll see paths like the following:

```
/pictures/vacation/florida
```

The equivalent path in Flash with a series of similarly named movie clips would be as follows:

```
_root.pictures.vacation.florida
```

Note   For those of you making the transition from Flash 4, the directory tree in Flash used to use the forward slash (/), but now the JavaScript-like dot syntax has replaced it.

In the preceding example, `florida` could be a variable inside the movie clip `vacation`, or it could be another movie clip inside of `vacation`. This example highlights why planning is so important in a Flash movie. Especially if you're doing a large, intricate Flash movie, you should plan out all your movie clip and variable names in advance. Mapping out a flow chart structure with movie clip instance names along with the names of the important variables they contain is always a good idea. If you need to add pieces and sections later on, you'll have a quick reference chart of where to access and/or modify all of your variables.

The _parent and _this syntaxes

Two additional path syntaxes to be aware of are `_parent` and `_this`. These syntaxes are both *relative* paths; `_root` and `_level` are *absolute* paths. You can use the `_parent` syntax when referencing the movie clip that contains the movie clip that your ActionScript statement is in. Suppose you have this sequence of movie clips:

```
_root.earth.atlantic.island.palmtree
```

If you want to put an ActionScript inside `palmtree` that targets the `island` movie clip and have it play a frame labeled `sunset`, you could use `_parent` instead of having to figure out the big, long, absolute `_root` path to `island`:

```
_parent.gotoAndPlay("sunset");
```

The `_parent` syntax is especially useful when using duplicated movie clips or multiple instances in general when it's too much trouble to be figuring out absolute paths, especially when all you want to do is control the movie clip that contains the current one. You also can combine multiple `_parent` statements, as in `_parent_parent.gotoAndPlay("waves");`, to reference a timeline that contains the parent of the current timeline.

Note   The `_parent` syntax is equivalent to the Internet (and former Flash 4) syntax of `../` that is used to denote the directory that contains the current one.

Instead of looking up the directory tree structure as _parent does, the this path reference looks down the directory tree. In the previous example, if you were to place an ActionScript inside the earth movie clip that is to reference island, you would use this code:

```
this.atlantic.island.gotoAndPlay("sunset");
```

Many developers leave off the this and just start with the name of the next nested movie clip because this is not necessary in many cases. You should, however, get into the habit of using it because, as you'll see in later chapters, some great shortcuts and dynamic feats need this in order to function correctly.

Globally accessible variables

This concept is very important: There is no such thing as a global variable within Flash! That's right; you heard it here. Even though the manual that comes with Flash talks about global variables, it misrepresents the truth. Although Flash does not have global variables, it does have *globally accessible* variables.

Anyone who comes to Flash knowing any other programming language (even BASIC from back in fifth grade) is fairly familiar with the concept of a global variable. Once a global variable is defined, its value is available anywhere just by referencing its name. In addition, if you change the global variable anywhere in the scripting, its new value will be returned whenever the variable is referenced thereafter.

Macromedia presents the concept of global variables in most of its texts, which would lead most developers to believe that if on the main timeline you defined the variable petName with a value of fluffy, that whenever you referenced the variable again anywhere in Flash, you would find that the petName variable's value was still fluffy. The reality is completely the opposite due to this fact: All variables are local to the timelines in which they're created, but they're globally accessible. So if you have eight movie clips on the main timeline, you could have eight variables named petName existing within those eight movie clips. If you stuck a dynamic text field on the main timeline and assigned it to reference the variable petName, it would remain empty until some ActionScript on the main timeline (whether in a frame or a button) defined petName within the scope of the main timeline or until you changed the reference on the text field to reflect one of the movie clips. Including the scope of the variable in a text field variable reference is an often-overlooked way to avoid creating additional ActionScripts. In the following example, we'll look at how Flash's variables are all local to the timelines in which they've been defined.

On the CD-ROM
In the following example, you'll need to open the file globalvariables.fla on the CD-ROM and save it somewhere on your local hard drive.

Upon opening the file globalvariables.fla from the CD-ROM, you'll immediately notice eight little houses placed on the stage. Each one of these houses represents an instance of the house movie clip. These instances are all named house1 through house8 sequentially. Click on any of these instances with your ActionScript panel open and you'll notice an onClipEvent statement like the following:

```
onClipEvent(load){
    this.petName="Fluffy";
}
```

These statements set a unique `petName` variable for each of the eight instances using the object `this` to designate that each instance should set this variable within itself. A text field in each movie clip is assigned the variable reference `petName`, so if you preview this movie choosing Control ⇨ Test Movie, you'll see that each house displays the name of its household pet. (If you'd like to customize this movie to use your pets' names, feel free to modify the `onClipEvent` statements at will.)

To understand how to gain access to these locally defined, but globally accessible variables inside each instance of the `house` movie clip, add a text field:

1. Select the first keyframe in the Text Field layer and use the Text tool in Flash to create a dynamic text field anywhere at the bottom of the stage.

2. With the text field selected, use the Text Options panel to designate it as a Dynamic Text field, Single Line, with Border/BG checked and HTML unchecked.

3. In the Variable Reference box in the Text Options panel, type in the variable name **petName.**

4. Preview the movie and notice that nothing appears in the text field. That is because the text field is on the main timeline and you have not defined `petName` anywhere on the main timeline. The only place it is defined is in each of the `house` movie clips.

5. Return to Flash and add a frame action to Frame 1 of the Text Field layer:

   ```
   petName="FishyWishy";
   ```

6. Preview the Flash movie again and you'll see that your text field reflects the great pet name `FishyWishy` because it was defined on the main timeline. The text field, having no reference before the variable name `petName`, looks to the timeline in which it sits as the default for where to retrieve a value for `petName` and finds `FishyWishy` because you defined it in Frame 1.

7. Return to Flash, and with the text field you created selected, change the variable reference in the Text Options panel to `_root.house3.petName` and preview the movie again.

Your text field now contains the `petName` variable defined in the third house in from the left, which should be `Candy`. You've suddenly created a 'window' to the variable in the timeline of that one movie clip instance. Try changing the number at the end of the `_root.house3.petName` reference to 4, 5, or 8 and preview again. By including a reference right in the dynamic text field, you've eliminated the need to add additional ActionScript to get variable values from other timelines displayed on the main timeline. Defining the variable reference in the Text Options panel effectively opens a pipeline to whatever timeline, movie clip, or level you desire. Pipelines tend to flow in both directions, so changing the text in the text field changes the variable in the movie clip instance that the text field refers to. To see this process in action, follow these steps:

1. With your dynamic text field selected, change its setting in the Text Options drop-down menu to Input Text. Make sure that the Border/BG box is checked as well.

2. Make sure to change the variable reference so that it associates this text field with one of the `house` movie clips, such as `_root.house3.petName`.

3. Preview the movie and notice that a value is initially present in your text field identical to that of the house you chose to specify. Start typing (or deleting) text in your text field and notice that the text field in the house you've referenced changes right along with it! Figure 1-4 shows how the screen looks when some text is deleted from the text field referencing the third house.

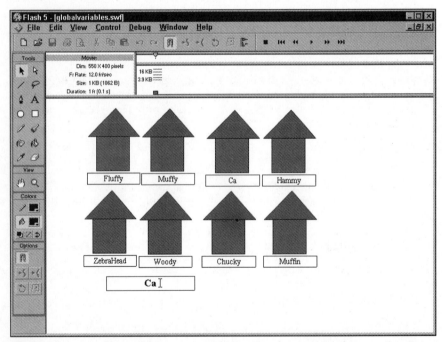

Figure 1-4: You can manipulate a variable that has been defined in any timeline as long as you know its path and attach that path to ActionScript code or, in this case, a dynamic input text field.

The most important point to take away from this example is that although the text field you're using to manipulate the variable is on the main timeline, the actual variable is stored on the timeline of the `house` movie clip you referenced. The variable is local to that movie clip, but it is globally accessible with another text field or piece of

ActionScript code, as long as you know the path to the variable. Even though in this example you added a path starting with _root to the variable reference in the text field, you could just as easily have added a path starting with another level number such as _level5 or even a reference beginning with _parent. All you've done is create another window to a particular variable. When you select Input Text on the Text Options panel, you have the added ability to reach through that window and make changes. Using a simple dynamic text field in this way makes it very easy to open up editable pipelines across timelines and levels.

Tip   A good way to store variables so that they stay organized if you really need the effect of a true global variable is to create a movie clip with no graphics and stick it somewhere on the main timeline. Give it an instance name of allVariables perhaps. Then anytime you're loading variables into Flash you could use the loadVariables statement and enter a target of _root.allVariables. Any variables loaded in from an external file would end up in this movie clip that would act as a kind of depot for all your variables. Then even if you had to display them in some fancy manner in some remote movie clip that was buried in your Flash movie, the ActionScript or text field present there would only have to reference _root.allVariables followed by the particular variable name for which you were looking.

Locally accessible variables

Although true global variables don't exist in Flash, Flash does have true local variables. You define a variable as local in Flash by preceding it with the var statement:

```
var howLong=25;
```

The var statement makes the variable definition that follows it local to the script that is using it instead of a timeline. This script is the one you see in the ActionScript panel when you're defining the variable. The var statement is most useful for multiple scripts in/on a movie clip that use common operators in multiple functions.

Caution   Declaring a variable as local using var works only if that declaration is inside the curly braces ({}) of a function block. Just declaring the variable using var outside of a function will not make it local. (Hopefully, Macromedia will rethink the var statement on its next release of Flash.)

For example, most developers tend to use the letter i when counting iterations of a loop:

```
for(i=0;i<100;i++)
```

If you have many scripts, all within one movie clip, that use loops but are present in many places such as frames, buttons, and clip events; it's easy for something to get messed up. With so many scripts setting and retrieving the same i variable, there's bound to occasionally be a mistake because there can be only one variable named i per timeline, and all the different scripts are operating on just that one variable.

The var statement changes that by letting each script use its own unique i variable that is shielded from interference by any other ActionScript that might also be doing something with i somewhere in the same timeline or movie clip. To use var you just have to define the variable once at the beginning of the script, and no matter how many times you use it from then on in that script, it's completely inaccessible anyplace else:

```
function countThings{
var i;
for(i=0;i<100;i++){
        //any scripting can go here
}
//The variable i, although incremented to 100 by the loop,
cannot be seen from anywhere outside this function.
}
```

The trade-off in using var is that it shields your variables so well that you can't access them from any global position or anywhere outside of that one chunk of ActionScript function code you're using var in. So if you need to make your variables accessible and sharable all over Flash, don't use var when setting them in a function; otherwise, it will seem as if they aren't there at all when you go looking for them!

Displaying and outputting arrays

The addition of array-handling capability to Flash 5 was a welcome addition for just about every Web programmer. Flash has powerful array-processing features, and you'll find yourself storing variables in them time and time again.

Arrays in action

An *array* is basically an associative list of variable definitions. Instead of a unique variable name for each value, an array value is referenced by the name of the entire array followed by the value's position in the array list. To review the necessary syntax, read the following quick example of an array in action. These steps describe how to create a list of items and then output their names one at a time into a text field:

1. Open a new Flash file.

2. Create a dynamic text field anywhere on the stage in Frame 1 and give it the variable reference output.

3. Select Frame 1 and attach the following ActionScript to it:

```
itemList=new Array("tomato","grapefruit",2346,"blue");
count=0;
```

Notice that string values in Flash arrays are enclosed in quotations (""); numerical values do not need quotations.

4. Create a button anywhere on stage in Frame 1 and attach the following ActionScript to it:

```
on(press){
output=itemList[count];
count+=1;
}
```

Preview the movie in Flash and click the button. Each time you click the button, Flash displays the next element in the array `itemList`. It does this in the button by incrementing `count` and then appending it to the end of the array name inside brackets. Brackets tell Flash to evaluate whatever value is inside them. In this case, Flash is evaluating which value in the array to send back. When you reach the last element in the array, you won't see anything in the output field because the variable `count` has been incremented past the number of elements in `itemList`.

Note

Change the `output` line in the button to the following:

```
output=itemList[3];
```

Preview the movie again and notice Flash displays the fourth element in the array, `blue`, and not the third element even though you've specified 3. The reason is because computers start counting with the number 0 and not with the number 1 like we do. Remember that the first element in an array is referenced by the number 0 and you'll always be able to reference the correct value.

Displaying arrays in a list

You can display all the elements in an array at once in Flash by using `join` to stick all the array elements into one long sequence that can then be displayed in a dynamic text field. Note that the process of joining an array does not refer to combining two different arrays together.

This example joins all the elements of an array into a vertical display list:

1. Open a new Flash file.

2. Create a large, multiline dynamic text field anywhere on the stage in Frame 1 and give it the variable reference `output`. Make sure it can support at least four lines of text and do not check the Word wrap box.

3. Select Frame 1 and attach the following ActionScript to it as a frame action:

```
itemList=new Array("tomato","grapefruit",2346,"blue");
```

4. Create a button anywhere on stage in Frame 1 and attach the following ActionScript to it:

```
on(press){
output=itemList.join(newline);
}
```

Preview your movie by choosing Control ⇨ Test Movie and then clicking the button. You'll see that all the elements have been pulled from the array `itemList` and displayed in the text field with a new line between each one.

The basic syntax for `join` is as follows:

```
arrayName.join(separator);
```

Replace `arrayName` with the name of your array and `separator` with whatever character you'd like Flash to stick in between the elements. In the example, we used the reserved ActionScript `newline` to put a line between each element, but you can put just about any character in between the elements. If you use a character, the output will be in one long string rather than on neatly formatted new lines and you'll also have to include that character in quotations (""). Try replacing the `output` line in the button code in this example with any of the following lines and note the results:

```
output=itemList.join("!!");
```

or

```
output=itemList.join("@");
```

or

```
output=itemList.join(chr(32));
```

Flash will put all the elements together in a row separated by whatever character you chose. The last sample code line using `chr(32)` joins the array elements together using a standard spacebar press, represented by the character code 32 with an output that looks like:

```
tomato grapefruit 2346 blue
```

Caution   The Flash 5 release introduced the use of the backslash (\) to designate certain escaped characters inside of strings you define. The escape character \r is used to denote a carriage return anywhere where one is needed. Although this character accomplishes the same purpose as `newline`, Flash recognizes it as a completely separate character. You can use either one to accomplish the task of creating a line break; they just can't be used interchangeably.

Processing arrays from a text file

In the earlier section "Loading external variables into Flash" in this chapter, you learned that the proper way to format an array inside your external text files is to separate the elements with commas (,). For example, an array with four car colors inside it is defined in the text file as follows:

```
&carColors=red,white,blue,green&
```

The problem is that once you load this array into Flash with any `loadVariables` command, Flash sees this array as one single variable named `carColors` and not an array with four separate elements inside it. In order to fix this problem, you must tell Flash to turn `carColors` back into an array and to break apart the string value `red,white,blue,green` into the separate array elements. The ActionScript `split` accomplishes this task for you.

When using `split`, you can basically split any string value into an array by designating the character inside the string that separates all the elements. For example, because our `carColors` example was formatted with commas, we can easily designate the comma (,) as the character that indicates where the string should be broken apart. When Flash uses `split`, it goes through the string and breaks apart all the elements at the defined separator and then removes the separator. The basic syntax for `split` is as follows:

```
stringName.split(character_to_split_at);
```

In this syntax, `stringName` is a string that you'd like to change into an array and `character_to_split_at` is the character you'd like Flash to look for inside the string and break apart the string at. You must enclose this character inside quotation marks unless you're specifying a Flash-reserved character such as `newline` or an ActionScript reference such as `chr(32)`.

Follow these steps to load an array into Flash from a text file (where it looks like a string) and convert it into an actual array inside of Flash:

1. Create a text file in your favorite text editor and save it in a directory on your hard drive as `arraysplit.txt`.

2. Inside this text file, put the following line of code and then save your changes:

   ```
   &carColors=red,white,blue,green&
   ```

3. Create a new Flash file and save it as `arraysplit.fla` inside the same directory as `arraysplit.txt`.

4. Create a single-line dynamic text field anywhere on the stage in Frame 1 and give it the variable reference `carColors`. Use static text to place the label "carColors - StringVariable" next to it.

5. Create a single-line dynamic text field anywhere on the stage in Frame 1 and give it the variable reference `carColorsArr`. This will be the name of the new array you create to hold the split variable from the text file string variable `carColors`. Place the label "carColorsArr - Array" next to the text field.

6. Create a large multiline dynamic text field anywhere on the stage in Frame 1 and give it the variable reference `output`. Make sure it can support at least four lines of text, and do not check the Word wrap box. Use static text to place the label "Output" next to it. Figure 1-5 shows the approximate layout of the stage.

7. Select the keyframe in Frame 1 and attach the following frame ActionScript:

   ```
   loadVariablesNum ("arraysplit.txt", 0);
   count=0;
   ```

   This script loads in the variable `carColors` from `arraysplit.txt` and makes it available on the main timeline.

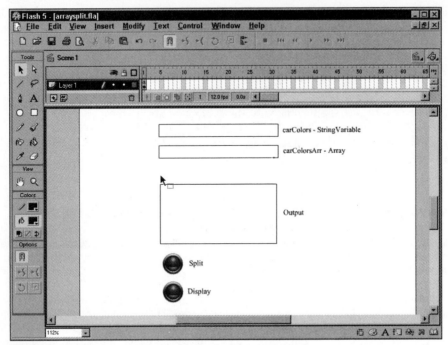

Figure 1-5: The layout of the stage for the file arraysplit.fla.

8. Create a button anywhere on the stage and use static text to label it "Split." Attach this ActionScript to the button:

```
on(press){
    carColorsArr=carColors.split(",");
}
```

This code creates an array with the name `carColorsArr` that contains the four values from the string variable `carColors` loaded in from the text file after Flash splits them apart. Flash removes the commas and places the four separate values into the array `carColorArr`.

9. Create a button anywhere on the stage and use static text to label it "Display." Attach the following ActionScript to the button:

```
on(press){
    output=carColorsArr[count];
    count+=1;
}
```

10. Preview the movie in Flash by choosing Control ➪ Test Movie. After Flash loads the variable `carColors` from the text file, you'll see it appear in the text field referencing `carColors`.

11. Click the Split button that you created. Flash has now created a true array named `carColorsArr` from the broken apart values of the string `carColors`. You'll see the whole array appear in the text field referencing `carColorsArr`, but notice that it looks exactly the same as the string variable `carColors`! Behind the scenes, the string variable `carColors` you have loaded in from the text file is still just a string variable, but the array `carColorsArr` that you created by clicking the Split button is a true array. So even though the two text fields are displaying what looks like two strings, rest assured they are not!

Note

When you just reference the array name in a dynamic text field, Flash automatically puts all the element values together for you to see. It's kind of like an automatic `join` being performed for your convenience.

12. Click the Display button you created. Flash steps through the elements inside the array one at a time, starting with the 0 element and incrementing the count each time. Now you see that even though the display of `carColorsArr` looks the same as `carColors`, it is actually an array created by using `split` You can prove this as well by changing the button code to reference `carColors[count]` and observing that it doesn't work, because `carColors` from the text file looks like a string to Flash and not an array.

13. You can now easily pull individual values from the array you created by just referencing them using their element numbers. You could also do a `join` on the array elements to place them into a list. Change the button code on the Display button to the following:

```
on(press){
     output=carColorsArr.join(newline);
}
```

You'll now see all the elements in the array joined together, one per line, in the Output field. Again, if you try to just reference the variable `carColors`, it won't work because that variable is just a plain old string variable to Flash. The text field labeled "carColorsArr - Array" is there to not only show you that Flash has performed an action when you clicked the Split button, but also to show you how Flash delivers an array as a whole when asked to just display the whole thing at once. This capability is important because Flash lists the elements all in a row by separating them with commas. This format is exactly how Flash sends an array to the server, as you see in the section "Sending variables to the server."

Checking for the arrival of variables

This section explains how to compensate for the reality of server lag. The reality is that Web servers experience delays and roadblocks on a consistent basis, and there's no way of ever telling precisely how long they can take to deliver a file requested by Flash. Internet conditions and bandwidth speeds also play a big role in determining how long it takes for someone at his or her home computer to receive a text file over a dial-up modem that a Flash movie in their browser requested from a slow server somewhere. The two methods of testing to see whether the variables requested by Flash have shown up yet are standard frame loops and the new Flash 5 onClipEvent(data) statement.

Standard frame loops

The standard frame loop was the only way in Flash 4 to effectively test to see whether any variables requested by loadVariables had shown up in Flash yet. This loop would usually consist of three keyframes placed one right after the other. The first frame would contain the loadVariable statement, the second frame would contain an if statement checking for the existence of a variable in whatever text file was called for, and the third frame would send the playhead back to Frame 2 to keep checking until the if statement proved true.

Although Flash 5 contains a simpler and more effective way to check for variables, this standard frame loop is still worth exploring because it paints a clearer picture of exactly what is happening when Flash is waiting for variables. The following example takes you through the process of building a simple frame loop to check for the existence of variables:

On the CD-ROM   The following example utilizes the files frameloop.fla and frameloopdata.txt found on the CD-ROM. Copy these files into the same directory on your hard drive and save them.

Start by opening the file frameloopdata.txt in your text editor. Notice that three variables are defined inside: name, occupation, and flag. The contents of the text file should look like:

    &name=Bob&

    &occupation=programmer&

    &flag=1&

The first two variables represent whatever data may be in any text file you normally load into Flash. The third variable flag is designed to be a signal to Flash that the end of all the data has been reached. You will set the value of this variable to 0 initially in the Flash movie. Then you'll keep checking to see if it equals 1. The only way it could eventually equal 1 is if Flash has read in all the other variables in the text file frameloopdata.txt to reach the very last variable named flag and load that in as well.

Note   You don't have to use the variable name flag when creating your own text files, but you should decide on a standard variable name that you'll use at the end of all your text files and remember to always check for that variable name in Flash. Other common end-of-data designators are variable names such as endvar or finished. You can also choose any value for them as well, such as true or yes. Remember to check for this value in Flash as well.

1. Open the file `frameloop.fla` in the Flash authoring environment. Notice the three keyframes at the beginning of the timeline in the Actions layer. In the Text layer, Frame 1 and Frame 15 each have one keyframe.

2. Reset the `flag` variable to 0 and load the text file by selecting Frame 1 in the Actions layer and adding this ActionScript:

```
flag=0;
loadVariablesNum ("frameloopdata.txt", 0);
```

3. To check to see whether the `flag` variable has arrived and, if it has arrived, send the timeline to a place that will operate on any variables loaded, select Frame 2 in the Actions layer and add this ActionScript:

```
if(flag==1){
     gotoAndStop("loadcomplete");
}
```

4. If the `flag` variable does not equal 1, Flash will continue to play on to Frame 3 where you'll send it back to Frame 2 to check again. To set up this process, select Frame 3 in the Actions layer and add this ActionScript:

```
gotoAndPlay(2);
```

5. Select Frame 15 in the Text layer and give it a label of `loadcomplete` by using the Frame panel.

6. With the playhead still at Frame 15, use the Text tool to put some words on the stage like "Load Process Complete." The example here uses 24-point bold Times New Roman.

7. Create two dynamic text fields below these words at Frame 15. Give one text field the variable reference `name` and the other text field the variable reference `occupation`. Select the Border/BG text box as well. Figure 1-6 shows the stage layout.

8. Return to Frame 1 in the Text layer and add some static text with the words "Loading Please Wait[el]." This text sends the user a message to wait while the variables are loading. The completed file is available on the CD-ROM as `flashloop_completed.fla` if you have any problems.

Preview the movie in Flash by choosing Control ⇨ Test Movie. Suddenly you're transported to Frame 15 where you'll see that the text fields already contain the two variables that Flash loaded in from the text file. What happened to the loop and the words "Loading Please Wait"?! What happened is that all the files are on your hard drive, so Flash got the variables from the text file the instant the `loadVariables` statement asked for them. It never got to play through the loop a few times.

Caution　The danger in testing Flash files that contain a dynamic text file from your local drive is that you can never get a sense of whether your failsafe mechanisms are working. Always upload these files to the Web to check how these files work under realistic conditions.

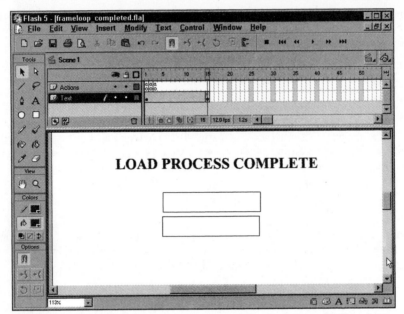

Figure 1-6: The stage layout for Frame 15 of the frameloop.fla file where the playhead is sent after Flash has received all the variables.

To remedy this situation, save the file `frameloop.fla` that you just created and then publish it as SWF and HTML files. Upload the HTML and SWF files to your Web server along with the file `frameloopdata.txt`. Make sure they're both in the same directory! Now open your browser and type in the URL to the HTML file you just uploaded. You should now see your loading script in action! If your Internet connection and server are really fast or there's no Internet traffic, you may miss it again. Keep hitting Refresh and sooner or later you'll get some lag and have to wait for the variables to arrive.

Keep in mind that you can substitute the `gotoAndPlay` action in the `if` statement in this example for any action you'd like to occur when your variables arrive. Also, although this example is built on the main timeline, you could easily put all these frames into a movie clip and load the variables from there. Just remember to load them into the movie clip using `this` as the target in the `loadVariables` statement, or if you still wanted to load the variables into `_level0`, you could change the `if` statement to read something like `if(_root.flag==1)`.

The onClipEvent statements

Flash 5 added some great new features to Flash. One of the more interesting additions to ActionScript is the `onClipEvent` set of statements. These statements sit outside and on top of a movie clip placed on the stage in much the same way that a button's actions reside outside and on top of the button. The `onClipEvent` has a few variations; this section focuses on the two that follow:

```
onClipEvent(load){
  //some ActionScript here
}
onClipEvent(data)
  //some ActionScript here
}
```

The onClipEvent(load) contains statements after it that will be executed only when the movie clip that they're sitting on shows up on the stage. Don't get this confused with loading variables or loading anything externally! All this statement means is that whenever that movie clip shows up on the stage, the statements in the onClipEvent(load) statement are executed. Think of the statement as onClipEvent(exists) and you'll be less confused.

The onClipEvent(data) statement works the same way except you need to wait for external variables in this one. This statement basically says that every time variables from an external text file show up in the movie clip that this statement's attached to, the statement will execute the statements that follow it. You don't need to set any flags in your text files anymore because Flash is smarter now and knows when all the data from a text file has been loaded.

Once onClipEvent(data) is attached to a movie clip and that movie clip is listed as the target in a loadVariables statement (from anywhere in Flash), the onClipEvent(data) statement will perform its duties once all the data has shown up. This statement is always waiting in background ready to see if the data has completely arrived. To see how this statement works, follow these steps:

1. On the CD-ROM, open the file clipeventdata.txt and save it to your local hard drive. This simple file contains two variable definitions:

   ```
   &name=Bob&
   &occupation=programmer&
   ```

2. Open a new Flash file and save it as clipevent.fla in the same directory that you saved clipeventdata.txt into.

3. In Frame 1, add some static text with the words "Loading Please Wait [el]." to give the user a message to wait while the variables are loading. Select this static text and then press F8 to turn it into a movie clip with a symbol name of "Load Check Clip."

4. Double-click the movie clip to get inside it and add a stop() action to Frame 1.

5. Create a keyframe inside "Load Check Clip" at Frame 15 by pressing F7 and give it the frame label loadcomplete.

6. Still at Frame 15 inside the movie clip symbol "Load Check Clip," create a static text field on the stage with the words "Load Process Complete."

7. Below that static text, create two dynamic text fields. Give one text field the variable reference name and the other text field the variable reference occupation. Select the Border/BG text box as well. These fields reference the two variables that will be loaded in from the text file clipeventdata.txt. Figure 1-7 shows what Frame 15 inside "Load Check Clip" should look like.

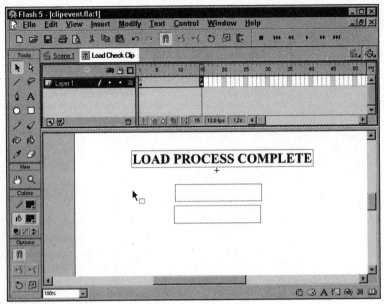

Figure 1-7: The layout of the timeline and stage on Frame 15 of the movie clip symbol "Load Check Clip."

8. Return to the main timeline and give the instance of "Load Check Clip" that you just edited an instance name of loadChecker using the Frame panel.

9. With loadChecker still selected, make sure the ActionScript panel is open and add the following ActionScript to the outside of it:

```
onClipEvent(load){
        loadVariables ("clipeventdata.txt", this);
}
onClipEvent(data){
        _root.gotoAndStop("loadcomplete");
}
```

This code accomplishes two things. First, as soon as the loadChecker movie clip loads (exists) on the timeline (which is right away because it's in Frame 1), it will load the variables from the file clipeventdata.txt into itself because it uses the self-reference path this as the target of the variables. Second, the onClipEvent(data) statement patiently waits until the data has fully arrived and then sends its timeline to stop at the frame labeled loadcomplete, which is Frame 15. Test the movie and see what happens. The completed file is available on the CD-ROM as clipevent.fla if you encounter any problems.

You should see the movie clip jump right to Frame 15 because you're testing it on your local hard drive. Upload the HTML, SWF, and TXT files to your Web server to get a better idea of the effects of the delay while loading the text file. A good way to make a longer lag is to go into the text file and make the variable occupation a very long paragraph of text, which will lengthen the load time for the file.

As you see, the movie clip instance `loadChecker` first loads the variables into itself and then waits until they arrive to perform an action. In this example, it's only sending its own timeline to a different frame where it displays the variables. In many dynamic applications, you're waiting for numerical data in order to operate on it later. Whatever the case, your data need to arrive in Flash before you can start adding up numbers or comparing user names and passwords to a list that you have in a text file.

Make a quick change to the file to see what happens:

1. On the main timeline, double-click the instance `loadChecker` to get into its symbol editing mode.

2. In Frame 15 (the frame labeled `loadcomplete`), delete one of the two dynamic text fields.

3. Change the remaining text field's variable reference to `approved` and extend its length on the stage so it will accommodate about 20 characters of text.

4. While still inside the movie clip, select Frame 15 (the frame labeled `loadcomplete`) on its timeline and add the following frame actions:

```
if(name eq "Bob" && occupation eq "programmer"){
    approved="You're approved!";
}
else{
    approved="Sorry, access denied!";
}
```

This code checks to see if the variables, once they've all arrived, match a certain criteria. Try changing the variable values in the text file to reflect something different, and you'll see the words "Sorry, access denied!" Just remember that if you're testing this on a server and you're making changes to the text file, your browser's probably cached the file, so it will seem not to work, even when the data is valid. To fix this problem, you need to institute the dynamic query string method described earlier in this chapter. The `onClipEvent` code for `loadChecker` would then need to look something like the following:

```
onClipEvent(load){
rn = Math.round(Math.random()*1000000);
    loadVariables ("clipeventdata.txt?reload="+rn, this);
}
onClipEvent(data){
    _root.gotoAndStop("loadcomplete");
}
```

The applications for using `onClipEvent(data)` are endless and include password checking, personalization of a Flash site, and checking to see if someone got the new high score in a game; the list goes on and on. Just remember that it does no good to use the `if` statement to start comparing variables that haven't arrived in Flash yet, so `onClipEvent(data)` is your new best friend!

Sending Variables to the Server

In order to use any of the server scripting languages described in this book, you need to have Flash send data to the server. When Flash sends data, it sends it out in the URL-encoded format automatically, so you have nothing to worry about there. You just need to be aware of which variables Flash sends and what the correct ActionScript is to send them.

Using loadVariables to send variables

The `loadVariables` ActionScript statement is responsible for sending variables to the Web server as well as loading them from external files into Flash. (Macromedia should have named the action something like `load/sendVariables`.) All you have to do to send some variables to a PHP, CGI, or ASP script is to specify the `GET` or `POST` option at the end of the `loadVariables` action. In the URL field, just enter the path to the script you're calling:

```
loadVariablesNum ("http://www.mydomain.com/myscript.php",
0, "GET");
```

This code would send variables using the `GET` method to `myscript.php` and would place any variables that are sent back into Level 0. But wait a second, precisely which variables is Flash sending to the script? The answer is all the variables in the timeline that executes the statement. If the `loadVariables` statement is executed from the main timeline, all the variables that are sitting on the main timeline are going to be shipped off to the server script. If the statement is inside a frame in the movie clip `_root.circus.car.clown1`, all the variables declared anywhere inside `clown1` are going to be converted to URL encoding and sent off to the server.

Many times, variables that you forgot about and may not want to send out are still lurking around. Little things like variables named `i` that you use to count iterations of a loop will be sent to the server with everything else. For this reason, you should put movie clip instances in your Flash movie that have no purpose other than to hold variables. You could then put the `loadVariables` action into that movie clip or, better yet, use the powers of object-oriented programming to let the command come from anywhere in Flash:

```
_root.ball.loadVariablesNum
("http://www.mydomain.com/myscript.php", 0, "GET");
```

That action could be executed from anywhere in Flash. It would take all the variables inside the `_root.ball` movie clip and send them to the server script `myscript.php`, at which point the server script would process them and send back some variables (not necessarily the same ones). These return variables would then arrive in Level 0 because the statement was a `loadVariablesNum` action with Level 0 specified. Powerful stuff! This code lets you place the action in one movie clip or timeline, send the variables contained within another, and have the returned variables placed somewhere else.

Watching out for objects and functions

When we mention that Flash sends all the variables present on the timeline that is executing (or referenced to execute) the `loadVariables` statement, we're not telling you the whole story. Flash also sends out all the objects and functions! Using `getUrl` is often a good way to check what types of things Flash is sending out. The following example shows this process in detail:

1. Open a new Flash file.

2. Create a button or drag one to the stage by choosing Window ➪ Common Library ➪ Buttons.

3. Add the following ActionScript to the button:

```
on(press){
name1="mark";
name2="bill";
function someFunc(){
            // any ActionScript here
}
checkMeOut=new Object();
getURL ("http://www.flashcore.com/defaultfile.html", "",
"GET");
}
```

4. Test the movie by choosing Control ➪ Test Movie.

A browser window should pop up (no Web page will display, though) with the URL specified and a query string filled with all kinds of excess junk! Then again as they say, "One man's trash is another man's treasure," although if you're not aware that every function and object on a timeline is going to be blasted out to the server, you're probably going to be leaning towards the "trash" opinion. Anyhow, the complete URL you see in the browser should look like the following:

```
http://www.flashcore.com/defaultfile.html
?someFunc=%5Btype+Function%5D&checkMeOut=%5Bobject+Object%5D
&name1=mark&name2=bill
```

You probably expected to see the following instead:

```
http://www.flashcore.com/defaultfile.html?name1=mark&name2=bill
```

In this example, Flash is sending out the names of all the functions and objects and their types. This example demonstrates another reason why you should create a movie clip whose sole purpose in life is to hold nothing but variables. Even though in this last example the functions and objects were defined in the button code and we used `getURL`, feel free to stick them on the timeline and/or use `loadVariables` to see what happens; the result is unfortunately the same. Thankfully though, Flash ignores all the movie clip instance names on any timelines.

Plan ahead where you'll be placing the important variables you need to send to the server and then just add the `GET` or `POST` method on to the end of any `loadVariables` statement to force Flash to start sending out the goods. This combination is the way to send e-mail form data to a CGI/Perl script or the information on a product order to a PHP page and MySQL database. You will be using `loadVariables` with `GET` and `POST` very often throughout the rest of the book.

Tip   If you ever need to send variables to another Flash movie that you're loading into the Flash Player via `loadMovie` or `loadMovieNum`, just specify `GET` at the end of the statement. Your variables will immediately show up ready for action on the main timeline of the SWF you're loading in. This procedure even works when replacing your Level 0 movie if you need to work with multiple frame-rate Flash movies but still retain your variables. Using `POST` in this case does not work, though.

Sending arrays to the servers

Besides the usual variables, objects, and functions that Flash takes from a timeline and converts to URL encoding in order to send them to a server, Flash sends any arrays as well. It does this in a fairly simple manner by automatically taking an array and joining its elements into a single string variable with the same name as the array and the values separated by commas. If you defined an array in Flash with this line

```
carColors=new Array("red","white","blue","green");
```

and then went on to execute a `loadVariables` statement to send the array to the server, Flash would send the entire array out in the form of a string like the following:

```
carColors=red,white,blue,green
```

This string does not in any way affect the array itself inside Flash. Flash just combines the elements on the way out to the server. Another important fact to note is that commas need to be URL-encoded as their value `%2C`; Flash does this encoding automatically. So the *actual* data Flash sends to the server when sending an array would look like the following:

```
carColors=red%2Cwhite%2Cblue%2Cgreen
```

This format is extremely important! On the server side, as you get into the server languages later in this book, you'll need to use that language's version of the `split` command if you want to operate on the array elements individually by first converting the URL-encoded `%2C` back into commas, and then creating a new array by splitting the string at each comma. What's interesting is that if your goal is to just store that array in a text file or database on the server to later send back to Flash, you can just leave the string alone. This works because when the server eventually takes what looks like a string and sends it back to Flash, you can use Flash's ActionScript `split` to transform the string back into an array!

This example uses `getURL` to show how Flash uses URL encoding on an array and sends it to the server:

1. Create a new Flash file.

2. Create a button on the stage or drag one in by choosing Window ⇨ Common Libraries ⇨ Buttons.

3. Attach the following ActionScript to the button:

```
on (press) {
        authors="Mark and Bill";
        carColors = new Array("red", "white", "blue", "green");
        getURL ("http://www.flashcore.com/nofile.html", "_blank", "GET");
}
```

4. Preview the movie in your browser and click the button.

You'll immediately see a window pop-up to a page that doesn't exist on FlashCore.com. What we're looking for here is to see the query string at the end of the URL for a visual representation of how Flash sends regular variables along with an array. The URL you see in your browser window should have this query string:

```
?authors=Mark+and+Bill&carColors=red%2Cwhite%2Cblue%2Cgreen
```

Whenever you use `getUrl` or a `loadVariables` statement, Flash sends any arrays to the server in the format of a string, with their elements combined and separated by commas that are URL-encoded as `%2C`. Just be sure to account for this formatting on the server scripting side to make sure you can break up the data the way you want.

Alternative Ways to Load and Send Variables

There are a few other ways to send data into and out of Flash. This section details some of them and even presents a secret piece of ActionScript code for writing variables directly onto the hard drive of a person viewing your Flash movie!

Loading HTML for display in Flash

Flash 5 introduced the capability to pull HTML code directly into Flash and place it into a text field complete with the correct link and text colors specified in your HTML code. Unfortunately, you can't just point Flash to the URL of a Web page and tell it to "go fetch." Many HTML tags confuse Flash, and you can load in only very basic HTML.

The way to designate a dynamic text field to parse HTML code in Flash is to check the HTML check box in the Text Options panel for your text field. A check in this box tells Flash to hunt for and parse any HTML code it finds inside the variable you've associated with the text field. That's right, you must have a string variable that contains all your HTML code.

Use these basic guidelines concerning Flash and HTML to help you use this feature successfully:

✦ Begin and end the code with the proper `<html>` and `</html>` tags, although this isn't completely necessary.

✦ Never include the `<head>` section; it confuses Flash, and it will display the page title and anything else right in the text field.

✦ Do not include any body attributes. Flash doesn't recognize code concerning background colors or default text colors and link colors. You'll have to specify them one at a time.

✦ Do not include any references to tables or other HTML layout items; Flash doesn't care. Yes folks, we're talking about bare bones HTML code here, circa 1993.

✦ Do not include any JavaScript or VBScript.

✦ Flash will parse any text and link colors, but you have to specify them directly for each block of text or link.

✦ Flash will make any links clickable inside the text field as long you have a properly formatted `<a href>` tag in the HTML code.

✦ Any `<p>` paragraph breaks are overly exaggerated; use line break `<br>` tags instead.

✦ Carriage returns in the text file containing the HTML code create line breaks in Flash. For this reason, you should usually have a server generate your HTML code for Flash and put it all on one continuous line.

✦ You must precede the opening `<html>` tag with the name of the variable you want to associate it with if you're loading your HTML code in from an external text file.

To see how Flash handles HTML, view the `htmlcode.txt` text file (it's on the CD-ROM) in your text editor. Notice that it contains no `<head>` section and that even though the body background is set to `black #000000`, Flash is going to ignore that setting. The most important part of the `htmlcode.txt` file is the variable reference `mycode` as the very first item followed by an equals sign and then all the HTML code. This reference basically defines all the HTML code as belonging to a variable named `mycode`:

```
mycode=<html>
```

On the CD-ROM   The files `htmlcode.fla` and `htmlcode.txt` are on the CD-ROM. Copy these files to your local hard drive and then open them to view their contents.

View the file `htmlcode.fla` in Flash and you'll notice a button with code to load in the data from the `htmlcode.txt` text file. You'll also notice the dynamic text field with the variable reference `mycode` and the HTML check box selected in the Text Options panel.

When you preview the movie in Flash or in your browser and click the button, you'll see the words Two Website Links: followed by links to the Web sites of Bill Sanders and Mark Winstanley. The links are fully clickable right inside the text field in Flash. Unfortunately, Flash doesn't underline them for you; so if you want to make your links more visible, color them a different color than any surrounding text. You'll have to do this for each link because Flash doesn't parse the HTML body attributes.

The raw line breaks in the text file create a lot of white space in text fields. If you'd like to go into the htmlcode.txt text file and delete every carriage return so that all the HTML code sits on one continuous line of text, you'll see all the three lines of text display one after the other in the dynamic text field with no extra white space. By dynamically generating your HTML code using a server script, you can force all the tags to sit on one line.

You can name the text file with any extension you'd like, such as html or txt, because Flash just looks inside whatever file you reference for properly formatted HTML code. You can embed links in regular variables by just including the <a href> and font color tags. If you have long pieces of text, you can embed links right inside the text fields for the convenience of the user. Just make sure the text field is set up to parse HTML by checking the appropriate box in the Text Options panel.

For example, if you open the additional CD-ROM file htmlcode2.txt, you'll see the variable mycode with some text and then all the tags for the links in between. Try changing the button code in the Flash file htmlcode.fla to point to htmlcode2.txt and then preview the Flash movie. You'll see how you can include HTML code in any variable as long as the dynamic text field is configured to receive it. If the box for HTML in the Text Options panel for the text field referencing mycode is not checked, you then see all the HTML tags and code present in the text field when you preview the Flash movie.

External ActionScript files

Flash 5 introduced the capability to save all your ActionScript in an external file and then use the ActionScript command #include to load the ActionScript into Flash. This procedure is as simple as putting any ActionScript you may want to use into a text file and then saving it with the as extension. This extension isn't absolutely required, but we recommend using it because it designates your file as containing ActionScript.

The same security rules apply as everywhere else in Flash: If you're including an http:// reference at the beginning of your filename, it must point to the same domain that your Flash movie is on if the movie is on the Web. Other than that, you can put as little or as much ActionScript as you'd like into a file. Then in whatever frame (or clip action) you'd like the actions to appear and execute, put an include statement with this syntax:

```
#include "filename.as"
```

Replace `filename` with whatever your filename is and the external ActionScript will be loaded in as if it were in that frame or clip action from the beginning. Make sure to enclose the filename in quotations. Note also that the `#include` ActionScript command is the only one that uses the pound sign (#) at the beginning of it. Don't forget the pound sign, or the script will not work correctly.

This set of steps demonstrates how this process works:

1. Create a new file in Flash and save it your hard drive as `include.fla`.

2. Select the keyframe in Frame 1 and add the following frame action:

```
stop();
#include "externalaction.as"
```

3. Create a new blank keyframe at Frame 10 in the same layer. Place a static text field here with the words "It Worked!!"

4. Open your favorite text editor and create a file named `externalaction.as` and save it in the same directory as your Flash movie `include.fla`.

5. Inside `externalaction.as`, place the following line of ActionScript and then save your changes:

```
gotoAndStop(10);
```

6. Preview the movie in Flash or in your browser and you'll see that the Flash playhead has jumped to Frame 10 and is displaying your text "It Worked!!"

Please note that what you put in your AS file has nothing to do with URL encoding. It is regular, straight-up ActionScript! In some instances, you may want to load in variables that you've defined like this because it's easier to denote their names and values in Flash ActionScript than it is with lots of URL encoding.

One drawback is that the `#include` command is not backwards compatible with any other version of the Flash Player. Another drawback is that if you constantly use this method you don't get as much experience using the Internet standard of URL encoding to operate on variables. Then again, URL encoding is only good for dealing with variable names and values, but external ActionScript files can contain any ActionScript you'd like!

Caution   The files pulled into Flash using `#include` seem to behave differently than regular text files that you would load using `loadVariables`. If you put all the files on your Web server and then view them through a browser, the external ActionScript files don't always appear in the browser cache. Even after you make changes to the external script and upload them to the Web server, Flash often seems to still acquire the old file data somewhere. If you're looking for consistent dynamic interactivity, use standard text files with the dynamic query string method described in this chapter or use server-side scripting as described in later chapters.

HTML and JavaScript variable loading

By using either JavaScript or direct HTML, you can pass variables into Flash directly from an HTML page where the Flash Player plug-in is embedded. This process works in all browsers. You can also have Flash send variables back to your HTML page, but this process often doesn't work with all browsers and all platforms.

In the following examples, you can use a file on the CD-ROM named `circus.fla`. Copy it to your hard drive and then publish it to get the files `circus.swf` and `circus.html`. You'll be modifying the HTML page code inside `circus.html` quite extensively. The Flash file contains no ActionScript; it just contains two text fields in Frame 1 referencing the variable names `clown1` and `clown2`.

Using HTML code to place variables into Flash

You can easily define variables right in your HTML page for Flash to use as soon as your Flash movie starts. If you're someone already using PHP, CGI, or ASP to generate your HTML pages where your Flash movies are embedded, you may have often wondered how to place variables in Flash directly upon generating your page. Either way, the process is very simple: Inside the `<object>` and `<embed>` tags of the HTML page holding your Flash movie, add a query string onto the end of the filename following the `swf` extension. That's it. As long as your query string is properly formatted in URL encoding, any variables you define will be ready and waiting on the main timeline of your Flash movie! You don't even need to check for them in any manner; Flash has no choice but to accept them and have them ready and waiting to go.

Suppose that you have a Flash movie named `circus.swf`. You want to include the variables and values `clown1=Happy` and `clown2=Honker` inside your HTML page or dynamically generate them with your HTML page if you're using a server scripting language. The filename as placed in the HTML code would become

```
circus.swf?clown1=Happy&clown2=Honker
```

The complete code for the HTML would look like this:

```
<OBJECT classid="clsid:D27CDB6E-AE6D-11cf-96B8-444553540000"
codebase="http://download.macromedia.com/pub/shockwave/cabs/flash
/swflash.cab#version=5,0,0,0" WIDTH=400 HEIGHT=300>
<PARAM NAME=movie VALUE="circus.swf?clown1=Happy&clown2=Honker">
<PARAM NAME=quality VALUE=high> <PARAM NAME=bgcolor VALUE=#FFFFFF>
<EMBED src="circus.swf?clown1=Happy&clown2=Honker" quality=high bgcolor=#FFFFFF
WIDTH=400 HEIGHT=300 TYPE="application/x-shockwave-flash"
PLUGINSPAGE="http://www.macromedia.com/shockwave/download
/index.cgi?P1_Prod_Version=ShockwaveFlash"></EMBED>
</OBJECT>
```

Marked in bold inside the code are the places where you'd normally have just the filename, but now you also have some variables tacked onto the end. You can include as many as you'd like, and they'll be instantly ready and accessible on the main timeline right when the first frame of your Flash movie loads. Because they're on the main timeline, the variable names will be accessible from anywhere in Flash by preceding the names with _root, as in _root.clown1 and _root.clown2 in this example.

Adding variables to the end of a filename is a great way to simply define some variables externally and have them available in Flash. But this method has two minor disadvantages:

✦ You have only one chance to define the variables because they are forced into Flash only when the plug-in is embedded in the HTML page. During later playback of your Flash movie, you'll have to use loadVariables to get any more external variables, unless you employ the JavaScript methods outlined in the next section.

✦ All your variable names and values are visible to the world! Anyone can view the source on your HTML page to see what variables you're defining and what values you're associating with those variables. Do not use this method for any variables that you need to keep secret and secure; instead use loadVariables and some server scripting to keep everything top secret!

As long as you're aware of the limitations involved using the HTML query string method, you can figure out when and where the appropriate variables you need to have ready and waiting in Flash will be there for you.

Forcing variables into Flash through JavaScript

JavaScript can be used to force variables into Flash much the same way the query string in the HTML page code can. The setup and syntax are only a slight bit different. JavaScript is by far the most popular object-oriented programming language. The Flash Player plug-in inside the Web page is just another object to JavaScript. If you specify a unique name for your Flash movie in the HTML code, you can then have JavaScript target that object and use the document.object.SetVariable syntax to transfer variables into Flash whenever you like.

Just like in the HTML query string, as soon as you set the variables using JavaScript, they are available on the main timeline whether Flash has asked for them or not. The great thing about using JavaScript is that you can set the variables after the Flash movie has already loaded.

First you need to set up the <object> and <embed> tags in the HTML page to make sure they reflect an object name that you'll be using to target your movie. Both these tags have a parameter that lets you specify an object name for your Flash movie. We'll use the circus and clown example again where the Flash movie is circus.fla and the variables and values clown1=Happy and clown2=Honker are to be set in Flash. The following code shows where to set the object name:

```
<OBJECT classid="clsid:D27CDB6E-AE6D-11cf-96B8-444553540000"
codebase="http://download.macromedia.com/pub/shockwave/cabs/flash
/swflash.cab#version=5,0,0,0" WIDTH=400 HEIGHT=300 name="circus">
<PARAM NAME=movie VALUE="circus.swf"> <PARAM NAME=quality VALUE=high>
```

```
<PARAM NAME=bgcolor VALUE=#FFFFFF>
<EMBED src="circus.swf" quality=high bgcolor=#FFFFFF  WIDTH=400 HEIGHT=300
name="circus" TYPE="application/x-shockwave-flash"
PLUGINSPAGE="http://www.macromedia.com/shockwave/download
/index.cgi?P1_Prod_Version=ShockwaveFlash"></EMBED>
</OBJECT>
```

In bold inside the code are the two places where you'll need to manually add the name you'd like to create for your Flash movie object to reference with JavaScript. Note that these places are right after where the `WIDTH` and `HEIGHT` are specified by the `<object>` and `<embed>` tags. In this example, `circus` is specified because the name of our hypothetical SWF file is `circus.swf`. Do not confuse specifying this object name in the page with any of the `<PARAM NAME>` tags. They are different. You can also name the object anything you'd like but be sure to enclose the specified name in quotations, as in `name="circus"`.

To set a variable on the main timeline of the file named `circus.swf` in the preceding code, you just have to reference it with some kind of JavaScript action or function. In general, you could include this JavaScript from anywhere inside the `<body>` tag after the Flash plug-in code on the HTML page:

```
<SCRIPT LANGUAGE=JavaScript>
document.circus.SetVariable("clown1","Happy");
document.circus.SetVariable("clown2","Honker");
</SCRIPT>
```

This code would immediately set two variables on the main timeline of the Flash movie referenced by the object `circus`, which is `circus.swf`: one variable with a name of `clown` and a value of `Happy` and another variable named `clown2` with a value of `Honker`. The important thing to watch out for when using JavaScript (like any language) is punctuation and capitalization. Make sure you specify the correct object reference in between the words `document` and `setVariable`. Also, note that the variable name is enclosed in quotations as well as its value. The variable name must always be in quotations, and the variable's value should be in quotations if it's a string. If it's a number, you can leave out the quotations, as in the following HTML example:

```
<SCRIPT LANGUAGE=JavaScript>
document.circus.SetVariable("clown1",56);
</SCRIPT>
```

You can also reference any other JavaScript variable and send that to Flash as well by using the same Javascript variable name or a different name, as shown in this HTML example:

```
<SCRIPT LANGUAGE=JavaScript>
var nameOfClown="Happy";
document.circus.SetVariable("clown1",nameOfClown);
</SCRIPT>
```

This code sets the JavaScript variable nameOfClown to the string value Happy and then passes that value to the Flash variable clown1 through plain old JavaScript.

Using JavaScript to set variables in Flash can come in very handy. If you're very familiar with JavaScript, you could have HTML page form values that can be sent into Flash, or you could put the SetVariable statements inside a JavaScript function in the <head> tag, call the function in the <body> tag with onLoad, and continually pass data into Flash. That's right, you can open a pipeline right into Flash through JavaScript and continually feed Flash new and updated information by using the JavaScript SetVariable. Be sure to coordinate elements in your Flash movie so Flash can do something with the data as it's arriving.

Caution   The one drawback to using JavaScript to send variables to Flash is that anyone can see what you're up to by viewing source on your page. Most people surfing the Internet won't have a clue, but if any security issues are involved, you should keep things inside of Flash using loadVariables and server scripting. For simple things and fun Flash movies it's a great tool to have in your bag though!

Calling JavaScript from Flash

Flash can be used to call any JavaScript function that you've defined in your HTML page or even to send JavaScript commands directly to the browser. The big drawback is that this doesn't work cross-platform and cross-browser, especially with Internet Explorer for the Macintosh. You may still want to use it in certain instances where you know that most people will be viewing your Flash movies on a PC or on a Macintosh using Netscape. You could easily implement some browser-sniffing JavaScript to test for these browsers as well.

The process of using Flash to talk back to JavaScript in the HTML page involves only the use of the getURL action. Instead of entering a URL, you enter javascript: and then the name of the function you want to call. If you defined a Javascript function named dateAndTime() in the HTML page holding your Flash movie, for example, and you wanted a button in Flash to execute it, the Flash button code would read:

```
on (release) {
    getURL ("javascript:dateAndTime();");
}
```

No space follows the colon in javascript: and that the semicolon for the JavaScript call is enclosed within the quotation marks of the getURL action where the URL would normally go.

In addition to calling a predefined JavaScript function, you can also use Flash to execute just about any valid JavaScript. You need to format the statement correctly because the Flash getURL action needs quotation marks in the right place as well as the JavaScript code. Suppose that you need a button in Flash to set a JavaScript variable in the HTML page named clown1 to a value of Happy. The Flash button code would read:

```
on (release) {
    getURL ("javascript:var clown1=\"Happy\";");
}
```

Notice the odd looking sets of quotations and semicolons near the end of the statement. The escaped quotation mark \" is needed to make sure that Flash is sending that quotation out to the HTML page and not interpreting it as a quotation signifying the end of the URL parameter in the `getURL` action. The last quotation in the statement signifies this and is not preceded with a backslash. Immediately following the last quotation is the closing parenthesis for the `getURL` action and then the ending semicolon for the Flash statement. The ending semicolon for the JavaScript statement is the one that follows `Happy\"` in the code line.

Secret Flash projector ActionScript

A Flash 5 projector file now has the ability to send variables right to the hard drive of whoever is viewing them by way of an undocumented FSCommand named `save`. This action creates a brand new text file on the computer of whoever is viewing the Flash projector movie. This text file contains all the variables from the main timeline of your Flash movie in a pseudo URL-encoded format. If you need to save variables to the user's hard drive that are located in other places in your Flash movie, you'll need to transfer them in Flash to the main timeline `_root` so that they may be saved as well.

Stand-alone only

I bet you're just ecstatic about this! This action opens the door to create stand-alone applications in Flash that can save data on a user's hard drive and retrieve it later on. You could build dynamic stand-alone projector games that save a player's high score and current place in the game or design a Flash multimedia kiosk application for a trade show that will let viewers register and be able to retrieve their names after the show! However, this secret action works only with stand-alone projector files with the `exe` or `hqx` extensions and not from the Web or in a Web browser.

This quick example will immediately create a text file on your hard drive and write some variables to it:

1. Create a new Flash file named `secretFS.fla` and save it on your local hard drive.

2. Select Frame 1 of this new Flash file and add the following frame actions:

```
author1="Mark Winstanley";
author2="Bill Sanders";
publisher="Hungry Minds";
```

3. Create a button on the stage in Frame 1 or drag one from the Standard library by choosing Window ➪ Common Libraries ➪ Buttons.

4. Attach the following ActionScript to the button:

```
on (release) {
    fscommand ("save", "fs_data.txt");
}
```

5. Under File ⇨ Publish Settings, check only the box for either Windows Projector or Mac Projector. Leave all the other boxes unchecked.

6. Press F12 to quickly launch the projector file. Click the button.

7. Using your Windows or Macintosh OS, navigate to the folder where you saved `secretFS.fla` and you'll see the `fs_data.txt` text file.

Upon opening this text file, you'll see this data:

```
&author1=Mark Winstanley&author2=Bill Sanders&publisher=Hungry
Minds
```

If you take a look at this data, you'll notice that the variables contain the proper ampersands (&) and equal signs (=), but they lack any other URL encoding such as converting the spaces between our first and last names into plus signs (+). Flash doesn't bother to convert spaces or any other nonletter characters for that matter into their URL-encoded equivalents. Flash knows that these characters are only going on a local hard drive and are not being sent out over the Web, so it skips that step.

Specifying a path

Now you can save variables to anyone's hard drive who happens to be viewing the projector movie you created. You can also specify any path you'd like for the text file containing the variables. If you don't specify a path, Flash automatically creates the text file in the same directory as the projector file. You could specify the parent directory of that file with this code:

```
fscommand ("save", "../fs_data.txt");
```

You could also specify any direct path on the hard drive:

```
fscommand ("save", "C:/My Documents/fs_data.txt");
```

Notice that example uses a Windows hard drive path. We don't know at this time what the correct paths may be for a Macintosh system and whether specifying a path on the Macintosh works. On Windows however, if you specify a path to a drive or folder that *already exists* (Flash can't create a directory), Flash will place the generated text file in that directory.

Also notice that normally on a Windows operating system the path to My Documents uses backslashes (\) and looks like the following:

```
C:\\My Documents\
```

Flash on the other hand finds its way to any directory on the hard drive using forward slashes (/) similar to a Web directory:

```
fscommand ("save", "C:/My Documents/CoolGames/gamedata.txt");
```

Specifying a file extension

Another interesting feature is that you can save the file with any file extension you'd like, including `vbs`, `html`, and even `exe`. There's not much purpose in doing this because the file is only going to contain sets of variables, but you can do it nonetheless. This capability means that you can write any type of file, including one with an `exe` extension that looks like an executable.

Caution   Because you can hypothetically configure the Flash projector to create an executable on a viewer's hard drive, you should exercise caution and always use the `txt` extension when creating these text files. Someone who is savvy at modifying the projector architecture could configure the Flash projector to contain harmful code and then write it somewhere deep on your hard drive. In general, you should never open an executable file sent you from someone you don't know, Flash or no Flash.

Here are some examples of this capability in action:

```
fscommand ("save", "C:/Windows/secretfile.exe");
```

or

```
fscommand ("save", "C:/My Documents/flashdata.html");
```

There isn't much of a reason to specify any extension other than `txt` unless another program running on the same machine uses the data, as in the case of a multimedia kiosk.

Loading the projector data into Flash

The text file you've dynamically generated and saved to the hard drive from Flash can be loaded back in the same way any other text files are loaded. Just use the ActionScript `loadVariables` and specify the filename (or path and filename) of the file you generated. Specifying a path could really come into play at this point, because you could hide a file somewhere on the user's hard drive where he or she may never find it, and therefore can't delete it. Use these features with fairness and respect and you'll never have anyone complaining that you've done sneaky things on their hard drive. Have fun!

Summary

Throughout this chapter, we have covered many facets of data formatting and sending and receiving that data to and from Flash. Go through the examples presented in this chapter carefully so that you'll be prepared to deal with data transfer in the later chapters. Many things presented in this chapter are basic Internet principles as well, and you'll now have a better understanding of the types of things that go on behind the scenes as data flies across the Internet. For those of you who are old hats at server scripting, you now see the ways that Flash deals with URL-encoded variable loading and sending along with its caveats and peculiarities. You're now ready to move onto the server languages and start making Flash truly dynamic and interactive!

✦   ✦   ✦

CGI/PERL: Quick and Easy Interactivity

✦ ✦ ✦ ✦

In This Chapter

Setting permissions
for your CGI scripts

Creating simple Perl
scripts

Transferring
information between
Flash and Perl

Using Flash and
CGI/Perl to develop
applications that
check passwords,
write and read text
files, and send e-mail

✦ ✦ ✦ ✦

*C*ommon Gateway Interface (CGI) is basically a doorway on the server through which the server can interact with scripts and then push data back out to the Web for the user to see. CGI is not a scripting or programming language, but rather the process through which scripts are accessed. The most common scripting language used with CGI is Perl. CGI scripts can be written in other languages, but 99 percent of the time Perl is the language used on the Web and is, therefore, the one that is used in this book to write scripts. When someone refers to a CGI script, that person is almost always referring to a script written in Perl; the terms "CGI script" and "Perl script" are used interchangeably and, for the purposes of this book, mean the same thing.

CGI scripts are the quickest and easiest way to add interactivity to your Flash movies and your Web site. These scripts can send e-mail messages, set and retrieve cookies, read and write to and from text files, and provide you with added security. CGI is the most common form of interactivity found on most Web host servers and is widely supported across the Internet. In this chapter, the many parameters and setup requirements that are unique to CGI are explained in detail. Once you get a few scripts up and running, you'll be using CGI all the time to enhance your Flash sites and make them perform amazing interactive feats!

Using CGI

CGI and Perl are almost always found exclusively on Unix or Linux Web servers. Perl scripts can be utilized on Windows NT hosts, but they require special modules. In contrast, installing Red Hat Linux on a Web server automatically installs Perl and makes the server ready to start executing any scripts. In most cases, you don't have to worry about these details. Just ask your hosting company, "Do you support and allow CGI/Perl scripts on your server?" Or if you are purchasing a new account, ask that your Web site be put on a Unix or Linux Web server that supports CGI and Perl.

Perl scripts have a wide variety of uses, including interacting with various types of databases. This interaction requires special modules regardless of the type of server software installed. Because the focus of this chapter is quick and easy inter-activity with CGI, the use of scripts to interact with mySQL is best left to the chapters on mySQL and PHP, which has become the de-facto standard for integrating with mySQL. Database design is also a world unto itself, and you'll see how with CGI/Perl and a standard text file you'll be able to emulate many of the read/write features of a database without all the additional setup steps. If you find Perl pro-gramming to your liking, check out *Perl for Dummies,* 3rd Ed. by Paul E. Hoffman (IDG Books, 2000) or *Perl: Your Visual Blueprint for Building Perl Scripts* by Paul Whitehead and Eric Kramer (IDG Books, 2000) for more information on the intricate details of this language.

Cross-Reference   To learn more about writing server scripts for MySQL and PHP, take a look at Chapter 4, "Using Flash 5 with PHP4 and MySQL."

Creating and uploading CGI scripts

CGI/Perl scripts are stored on the server in a CGI directory folder almost always named `cgi-bin` or occasionally just `cgi`. The presence of a CGI directory folder generally indicates that your host has set up and configured Perl correctly. The Perl program itself, which secretly lives on the server, is responsible for recognizing Perl scripts and executing them correctly. Perl scripts usually end in the extensions `pl` or `cgi`. We'll be using the Perl `pl` extension because it is the most common.

A Perl script is just a list of programming instructions inside a text file for the server to read and then execute. You can use any common text editor, such as Notepad or Wordpad (Windows) and SimpleText (Macintosh), to create a Perl script. You could use a more complex program, such as Word, although the file must be saved in plain text format with the extension `pl` added to the end. For example, you'll be creating two Perl scripts in this chapter named `setCookie.pl` and `getCookie.pl`.

Note   To modify a Perl script from this chapter that is on the CD-ROM, you first need to transfer the script to your hard drive and then upload it to your Web server. You may even want to copy all the Flash FLA files and all the Perl PL files to a new directory on your hard drive and open them from there.

Uploading and configuring Perl scripts on the server is a two-part process. The first part is to upload your script file into the `cgi-bin` directory; this process is no different than uploading any file to your Web server. Open up your favorite FTP program and upload the file just like any other Web page or graphic file.

Caution Using an FTP program to upload your Perl scripts is important. Uploading a Perl script to your Web host by using a program such as FrontPage or Dreamweaver is not recommended because most programs like these usually do not support the configuring of your script. Make sure to always select ASCII format in your FTP program as well. Most FTP programs upload in a binary format by default, but you want to upload Perl scripts using ASCII. The documentation for your FTP program can help you properly configure the program for this format.

Configuring CGI scripts

All Perl scripts that are uploaded to a Web server subsequently need to be configured before the server will execute them when they are called for by Flash or a Web page. If you are new to server scripting, the analogy would be that of going into a bakery and asking the baker for a chocolate cake and being handed the recipe for it. You do not want the set of instructions for making the cake; you want the baker (who represents the Web server) to execute the instructions and hand you the output, which is the chocolate cake. A special CGI command configures scripts inside the CGI directory to be executed when they are called for. This command is named `CHMOD`.

`CHMOD` stands for "change mode," and people usually call it by this name or say, "c-h-mod." This command sets the file permissions on the server for each CGI script so that when Flash or a Web page calls for the script, it either receives the script itself (which you don't want) or the parsed and executed output of the script (the chocolate cake). `CHMOD` can also configure files in the `cgi-bin` directory so that the Web server can write to and dynamically update them, thus making for a quick and easy mock database.

The `CHMOD` command is usually accessed in a FTP program by highlighting/selecting the CGI script in the remote Web directory after it has been uploaded and then finding the `CHMOD` command on a drop-down menu or Ctrl-clicking or right-clicking on the file. A dialog box will usually appear asking for the three-digit permissions number. Avoid the check boxes in the dialog box, if there are any, because determining which boxes correspond to which permission numbers becomes very confusing. Figure 2-1 shows the CHMOD window in CuteFTP (FTP software that is available from `www.cuteftp.com`) that appears after a user highlights a Perl script on the Web side and then chooses Commands ➪ File Actions ➪ CHMOD.

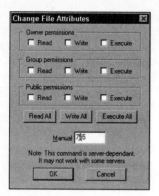

Figure 2-1: Accessing the CHMOD window to configure Perl scripts in the FTP program CuteFTP.

Each CGI script you upload has to be individually configured with a CHMOD command to designate what the server is to do with it when it receives a request for that file. The CHMOD command is followed by a three-digit number that represents the type of permissions to be set. The two you need to know are 755 and 666.

CHMOD 755 represents the permissions to set for a CGI script that you want the server to execute and then provide you with an output. CHMOD 666 is the permission to set for a data file that is going to be updated and written to by another script. Almost all scripts will be CHMOD 755, unless they contain raw data that needs to be dynamically updated; in those cases, the file will be CHMOD 666. Files that are CHMOD 666 usually contain nothing but data and end in the extension dat or txt, which marks them as dynamic text files. When a file's permissions are set to 666, the server is allowed to dynamically write to a text file. Figure 2-2 illustrates how this process works on the server and returns data to Flash.

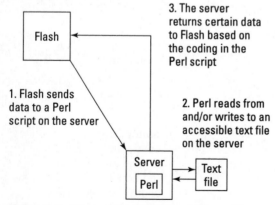

Figure 2-2: The process of Flash working with multiple scripts and text files on the server.

Note   Each script you upload needs to be individually configured with the CHMOD command for its intended purpose. The server, however, stores these permission settings as an association to the filename. This means that when you first upload a script you must use CHMOD, but when you upload revisions to the script, you do not need to use CHMOD again as long as the filename is the same. This takes the hardship out of making lots of changes and then quickly uploading and testing their effects.

Accessing your CGI scripts

Calling out to a CGI script requires an http reference in either a Web page or a Flash movie. The reference to use is http://yourdomain.com/cgi-bin/ scriptname.pl where yourdomain.com is your Web site address, cgi-bin is the designated CGI directory (usually cgi-bin), and scriptname.pl is the name of the script your are trying to reference, which ends in the Perl script file extension pl.

Troubleshooting potential CGI problems

You may run into a few problems when you initially contact your hosting company about using CGI with Perl scripts. One common problem is that your host does not allow CGI use at all or allows you to use only the prewritten scripts it has made available to you. If you have this problem with your host and you are paying for this hosting, switch immediately to a better company! Hosting companies today have no excuse for not allowing their users access to CGI/Perl other than incompetence on their part and lack of knowledge on how to properly protect their servers (because CGI can present somewhat of a security risk).

Tip   A great hosting company like jtlnet.com is the place to go for good service at a reasonable cost. With accounts starting at $7.95 per month, this company provides full CGI/Perl support along with PHP 4.0 and mySQL. We are baffled as to why other hosts give their paying customers a headache concerning CGI.

Another problem may occur after you've uploaded your scripts to the designated cgi-bin directory and are unable to use the CHMOD command with the files. This problem usually occurs when a host has given you limited CGI access because setting certain file permissions might wreak havoc on their servers. Full CGI access would allow you to run executable scripts such as CHMOD 755 because this server is generally configured to automatically execute all scripts in the CGI directory. The downside to having limited CGI access is that you cannot designate DAT files to write and append data to. Unless you're intimately connected to a host like this, we suggest seeking a different host or asking the host to give you a CGI directory with full access to file permissions. You would be surprised how many hosting companies with multimillion-dollar clients have these problems. Educating your clients is a good way to get them to switch hosts, especially when the result is a dynamic, interactive Web site.

Tip You can also set CHMOD permissions with Telnet. Fewer and fewer hosts allow Telnet access these days, but if you can find one (like jtlnet.com), the command once you change to the right directory is chmod 755 *filename* where *filename* is the name of your Perl script or dat file.

Writing Basic Perl Scripts

The best way to see how a server deals with a Perl script is to write one and get it up on the server for testing. Open your favorite text editor and create a new file. Save it as testing.pl and then enter the following code:

```
#!/usr/bin/perl
$somenumber=5;
#This sets a variable we can access
print "Content-type:text/html\n\n";
print "This is where we can send some data to Flash<br>";
print "For example the number $somenumber";
exit;
```

Save your changes and upload this script into the cgi-bin directory on your server. Use the CHMOD command in your FTP program to set the permissions of testing.pl to 755. If you're experiencing problems, use the copy of this file that is on the CD-ROM'. To test your script, open your Web browser and enter the URL

```
http://www.yourdomain.com/cgi-bin/testing.pl
```

where yourdomain.com is the name of your Web site and cgi-bin is the correct name of the CGI directory. Hit Enter and observe the Web page that is generated. The output on your browser screen is displayed in Figure 2-3 and should read

```
This is where we can send some data to Flash
For example the number 5
```

The small script you've just written contains the very basics of a Perl script that you will use to integrate with Flash!

Perl syntax

To ensure your scripts properly execute, you must follow some simple rules. Let's dissect some lines of code in testing.pl to see the basic syntax rules required for a properly functioning Perl script.

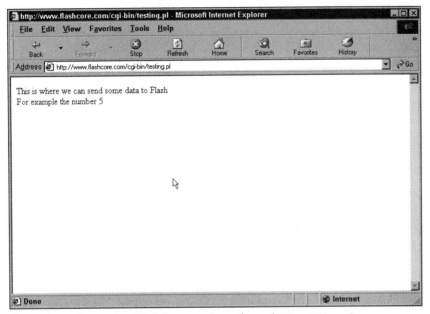

Figure 2-3: Output in a Web browser from the script `testing.pl`.

Path to Perl

All Perl scripts must begin with this line that designates the path to Perl. This line always begins with the two characters #! and does not need a semicolon at the end:

```
#!/usr/bin/perl
```

The path to Perl is the location on the server where the Perl program is installed and waits ready to parse Perl scripts. The path shown here is the normal default for most servers. If `testing.pl` doesn't work after you install it and you're sure you've used the CHMOD command correctly, the path to Perl on your server may be different. E-mail or call your hosting company to find out the correct path to use.

Semicolons

All lines of code in Perl must end with a semicolon. For example, look at the command in `testing.pl` that sets a string named `somenumber` to be equal to 5:

```
$somenumber=5;
```

If you forget even one semicolon, the Perl script will probably not function.

Comments

All comments in Perl start with the pound sign (#), as you can see in the following example:

```
#This sets a variable we can access
```

A comment line is an exception to the semicolon rule in Perl. Comment lines do not need a semicolon at the end. Comment lines can also contain many pound signs in a row (######) to block off an area of code.

Comments in Perl in this chapter are provided for convenience; they are not required for the code to function properly. When you start modifying the scripts or making your own scripts, add as many comments as you deem necessary.

Content-type

Another essential line of code is the content-type line.

```
print "Content-type:text/html\n\n";
```

In order to display data on a Web page or get it back into Flash correctly, you must set the type of data you are outputting. In this case, we are specifying in the script that the output of our script is meant for use on the Internet in a text or HTML format. If you view the source code on the Web page when you execute `testing.pl`, you'll see that this line is nowhere to be found because it is a necessary scripting element and not something being output to the Web page.

Print command

The command most commonly used for displaying data is `print`. The `print` command is used to not only display data from Perl on Web pages or to send data to Flash, but also to write data into e-mails and text files generated by Perl. These lines are standard `print` statements in Perl that write data for output:

```
print "This is where we can send some data to Flash<br>";
print "For example the number $somenumber";
```

These `print` statements wrote the two lines that were displayed on your Web page. Notice the quotation marks at the beginning and end of the text to be displayed and the semicolon at the end of the statements; these elements are required.

Also note how the `$somenumber` statement was included and parsed to display the number 5 on the Web page from within the `print` statement. Unlike in ActionScript, you don't need to concatenate variables with quoted text in Perl to display multiple data types together. Perl recognizes strings present within a quoted `print` statement.

Suppose you had a variable named `pet` and you wanted to set its value as `Jaguar` and display this output:

```
Jaguar=A great pet to own.
```

The ActionScript syntax and Perl syntax for this example would look different. Here is the Perl code:

```
$pet="Jaguar";
print"$pet=A great pet to own.";
```

The same effect in ActionScript code with a text filed named `output` on the stage:

```
_root.pet = "Jaguar";
_root.output = _root.pet+"=A great pet to own."
```

Escaping characters

Perl automatically parses strings within `print` statements because it searches for the dollar sign ($) and then parses the string that follows. If you wanted to output a dollar sign in a `print` statement, you must use an escape character. In this case, you would precede the dollar sign with a backslash (\). For example, to output the following line in Perl

```
I like to make lots of $MONEY$
```

you would need to escape the dollar signs so Perl doesn't think `MONEY` is a string needing to be parsed:

```
print"I like to make lots of \$MONEY\$";
```

Knowing when to escape a character is important to keep Perl from getting confused. The standard rule is that anywhere you need to output and display a Perl reserved character such as a quotation, semicolon, or dollar sign, you must precede the character with a backslash. The same rule applies to certain characters in ActionScript as well.

Exit

The `exit` statement is always the very last line in a Perl script:

```
exit;
```

Make sure this statement always ends up at the very bottom of your script.

Basic Perl commands and operators

The basic operators in Perl are very similar to those in ActionScript. Table 2-1 lists some of the Perl operators and describes how they are used.

	Table 2-1 Basic Perl Operators	
Operator	*Use*	*Format example*
=	assignment	`$posMX =100;`
+	add	`$sumNow = $firstVal + $secondVal;`
-	subtract	`$sumLoss = $firstVal - $secondVal;`
*	multiply	`$taxCalc = $item * .07;`
/	divide	`$centLoad = $loadNow / $loadTotal;`
==	equal to (compare)	`if ($firstTry == $secondTry) ...`
===	equal to plus data type	`if($typeA === $typeB) ...`
!=	not equal to	`if ($better != $worse) ...`
>	greater than	`if ($most > $more) ...`
<	less than	`if ($least < $less) ...`
>=	greater than or equal to	`if ($now >= $then) ...`
<=	less than or equal to	`if ($fun <= $work) ...`
+=	compound assign add	`$sum += 6; #Adds 6 to $sum`
-=	compound assign subtract	`$refund -= $item;`
.	concatenation	`$wholeName = $firstName.$lastName;`
.=	compound concatenation	`$firstName .= $lastName`
&&	logical AND	`if ($a == $b && $c <= $d) ....`
||	logical OR	`if ($x == $y || $a == $z)....`
++	increment (pre or post)	`$ct++   #increments $ct`
--	decrement (pre or post)	`$ls--   #decrements $ls`

Table 2-2 lists some basic Perl commands that will be detailed in this chapter.

Table 2-2
Basic Perl Commands

Command	Description
print	Prints data to the Web or to an e-mail
open	Opens a file or e-mail for reading, writing, or appending
for	A for loop with same syntax as ActionScript
foreach	A for loop that iterates over the contents of an array
sort	Sorts the values in an array into alphabetical order
split	Splits data in an array based on the character(s) specified
if	An if statement with same syntax as ActionScript
else	An else statement with the same syntax as ActionScript
elsif	The Perl version of else if, but notice in Perl it's abbreviated elsif with the missing e
read	Reads the STDIN (standard input), which usually consists of data received via POST
\n	An important escaped character used to designate a new line or carriage return

Perl variables and arrays

To define and reference variables in Perl, you precede them with the dollar sign ($). For example, to set a variable named customColor equal to blue, you would use this code:

```
$customColor = "blue";
```

Arrays are created using the @ symbol and then a set of parentheses containing the array elements separated by commas. Individual elements of the array are then referenced using the $ sign and brackets. To create an array named favColors and then display it, you would use this code:

```
@favColors = ("red","green","blue");
print"$favColors[0]"; #prints the word "red"
print"$favColors[1]"; #prints the word "green"
print"$favColors[2]"; #prints the word "blue"
```

Another array type is a *hash* or *associative array*. This array is referenced with keys instead of numbers. Each key is a word, referencing a position in the array where a value is to be defined to or drawn from. In a standard array, values are stored in sequential positions and a numerical value (starting at 0) is used to reference a variable's position in the array.

The hash array as a whole is defined using the percent sign (%), and then values are retrieved using the dollar sign ($) preceding the name of the whole array along with curly braces and apostrophes to denote the key. To define a hash array and then display an element from it, you would use this code:

```
%carColors = ("Camaro","Red",
              "Mustang","Blue",
              "Corvette","Yellow");
print"$carColors{'Corvette'}";
```

or

```
%carColors = (Camaro => "Red",
              Mustang => "Blue",
              Corvette => "Yellow");
print"$carColors{'Corvette'}";
```

Individual elements in this hash array can then be changed with this code:

```
$carColors{'Corvette'}="White";
```

In these examples, the words `Corvette`, `Camaro`, and `Mustang` are keys in this hash array, and `carColors` is the name of the entire array. A key can be referenced with another variable, in which case the apostrophes are not used:

```
$someCar="Mustang";
print"The color of the $someCar is $carColors{$someCar}";
```

This code would result in this output:

```
The color of the Mustang is Blue
```

On the CD-ROM You can start testing these scripts by inserting the code segments into the CD-ROM file `perltemplate.pl` and then saving it under a new name, uploading the file, using `CHMOD 755`, and typing in the URL to the new script from your browser.

Variables Warning

Unlike ActionScript, Perl is case-sensitive. For ActionScript, the following variables are treated as the same:

```
SalesTax
Salestax
SALESTAX
```

However, all of these variables are different in Perl. So you should make sure that all the ActionScript variables you are using in conjunction with Perl are case-sensitive. That way, you won't run into a problem because you expect a variable named $Salestax to read your ActionScript variable named SalesTax. Other than case-sensitivity, other naming conventions are pretty much the same in ActionScript and Perl. For example, the Hit_Score variable in ActionScript will be equated with the $Hit_Score variable in Perl.

Special Perl environment variables

Perl has some special variables that are used to retrieve data about the current Web environment. These variables have specific names that cannot be changed. Table 2-3 lists the most pertinent environment variables and the types of data they reference when called for.

Table 2-3
Perl Environment Variables

Variable	Data referenced
HTTP_COOKIE	The list of all cookies set for the current domain
HTTP_REFERER	The URL of the Web site and page that requested the script
QUERY_STRING	Data string sent by a GET request from Flash or a Web page
CONTENT_LENGTH	Length of data string sent by a POST request

The information in these variables is always available as long as the data exists. (If no cookies have been set, there are obviously none to retrieve.) To retrieve data in any of these variables, use the following syntax:

```
$ENV{'environment_variable'}
```

For example, to find out where the current script was called from, write a Perl script in your text editor containing the following code:

```
#!/usr/bin/perl
#This displays the URL from where
#this script was called
print "Content-type:text/html\n\n";
print "This script was called from $ENV{'HTTP_REFERER'}";
exit;
```

Name the script environment.pl, upload it to your server, and configure it withCHMOD 755. Now create a simple HTML Web page with a link to this script. Upload this Web page to the normal place on your host where Web pages are stored (or, even better, another domain if you have one). Open your Web browser and surf over to this page. Click the link you created to your script. The page should display the URL of the HTML page from whence you came. This script is on the CD-ROM.

These environment variables are powerful tools not only for seeing the data they contain but also to test for certain conditions such as whether cookies exist or if the script was called from only a particular Web page on your server. Knowing this information could help you prevent people from calling your scripts from their own Web sites or from their desktops. We will be making good use of these environment variables.

Moving Data Between Flash and Perl

Moving data between Flash and Perl is a fairly straightforward process. The first part of that process is to send some data from Flash to the CGI script. Once the script receives the data, it must parse either the query string (if Flash used GET) or the post header (if Flash used POST) to split and separate the variables and their values.

On the CD-ROM   To make the most of the material in this section, go first to the CD-ROM found at the back of this book and locate the Flash movie called favoritecolor.fla and the Perl script named favoritecolor.pl.

Sending data from Flash to Perl

Open the Flash movie on the CD-ROM named favoritecolor.fla. Open the ActionScript palette and look at the ActionScript attached to the button marked Send (ignore the other button for the time being):

```
on (release) {
getURL ("http://www.yourdomain.com/cgi-bin/favoritecolor.pl", "_blank", "GET");
}
```

Change the words `yourdomain.com` to reflect your Web site. Notice that the code references a script named `favoritecolor.pl`. Find the Perl script on the CD-ROM named `favoritecolor.pl` and upload it to your Web server. Then configure the script as `CHMOD 755`. The Perl code in `favoritecolor.pl` reads as follows:

```perl
#!/usr/bin/perl
print "Content-type:text/html\n\n";

if ($ENV{'REQUEST_METHOD'} eq "GET"){
    print"$ENV{'QUERY_STRING'}";
}
elsif ($ENV{'REQUEST_METHOD'} eq "POST"){
    read(STDIN, $allPostData, $ENV{'CONTENT_LENGTH'});
    print"$allPostData";
    }

exit;
```

Return to Flash and preview the movie in your Web browser while you're connected to the Web. Type in any colors (or words for that matter) in the text fields and click the Send button. A window will pop up showing the variables in one long string, which is how Flash sent them to the Perl script. Potential results are displayed in Figure 2-4.

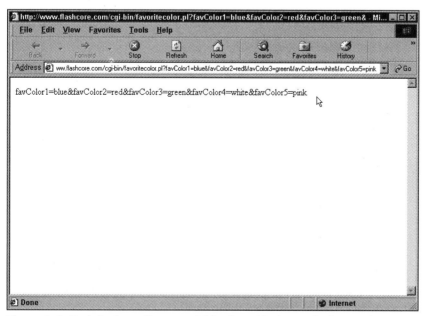

Figure 2-4: Perl displays all your variables from Flash exactly the way it received them, in one long string.

Notice the environment variable is tested for to determine GET or POST and then either the query string (QUERY_STRING) or the post header (CONTENT_LENGTH) is subsequently displayed. Change the code in the Flash movie Send button to reflect the POST method and test the script again in your Web browser. The same script recognized the method as POST and displayed the same data as it did using the GET method.

This following line is necessary in Perl to extract data from the post header.

```
read(STDIN, $allPostData, $ENV{'CONTENT_LENGTH'});
```

It takes the data in the post header and sticks it in a variable named allPostData. You can replace this variable name with anything you want for referencing later in the same script. The rest of the line must remain as is.

Keep testing the script using characters such as spaces, ampersands, and asterisks in the text fields. Try leaving every other field blank. Try leaving all the fields blank or just one. Every time you click Send, the script throws the data you sent right back at you 'as is'. In order for Perl to operate individually on those variables, you need to break up that big long string.

Splitting up sent variables

Perl looks at the query string or post header sent by Flash as being one big lump of data, one whole string. When Flash receives such data, it is smart enough (thanks to Macromedia) to be able to sort through the data and automatically separate it into individual variables. Perl can do this task, too, but you must write your own routine for it. In the following exercise, you will see how you must program Perl to take the incoming singular data stream and divide it up into individual variables.

Open the CD-ROM file colorsplitter.pl in your text editor (see Listing 2-1). Upload the file to your server and configure it as CHMOD 755. Change the ActionScript in the Flash button labeled SPLIT UP to reflect your Web domain. Save your changes to your hard drive; you'll be using this file again.

Listing 2-1: **The colorsplitter.pl File**

```perl
#!/usr/bin/perl
print "Content-type:text/html\n\n";

# Test for method and collect all the variables
if ($ENV{'REQUEST_METHOD'} eq "GET"){
    $allWebData=$ENV{'QUERY_STRING'};
}
elsif ($ENV{'REQUEST_METHOD'} eq "POST"){
    read(STDIN, $allWebData, $ENV{'CONTENT_LENGTH'});
    }
```

```
#Now split that big, long string into individual variables

@variables = split(/&/, $allWebData);
   #Split up the pairs at each ampersand

foreach $pair (@variables) {
   ($name, $value) = split(/=/, $pair);
      $value =~ tr/+/ /;
         #Translates spaces back into spaces
      $value =~ s/%([a-fA-F0-9][a-fA-F0-9])/pack("C",
hex($1))/eg;
         #Translates all URL-encoded characters back to
themselves
      $DATA{$name} = $value;
}

#Display the final output on the Web page
foreach $i (keys %DATA) {
print "$i: $DATA{$i} <br><br>";
}
```

Test the Flash movie in your browser and click the SPLIT UP button to see what happens. The result should look like what is displayed in Figure 2-5.

Note   The results may not be listed in the order that you're viewing them in Flash. The reason for this is that the Perl script deals with the variables in a random order, not the order they're graphically displayed in your Flash movie. For the purposes of this book, this difference doesn't matter because eventually you'll just be sending them back to Flash, not to a Web page for a listed display.

The split command in detail

The next sections dissect the more complex parts of colorsplitter.pl. The first section of colorsplitter.pl is identical to favoritecolor.pl with the exception of naming the initial big, long string allWebData for both GET and POST methods.

The next section of colorsplitter.pl uses the split command to split $allWebData into the array @variables; this array now contains name/value pairs. The syntax for the split command is

```
@new_array_name=split(/character_to_split_at/, $your_string_here);
```

The line of code for the split command in the example is

```
@variables = split(/&/, $allWebData);
```

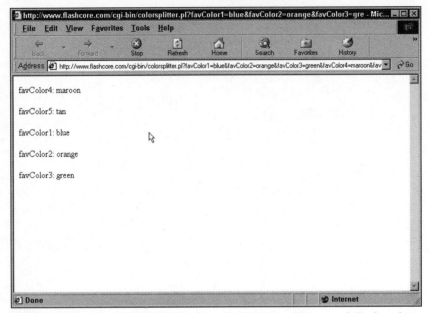

Figure 2-5: Results of the variables from Flash being split up and displayed on a Web page.

Perl takes the long string and breaks it at every ampersand, ending up with pairs in @variables that look like the following:

```
favColor1=Blue
favColor2=Green
```

These pairs still look like single strings to Perl (not actual variable names and values), and you need to break them again into variables that Perl can operate on. The following chunk of code splits the data again and properly puts it into an associative hash array named DATA:

```
foreach $pair (@variables) {
    ($name, $value) = split(/=/, $pair);
     $value =~ tr/+/ /;
        #Translates spaces back into spaces
     $value =~ s/%([a-fA-F0-9][a-fA-F0-9])/pack("C",
hex($1))/eg;
        #Translates all URL-encoded characters back to
themselves
    $DATA{$name} = $value;
}
```

Foreach

The foreach command goes through every value in the array specified in parentheses and performs the operations inside the curly braces on each value. The syntax of the foreach statement is

```
Foreach $item (@array_name) {
    #Perform some action here on each item by referencing $item
    #You can rename $item to any name you want as long as it's
    #a name you again reference inside these curly braces
}
```

Back to our example, the temporary holding variables $name and $value are each assigned one half of each pair in the array, which happens to be each variable's name and its value:

```
foreach $pair (@variables) {
    ($name, $value) = split(/=/, $pair);
```

The translate function and a regular expression then convert all spaces back into themselves and change special characters that were URL encoded into themselves (on the value side of each pair):

```
    $value =~ tr/+/ /;
    $value =~ s/%([a-fA-F0-9][a-fA-F0-9])/pack("C",
hex($1))/eg;
```

The last line of the foreach statement loads the final, usable name and value variables into a hash array:

```
    $DATA{$name} = $value;
```

Notice the mixed use here of variable names that are already defined being loaded into an array that is undefined. In Perl, you don't need to define variables, arrays, or hash arrays before you use them. In this code, the new hash array %DATA is being loaded one value at a time with the predefined variable name from Flash, which happens to be the hash array's key ($name) and its value ($value). For example, you could now rename favColor1 by inserting

```
$DATA{'favColor1'}="Pink";
```

after the closing curly brace of the foreach statement.

Keys

Keys are the name part of an associative hash array, as shown in the following string:

```
    $arrayname{$keyname} = $somevalue;
```

The last section of `colorsplitter.pl` uses `foreach` along with a reference to each key to go one by one through the hash array and display the variable name and its value. The reserved word `keys` in Perl references each key in the array name following it, in this case `%DATA`:

```
# Display the final output on the Web page
foreach $i (keys %DATA) {
print "$i: $DATA{$i} <br><br>";
}
```

> **Note**   The `<br>` tag is used here for Web page display only and inserts standard line breaks to separate the data. When dealing strictly with Flash, you don't need to include tags like these, and they're here just to illustrate basic concepts. Any data sent back to Flash will have to be sent back in the form of a query string, in one piece, with no line breaks in between.

To illustrate how Perl can now treat the variables on an individual basis and operate upon them, change the last section of code in `colorsplitter.pl` to read

```
foreach $i (keys %DATA) {
$DATA{$i}+=$DATA{$i}; #This adds each variable to itself
print "$i: $DATA{$i} <br><br>";
}
```

Upload the modified Perl script (remember, you don't need to use the `CHMOD` command again) and preview the Flash movie in your browser. This time, enter numeric values in all the text fields. Click the SPLIT UP button once again to see what happens. Perl is now operating on your variables individually and adding each one to itself.

These examples are here to show you what is going on behind the scenes with Flash and Perl and how Perl must divide up data in order to deal with it effectively. Sometimes breaking up the data is unnecessary, but you must know how it works, nonetheless. You have been displaying the output of your CGI/Perl scripts so far in a pop-up window to illustrate what Perl is doing to all the data. We can now move on to seamlessly and invisibly sending the data back into Flash from Perl to create a truly dynamic Flash experience!

Sending data from Perl back to Flash

Sending data back to Flash from a Perl script is now as simple as deciding what you want to do to the data in Perl and then making a minor formatting change so Flash can read it. Your Perl script can send back brand-new data that is either dynamic or hard-coded into the Perl script itself.

Cross-Reference Flash can read text files! In Chapter 1, we discuss how to get Flash to read data from a text file. We're doing the exact same thing here except that the text file is being dynamically generated by Perl each time it is called.

Sending data back to Flash

In this exercise, you first see the format of the data to be sent from Perl back to Flash. Then with a minor change to the ActionScript, this data will become invisible to the naked eye and travel seamlessly back to Flash, where a user will never realize that any server interaction has occurred! First we'll upload and test the files to see the effect and then dissect the new code that is responsible for the correct return of the data to Flash.

1. Open the version of `favoritecolor.fla` you saved from the last exercise.

2. Copy the button labeled SPLIT UP and move it over so it is clearly visible. Label this new button SEND BACK.

3. Locate the CD-ROM file `returncolors.pl` and upload and configure it as `CHMOD 755` on your Web server.

4. Change the name of the SPLIT UP button's `getURL` ActionScript statement to reflect your server URL and the Perl file named `returncolors.pl`.

5. Preview the movie in your Web browser and test it by entering some color names in the fields and pressing the new SEND BACK button.

A window will pop up once again showing you exactly what is going to be returned to Flash, in this case the color names you entered with the words `The color is` preceding each one.

The only change you need to make to stop that window from appearing and to send the data transparently back into Flash is to change the ActionScript on the SEND BACK button to a `loadVariablesNum` statement instead of `getURL`. The new code on the SEND BACK button should read

```
on (release) {
loadVariablesNum ("http://www.yourdomain.com/cgi-bin/returncolors.pl",
0, "GET");
}
```

Make this change and be sure to retain the reference to your Web domain and `returncolors.pl`. Select `GET` or `POST`, and leave the level set to 0. Then preview the Flash movie in your browser once again. The pop-up window is gone, and any color names you enter are preceded by `The color is` after you press the SEND BACK button (see Figure 2-6). Congratulations! You've completed a full round trip of data!

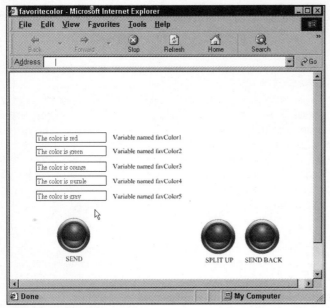

Figure 2-6: The data has made its way back to Flash after being modified by Perl.

When you press the SEND BACK button, the following happens:

✦ Flash converts all the favColor variables to URL encoding and sends them to the Perl script.

✦ The Perl script on your host server receives the variables and separates them.

✦ The Perl script then prints a text file, which is invisible to the user, with the new data in a format Flash can read.

✦ Flash reads this data and replaces the existing variables with the changed ones.

Outputting data in Perl that Flash can read

The Perl script returncolor.pl you just executed is the same as colorsplitter.pl with the exception of the last section that outputs the data. The difference is that now the data is being output in a format that Flash can read; the URL-encoded format. This format outputs the data all in one continuous string that is not broken up by any white space or <br> tags, as in colorsplitter.pl. To format one long URL-encoded string, Perl executes the code at the end of returncolor.pl:

```
# Send the final output back to Flash
foreach $i (keys %DATA) {
```

```
    print "$i=The color is $DATA{$i}\&";
    #Add some text before each variable
    #and an escaped ampersand after it
}
```

The important factor in getting Flash to recognize the returned data is this `print` statement:

```
    print "$i=The color is $DATA{$i}\&";
```

It references each variable's name with $i and prints the equal sign (=) followed by some text and the actual variable value referenced by $DATA{$i}. The very last and most important piece is the escaped ampersand (\&) at the end. This escaped character enables all the variables to be strung together in the query string format Flash is happy to read.

Tip   If you experience a problem at any time when you test Perl script outputs for invisible return into Flash, just change the `loadVariables` statement in Flash into a `getURL` with a `_blank window` target. This change will display exactly what is being sent to Flash in a pop-up browser window and allow you to make corrections to your Perl script if it's not printing the final variable list correctly. It's a valuable tool for troubleshooting.

At the end of the `returncolors.pl` file, right before the `print` statement, try inserting this statement

```
    $DATA{$i}.=$DATA{$i};
```

or this one

```
    $DATA{$i}+=$DATA{$i};
```

For instance, look at this code:

```
# Send the final output back to Flash
foreach $i (keys %DATA) {
    $DATA{$i}.=$DATA{$i};
    print "$i=The color is $DATA{$i}\&";
    #Add some text before each variable
    #and an escaped ampersand after it
}
```

The . = statement concatenates each variable with itself while the += statement adds each variable to itself if you again try inputting numeric values in the Flash text fields. Try out these code variations with both numeric and string values to see what effect they have.

Sending completely new variables

So far we've been sending Flash the same variables as it sent to the Perl script, but there's no reason why Perl can't send whole new sets of variables back to Flash. For example, use the same `favoritecolor.fla` file and duplicate all of the text fields on the left over to the right side of the stage so that they mirror the ones on the left side. Rename each right side variable text field so it has the word *new* at the end, for example, `favColor1new` and `favColor2new`.

Replace the last block of code in `returncolors.pl` with the following code:

```
# Send the final output back to Flash
foreach $i (keys %DATA) {
    $newVar=$i."new";
    #Creates a new variable that has the same name
    #but with the word 'new' appended to the end
    print "$newVar=$DATA{$i}\&";
    }
```

The `$newVar=$i."new";` statement creates a new variable name that is the same as the original one with the word *new* appended to the end. In other words, it is taking the variable name `favColor1` and creating a string named `favColor1new`. It then outputs this new variable name in the last statement for Flash to read along with an equals sign (=) and then the value attached to the original variable.

Upload these script changes and test the Flash movie in your browser. Upon clicking the SEND BACK button, you now get all your variables renamed into new variables and displayed on the right side of the screen. Figure 2-7 shows how this should look. If you encounter any difficulty, this Flash file is available on the CD-ROM as `favoritecolor_part2.fla`.

 Note As we showed you earlier in this chapter using the sample script `testing.pl`, Perl can easily generate and display variables that have nothing to do with any that were sent by Flash.

If the code segments in the last code example seemed too complicated, create a brand-new dynamic text field anywhere on the stage of `favoritecolor.fla`, name it `finalOutput`, and make sure it will hold about two lines of text. Replace the last block of code in `returncolors.pl` with the following:

```
# Send the final output back to Flash
$scriptName="Perl";
print"finalOutput=$scriptName has done nothing with the data
you sent it";
```

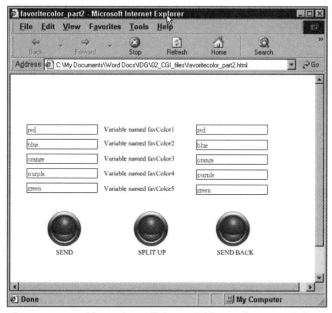

Figure 2-7: Perl has taken all the variables and renamed them, attaching the same values, and sent them back to Flash.

Save and upload your script changes and test the Flash movie in your browser. When you click the SEND BACK button, Flash still sends all the data to the Perl script. But after the Perl script splits the data, it chooses to ignore it and return something completely different to Flash. This process is how you would test in Perl if a password you've defined in Perl matches one that a user submitted through Flash and then returned an approval or denial. We'll discuss this topic in more detail in the next section. For now, congratulations on successfully completing the basics of integrating Perl with Flash! Let's move on to some great dynamic applications with our dynamic duo: Flash and Perl

Creating Dynamic Applications for Flash and CGI/Perl

Now that you've seen the basics of Flash and Perl working together, we can explore real-world applications for calling CGI scripts from Flash. You will learn how to check passwords; set and retrieve cookies; read, write, and append text files to mimic a database; send e-mails, and all the other things you always wished you could do from Flash but couldn't quite figure out how. Each section covers Perl code specific to the objective, and some new commands are introduced; however, most of the code should be familiar from the previous sections.

Checking passwords

Checking for passwords is a common feature on many sites to keep out unwanted visitors or to direct specific visitors to a certain section of your Flash site based on who they are. One way to do this is by creating a text file of all the passwords, loading the file into Flash, and then using Flash to search through and match each one against a password submitted by the user. The big downside to doing it this way is that this process is not very secure. Because the call for the text file containing the passwords was made through an HTTP request, that text file is now in the user's browser cache and he or she can easily open up his or her cache and view all the passwords along with any other variables you've stored.

Security has become even more important since the Flash Player SDK was released because many companies have come up with ways to compromise the security of compiled and published Flash movies. Available programs can reveal all of your ActionScript code and target names for the entire world to see, regardless of whether you've checked the Protect From Import option. This capability represents a huge security risk for your Web site and Flash movie. If this problem sounds far-fetched, just check out the ActionScript Viewer from www.buraks.com and see what I mean. This program shows anyone the entire contents of your Flash movie. Server-side scripting takes on a whole new level of importance in keeping sensitive information away from the prying eyes of unscrupulous individuals.

Perl to the rescue! The simplest way to strengthen security around passwords or other sensitive dynamic data is to make sure it all stays on your server where it belongs. Perl receives a password submitted by a user through Flash and compares it to an array list of all passwords. Perl then determines if a match exists and returns a simple approval or denial message. The user never sees anything except this final answer. The details surrounding the processing of the question happen on your Web server where the user never sees or knows precisely what is going on. Even if the user types a direct URL to your script, he will only get the cake and never the recipe!

On the CD-ROM

In the following exercise, you'll use a Flash movie file called `simple_login.fla` and Perl scripts named `simple_login.pl` and `perltemplate2.pl`. You'll find these files on the CD-ROM located at the back of this book.

In this example, you'll see how a Perl script is used to integrate password protection into a Flash movie. Follow these steps:

1. Open the Perl script `simple_login.pl` on the CD-ROM and upload it to your server using `CHMOD 755`.

2. Open the Flash file `simple_login.fla` on the CD-ROM.

3. Change the LOGIN button `loadVariables` ActionScript to reflect your Web domain.

4. Test the Flash movie in your Web browser.

5. Enter different passwords and observe the denial message.

6. Enter either **Winstanley** or **Sanders** for the password and you will see the word ACCEPTED!

You have just observed passwords being checked by Perl and only the approval or denial being returned to Flash. To take an in-depth look at all the code, open simple_login.pl in your text editor and notice that it uses the standard input parser that has been present in many scripts up to this point. The CD-ROM file perltemplate2.pl contains these core parsing pieces, and we'll be using them in most scripts from here on out. Take a moment to look at perltemplate2.pl. It contains a commented main code section, which is where you should put your main body scripting elements.

The simple_login.pl script uses the standard elements in perltemplate2.pl to separate out all the variables. The main code section utilizes the following code to define the passwords, check for a match, and then send an approval or denial to Flash:

```
#Define the password array and then test user input
@passwords=("Winstanley","Sanders","Flash5","ActionScript");
$approval="no"; #Set a flag to reflect a nonmatch#
foreach $checkme (@passwords){
    if ($DATA{'userPassword'} eq $checkme){
        $approval="yes";
        #Set flag to true if a match
        #to any password is made
    }
}

print"approved=$approval";
#Print the variable 'approved' to Flash
#containing either yes or no
```

The Flash movie contains only one input text field named userPassword. This input is sent out to Perl where the preceding coding section checks for a match. During this process, Perl performs these actions:

1. Defines the master password array in @passwords

2. Sets a flag named $approval to its default no before it starts checking for matches

3. Starts checking each password defined in Perl in @passwords against the variable userPassword sent from Flash that was defined inside the DATA array in the standard parser section

4. Prints back to Flash the variable name approved followed by an equals sign and then a value of yes or no held in $approval

Flash receives this data and then decides, based on the approval variable being yes or no, whether to accept or decline the user access to the site.

Creating your own login script

To create `simple_login.fla` for yourself, follow these steps:

1. Open a new Flash movie.

2. Create a static text field on the screen containing the words **Please Enter Your Password,** and with this text field selected, press F8 to turn it into a movie clip named **processor**.

3. Double-click the Processor movie clip to edit it and add a `stop()` action to Frame 1.

4. While still editing the Processor movie clip, extend the timeline in the layer with the text field (the only layer) and make keyframes at Frames 10 and 20.

5. Label Frame 10 **accepted** and Frame 20 **declined** and then change the static text box in each of these frames to reflect a message to be displayed upon acceptance or decline.

6. Return to the main stage, and after selecting the Processor movie clip, give it an instance name of **process**.

7. Name the layer it sits on **Processing Clip**.

8. Create a new layer named Button. Place a button on the stage from the standard button library, which you can access by selecting Windows ➪ Common Libraries ➪ Buttons. The circle LED buttons usually look decent.

9. Attach the `loadVariables` ActionScript to the button so that it points to `simple_login.pl` on your Web server, targets the movie clip `_root.process`, and has a method of `POST`.

10. To check for data coming into `_root.process`, select it, and in the ActionScript window, add an `onClipEvent(data)` statement containing the following code:

```
onClipEvent (data) {
    if(this.approved eq "yes"){
        this.gotoAndStop("accepted");
    }
    else {
        this.gotoAndPlay("declined");
    }
}
```

11. Create a new layer on the main timeline named Input Field, and then put a dynamic input text box with the variable name `userPassword` into this layer.

The Flash logic that occurs when you click the button starts with the `loadVariables` statement. Because it designates `_root.process` as the target, this movie clip will contain any variables that come back from Perl. However, the variables that are sent are on the main timeline because the main timeline is where the button sits and where the statement is executed from. The only variable existing on the main timeline is the `userPassword` field, which Flash whisks off to the server.

The `onClipEvent(data)` statement on the `_root.process` movie clip patiently waits the whole time to receive any variables. When it receives a variable, it executes the `if(this.approved eq "yes")` statement to check whether an approval was sent from the Perl script. This movie clip then sends itself to the appropriate frame. As with anything in Flash, you can house and nest these movie clips in a number of ways. This is just one.

Modifying your login script

In Flash, you can often do the same task in 20 different ways, and this section is just one example of a variation on the password-checking project. Try putting a `stop()` action on Frame 1 of the main timeline and then add some keyframes to the timeline labeled **accepted** and **declined** further on down. Put some nifty graphics in those keyframes and change the `onClipEvent(data)` statement to read `_root.gotoAndStop("declined")` instead of using the `this.gotoAndStop` statement.

Now your main timeline is jumping to a new place instead of the Process movie clip moving its timeline. You could change those statements to reflect anything you'd like to happen in Flash when someone is approved or declined based on their password. Now the Process movie clip is nothing but a robot clip whose job it is to wait for variables and then redirect the main timeline. You can easily hide a movie clip like this off the main stage while it waits to accept and process data.

In the following exercise, you'll use a Flash movie file called `complex_login.fla` and the Perl script named `complex_login.pl`. You'll find these files on the CD-ROM located at the back of this book.

A more complex variation of this project is to have Perl check for both a username and a password. This variation is illustrated in the files `complex_login.fla` and the Perl script `complex_login.pl` that accompanies it. The only change in the Flash movie is the addition of a text box on the main timeline with the variable name `userName`. The Perl script looks very similar except for some changes to the last processing section:

```
# Define the password array and then test user input
%passwords=(Mark => "1234",
      Bill => "AABB",
      Mike => "XYZ"
      #Add more usernames and passwords here
);
$approval="no"; #Set the flag to 'no-match'#
foreach $name (keys %passwords){
if ($name eq $DATA{'userName'} && $passwords{$name} eq $DATA{'userPassword'}){
      $approval="yes";
      #Set flag to true if a match
      #between both userName and userPassword
   }
}
```

```
print"approved=$approval";
#Print the variable 'approved' to Flash
#containing either true or false

exit;
```

In this case, the usernames are the keys in the %passwords array. The foreach and if statements then make sure that when and if a valid username is entered, it is matched against its associated password on the value side of the %passwords array. This coding delves deeper into the world of Perl, and an in-depth explanation is beyond the scope of this book. The good thing is that you can use this script as-is in all your Flash movies. Just add more usernames where the commented line says to do so. The syntax is as follows:

> *username* => "*password*"

Remember to add a comma after each line unless it's the last element in the array definition, like Mike is in the previous example.

You can use either the simple or complex login scripts along with your Web site by modifying your Flash movie to submit the correct variable names and wait for the approved variable to return. Just be sure to change the passwords in the simple_login.pl script or the usernames and passwords in the %passwords hash of complex_login.pl. Making changes and spending lots of time testing is the way to become a true master of server interaction.

Baking cookies is an excellent way to store personalized data about someone who visits your Web site and retrieve that data at a later time. The neat thing about cookies is that they're not stored on the server in any sort of database but on each user's computer, where they stay for as long as you specify. You can use them to create a truly personalized experience for the user without the user having to log in to any type of database. You could store a person's name and personal preferences that you would then use in Flash to greet that person or configure a menu structure a certain way. Cookies are also a great way to store a high score for each person playing a Flash game or even to track a player's progress and let that player return to the same area of a game he or she was playing the last time he or she was at your site!

A *cookie* is nothing more than a text file containing some sort of data that is stored in a special temporary directory on each user's hard drive. This text file can be read by and written to via any Web browser and, in turn, the data can be passed back and forth to Flash. A separate cookie text file is stored on a user's computer for each Web site he or she visits that sets a cookie. Inside that text file are name/value pairs, and each individual pair can be considered and referred to as an individual cookie.

Cookies have a limited time that they're good for, which is referred to as the *expiration*. When asked to read and return the data contained within a cookie, the Web browser first checks to see if the cookie has expired. If it hasn't, all the data within the cookie will be returned to whatever type of script was asking for it; in our case a CGI/Perl script. Perl is a great way to set and retrieve cookie values and pass them back and forth to and from Flash because all the scripting happens on the server side. Many times JavaScript is used for cookies, but it's often unreliable and exposes all your code because JavaScript is in the HTML page. Using a Perl script via the `loadVariables` actions in Flash to set and retrieve cookie values enables you to store Flash variable values on the computer of anyone viewing your Flash movie without that person even knowing it.

Caution   Most people have cookies enabled in their Web browser. Those who are particularly security-conscious (or just plain paranoid) have cookies turned off or have their browser prompt them each time a cookie is being set. If the user's cookies are disabled, you won't be able to use your Flash/Perl/cookie scripts when that person is viewing your site. If you need everyone viewing your site to have access to the cookie scripts you're using, you should place a message on your Flash site prompting users to enable their cookies. If the users' cookies are set to prompt them when they are being set, those users will know each time you're setting a cookie via Flash, so be forewarned.

Setting cookies

The explanations of some core elements of a Perl script that effectively sets cookies in Flash are beyond the scope of this book. Therefore, we're going to just provide you with a great cookie script for Flash and explain only the areas that you need to change in order to set the expiration date you desire. Listing 2-2 outlines the code inside `cookset.pl` with some of the key sections in bold.

On the CD-ROM   Locate the files `cookset.pl`, `cookread.pl`, and `cookdelete.pl` on the CD-ROM and transfer them to your hard drive. Open `cookset.pl` in your favorite text editor to examine and modify it.

Listing 2-2: **The cookset.pl Code**

```perl
#!/usr/local/bin/perl

srand(time);

$numberOfDays=7; ##Replace this number with 1-365 days##

$expiration = setGMT(time+(86400*$numberOfDays));

##################################################
# Test for method and collect all the variables
if ($ENV{'REQUEST_METHOD'} eq "GET"){
    $allWebData=$ENV{'QUERY_STRING'};
}
```

Continued

Listing 2-2 *(continued)*

```perl
elsif ($ENV{'REQUEST_METHOD'} eq "POST"){
   read(STDIN, $allWebData, $ENV{'CONTENT_LENGTH'});
   }
##################################################
# Split up variable pairs and set a cookie for each variable

@variables = split(/&/, $allWebData);
foreach $pair (@variables) {
    ($name, $value) = split(/=/, $pair);
    print "Set-Cookie:$name=$value;expires=$expiration;\n";
}


##################################################
# Output in web browser - for testing only via getURL

print "Content-type:text/html\n\n";
print "Cookies were just set that expire on $expiration";


##################################################
# Subroutine to set GMT expiration time

sub setGMT {
   ($inTime) = @_;
   @monthArr = ("Jan","Feb","Mar","Apr","May","Jun","Jul","Aug",
           "Sep","Oct","Nov","Dec");
   @dayArr = ("Sun","Mon","Tue","Wed","Thu","Fri","Sat");

   ($second,$minute,$hour,$monthday,$month,$year,$weekday,$yearday,$ldat) =
   gmtime($inTime);

$finalTime = sprintf("%3s, %02d-%3s-%4d %02d:%02d:%02d GMT",
$dayArr[$weekday],$monthday,$monthArr[$month],$year+1900,$hour,$minute,$second);
return $finalTime;
}


exit;
```

The only line in this entire script you're going to need to change is the line of code dealing with setting the expiration date:

```perl
$numberOfDays=7; ##Replace this number with 1-365 days##
```

The variable numberOfDays is set to 7 in this line, meaning that the cookie will expire seven days following the day it is set. After the cookie has expired, it disappears and is no longer readable by the cookread.pl script, which is explained in the next section. For now, just realize that all you have to do is replace the number 7 in this code line with any number between 1 and 365 for the number of days you'd like the cookie(s) to remain available.

The rest of the script contains code to break apart any query string or post header sent from Flash, break apart the name/value pairs, and set the name/value pairs as cookies on the user's computer. You can see from the line

```
print "Set-Cookie:$name=$value;expires=$expiration;\n";
```

that the command in Perl for setting cookies is Set-Cookie. The tricky part is the expiration date, and that's where the extra functions and subroutines in the script come into play to set the date in the GMT time that most Linux/Unix servers demand. The code provided here does it all for you, so you have nothing to worry about.

The section of code that notifies you of the successful setting of the cookies begins with the following comment:

```
# Output in web browser - for testing only via getURL
```

The code in this section gives you a confirmation message if you're testing the script initially using getURL instead of loadVariables, which is a good idea.

The following steps show you how to implement cookset.pl on your Web site with a Flash movie. When called from Flash, the script will take every variable defined in the query string or post header and set it as an individual cookie that expires in the number of days you specify in the numberOfDays variable.

1. Upload the cookset.pl Perl script to the cgi-bin directory on your Web server and set its permission as CHMOD 755.

2. Create a new Flash file named firstcookies.fla and save it on your hard drive. On the stage in the initial layer, create three input text fields and place them anywhere you want. Use the Text Options panel to give the first text field the variable reference **var1**, the second field a variable reference of **var2**, and the third field a variable reference of **var3**, making sure to also check the Border/Bg check box for each field.

3. Create a button on the stage or use one from Window ⇨ Common Libraries ⇨ Buttons. (The firstcookies.fla file is available on the CD-ROM if you want to reference it for layout or coding purposes.) Attach the following action to your button, making sure to replace www.mydomain.com with the proper path to the cookset.pl script on your server:

```
on (release) {
    getURL ("http://www.mydomain.com/cgi-bin/cookset.pl",
 "_blank", "GET");
}
```

4. Save your changes to firstcookies.fla and preview the movie in your Web browser by pressing F12. Enter any values in the three fields that you want, for example, **red, green,** and **blue.**

5. Click the button you created and a new browser window should pop-up with a confirmation message telling you that cookies were set and they expire on the date consistent with the `numberOfDays` variable set in the `cookset.pl` script. Here is an example of the message that should appear:

```
Cookies were just set that expire on Wed, 18-Apr-2001
10:13:46 GMT
```

Your cookies have now been set. You can see from the query string in the pop-up browser window the variable names and values sent by Flash. These have now become the cookie names and values set by the browser on your hard drive specific to the Web domain where you uploaded the Perl script. If you entered the three colors specified in step 4, your hard drive would contain the following cookies:

Cookie name	Cookie value
var1	red
var2	green
var3	blue

The cookies remain available on your hard drive to have their values returned up until the date you saw in the confirmation message. Keep in mind also that even though you used `getURL`, all you have to do is implement `loadVariablesNum` instead to make the setting of the cookies happen invisibly in the background.

Retrieving cookies

The code involved to retrieve the values of cookies that you've set is much simpler than the code to set them. Open the `cookread.pl` file in your text editor. This code will retrieve any cookies that were set by the server for the current Web domain and display them in a Flash-friendly format with name/value pairs separated by ampersands:

```
#!/usr/local/bin/perl
print "Content-type:text/html\n\n";

############################################
#Pull in all the available cookies
$allCookies = $ENV{'HTTP_COOKIE'};

############################################
#Output each cookie name/value pair
#with an ampersand between them
#
```

```
@cookies = split(/; /,$allCookies);
foreach $i (@cookies) {
    ($cName,$cValue) = split(/=/,$i);
   print"$cName=$cValue&";
}
###########################################

exit;
```

The first section highlighted in bold contains the line needed for Perl to read in all the cookie names and values from the user's hard drive. The big time saver in this system is the Perl environment variable HTTP_COOKIE. Anytime a request is made to the server for a Perl script, any cookie names and values are always present in this environment variable. All we had to do in this code is assign this variable to the $allCookies variable and then perform a simple split action, just like the splitting of a query string. The only difference is that the separator in this code is a semicolon, as evidenced in the following line:

```
@cookies = split(/; /,$allCookies);
```

After the names and values of the cookies have been separated into the variables $cName and $cValue, the only thing left to do is output them in a format that Flash can read:

```
print"$cName=$cValue&";
```

You don't have to modify anything in this script. It will find all the cookies associated with the Web domain where the Perl script resides and output all the name/value pairs for Flash to use. Before completing the following steps to use cookread.pl, make sure you've set some cookies as you were instructed to in the last section; otherwise, there won't be any cookies to read.

1. Upload the Perl script cookread.pl to the cgi-bin directory on your Web server and set its permission as CHMOD 755.

2. Open the Flash file firstcookie.fla that you created in the previous section "Setting cookies," or use the one provided on the CD-ROM. Make sure you have used it to set some cookies.

3. Change the code on the button to the following, making sure to replace www.mydomain.com with the path to the cgi-bin directory where you uploaded the Perl script:

```
on (release) {
    getURL ("http://www.mydomain.com/cgi-bin/cookread.pl",
 "_blank");
}
```

4. Preview the movie in your Web browser by pressing F12. Click the button inside of the Flash movie and a new window should pop up displaying a URL-encoded string with the three variables you previously set as cookies.

Note

You may see additional cookie names and values in the pop-up window as well. Some could have been already set on your domain, and others may be set automatically by the server. For example, if you are using the complimentary JTLNet hosting account included with this book, you will see all of your previously set cookie variables plus a variable named WEBTRENDS_ID:

```
var1=red&var2=green&var3=blue&WEBTRENDS_ID=xxxx-xxxxxxx
```

You can't do much about something like WEBTRENDS_ID because it's there to automatically track server traffic. Anyway, these extra variables are nothing to worry about unless they conflict with variable names you're using in Flash. Your best bet is to run this Perl script and see what kind of extra variables come back and make sure to avoid those variable names in Flash.

5. Return to the stage of firstcookies.fla and change the button code to reflect the following loadVariables action. This action enables Flash to invisibly load the variable names and values provided by the Perl script that found them in the cookies:

```
on (release) {
    loadVariablesNum ("http://www.mydomain.com/cgi-
bin/cookread.pl", 0);
    }
```

6. Preview the movie once again in your Web browser by pressing F12 and then click the button inside the Flash movie. Within a few seconds, all the variable values should appear in the appropriate text fields. If they don't, make sure that your text fields reflect the same variable references as the variable names you saw when the browser window previously popped up in step 4.

You are now ready to set all kinds of cookies! The two scripts cookset.pl and cookread.pl automatically set and retrieve cookies comprised of the variable names and values sent by Flash. Keep in mind that you don't have to attach the loadVariables action to a button; you can hide it in a frame or movie clip action. This way, the end user usually won't know that any cookies are being set and/or retrieved.

Deleting cookies

Sometimes you may just want to get rid of all the cookies set for your Web domain on a user's hard drive. This way, you're sure that no spare cookies are hanging around that user's hard drive. The Perl script cookdelete.pl on the CD-ROM will perform this task for you. The script requires no modification or variables passed to it in order to function. Just upload it to your cgi-bin directory and configure it as CHMOD 755.

Anytime that the script is called from a user's Web browser via an http request, a getURL command, or a loadVariables action, it effectively deletes all the cookies present on the user's hard drive for the Web domain where the script is located. The cookdelete.pl script is a combination of the two scripts cookread.pl and cookset.pl in that it first looks for all the cookies present and then resets them to have an expiration date of yesterday. It does this by using a negative number for the numberOfDays variable. Feel free to employ this script in any means you deem necessary because sometimes cookies have a way of piling up.

Writing and reading text files

When you first read through the capabilities of ActionScripting as presented by Macromedia, it's easy to get excited over the fact that you can load data in from a text file. This excitement is quickly stymied by the fact that Flash had no way to write to a text file. A server script, such as one written in Perl, is needed to accomplish this task because a Flash movie sits in a Web browser and a Web browser doesn't have the authority to go into servers and make changes to files. The instructions for making changes must be inside a script already uploaded to the server. All Flash has to do is call out to that script and say, "Hey, take these variables and write them to a text file!" The script then handles the chore of opening a text file and writing the data to it.

Writing to a file in Perl

Perl has some simple ways of dealing with text files that will be written to. These files almost always must be in the cgi-bin directory next to the scripts that will operate on them. Usually files that will be written to need to be configured using CHMOD 666. In order to write to a text file on the server that can later be read and have its data returned to Flash, you need to understand a few key concepts and commands in Perl.

Opening the file

Before a file can be written to, the file must be open. To open a text file in Perl, use the open command with this syntax:

```
open(filehandle, "filename");
```

When you open a file, you also associate a file handle with it. *File handles* are names in Perl that refer to a specific file much like your nickname in an Internet chat room refers to you. For instance, you usually never use your first and last name when you log into a chat room. You pick some easy one-word nickname like "Coolguy," and when people in the chat room say, "Hey Coolguy!" you'll know they're referring to you. File handles in Perl work the same way. Once you've defined the file you're going to work with, you associate it with a simple nickname. This nickname is used in reading data from the file and in print statements to print data into the text file, which accomplishes the task of writing into it. We recommend using all capital letters for file handles to make them stand out when you're reading the code.

Filenames are usually just the name of the file enclosed in quotes, such as "highscores.txt". But they need to be preceded by either a right bracket (>) to designate that you are opening the file in order to overwrite it or by two right brackets (>>) to designate that you are going to append data to the file. Note that the brackets must be within the quotation marks. If Perl is just opening the file to read in some data, you do not need to include any right brackets.

Suppose you've uploaded a text file in your `cgi-bin` named `webdata.txt` and configured it with `CHMOD 666`. To open that file and associate the file handle `STUFF` with it, you would use this code:

```
open(STUFF,"webdata.txt");
#Opens the file for reading only
```

Notice the file handle `STUFF` is not in quotes but the actual filename is. No bracket is present before the filename, which means Perl is opening the file to read it only.

To open the same `webdata.txt` file for the purpose of overwriting it, you need to add a bracket before the filename. Note the bracket is within the quotation marks:

```
open(STUFF,">webdata.txt");
#Opens the file for overwriting
```

When you append data to a file, the data is added at the very end of the last line of text currently in that file. To open a file for appending, add two brackets before the filename in the quotation marks:

```
open(STUFF,">>webdata.txt");
#Opens the file for appending
```

Reading, writing, and closing

To read data into Perl once Perl has properly opened the text file, you assign the data to a string or array using the file handle enclosed in brackets:

```
@myarray=<filehandle>;
```

The typical Perl `print` statement needs only the addition of the file handle in order to write data into the text file. This file handle immediately follows the `print` statement and is not enclosed in any parentheses, brackets, or quotes. The syntax is as follows:

```
print filehandle "any text here";
```

When you've finished writing to the text file, you need to close it with the `close` command:

```
close(filehandle);
```

Appending data to a file

Look at the following code example taken from the CD-ROM file `open_close.pl`:

```
#!/usr/bin/perl
print "Content-type:text/html\n\n";

open(STUFF,">>webdata.txt");
#Opens the file for appending
```

```
print STUFF "We are appending some text to the file";
#Appends the quoted text to the file

close(STUFF);
#Properly closes the file on the server

print"The text file was properly appended.";
#Displays some Web page data confirming the write

exit;
```

This Perl code opens the file `webdata.txt` (also on the CD-ROM) for the purpose of appending data to it. Try it out:

1. Upload the `open_close.pl` file to your `cgi-bin` directory and configure it with `CHMOD 755`. Remember that this is the script being executed.

2. Open the text file `webdata.txt` in your text editor just to see what it contains.

3. Upload the file `webdata.txt` to the same `cgi-bin` directory and configure it with `CHMOD 666`. This code designates the text file as readable and writeable.

4. Open your Web browser and type in the URL to `open_close.pl`.

You should see the words `The text file was properly appended.` appear in your Web browser. Hit your Refresh button three or four times. Every time you do this, Perl opens the file and then appends the words, `We are appending some text to the file`, to the end of the current line. Download `webdata.txt` from your Web server and open it in your text editor to view the results.

Try changing the append `open` command in the script to the overwrite `open` command by removing one bracket. Test and view the results again and notice that no matter how many times you refresh the script the text file contains only one line because Perl is now overwriting the entire file each time.

Creating a script to view your most recent visitor

To practice building Perl scripts that read and write text files, try this project. This Flash project will display the most recent visitor to your Flash site and offer the person viewing it the opportunity to post his or her name as most recent visitor.

On the CD-ROM The files required for this project are on the CD-ROM located at the back of this book. The files you'll need are `visitor.fla`, `readvisitor.pl`, `writevisitor.pl`, and the data file `visitordata.txt`.

`Visitor.fla` contains two text fields on the stage. One is for the `personName` variable, and the other is for the `personEmail` variable. An ActionScript in Frame 1 calls out to `readvisitor.pl`, which in turn opens `visitordata.txt` on the server and sends the information contained within this file back to Flash. If the site viewer wants to leave his or her name and e-mail address, the viewer can enter his or her data into the input text fields in the Flash movie and click the Submit button. The

ActionScript on the Submit button sends the new variables to `writevisitor.pl` on the server, which opens `visitordata.txt` and writes the new information to it, replacing whatever was there before.

We'll test this project first and then analyze the components:

1. Upload the files `readvisitor.pl` and `writevisitor.pl` to your `cgi-bin` folder and configure them both with `CHMOD 755`.

2. Upload the data file `visitordata.txt` to the same `cgi-bin` folder and configure it with `CHMOD 666`.

3. Open `visitor.fla` in Flash and change the `loadVariables` ActionScript statement in Frame 1 to reflect your Web domain.

4. Change the `loadVariables` ActionScript statement on the Submit button to also reflect your Web domain.

5. Preview `visitor.fla` in your Web browser.

The first thing that happens is that Flash displays `default` in the text fields. Flash received this data courtesy of Frame 1 calling `readvisitor.pl`, which retrieved the data from the `visitordata.txt` data file on the server. Even though three elements are involved in this process, it happens mighty fast. `Visitordata.txt` contains only this code:

```
personName=default&personEmail=defualt&
```

The code in `readvisitor.pl` reads this code and sends it back to Flash by using the following Perl code:

```perl
#!/usr/bin/perl
print "Content-type:text/html\n\n";


####### File operations #######

open(VISIT,"visitordata.txt");
#Opens the file for reading

@visitordata=<VISIT>;
#Puts the data from the text file
#into the array @visitordata

close(VISIT);
#Properly closes the file on the server

print "@visitordata";
#Sends the data from the text file
#back out to Flash


exit;
```

This code opens the `visitordata.txt` file and puts the entire contents into the array `@visitordata`. The final `print` statement prints the entire array in one lump back out to Flash. There is no need to break up the data in any way because Flash automatically breaks up the data when it receives the data. The true power in this script is that it is fully modular. You can store any amount of variables by using this script along with `writevisitor.pl`!

When the user in the Flash movie wants to submit his or her own name and e-mail address, the user types it in and clicks the Submit button, which sends this new data to `writevisitor.pl`, which in turn overwrites `visitordata.txt` with the new name and e-mail address. A brief message is displayed in the sample file to confirm the process, and then the timeline plays through and stops at the beginning. Here is the code in `writevisitor.pl`:

```perl
#!/usr/bin/perl
print "Content-type:text/html\n\n";

#Test for method and collect all the variables
if ($ENV{'REQUEST_METHOD'} eq "GET"){
    $allWebData=$ENV{'QUERY_STRING'};
}
elsif ($ENV{'REQUEST_METHOD'} eq "POST"){
    read(STDIN, $allWebData, $ENV{'CONTENT_LENGTH'});
    }

####### File operations #######

open(VISIT,">visitordata.txt");
#Opens the file for overwriting

print VISIT "$allWebData";
#Overwrites the entire file with the
#new data sent from Flash

close(VISIT);
#Properly closes the file on the server


exit;
```

Take a look at the section that reads the query string or post header. Notice that it does not break up the data with the `split` command! Herein lies the power inherent in these scripts. Perl is just taking the entire string of data sent from Flash and writing it onto `visitordata.txt`. This script essentially takes a snapshot of any data sent from Flash and pops it into the text file of your choice. Simply rename any references to `visitordata.txt` to reflect the text file you wish to read/write to and make sure that text file is configured with `CHMOD 666` on the server.

If Flash sends 38 variables to this script, the script will simply take all 38 variables and put them in the text file. The read script then retrieves all the variables and sends them back to Flash exactly as they were sent in the first place. Flash even recognizes the URL encoding and does the proper conversions for you when the data is returned!

I bet your mind is reeling from the possibilities now. Try out the code:

1. Inside `visitor.fla`, create as many more input text fields as you'd like and make sure to name them each with new unique variable names. These text files can be as big or as small as you'd like.

2. Preview your movie in your browser.

3. Enter any values you want in all your new text fields and click the Submit button.

4. Close your browser.

5. Download and open `visitordata.txt` from your server and observe the beauty of the big, long string containing all your variables.

6. Preview the Flash movie again in your browser and notice that every variable is exactly as you entered it!

Now you have a way to read and write any amount of data from Flash with a text file. When this data comes back to Flash, you can use it in any way you'd like.

The `loadVariablesNum` statement in the first frame of the movie can just as easily be attached to a button so that a user could retrieve data on demand. Nesting the statement inside an `if` statement makes for even more conditional possibilities, such as only allowing a user to write to the text file if he or she has already logged in with a username and password.

Caution   Make sure to test for the data's existence (see Chapter 1) before operating on it.

Even though the snapshot method was demonstrated in this example, once Perl opens your text file for writing you can use a `print` statement to enter any kind of data. For example, the `split` command was not used to split the incoming data string from Flash. You could easily add this code section to the write script and write only the variables you want to a text file. This code is very useful if Flash is sending out 15 variables and you want only two specific ones to be stored in the data text file. After adding the `split` command segment, you would just change the `print` code block in the Perl script to something like the following:

```
print VISIT "$DATA{'personEmail'}\&$DATA{'personAddress'}\&";
```

Notice the escaped ampersands (\&). These are used so that the data is stored in one long string in the text file and later sent in one correctly formatted chunk back to Flash. If you'd like to make a text file that keeps accumulating data, just open it for writing in append mode. Because the data already ends in an ampersand, the file will keep accumulating data. This kind of text file can get big really fast and is not recommended unless you plan on manually cleaning it out or writing Perl code to do it for you.

Sending e-mail messages from Flash

Sending e-mails from Flash is undoubtedly the most common request among those new to Flash and server-side scripting. This example is presented last because it uses every Perl concept presented thus far. Unlike reading and writing to text files, which involves a myriad of files, sending an e-mail takes only one Perl script. The only new concept is using a file handle to refer not a text file, but to the mail program on the server.

The Unix e-mail program

Each Unix/Linux server (usually) has an e-mail program called `sendmail` sitting on the server in the background that is responsible for sending e-mail messages. You can talk to this mail program using Perl and send e-mail directly from the server. This capability is especially useful for processing forms sent from Flash and sending the results to someone who will read and interpret them.

There is a technical path to this program just like there is a path to Perl. The most common path is `/usr/lib/sendmail`, and this path is used in the following examples although another common path can be `/usr/sbin/sendmail`. If these examples completely fail to work for you, the path to your mail program may be different; a call to your friendly hosting company should provide you with the correct path to `sendmail`.

File handle for sendmail

The file handle for `sendmail` can be anything you'd like, but it's best to keep it simple and just use the word EMAIL. Also, opening `sendmail` requires a slightly different syntax than opening a text file. In the examples that follow, a standard set of commands precedes the sending of e-mails:

```
#Reference the location of sendmail
$sendmail='/usr/lib/sendmail';
#Open the e-mail program
open(EMAIL , "|$sendmail -t");
```

The `-t` and other characters are needed to open a tunnel to the `sendmail` program. Any `print` statements made after this code block print directly into an e-mail that is sent as soon as the `close` command is issued:

```
close(EMAIL);
#Closes and sends the e-mail
```

E-mail requirements

Only two elements are required to send e-mail successfully: a recipient and some body text. These elements are defined in standard Perl `print` statements after the e-mail program has been opened. To specify the recipient and, optionally, a sender, reply-to, or subject, use this syntax:

```
print EMAIL "To: data here \n";
print EMAIL "Reply-to: data here \n";
print EMAIL "From: data here \n";
print EMAIL "Subject: data here \n\n";
```

Replace `data here` with either the actual text you are hard-coding into the script or with variables sent from Flash. This code

```
print EMAIL "To: $DATA{'recipient'}\n";
```

will send the e-mail to an e-mail address that Flash sent in a variable named `recipient`.

Note The \n escape character is used to designate a new line or carriage return. This character is required here make sure things such as the sender and the subject are on separate lines when the code interacts with the `sendmail` program on the server. The escaped new line character (\n) should appear inside the quotation marks of the `print` statement. If you're going to include a subject, it should be the last item, and it should be followed by two consecutive \n characters.

The body text is delivered by just using `print EMAIL` and either hard-coded text or a variable name in the quotes:

```
print EMAIL "Dear John, very nice to see you today\n";
print EMAIL "I hope you are feeling better\n";
print EMAIL "Mark";
```

or

```
Print EMAIL "$DATA{'message'}";
# Prints a variable from Flash named "message"
# as the body of the e-mail
```

Your own Flash e-mail application

In this section, you'll create a quick little application in Flash that lets anyone send an e-mail to someone else. Although you can put this application on your Web site, we don't recommend doing so because then anyone can send e-mail using your domain! If this application is going to be part of your Flash site, it should be password-protected to prevent anyone from gaining easy access to it.

For this project, you'll need the Flash movie file `quickemail.fla` and the Perl script files `emailtemplate.pl` and `quickemail.pl`, which are found on the CD-ROM located at the back of this book.

First, you'll set up an e-mail script on the server to receive the variables from Flash and create and send an e-mail:

1. Open the CD-ROM Perl script file `emailtemplate.pl` This file is nearly identical to `perltemplate2.pl` except for the addition of the e-mail–sending section at the end.

2. Replace the commented code section in the e-mail section of the script with the following `print` statements:

```
print EMAIL "To: $DATA{'recipient'}\n";
print EMAIL "From: $DATA{'sender'}\n";
print EMAIL "$DATA{'message'}";
```

   Make sure to leave the `open` and `close` e-mail statements above and below the commented code block you're replacing.

3. Save this file on your hard drive as `quickemail.pl` (this file is available on the CD-ROM if you have any problems).

4. Upload this file to your server `cgi-bin` folder and configure it with `CHMOD 755`.

This Perl script is now configured to use three variables from Flash named `recipient`, `sender`, and `message`. Next, you must configure the Flash movie:

1. Create a new file in Flash and save it as `quickemail.fla` (or just pop open the CD-ROM file `quickemail.fla`, reference your Web domain in the button code, and skip to step 11).

2. Add a `stop()` action to the first frame.

3. Create three input text fields on the stage.

4. Assign the variable names `recipient`, `sender`, and `message` to the text fields. The `sender` and `recipient` fields can be single line and should support enough characters to contain an e-mail address. The `message` field should be multiline with word wrap.

5. Use static text fields to provide the proper labels next to the dynamic entry fields.

6. Create a button on the stage or use one from the standard Flash button library and use a standard text field to label it **Send Now!**

7. Attach a `loadVariablesNum` statement to this button specifying the `quickemail.pl` file on your server as the URL, a method of `POST`, and a level of 0.

8. Below the `loadVariablesNum` statement, add a `gotoAndPlay(10)` statement.

9. Create a blank frame around Frame 10 and then fill it with a static text field containing the text **"Your message has been sent!"** Put 10 standard frames out in front of it. Figure 2-8 shows the layout of the stage and timeline.

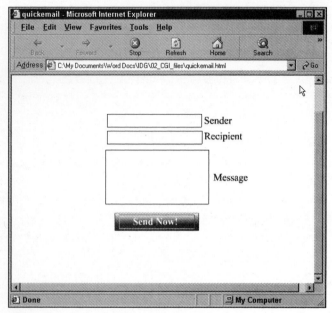

Figure 2-8: Stage layout and timeline setup for CD-ROM file `quickemail.fla`.

10. Preview the movie in your Web browser.

11. Enter an e-mail address in the Recipient field (preferably your own so you can test the program) and then enter any valid e-mail address in the Sender field and any text in the Message text box.

12. Click the Send Now! button and check your e-mail in a minute or so (some servers can take up to 10 minutes or more if they're slow). You should receive the exact contents of the `message` field sent from whatever address you entered in the Sender field.

Perl compiles and sends an e-mail according to the three variables sent from Flash, one each for sender, recipient, and the message body. Perl opens the `sendmail` program and provides the data, at which point the server compiles and sends the e-mail. Although this script lets anyone using this Flash movie send an e-mail to anyone else, what you probably will want to use it for most of the time is as a standard form-processing application.

A Flash form-processing Perl script

The most common use for Perl scripts that send e-mails is form processing. You've filled out such forms countless times online. You're probably used to seeing them in HTML format, but building a form using Flash and Perl is just as easy. The project in this section uses the CD-ROM file quickemail.fla as a starting point to illustrate how to make certain parts of the form accessible to the user while other parts remain secret, such as the address of the recipient.

On the CD-ROM For this project, you'll need the Flash movie file quickemail.fla and the Perl script file emailtemplate.pl, both of which are on the CD-ROM located at the back of this book.

First you'll set up an e-mail script on the server to receive the variables from Flash and create and send an e-mail:

1. Open the CD-ROM Perl script file emailtemplate.pl.

2. Replace the commented code section marked for replacement in the e-mail section of the script with the following print statements:

```
print EMAIL "To: $DATA{'recipient'}\n";
print EMAIL "From: $DATA{'senderemail'}\n";
print EMAIL "Subject: $DATA{'subject'}\n\n";
foreach $i (keys %DATA) {
    print EMAIL "$i: $DATA{$i}\n\n";
    }
```

   Make sure to leave the open and close e-mail statements above and below the commented code block you're replacing. This new code sends the Perl-generated e-mail to a variable named recipient defined in Flash and makes it appear to come from whatever e-mail address is defined in a variable in Flash named senderemail. The subject is also defined in Flash and used here as well. The foreach statement then references the keys in the %DATA array, which are all the variable names sent from Flash. Each one it finds is printed into the body of the e-mail followed by a colon (:) and then its value.

3. Save this file on your hard drive as flashform.pl (this file is available on the CD-ROM if you have any problems).

4. Upload flashform.pl to your server cgi-bin folder and configure it with CHMOD 755.

Next you must configure the Flash movie:

1. Open the file quickemail.fla found on the CD-ROM or use the one you created in the previous example, "Your own Flash e-mail application." You can also open the finished file flashform.fla on the CD-ROM and skip to step 7.

2. Delete the Recipient text field and its label (the word Recipient) on the stage.

3. Change the word `Sender` on the stage to read **Email Address**. Change the variable name referenced in the text box next to it from `sender` to `senderemail`.

4. Select both the `senderemail` text field and the words `Email Address`. Drag them to the top of the stage. This field is where someone enters his or her own e-mail address when filling out your form.

5. Below that text field, create another dynamic text field similar to the Email Address field and assign it the variable `sendername`. Enter **Name** as regular text next to the field.

6. Create a larger multiline dynamic text field below the Name field you just created. Assign it the variable `streetaddress`. Enter **Street Address** as regular text next to the field. The stage layout should look something like Figure 2-9.

Figure 2-9: The stage layout for a simple Flash form that will deliver its contents to a Webmaster using Perl to put all the data in an e-mail.

7. Select the button at the bottom of the stage and view its attached ActionScript. Change the URL to reflect your domain and the Perl script `flashform.pl` that you uploaded.

8. Immediately before that `loadVariablesNum` statement, enter the following lines of ActionScript:

```
recipient="your email address";
subject="Result from Flash Form!!";
```

9. Replace the text inside the quotes of the `recipient` variable with your e-mail address. If you were developing this application for a client, you would enter the e-mail address of the person who is to receive the form results here.

10. Publish and preview this movie inside your Web browser and fill in the appropriate text fields with whatever data you'd like. Then click the Send Now! button.

11. Wait a few minutes and check your e-mail. All of the form data should have arrived.

12. Save your new Flash movie as `flashform.fla`. If you're having any problems, the movie is available on the CD-ROM in its completed state.

The button code in Flash in this example sets the recipient of the e-mail and the subject right before it executes the call to the Perl script. This means that people using this Flash movie can enter any data they want, but they can send it only to the address specified in the `recipient` variable in the button code!

The other great thing about the Perl script `flashform.pl` is that it's modular and can support any number of variables sent from Flash, because it's using the `foreach` statement to reference them all. Try it out:

1. Add as many other dynamic text fields as you'd like to the Flash movie you just created.

2. Make sure each one has a unique variable name and label each text field with some plain text for reference.

3. Click the Send Now! button and watch all your variables get delivered right to your e-mail box, courtesy of Flash and Perl.

Tip   You can easily take all the elements on the stage (the text fields and the button) and put them into any movie clip. This movie clip can then appear on-screen when a user clicks a button to fill in the form. Because the `loadVariablesNum` statement sends every variable in the timeline that it resides in, this setup is a good idea because it separates your e-mail form variables from any others hanging around the main timeline of your Flash movie.

The more you learn about Perl, the more you can customize the e-mail script. You could have Perl alphabetize the fields or remove unwanted fields from the body of the message. A simple way to remove unwanted fields would be to list only the variables you want to see in the body of the e-mail, as in this example:

```
print EMAIL "To: $DATA{'recipient'}\n";
print EMAIL "From: $DATA{'senderemail'}\n";
print EMAIL "Subject: $DATA{'subject'}\n\n";

#Display only specific variables below
print EMAIL " $DATA{'sendername'}\n\n";
print EMAIL " $DATA{'streetaddress'}\n\n";
print EMAIL " $DATA{'message'}\n\n";
```

This code would eliminate the `subject` and `recipient` variables from being present in the body of the e-mail message. In addition though, it makes the Perl script specific to only the one Flash movie you're using it with.

You can use Flash to improve the whole system as well. If you're really handy with ActionScript, you could add validation code to validate entries in any of the fields to make sure they're actually e-mail addresses. Another obvious addition is to add some sharp-looking graphics.

Summary

As you've seen throughout these examples, Flash and Perl make for a very happy couple. After you get used to the Perl syntax and the extra code it needs to split up variables from Flash, you can operate on those variables in any way you choose. You can pop them into text files or cookies and send e-mail messages from Flash forms with ease. Regardless of what new technologies arise in the near future, CGI and Perl will be present on the majority of Web hosts you find. Perl is the most common language on the Unix/Linux servers of the world, and these servers, being less expensive to install and maintain by hosting companies, will be the standard for years to come.

✦   ✦   ✦

Linking Flash to Active Server Pages and Access Databases

Active Server Pages (ASP) provide you with a primary back end server-side solution. ASP can act either as a middleman between your browser pages and a database or provide added dynamic interaction between your browser client and server. In either role, Flash is an excellent display platform when compared to HTML. ASP pages give you far more options when using Flash, and you quickly see how easily you can make the ASP-Flash 5 connection.

ASP resides on NT Servers, and we have made arrangements for a month of free hosting on HosTek's NT Servers (www.hostek.com). The trial hosting will enable you to learn how to use ASP with Flash 5. Both Windows and Macintosh users can take advantage of the trial hosting service. Therefore, in explaining how to set up the server-side scripts, a single common reference can be used.

ASP and VBScript Scripting Language

For Flash 5 users, ASP is a great introduction to a server-side Web scripting language. Visual Basic Scripting Edition (VBScript) is the default scripting language for ASP. So learning to use ASP is learning to write VBScript. However, so as not to clutter and confuse references in discussing ASP, the assumption in this chapter is that the language in question is VBScript unless otherwise stated. In other words, "writing an ASP page" is really writing VBScript to create an ASP page.

ASP pages run either as a mix of HTML and VBScript or VBScript alone. ASP pages can contain XML or JavaScript as well, but in this chapter we focus on using VBScript in ASP pages. In any case, ASP is saved in the Web server's root directory with the `asp` extension. The root directory varies with the setup of your system. If you are using your HosTek account, put your files into the root folder (directory) or a directory within the root folder and use your domain name (or IP address if you have no domain name) as the root. The following line calls an ASP program where the domain is `your.URL.com` and the ASP program is in the root directory:

```
http://your.URL.com/myProgram.asp
```

To keep the root directory uncluttered, you may want to create additional directories for different projects. To learn how to use Flash 5 with ASP, for example, you may want to add a directory in your Web server root directory named `FlashASP` and put all your ASP programs there. With this added directory, the preceding example changes to the following line:

```
http://your.URL.com/FlashASP/myProgram.asp
```

The addressing process is identical to that for HTML files, but you must keep in mind the relative relationship to the Web server's root directory.

If you are using an IP address as a root directory because you have no domain name, all you need to do is use the IP address. If your IP address is 234.56.78.910.11, for example, your access to the ASP page shown above is as follows:

```
http://234.56.78.910.11/FlashASP/myProgram.asp
```

Either method of addressing your ASP page follows the same slash format for any URL.

Note   Because this introduction to ASP is designed to get you up and running as quickly as possible, using Flash as the front end and ASP as the back end, we're covering just the essentials of ASP to help you get started using VBScript to create ASP pages. If you decide that ASP is what you need as a server-side language, take a look at *Active Server Pages Bible* by Eric Smith or *Active Server Pages For Dummies* by Bill Hatfield (both by IDG Books Worldwide, Inc.) for more information.

The basic ASP format

Setting up an ASP page is simple. A beginning tag, `<%`, and an ending tag, `%>`, demarcate the ASP code in a page. You can mix HTML with VBScript and save the whole page with an `asp` extension, and it works fine. For the most part, though, we wanted to avoid HTML as much as possible and have all ASP operations communicate directly with the SWF page. As a result, the only HTML included in the examples is just to show how ASP works in general. The front end, then, is Flash and not HTML. As a result, most of the scripts show the following format:

```
<%
script
%>
```

Use a text editor such as Notepad or WordPad (Windows) or SimpleText (Macintosh) to write your ASP scripts. To get started, write the following script:

```
<%
Dim Hello
Hello="HiYa George"
Response.write Hello
%>
```

Caution   If you use Notepad, make sure that Notepad doesn't add a `txt` extension in addition to your `asp` extension if you save your file as a text file (Text Documents) with an `asp` extension. Place quotation marks around the name of your file when you save it to prevent Notepad from adding an unwanted `txt` extension.

Save the file as `hello.asp` in your server root directory or subdirectory. For this example, we saved the ASP file in a folder (directory) named `FlashASP` in the Web server's root directory, `your.URL.com`. To launch the program, we type the following:

```
http://your.URL.com/FlashASP/hello.asp
```

Substitute your domain name for `yourURL.com` and your subdirectory name for `FlashASP`. After you launch the program, you should see the following in the browser window:

```
HiYa George
```

If you get an error, double-check your code and check whether you placed your script in the correct root directory or subdirectory. If you're using your own computer as a server and client, make sure that your server is running and the rest of your software is in place and set up correctly.

Data display

Throughout this chapter, you see the `Response.write` command in use. This command works something like a `print` command in Basic. The `Response.write` command takes the materials to the right of the command and displays them in a Web page. Generally, the `Response.write` command uses the following format:

```
Response.write "Display this message."
```

You can also use the `Response.write` command to display functions, as in the following example:

```
Response.write sqr(250)
```

The output shows the square root of 250, which is 15.8113883008419. Throughout the rest of this chapter, you see the `Response.write` command used often, because this workhorse command is used to send information to the user through Web pages or Flash.

Comments

As in all programming languages, comments in code help developers remember what they were doing with the code as they were developing it. VBScript uses a single quote mark (`'`) to flag a line as a comment, as in the following example:

```
<%
Dim item
item=49.85
'The item must include a 7% sales tax.
item = item + (item * .07)
Response.write item
%>
```

Variables

Declaring a variable in ASP is different from declaring a variable in ActionScript. In ActionScript, you define the variable with a value, and that action takes care of both the declaration and assignment. In ASP, you need to declare variables with the `Dim` keyword and then assign a value to the variable. The following example shows how to declare a variable by using VBScript in an ASP block:

```
<%
Dim score
score = 50
%>
```

The script requires that the variable `score` first be declared using `Dim`. To declare several variables, you can declare them by using multiple `Dim` keywords, as follows:

```
Dim Ned
Dim Mo
Dim Homer
```

Or you can use the following shortcut:

```
Dim Ned, Mo, Homer
```

Whatever method you prefer, ASP requires a variable declaration prior to your using the variable in the script.

Data types

A variable is not limited to a single data type in VBScript. Instead, a variable can change from one type of data to another, not unlike in ActionScript. You can also mix different types of data in a single variable.

The following script shows three data types entered into ASP variables: integers, doubles (floating point numbers), and a string literal. However, to format the variables into three lines for output, you must concatenate an HTML tag, `<br>`, to create a line break. The tag is placed into a variable named `lnBreak`, and the `lnBreak` variable is placed between the `Response.write` statements to place output on different lines, as in the following example:

```
<%
Dim wholeThing, someFractions, stringBean, lnBreak
lnBreak = "<br>"
wholeThing = 6744
someFractions=22.95
stringBean= "Eat your vegetables!"
Response.write wholeThing
Response.write lnBreak
Response.write someFractions
Response.write lnBreak
Response.write stringBean
%>
```

The output of this example is as follows:

```
6744
22.95
Eat your vegetables!
```

For the most part, in dealing with ASP and Flash, you format the output by placing it in the appropriate variable or movie clip, and you don't need to worry about formatting the output in ASP scripts. What is viewed on-screen depends on whether you are placing the output from ASP into a variable associated with a dynamic text field or a movie clip.

If you need to know the data type of a variable at any given moment, you can use the `VarType()` function. This function returns the variable as 1 of 16 coded values. For example, in the following listing, a variable named `uniVar` is first defined as a floating-point number, and the `VarType()` function returns the code for a double-precision floating-point number. Then the variable `uniVar` is concatenated with a string, changing the variable to a string. As a result, the code for a string is returned.

```
<%
Dim uniVar, lnBreak
lnBreak="<br>"
uniVar=123.45
Response.write VarType(uniVar)
```

```
Response.write lnBreak
uniVar= uniVar & "A Word"
Response.write VarType(uniVar)
%>
```

After the program executes, the following appears on-screen:

```
5
8
```

Those two codes are for the variable's first incarnation as a double and then its second incarnation as a string. Table 3-1 shows the entire list of code for the different types of data using the VarType function.

Table 3-1 VarType Codes	
Code	Data Type in Variable
0	Empty
1	Null
2	Integer
3	Long integer
4	Single
5	Double
6	Currency
7	Data
8	String
9	Object
10	Error
11	Boolean
12	Variant (arrays only)
13	Nonautomation object
17	Byte
8192	Array

The codes are handy for conditional statements that look for the different types of data you may have in your variable. If you want a string instead of a code returned, use the `TypeName()` function.

For example, we made a couple changes to the previous listing, substituting `TypeName()` for `VarType()`. Instead of seeing codes, you see descriptive words for the variant type in the following example:

```
<%
Dim uniVar, lnBreak
lnBreak="<br>"
uniVar=521
Response.write TypeName(uniVar)
Response.write lnBreak
uniVar= (20 > 19)
Response.write TypeName(uniVar)
%>
```

Your computer screen should show these two lines:

```
Integer
Boolean
```

Operators

The VBScript operators used in ASP 3.0 are different in places from those found in Flash 5 ActionScript, but you find many similarities as well. VBScript has its origins in Microsoft Visual Basic, whereas ActionScript has an appearance and structure more like that of JavaScript. Remember also that the VBScript in ASP 3.0 was not written with Flash in mind, while ActionScript very much was. (In other words, don't expect to find a `gotoAndPlay()` statement in VBScript.) Table 3-2 shows the VBScript operators used in ASP.

Table 3-2 ASP Operators		
Operator	*Use*	*Format Example*
=	assignment	posMX =100
+	add	sumNow = firstVal + secondVal
-	subtract	sumLoss = firstVal - secondVal
*	multiply	taxCalc = item * .07
/	divide	centLoad = loadNow / loadTotal
\	integer divide	whole = 99.2 \ 11 (Results=9)

Continued

Table 3-2 *(continued)*

Operator	Use	Format Example
Mod	modulus	remain = 75 Mod 4
^	exponentiation	squareIt = sum ^ 2
&	concatenation	FullName = "Bleeding" & " " & "Gums"
=	equal to	if firstTry = secondTry Then ...
<>	not equal to	if better <> worse Then ...
>	greater than	if most > more Then ...
<	less than	if least < less Then ...
>=	greater than or equal to	if now >= past Then ...
<=	less than or equal to	if fun <= work Then ...
Not	negation	if not (a=b) Then...
And	logical AND	if (a = b) And (c <= d) Then ...
Or	logical OR	if (x = y) Or (a = z) Then...
Xor	logical XOR	if (soup = nuts) Xor (duck = chicken) Then...
Eqv	logical equivalence	if (high > low) Eqv (sky > earth) Then...
Imp	logical implication	if right Imp correct Then...

Conditional statements

The conditional statements in both ActionScript and VBScript accomplish similar goals, but they are written differently. If you are familiar with just about any version of Basic, especially Microsoft Visual Basic, you are on very familiar ground with VBScript. If, however, your scripting background is more on the lines of JavaScript and ActionScript, pay close attention to the differences.

The if/then/else and elseif statements

VBScript uses the if/then/else statement. This statement uses then instead of the curly braces to separate the condition from the consequence, as does ActionScript. If the condition in the first part of the statement is met, the program executes the portion of the line after the word then. If the condition is not met, the code after then is ignored. For example, the following code triggers the

Response.write portion of the line because the first portion of the line is evaluated as true:

```
<%
Dim apples, oranges
apples=10
oranges=20
if apples <> oranges then Response.write "I didn't think so."
%>
```

If you have an alternative to the conditional statement using else, the else clause is initiated automatically if the if condition is not met. The following script shows how else works:

```
<%
Dim suzy, ralph
suzy="smart"
ralph="strong"
if (suzy="smart") And (ralph="smart") Then Response.write "Off
to gifted class" Else Response.write "To each his or her own."
%>
```

Notice how the logical AND operator is used in the script. And the line beginning with if does not end until own. Both the then and else statements are part of the same line. To make the code clearer, you can use an underscore (_) as a continuation character. For example, you can add underscores to the preceding listing to make it clearer, as the following example shows:

```
<%
Dim suzy, ralph
suzy="smart"
ralph="strong"
if (suzy="smart") And (ralph="smart") _
Then _
    Response.write "Off to gifted class" _
Else _
    Response.write "To each his or her own."
%>
```

Either way works, but some people find the underscores to be distracting. If you do use the underscores as a continuation character in your scripts, make sure that you put a space between the underscore and the previous character in the line.

You can use the ElseIf keyword if you have several different conditions to list, as in the following example:

```
If A=1 Then do this
ElseIf A=2 Then do that
ElseIf A3 Then go home
Else Give up and go back to work
End If
```

The Select Case statement

An alternative to using several ElseIf statements with the If...Then structure is using the Select Case statement. Depending on the contents of a variable, the Select Case statement launches different responses. Suppose that you have an e-business with a list of available products or services. After the customer clicks one of the choices, the script matches his or her selection with one of several options that are available. If the customer's selection is not on the list, an Else option specifies how to inform the viewer. The basic structure of the statement is as follows:

```
Select Case variable
Case "One" Condition 1
Case "Two" Condition 2
Case "Three" Condition 3
Case Else None of the above
End Select
```

The Select Case structure makes scripting several conditions much clearer, and the Case Else statement provides an automatic alternative for none of the conditions being met. The End Select statement acts as a terminator for the structure.

The following example shows how Select Case might be used. In an application, the contents of the variable would be provided by a user visiting an e-commerce site rather than defined in the script.

```
<%
Dim product
product="Laptop"
Select Case product
Case "Desktop" Response.write "We have PCs and Macs."
Case "Laptop" Response.write "Several brands of laptops are
available."
Case "Software" Response.write "We have utilities,
applications, and games."
Case Else Response.write "We do not carry that product or
service."
End Select
%>
```

ActionScript does not have an equivalent to the Select Case statement, but passing data between an ASP Select Case statement and Flash is simply a matter of formatting any outcome from a Select Case structure to be read by Flash 5 ActionScript. We examine how to do that in the next section.

Conditional statements are important for server-side scripts because such statements are the decision-makers. If you create a dynamic site, the data from the Flash 5 front-end often must be analyzed in an ASP script, so seeing the similarities and differences between formatting conditional statements in ActionScript and formatting them in ASP is important.

Loops

ASP has two basic loop structures: `For...Next` and `Do...`. You find some similarities between ActionScript loops and those in VBScript, but VBScript loops are formatted more along the lines of Basic than either ActionScript or JavaScript.

Do loop structures

VBScript provides a number of variations on the `Do` loop. Depending on what you need from a loop and your programming style, each has a slightly different function and format.

Do...While loop

At the beginning of the `Do...While` loop, a statement specifies the conditions under which the loop terminates. All loop actions take place between the defining conditions of the loop and the `Loop` statement that terminates the loop, as follows:

```
<%
Dim counter, lnBreak
lnBreak="<br>"
counter=1
Do While counter <=5
    Response.write ( "Loop" & " " & counter)
    Response.write lnBreak
    counter = counter + 1
Loop
%>
```

Do...Until loop

About the only difference between the `Do...While` loop and the `Do...Until` loop is that the former guarantees at least one pass through the loop even if the termination condition matches the counter variable value. As soon as the `Do...Until` loop encounters the termination condition, it exits the loop without executing the statements in the loop. Compare the `Do...While` loop example with the following to see the differences:

```
<%
Dim counter, lnBreak
lnBreak="<br>"
counter=1
Do Until counter =5
    Response.write ( "Loop" & " " & counter)
    Response.write lnBreak
    counter = counter + 1
Loop
%>
```

The For...Next structure

The `For...Next` loop expects a loop variable, a beginning value, and a terminating value. Unlike ActionScript's `for` loop, VBScript does not have pre- and post-incremental variables. All termination occurs after the terminating value is reached and the loop makes a final pass. The following example shows how the loop is structured; compare it to the previous two examples of loops:

```
<%
Dim counter, lnBreak
lnBreak="<br>"
For counter = 1 To 5
    Response.write ( "Loop" & " " & counter)
    Response.write lnBreak
Next
%>
```

The `For...Next` loop is the easiest to use if you know the beginning and terminating values. If those values are unknown, we prefer using the `Do...While` structure that looks for the termination condition rather than defining that condition at the outset instead of using the `Exit For` procedure in a `For/Next` loop to exit the loop.

Step feature

A nice feature of VBScript `For...Next` loops is the `Step` keyword. Using `Step`, you can make the loop increments in a number of positive or negative steps. The following script illustrates this feature:

```
<%
Dim counter, lnBreak
lnBreak="<br>"
For counter = 20 to 1 Step -4
    Response.write ( "Loop" & " " & counter)
    Response.write lnBreak
Next
%>
```

Arrays

Arrays in ASP and ActionScript differ in several ways, but the concepts are identical. Arrays are especially important in ASP for organizing database information. VBScript has a number of different ways to create an array in ASP. First, you can just use an array name and assign literal values to each element in the array. As with variables, you must first establish a dimension for the array. For example, the following is a simple array in ASP:

```
<%
Dim item(4)
item(0) = "monitor"
item(1) = "keyboard"
item(2) = "motherboard"
item(3) = "mouse"
Response.write item(2)
%>
```

Like arrays in other scripting and programming languages, the initial element is the zero (0) element, and not one (1). Also notice that, in VBScript, the array elements are in parentheses and not in brackets as in ActionScript.

Multidimensional arrays

Especially if you work with databases, one of the nice features of VBScript's arrays is the ease with which you can declare them to more than a single dimension. Suppose that you have a service database that contains all the different service costs a company has. Each record is a client, and each field is a different service cost. To arrange the data from that database, you can place it in a two-dimensional array. The first element is the client, and the second is the service cost. The company has five different services and 300 clients, so the array can be dimensioned as follows:

```
Dim arrService (300,5)
```

Think of this line as equivalent to the following line:

```
Dim arrService (Row,Column)
```

Or consider it as follows:

```
Dim arrService (Client,Service Cost)
```

If you want to look at output showing what a particular client is billed broken down by service cost, you can write a script that looks at the client's name associated with the value of the first dimension and a service cost associated with the value of the second dimension. The following script shows how the parts of the two-dimensional array work with a client with the ID number of 259:

```
<%
Dim arrService(300,5), lnBreak
lnBreak="<br>"
arrService(259,0)=345.95
arrService(259,1)=0
arrService(259,2)=1342.87
arrService(259,3)=904.22
arrService(259,4)=0
Response.write ("Artwork = " & "$" & ArrService(259,0))
Response.write lnBreak
Response.write ("Consulting = " & "$" & ArrService(259,1))
Response.write lnBreak
Response.write ("Flash = " & "$" & ArrService(259,2))
Response.write lnBreak
Response.write ("Design = " & "$" & ArrService(259,3))
Response.write lnBreak
Response.write ("Hosting = " & "$" & ArrService(259,4))
%>
```

The output looks like what you see in the following example:

```
Artwork=$345.95
Consulting=$0
Flash=$1342.87
Design=$904.22
Hosting=$0
```

With this structure, you don't need 300 different scripts to get through 300 records.

Looping through arrays

In most computer languages, if you set up an array, pulling out elements is a matter of looping through the array until the element you're seeking matches a condition. The same is true of ASP. For example, the following script places values in five elements and then looks for one using a loop:

```
<%
Dim city(5), counter, search
city(0)= "London"
city(1)= "Paris"
city(2)= "New York"
city(3)= "Tokyo"
city(4)= "Bloomfield"
Do While search <> "New York"
search = city(counter)
counter = counter + 1
Loop
Response.write search
%>
```

In organizing databases, keep in mind that, at some point, data needs to be entered and retrieved, and using arrays in an ASP page can aid this process. Notice how the preceding loop takes advantage of the index beginning with 0. Initially, counter is 0 (undefined), so the index picks up the first element in the array the first time through the loop and keeps on going until the search condition is met.

Functions

As does ActionScript, VBScript has both built-in functions and user functions. For example, the VarType() function, used previously in this chapter, is built into VBScript. Similarly, a number of other functions are built into VBScript, but only a small subset of these that can be used with Flash 5 are going to be discussed in this book. (See VBScript Language Reference at http://msdn.microsoft.com/scripting/default.htm?/scripting/vbscript for a full listing of functions in VBScript, along with detailed explanations.) User functions in both ActionScript and VBScript are similar in structure and application. A user function is defined with a word using optional arguments and then a list of statements and is terminated with an End Function statement. For example, a function to add tax and shipping to an item can be written as follows:

```
<%
Function taxShip(item)
taxShip = item + (item *.07) +4.95
End Function
Response.write taxShip(19.95)
%>
```

The trick is, of course, to get the input from Flash 5 and use the data to do something. Eventually, you want to use ASP to take Flash 5 data and put it into a data file and pull data out of a file and output it in a Flash 5 movie.

Moving Data Between Flash 5 and ASP

Passing data between a server-side script, ASP, and Flash 5 is relatively simple. The variable names generated in Flash 5 are recognized by the same variable names in ASP and vice versa. If you pass a variable named item from Flash to ASP, the variable with the identical name in an ASP script takes on the value generated in Flash. A variable from ASP must be passed to Flash using a special Flash formatting protocol, explained in the next section.

All the files that are used to create the Flash movies and ASP files in this section are available on the CD-ROM.

Sending data from ASP to Flash 5

Flash 5 uses the loadVariablesNum() action to bring in data from remote sources. The action expects a URL containing the target data source and a level to load the data. The target can be a text file in the same directory as the Flash movie, or it can be remote target. For example, the following ActionScript targets an ASP file on an NT server at the specified URL:

```
loadVariablesNum ("http://www.sandActive.com/ASP/data.asp", 0)
```

The variable names are created in the external source. The format for external variables in a text field loaded using loadVariablesNum() is as follows:

```
VariableName=Data in the variable.&NewVariable=More data.
```

No spaces are allowed between the variable name, the equal sign (=), and the variable's contents. New variables are separated by an ampersand (&) and follow the same rules as the initial variable, and no spaces are allowed between the end of the first variable's data and the ampersand.

In ASP script, all the variables are placed between quotation marks. The ASP Response.write command sends the text block to Flash. For example, the following script places a variable named myHotVariable into Flash after the loadVariablesNum() action targets the ASP file:

```
<%
Response.write "myHotVariable=This message is from a server-side script."
%>
```

Optionally, you can place an ampersand before the initial variable name. Some developers like to place an ampersand before the first variable to ensure that all the variables contain a leading ampersand and are, therefore, easier to identify.

Creating the Flash movie

The Flash movie described in the following sections shows the steps involved in pulling in data from an ASP script and displaying it in Flash 5. Open up a new Flash movie, add and rename the following three layers, and save the movie as ASP2Flash.fla:

✦ Text Field

✦ Button

✦ Labels

Color palette

All color palettes come from a set of color combinations that compliment one another and help improve the general appearance of the movie. You add each color by first using the values (hexadecimal) for each color in the Mixer panel and then selecting Add Swatch from the pop-up menu in the Mixer panel's upper right corner. To create the color palette for ASP2Flash.fla, you need to add three colors, **Red**, **Green**, and **Blue**, with the values specified in the following table.

Color	R Value	G Value	B Value
A	E6	00	00
B	00	F3	00
C	FF	E6	00

Labels layer

Follow this next set of steps to create the background color and elements for the layer:

1. The background color is set to yellow. Choose Modify ➪ Movie and select Color C from the movie's color palette.

2. Draw a red rectangle using Color A for fill and stroke. Make the rectangle roughly W=150, H=30. Use Color B and a bold 12-point Verdana font to write the label **From ASP to Flash** on top of the rectangle.

3. Draw a green rectangle using Color B for fill and stroke. Set the rectangle dimensions to W=230, H =36.

4. Use as 12-point red Verdana font and type **Click Button** to the left of the bottom rectangle. Leave room between the label and the green rectangle for a button. See Figure 3-1 to see the placement of the different objects on the stage. Lock the layer after you finish.

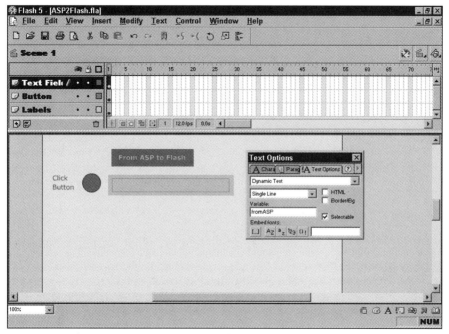

Figure 3-1: The stage area contains a single text field and a button for the ActionScript.

Text Field layer

The text fields in Flash can act as input and output windows. Both dynamic and input text fields can be associated with a variable name in the Text Object panel. Notice in Figure 3-1 how the name fromASP is used (in the Text Options panel) as the variable name associated with the dynamic text field. Set up the Text Field layer with the following steps:

1. With Figure 3-1 as a guide, use the Text tool to draw a text field over the bottom rectangle.

2. Select the text field and open the Character panel by clicking the text icon on the launcher bar and then clicking the Character tab. Select the Color A Red for the font color and choose a 12-point Verdana font.

3. Click the Text Options tab and select Dynamic Text from the top pop-up menu in the Text Options panel.

4. In the Variable window, type **fromASP** to indicate the name of the variable associated with the text field. Any variable named `fromASP` passing to Flash from the ASP script appears in the text field associated with that variable name.

Button layer

The button holds the ActionScript that loads the variables from ASP. The following set of steps shows how to set it up:

1. Use the Oval tool to draw a circle, using Color A for the fill and black for the stroke.

2. Select the circle and text and press the F8 key to open the Symbol Properties dialog box. Select Button for the Behavior and, in the Name window, type **ASPgetter**. Click OK to create a button symbol.

3. Select the button instance and click the Action panel icon (arrow) on the launcher bar to open the Objects Action panel. Enter the following script, substituting the URL with the one you use as your root directory and subdirectory in your root directory:

```
on (release) {
    loadVariablesNum
("http://your.URL.com/FlashASP/flash1.asp", 0);
}
```

While entering the ActionScript in the Normal mode, place the parameter values as shown in Figure 3-2. Use the default Level value of 0, and type the URL in the URL window. You do not want to send any variables to ASP, so leave the Variable pop-up menu in the default state of "Don't send."

Figure 3-2: In the Normal mode, the parameter values are placed at the bottom of the ActionScript editor.

That step concludes the Flash portion of the project.

Using ASP to create variables

This first ASP script does one thing: It passes a variable to Flash. The format is fairly straightforward. The variable format consists of an ampersand followed by the variable name, an equal sign, and the contents of the variable. After you write the following script, save it in the root directory or a subdirectory of the root directory under the name data.asp:

```
<%
Dim fromASP
fromASP = "fromASP=Greetings from ASP"
Response.Write fromASP
%>
```

Figure 3-3 shows the output in Flash.

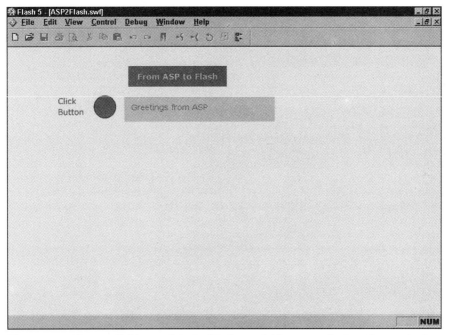

Figure 3-3: The text field associated with the variable name displays the contents from the server-side script.

Sending data from Flash to ASP

To send data from Flash to ASP, you need some way of directing the data out of Flash and making it go somewhere else. As does HTML, Flash provides two methods for this action: GET and POST. The POST method has proved the best cross-platform method, so we use it throughout the book.

The general format for sending data from Flash to a server script is as follows:

```
loadVariablesNum ("http://your.URL.com/ASP/grand.asp", 0, "POST")
```

The format looks identical to the format for loading variables into Flash, except that `"POST"` is added after the level value.

Which variables are sent from Flash? All variables are sent. However, each one must be captured in ASP separately. The VBScript `Request.Form()` function works great with Flash forms. All you need to do is place the name of the Flash variable you're sending into a VBScript variable using the `Request.Form()` function. Suppose that two variables, `item` and `price`, are sent from Flash to an ASP page. To retrieve those two variables and place them into ASP variables, you use the following script:

```
<%
dim item, price
item=Request.Form("item")
price=Request.Form("price")
%>
```

After the data passes from Flash to variables in an ASP page, the data can be used for further calculations, for formatting, or passed to a database.

Creating the Flash movie

This next Flash movie demonstrates how a variable in Flash is sent to an ASP script, concatenated with an ASP literal, and sent back to Flash. The purpose of sending the variable back to Flash is to show that it is the value that came from Flash in the first place. By adding a bit of material, you can begin to see how data in the server-side script can interact with the data sent from Flash. Open a new movie and add the following layers:

✦ Background

✦ Text Fields

✦ Button

Use the steps in the following sections to create the Flash movie and save the movie as `Flash2ASPnBack.fla`.

Color palette

Use the color palette in Table 3-3 for the movie. Use Color F for the background color.

Table 3-3 Color Palette for Flash2ASPnBack.fla			
Color	**R Value**	**G Value**	**B Value**
A	A6	F3	C0
B	07	99	33
C	A6	A6	40
D	80	33	33
E	FF	FF	80

Background layer

Begin with the bottom layer. By placing all the labels and backdrops for the movie, you can get a better feel of where everything else goes. Just follow these steps:

1. Choose Modify ⇨ Movie and, in the Background Color well, select Color F (yellow) for the background.

2. In the middle of the stage near the top, draw two backdrops using the Rectangle tool. Use Color A for both the fill and stroke colors and give each rectangle the dimensions W=134, H=32.

3. To the right of the top backdrop, type **Input** using a bold 12-point Verdana font in Color D. Using the same font and color, type **Output** to the right of the bottom backdrop. (See Figure 3-4 to give you a clear idea of what this looks like.)

4. To the left of the two rectangles, type a **Click Button** label using a 12-point Verdana font in Color C, as shown in Figure 3-4. Leave space for the button that goes between the label and the text field backdrops.

5. Lock the layer.

Text Fields layer

In this movie, both an input and output layer are required. The input field is placed over the top backdrop, and the output field is placed over the bottom. The following set of steps covers the process for creating the two text fields:

1. Select the Text tool and draw a text field over the top backdrop rectangle (refer to Figure 3-4). Open the Character panel and select a bold 12-point Verdana font using Color B.

2. Open the Text Options panel and select Input Text from the top pop-up menu. Check the Border/Bg box.

3. In the Variable box on the Text Options panel, type **input** for the variable name to be associated with the text field.

4. Repeat steps 1, 2, and 3, except select Dynamic Text as the type of text field and deselect the Border/Bg box. Use the name **output** for the variable name in the Text Options panel.

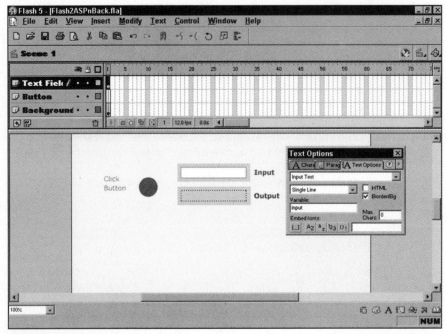

Figure 3-4: Two text fields provide an entry portal (input) and return data window from the ASP page (output); a button contains the ActionScript to launch the process.

Button layer

The button holds the ActionScript that loads the variables from ASP. The following set of steps shows how to set it up:

1. Use the Oval tool to draw a circle using Color B for the fill and Color D for the stroke.

2. Select the circle and press the F8 key to open the Symbol Properties dialog box. Select Button for the Behavior and, in the Name box, type **InAndOut**. Click OK to create a button symbol.

3. Select the button instance and click the Action panel icon (arrow) on the launcher bar to open the Objects Actions panel. Enter the following script, substituting your own path:

```
on (release) {
  loadVariablesNum
("http://your.URL.com/FlashASP/flashback.asp",
0, "POST");
}
```

4. In the Object Actions panel, type the URL in the URL box. Use the default Level value of 0. In the Variables drop-down list box, select Send using POST. These parameter values are as shown in Figure 3-5.

The Flash side of the equation is now complete.

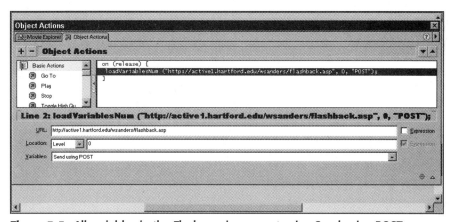

Figure 3-5: All variables in the Flash movie are sent using Send using POST.

Setting up ASP to catch variables

The data sent to ASP is the contents of the text field associated with the variable named `input`. Therefore, you want a mirror variable named `input` in the ASP script to store the data sent from Flash. If you had 10 or 100 variables in the Flash movie, ASP could handle them all as long as you included an ASP mirror variable to hold the contents passed from Flash. The following script takes the data entered into the input text field and stores it in a variable named `backFlash`. Then you can do with it what you want. In this case, the contents of the variable are concatenated with the phrase `" from ASP."` with a space between the first quotation mark and the first word. Otherwise, the data would run together.

To send the data back to Flash with the new phrase, use the output variable associated with the second text field. An ASP variable, output, is defined to contain the necessary data for Flash. The new contents of input are defined in the variable to be sent back to Flash. The Response.write command then sends the variable output back to Flash. Save the following script under the name flashback.asp in your root directory or the appropriate subdirectory in the root directory:

```
<%
Dim fromASP, backFlash
backFlash=Request.Form("input")
backFlash = backFlash & " from ASP"
fromASP = "output=" & backFlash
Response.Write fromASP
%>
```

Run your SWF file and enter some text in the input text field. As shown in Figure 3-6, whatever you enter in Flash is bounced back from ASP with the concatenated message.

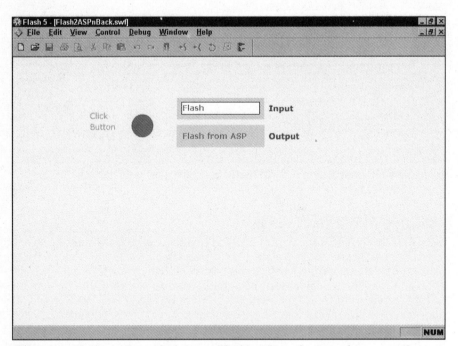

Figure 3-6: The input from Flash is modified in ASP and returned as output in Flash.

Using Flash data and ASP calculations

The next step is to see how data gathered in a Flash front end can be used in calculations generated by ASP. The calculations can be simple or complex, and most can be accomplished by client-side scripts in ActionScript. But seeing how to pass calculated data from a ASP script with data originating in Flash is the first step in using wholly ASP-generated data for output in Flash.

Creating the Flash movie

This Flash movie is similar to the previous one, but it takes the data sent from Flash, performs a calculation, and then returns the calculated results back to Flash. With this example, you can begin to see the benefits of ASP. Several different Flash movies can use the same ASP script, and if values need to be changed (tax rates or shipping costs), a single change in the ASP script suffices to change the output in all the Flash movies that need the same data calculated. Open a new movie and create the following layers:

- ✦ Input
- ✦ Button
- ✦ Output

Use the steps in the following sections to create the movie and save it as ASPcalc.fla.

Color palette

Use the color palette in Table 3-4 for the movie. Use Color B (deep red/brown) for the background color. Set Color D as black and Color E as white.

Table 3-4			
Color Palette for ASPcalc.fla			
Color	*R Value*	*G Value*	*B Value*
A	FF	BD	33
B	99	00	19
C	B3	FF	CC

Input layer

Like the last movie, the input field is used to provide data associated with a variable that will be sent to the ASP script on the server. The following set of steps covers the process for creating the input text field:

1. Select the Text tool and draw a rectangle text field near the top of the stage, as shown in Figure 3-7.

2. Open the Text Options panel and select Input Text from the top pop-up menu. In the Variable box, type **input** for the variable name to be associated with the text field.

3. In the Character panel, select Verdana as the type and black for the text color.

4. Using Color C and a bold Verdana 12-point font, type **Enter item price:**, as shown in Figure 3-7.

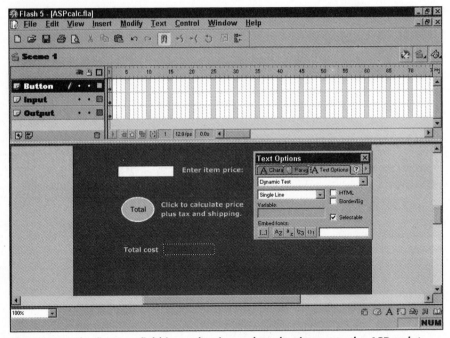

Figure 3-7: The first text field is used to input data that is sent to the ASP script, calculated, and then returned to Flash in the output window.

Button layer

The ActionScript in the button sends data to VBScript script, but it does no calculation itself. The script is almost identical to the previous Flash movie, but the button is a little different; follow these steps:

1. Use the Oval tool to draw an oval using Color A for the fill and white for the stroke. Type **Total** on top of the oval.

2. Select the oval and the text on the oval and press the F8 key to open the Symbol Properties dialog box. Select Button for the Behavior and, in the Name box, type **calcToASP**. Click OK to create a button symbol.

3. Select the button instance and click the Action panel icon (arrow) on the launcher bar to open the Object Actions panel. Enter the following script, substituting your own path:

```
on (release) {
     loadVariablesNum
("http://your.URL.com/FlashASP/dataBack.asp",
 0, "POST");
}
```

4. Type the URL in the URL box and use the default Level value of 0. In the Variables drop-down list, select Send using POST.

Output layer

The Output text field goes below the button (refer to Figure 3-7). Follow the steps for the Input layer except select Dynamic Text from the pop-up menu in the Text Options panel and type **output** for the variable name to associate with the field.

Using ASP to Calculate Values

This next VBScript does the relatively mundane chore of adding tax and shipping costs to a value. As does the script in the previous movie, the following script wraps the completed calculation into a variable and sends it back to Flash with the `Response.write` command:

```
<%
Dim input, output
input=Request.Form("input")
input = input + (input * .07)
input = input + 5.99
output = "output=" & "$" & input
Response.Write output
%>
```

Save the ASP file as `dataBack.asp` and place it in your root directory or a subdirectory in the root directory. After you launch your Flash SWF file, the value you enter into the input text field is put into the calculations of the ASP script. Because the text field is associated with the input variable in Flash ActionScript, the data is passed to the input variable in ASP. The calculations are carried out and the results are returned to the output variable in Flash. Because the second text field is associated with output, the results appear in the text field window.

Passing data generated in ASP functions

Using ASP functions to pass data to Flash requires arranging your ASP code so that the function contains everything required to organize and send the data to Flash, including everything for calculations and formatting data for Flash and a `Response.write` command. The generic format looks as follows:

```
<%
Function funcName (arguments)
'Calculations and formatting stored in variable
backToFlash="FlashVariable=" ASPvariable
Response.write backToFlash
End function
funcName(input from flash)
%>
```

The function name and arguments are standard, as are the calculations and formatting statements. However, after all the formatting is completed and stored in ASP variables, the Flash variables must be formatted to read the ASP variables within the function's parameters. For example, the following function is another tax and shipping one with the Flash formatting added. After the function is called from Flash, it returns the input value from Flash with the tax and shipping added.

```
<%
Function taxShip(item)
    taxShip = item + (item *.07) +4.95
End Function
Dim results, output
results=taxShip(Request.Form("input"))
output="output=" & "$" & results
Response.write output
%>
```

Save the ASP file as `taxShipFlashFunction.asp` and save it in your root directory on the server. Then, using the movie from the previous example (`ASPCalc.fla`), change the button script to read as follows:

```
on (release) {
    loadVariablesNum
("http://your.URL.com/FlashASP
/taxShipFlashFunction.asp", 0, "POST");
}
```

Try out the movie by pressing Ctrl+Enter (in Windows) or Cmd+Return (on the Macintosh). After the SWF file appears, type a value and click the button. You should see the value you entered returned with tax and shipping costs added, as shown in Figure 3-8.

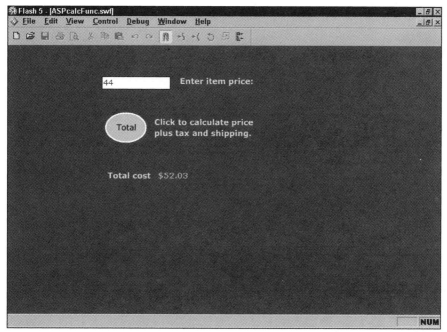

Figure 3-8: All the calculations in the Total cost are generated in a VBScript function on an ASP page and returned to Flash for output.

Passing array data between Flash and ASP

Data from a database can be placed into an array for transfer to and from Flash and ASP. In looking at how arrays behave, you quickly see that they are treated no differently than variables. The great advantage of an array, though, is that a series of numbers can be used to access the array, and by understanding how to use array elements and associated values, you can better establish a way to organize and pass data between Flash and ASP.

On the Flash side, the arrays can be associated with text fields for displaying any or all elements of the array. On the ASP side, the array elements can be coordinated to the text fields. In this way, whatever value is passed from Flash to ASP can be used to coordinate ASP data and Flash output.

Creating the Flash movie

This next movie contains five text fields and five buttons associated with the text fields. Each of the text fields is an element in an array, and each button contains a script that sends information to an ASP script that uses its own array to verify that a button is clicked. Open a new movie and create the following layers:

✦ Background

✦ Buttons

✦ Text Fields

Create this movie by performing the steps in the following sections and then save the movie as `ASParray.fla`. Figure 3-9 provides an overview of the movie and its major components:

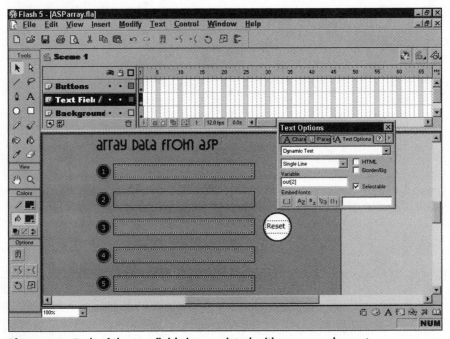

Figure 3-9: Each of the text fields is associated with an array element.

Color palette

The movie uses a simple gray, purple, black, and white color palette whose values are shown in Table 3-5. Color C is black, and Color D is white.

Table 3-5 Color Palette for ASParray.fla			
Color	*R Value*	*G Value*	*B Value*
A	A6	99	E6
B	A6	A6	A6

Background layer

Follow these steps to create the Background layer:

1. Choose Modify ➪ Movie and then select the color palette's purple color (Color A) for the background.

2. Draw a gray rectangle with black strokes to serve as a backdrop to a text field. Use the Info panel to set the rectangle dimensions to W=259 and H=28.

3. Select the rectangle and then choose Modify ➪ Group so that the stroke and fill are grouped.

4. Make four identical copies of the rectangle and line them up vertically using the Align panel to space and align them (see Figure 3-10).

Buttons layer

Create five buttons and label them from 1 to 5, as shown in Figure 3-10. These buttons contain scripts that send data to the ASP script and fire the ASP script. The value of the variable myData is the array element value of the text field adjacent to the button. In the ASP script, you see how that value is used to return the correct message after the button is clicked. Substitute your URL for the one provided in the following example:

```
on (release) {
    myData = 1;
    loadVariablesNum
("http://your.URL.com/FlashASP/arrayData.asp", 0,
"POST");
}
```

Create a sixth button and label it Reset. The Reset button launches an ASP script that places a space in each of the five text fields, effectively resetting them all:

```
on (release) {
   loadVariablesNum
("http://your.URL.com/ASP/clearArray.asp", 0)
}
```

Text Fields layer

The text fields are all associated with the same array: out[n]. Use the following steps to set them up:

1. Lock the Background layer so that you don't select the background rectangles. In the Character panel, set the font to Verdana, selecting black for the color and 12 for the font size.

2. Create the first text field adjacent to the button numbered 1 over the text field background (rectangle). Using the Info panel, make sure that the width (W:) is 250. Center the text field over the background rectangle (which requires you to temporarily unlock the background layer) by using the Align panel.

3. With the text field selected, open the Text Options panel and select Dynamic Text from the drop-down menu. In the Variable box, type **out[1]**. That variable (array element) is now associated with the text field.

4. Repeat steps 1 through 3 for four more text fields. In the Variable window in the Text Options panel, use the array element names out[2] through out[5].

Tip   You can save some time by selecting the first text field and then using Alt+drag (in Windows) or Option-drag (on the Macintosh) to make copies of the text field. Then all you need to do is to align the new fields and rename the elements in the Text Options panel.

Writing the ASP scripts

Two ASP scripts are required for the movie. The first script generates an array and then, depending on the button clicked in the Flash movie, sends an array element back to Flash in the appropriate text field associated with an output array (out[n]). The important part of the script is where the output variable uses the value of flashData, which was sent as myData from Flash. Each numbered button's script sent a value in myData consistent with the text field's element number next to the button. The value is also linked to a value in the array in the ASP script. Thus, the button numbered 3 sends a value of 3 in the myData variable. In the ASP script, item(3) states, "You clicked the third button." and appears in the text field associated with out[3] in the Flash movie. All these elements are placed in the output variable by concatenating the array element out[myData] with the equal sign (=) and the ASP array element item(flashData). Then the whole thing is sent back to Flash using Response.write. Save the script in the server's root directory or a subdirectory in the root directory under the name arrayData.asp.

```
<%
'Create a simple array.
Dim item(5), flashData, output
item(1) = "You clicked the first button."
item(2) = "You clicked the second button."
item(3) = "You clicked the third button."
item(4) = "You clicked the fourth button."
item(5) = "You clicked the fifth button."
```

```
'Get the element number from Flash and
'concatenate the output as an array element
'in Flash 5 format.

flashData=Request.form("myData")
output = "out[" & flashData & "]=" & item(flashData)
Response.write output
%>
```

The second ASP script clears out all of the text fields by placing a space in the field. In the following script, make sure that you put a space between the equal sign (=) and the ampersand (&). Save the script in the server's root directory or a subdirectory in the root directory under the name " clearArray.asp.

```
<%
Dim output
output = "out[1]= &out[2]= &out[3]= &out[4]= &out[5]= &"
Response.Write output
%>
```

Figure 3-10 shows the SWF file where three of the buttons are clicked.

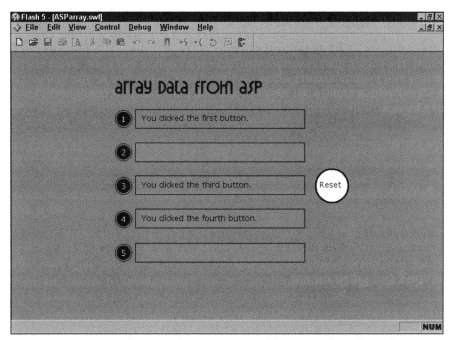

Figure 3-10: Arrays written in ASP can connect with an array in ActionScript.

Microsoft Access, ASP, and Flash

One of the most popular database programs in use is Microsoft Access. Using Access 2000, this section shows how to use Flash 5 as a front end to display, search for, and add records to an Access 2000 file on a server. Most of the work is done using VBScript and SQL (Structured Query Language) commands to query an Access 2000 file on a server using variables in a Flash 5 movie for showing what is in the database and as an input source for adding new records. We decided to use a simple database made up of names and e-mail addresses along with an ID number to focus on the script needed to send data between Flash and the Access 2000 file.

Figure 3-11 shows the basic relationship between Flash, ASP pages, and the database. To read data from the Access 2000 database, the Flash movie sends a `loadVariableNum()` command to the ASP page. The ASP page opens the database and retrieves the data from the one or more tables in the Access 2000 file. The data is then translated into a format that can be read by Flash 5, placed into variables, and sent back to Flash. After data is added to the database, the information is entered into a Flash 5 text field or other output object (a button or movie clip) and sent to the ASP page. Through the use of SQL and VBScript in the ASP page, the data from Flash is inserted into the database.

Figure 3-11: Three different files are involved in sending data between Flash 5 and a database.

Setting up the Access 2000 file

Before doing anything else, you need to create an Access 2000 database file and table. A good resource for learning about using Access 2000 is *Microsoft Access 2000 Bible,* Gold Edition, by Cary N. Prague and Michael R. Irwin (published by IDG Books Worldwide, Inc.), but for now, all you need to do is create a simple Access file. This file is used to show how to access the data in the file as well as add data to it and pass information between Flash 5 and the database. The following steps show how to set up the database file used in this example:

1. Open Access 2000, and select Blank Access database in the dialog box. Click OK.

2. In the File New Database window, select the Desktop as the folder and then enter the filename **emailFlash.mdb** in the File Name text box at the bottom of the window. Click the Create button.

3. Double-click the Create Table in Design View option in the Database window. In the Design View window, enter the following in the Field Name and Data Type columns (and use the pop-up menu in the Data Type column to select the data type):

> *ID:* AutoNumber (click the key icon to make this field the primary key)
>
> *Name:* Text (default)
>
> *Email:* Text (default)

4. Choose File ⇨ Save (or click the diskette icon on the toolbar) and save the table using the name `EmailTable`. Then choose File ⇨ Close from the menu bar.

5. After you close the Design view window, you see a window with your new table in the emailFlash: Database window. Double-click the EmailTable icon to open it. Enter three names and e-mail addresses in the table. You can ignore the ID column because it automatically provides a unique ID number as you enter data into the other two fields.

6. After entering the names and e-mail addresses, click the Save icon (diskette in the toolbar) and then choose File ⇨ Exit. You're all finished with entering data directly into the Access 2000 database table and file.

Placing the Access 2000 file on the server and preparing the DSN

The next step is to open the root folder where you have been placing your ASP pages and place your database file there. If you are using a remote server, just use FTP to move the Access 2000 file to the root folder or subfolder on the NT Server.

Next, you need to create a data source name (DSN) connection to the database on the server. This connection enables your ASP application to interact with the database. After you enter the database filename in an ASP script, the server software uses the DSN name to enable a connection.

For Windows 2000 and Windows NT, use the following steps:

1. Choose Start ⇨ Settings ⇨ Control Panel. In the Control Panel, double-click the ODBC Data Sources icon to open the ODBC Data Source Administrator.

2. Click the File DSN tab, click Add, and then select Microsoft Access Driver (*mdb) from the menu and click Next.

3. Type a descriptive name. We used `EmailFlash` for the file DSN name. Click Next.

4. Click Finish and then click Select. Navigate to the directory of your database file; it appears in the left window under Database Name. Click your database (for example, emailFlash.mdb) to select it and then click OK.

5. Click OK twice. In the ODBC Data Source Administrator window in the File DSN tab, you see your new DSN name with the extension `dsn` added.

Setting up your connection on your ASP file

This next set of steps requires that you know the path in your server that is used to make the connection to your database file. On the face of it, the process is quite simple, but in practice, the process can be quite confusing. After you get the formula, however, you can reuse it on any database within the same server. For example, two different servers we used in developing the material for this book had different internal paths to the data. The HosTek hosting service provided one server. The HosTek paths look something like the following example:

```
d:\home\hnt1a234\ASPbase\emailFlash.mdb;
```

A different server used the following path, which is probably very similar to what those who use their own computers as servers and clients use:

```
d:\Inetpub\Wwwroot\ASPbase\emailFlash.mdb;
```

The fact that both servers use Drive D is coincidental and not a requirement. They could just as well have used Drive C or E or any other drive. The important fact to notice in both the paths is that they are internal paths to the root directories. Although a different address needed to be used to access the ASP pages (for example, `http://your.URL.com`) that contained the code, the path in the ASP page referenced a local, internal path for the server.

The path is just part of a longer driver definition required to connect the ASP script to the database and the data within it. Generally, the path is defined in a variable, and then the VBScript uses that variable in other commands to make the connection. First, the provider needs to be defined. The following line defines the driver in the variable named `Serv`:

```
Serv= "Driver={Microsoft Access Driver (*.mdb)};
DBQ=d:\Inetpub\Wwwroot\ASPbase\emailFlash.mdb;"
```

Because the provider information has been placed into a variable, you can use only the variable name instead of the long line of code if the provider must be used.

The rudiments of setting up an ASP page to make a connection to a database and pull out data to be sent to Flash can best be seen in a complete page and example. In that way, you can better understand the context of the required code. The following Flash 5 movie and ASP page pull together the different parts needed to see the contents of a database on a server.

Reading an Access 2000 database with Flash and ASP

After the Access 2000 database is set up and a DSN established for it, you are all set to create an ASP page to pull data from the Access file and send it out to Flash. To begin, enter the following ASP script and save it in the root directory or a subdirectory within the root directory of your server. Save the file using the name EmailFlashList.asp.

```
<%
Dim Serv, Conn, RecordView, Ename, output, collect, SQL
Serv= "Driver={Microsoft Access Driver (*.mdb)}; _
DBQ=d:\Inetpub\Wwwroot\ASPbase\emailFlash.mdb;"
Set Conn = Server.CreateObject("ADODB.Connection")
Set RecordView = Server.CreateObject("ADODB.Recordset")

Conn.Open Serv
SQL="SELECT * FROM EmailTable"
RecordView.Open SQL, Conn

Do While Not RecordView.EOF
Ename=RecordView("Name") & "<BR>"
collect =collect & Ename
RecordView.MoveNext
Loop

output="output=" & collect
Response.Write output

RecordView.Close
Conn.Close
Set RecordView = Nothing
Set Conn = Nothing
%>
```

The script is divided into five blocks. Each block is considered separately. The first block is for dimensioning the variables, defining the connections, and then setting the connections. Several variables are defined using the Dim statement. Next, the driver and provider are placed into the Serv variable. The ADODB connection object is placed into the Conn variable, and the ADODB recordset object is placed in a variable named RecordView.

On the CD-ROM All the files that are used in the examples in this and the following sections are available on the CD-ROM.

The second block opens the connection and defines an SQL command. (The variable name SQL is used to emphasize the fact that the variable contains an SQL command, but you could use any variable name you want.) The command (or action query) selects all the records (* = wildcard) from the table named EmailTable in the Access 2000 file named emailFlash.mdb. The next line opens up the recordset in the database defined in the connection and issues the SQL command.

A loop dominates the third block. One of the nicer features of VBScript is that it can loop through a recordset until it encounters the EOF (end of file) of the recordset. Another feature to note in this block is the use of the `<BR>` tag. Used in HTML as a line break, this tag works just as well as a line break in a Flash 5 text field. The `collect` variable concatenates the data with the line break tag through the entire loop. To keep this first example simple, only one of the three fields, `Name`, is passed to a variable that is sent to Flash.

The fourth block transforms the accumulated variable, `collect`, into a format that can be read as a variable by Flash. Although the `output` variable is not declared in the VBScript, the variable is recognized as a Flash variable because of the = sign attached to it. Finally, the last block of code closes up the connection and recordset and resets the variables.

Receiving the data from the database in Flash 5

Making the Flash movie is easy. All the movie needs is a single dynamic text field to receive the data and a button with ActionScript to load the variables. The movie, named `Access2Flash.fla`, has three layers:

✦ Background

✦ Text Field

✦ Action Button

Table 3-6 provides the color palette and Figure 3-12 shows the initial stage. Notice that, in Figure 3-12, the Text Options panel contains the variable name for the data that is sent from the database via the ASP page.

Table 3-6
Color Palette for Access2Flash.fla

Color	R Value	G Value	B Value
A	00	80	B3
B	B3	33	4C
C	B3	73	40
D	FF	D9	19

Background layer

Use Color A as the background color. Draw a rectangle with the Rectangle tool, using Color B as the fill color and Color D as the stroke to create a backdrop for the text field. The rectangle should have these dimensions: W=200, H=166. Using Figure 3-12 as a guide, type **Click to view data** to the left of the rectangle.

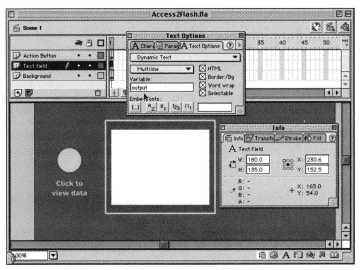

Figure 3-12: The text field dominates the stage because it is where all the data is sent.

Text Field layer

Use the Text tool to create a text field with the dimensions W=180, H= 135. In the Text Options panel, select Dynamic Text for the type of field, enter **output** for the variable name, and check all the check boxes.

Action Button layer

Use the Oval tool to draw a circle, using Color D as the fill and Color B as the stroke. Select the circle and press F8 to transform the drawing into a button. Select the button and enter the following script, substituting your own server's address for the one shown:

```
on (release) {
    loadVariablesNum
("http://your.URL.com/ASPbase/EmailFlashList.asp", 0);
}
```

Test the program and, depending on what names you put into the database, you see something like the example shown in Figure 3-13.

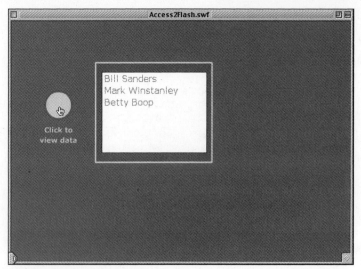

Figure 3-13: The formatting of the names in the Flash text field is accomplished through the <BR> tag added to each name from the database in the ASP page.

Reading and displaying multiple fields

By making a few changes in the ASP script and the Flash movie, you can easily show more than a single field. The SQL command opened all the data in the database, so all you need to add to the VBScript is a second variable that loads data from a second field. The following script should be saved in the root directory as Name_Email_List.asp. The DBQ variable should be changed to your home path (for example, ...DBQ=d:\home\hnt1a234).

```
<%
Dim Serv, Conn, RecordView, Ename, Email, output, collect
Serv= "Driver={Microsoft Access Driver (*.mdb)}; _
DBQ=d:\Inetpub\Wwwroot\ASPbase\emailFlash.mdb;"
Set Conn = Server.CreateObject("ADODB.Connection")
Set RecordView = Server.CreateObject("ADODB.Recordset")

Conn.Open Serv
SQL="SELECT * FROM EmailTable"
RecordView.Open SQL, Conn

Do While Not RecordView.EOF
Ename=RecordView("Name")
Email=RecordView("Email")
collect =collect & Ename & " -> " & Email & "<BR>"
RecordView.MoveNext
Loop
```

```
output="output=" & collect
Response.Write output

RecordView.Close
Conn.Close
Set RecordView = Nothing
Set Conn = Nothing
%>
```

The new variable, `Email`, examines the recordset of the field in the database with the same name. Both it and the other variable are formatted into a variable named `collect` and then gathered up into an `output` variable and sent back to Flash with the `Response.Write` statement. The Flash movie requires a wider text field and the button moved out of the way, but otherwise, it is identical to the first one. A different color palette, provided in Table 3-7, helps to distinguish this movie from the first movie. Use the same layers, as shown in the following list:

✦ Background

✦ Text Field

✦ Action Button

Table 3-7
Color Palette for Access2FlashAll.fla

Color	R Value	G Value	B Value
A	FF	CC	00
B	D1	00	55
C	6B	00	55

Background layer

Use Color B for the background color. Draw a rectangle with Color A for the fill and Color C for the stroke in the dimensions W=450, H-166. Then enter a **Click Button** label near the top and a **Name -> Email address** label near the bottom, using Figure 3-14 to judge placement.

Text Field layer

Using the Text tool and Text Options panel, create a Dynamic Text field in the dimensions W=400, H=135. Place the text field over the backdrop rectangle created in the Background layer. In the Text Options panel, enter the variable name **output** and check all the check boxes. Select Multiline from the pop-up menu.

Action Button layer

Draw a circle with Color A for the fill and Color C for the stroke color. Select the circle and press the F8 key to create a button symbol. With the new button selected, open the Object Actions window and enter the following script, substituting your own server URL:

```
on (release) {
    loadVariablesNum
("http://your.URL.com/ASPbase/Name_Email_List.asp", 0);
}
```

After you execute the ActionScript, you can see both the names and the associated e-mail addresses, as shown in Figure 3-14.

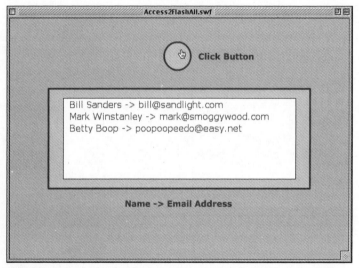

Figure 3-14: Using simple formatting and a single output window, Flash can display multiple fields from a database.

Ordering data in an array and passing it to Flash

Formatting data into a single field is quite legitimate and useful, but it fails to take advantage of Flash's own design features and capability to arrange the data output as you want. One way to help order data is to place it in an array in the ASP page and pass it to another array in ActionScript. In the script for this section, you notice that the script opens and closes like the others passing data to a Flash output. But this script breaks up the six pieces of data (three names and three e-mail addresses) into two arrays, one each for names and e-mail addresses. The trick is not in setting up arrays in VBScript but formatting them so that they are separate array elements when returned to Flash. Before you look at the script, look at the following lines to see how data is brought into an array in the ASP page and then translated for Flash use.

```
. . .
Ename(Counter)=RecordView("Name")
. . .
output(Counter)="&output["& Counter & "]=" & Ename(Counter)
. . .
```

Both lines are in a middle of a loop that reads records from the database until the database runs out of data. The first time through the loop, the script has the following literal values:

```
Ename(0)=RecordView("Name")
. . .
output(0)="&output["& 0 & "]=" & Ename(0)
. . .
```

The first line puts the first record of the Name file into the array element Ename(0). After the program reaches the output array element, it is in the first round of the loop, so the output element is output(0). The results are concatenated, so the contents of output(0) are as follows:

```
&output[0]=DBname1
```

After the program reaches Response.Write output(Counter) for the first time, Flash receives the first concatenated results. Flash treats the ampersand as a variable demarcation and places the value of the first database name into the array element output[0].

Note   VBScript uses parentheses (x) to enclose the element value of an array while ActionScirpt uses brackets [x]. So in addition to translating the data into Flash format, you must also translate the array elements into the ActionScript format.

The second time through the loop, the concatenated value is as follows:

```
&output[1]=DBname2
```

Because the text begins with an ampersand, Flash treats it as another new variable or, in this case, a new array element. Without the leading ampersand, Flash would assume that everything else was part of the first array element. By using array names for text fields, you can place the data anywhere that you want on the stage.

Save the following script as `ArrayOutput.asp` in your server's root directory or subdirectory in the root directory. The arrays were dimensioned for 10 elements arbitrarily; you can change that value to the number of elements in your database.

```
<%
Dim Serv, Conn, RecordView, Ename(10), Email(10)
Dim Counter, output(10), eoutput(10), SQL
Serv= "Driver={Microsoft Access Driver (*.mdb)};
DBQ=d:\Inetpub\Wwwroot\ASPbase\emailFlash.mdb;"
Set Conn = Server.CreateObject("ADODB.Connection")
Set RecordView = Server.CreateObject("ADODB.Recordset")

Conn.Open Serv
SQL="SELECT * FROM EmailTable"
RecordView.Open SQL, Conn

Counter=0
Do While Not RecordView.EOF
    Ename(Counter)=RecordView("Name")
    Email(Counter)=RecordView("Email")
    output(Counter)= "&output
    [" & Counter & "]=" & _ Ename(Counter)
    eoutput(Counter)= "&eoutput
    [" & Counter & "]=" & _ Email(Counter)
    Response.Write output(Counter)
    Response.Write eoutput(Counter)
    Counter=Counter +1
    RecordView.MoveNext
Loop

RecordView.Close
Conn.Close
Set RecordView = Nothing
Set Conn = Nothing
%>
```

On the Flash 5 side of the equation, all you need to do is to provide arrays to receive the data and some ActionScript to load the data into Flash. The movie is similar to the first two examined for bringing in the variables from ASP and the Access 2000 database, except that more fields are used and array elements are used instead of variables in the text fields. The movie uses the following three layers and the color palette in Table 3-8:

✦ Background

✦ Action Button

✦ Text Fields

Table 3-8 Color Palette for AccessArray.fla			
Color	R Value	G Value	B Value
A	A6	B3	59
B	94	14	00
C	CC	E6	73
D	E6	F5	CC
E	F3	8C	00

To get started, take a look at Figure 3-15. The three text fields in the left column are associated with the three array elements in the Name field, and the three text fields in the right column are associated with the three array elements in the Email field.

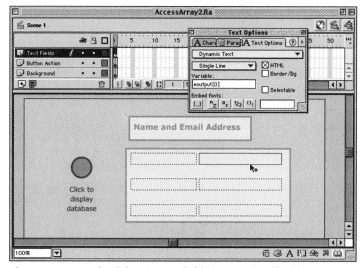

Figure 3-15: Each of the six text fields is associated with a different array element.

Background layer

The Background layer contains the rectangular backdrops for the text fields and labels. Complete these steps to create the Background layer:

1. Use Color C for the background color.

2. Draw two rectangles with Color D as the fill and Color A as the stroke, using Figure 3-15 as a guide.

3. In the top, smaller rectangle, type the label **Name and Email Address** using Color E for the text color and a bold Verdana font.

4. Below where the button is placed, type **Click to display database**, using Color B for the text color.

5. Lock the layer.

Action Button layer

Use the Oval tool to draw a circle, using Color E for the fill and Color B for the stroke. Select the circle and press the F8 key to transform it into a button symbol. Select the button and enter the following script:

```
on (release) {
    loadVariablesNum
("http://your.URL.com/ASPbase/ArrayOuput.asp", 0);
}
```

Position the button to the left of the larger of the two rectangles on the background layer.

Text Fields layer

The key to this movie is getting the text fields right. Take the following steps to create the fields correctly:

1. Lock the other layers. Open the Text Options panel and select Dynamic Text and Single Line from the pop-up menus.

2. Create three text fields with the dimensions W=120, H=20. Use the following variable names:

   ```
   output[0]
   output[1]
   output[2]
   ```

3. Align the three text fields over the larger of the two background rectangles, as shown in Figure 3-15.

4. Repeat steps 2 and 3 using the dimensions W=150, H=20 and these variable names:

   ```
   eoutput[0]
   eoutput[1]
   eoutput[2]
   ```

5. Align the fields in the right column, as shown in Figure 3-15.

As you run the Flash movie, each data element is positioned independently. As you can see in Figure 3-16, both the left and right columns are left aligned and look more professional than a single large text field.

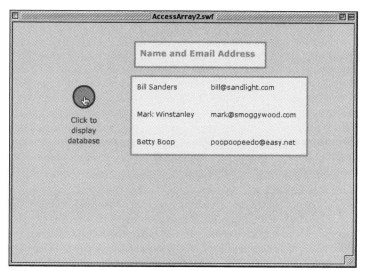

Figure 3-16: Spacing and alignment can be more precisely controlled if output is placed into individual text fields.

Inserting records into Access from Flash

The last step in this introduction to using Flash with ASP and Microsoft Access 2000 is to see how to insert records into an Access database from Flash. When inserting records into an Access database, you must insert data into all fields, or you generate an error. In the example used of a three-field database that has an automatic numbering system for the ID field and text for both the Name and Email fields, the procedure is relatively simple.

As you're adding, deleting, and modifying records in Access from your desktop, you can use all the tools provided with Access to make the job fairly simple. However, in adding data to a remote Access file, you need to build an ASP page to handle the data coming from Flash and writing to the data file. Included in this page is a script to automatically increment the ID field and a way to check to make sure that your record is indeed in the database.

To show how everything works, we chose to generate three small ASP files instead of creating a big ASP file and launch the scripts using three buttons in the Flash movie. One ASP script finds the value of the highest ID number, adds one to it, and uses that value as the next number in the automatic numbering of the ID field. A second ASP page takes input from Flash and writes to the three data fields. Finally, a third ASP page rummages through the database and checks whether the file you just entered is there and prints it on-screen for you.

To provide a context for inserting records into an Access file on a server with Flash and ASP, we begin with the Flash movie. The movie contains three buttons, each to launch a different ASP script. In addition, the movie has four text fields, one each for the three fields in the database and one to return the most recently entered record. Figure 3-17 shows the initial stage for the movie.

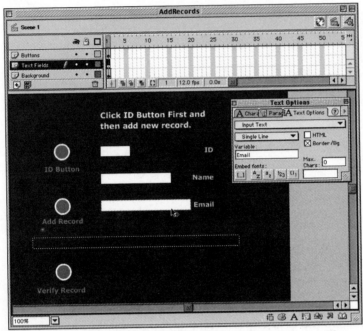

Figure 3-17: Several buttons launch different ASP scripts to either get information from the database or add records to it.

The movie's color palette is in Table 3-9, and the movie contains the following layers:

✦ Background

✦ Button

✦ Text Fields

	Table 3-9		
	Color Palette for AddRecords.fla		
Color	**R Value**	**G Value**	**B Value**
A	4C	00	00
B	FF	66	33
C	EE	E6	A1
D	00	99	00
White	FF	FF	FF
Black	00	00	00

Background layer

In the background color well (choose Modify ➪ Movie), select Color A to give the movie a rich brown background. Using Figure 3-18 for a guide, enter the following labels:

✦ Use a 14-point bold white Verdana font to enter **Click ID Button First and then add new record**.

✦ Use Color C to type the **ID**, **Name**, and **Email** labels to the right of the text fields you are placing.

✦ Use Color B (orange) to type the button labels: **ID Button**, **Add Record**, and **Verify Record**.

Button layer

Each of the three buttons is associated with an ASP page, so we first look at the ASP page and then the button associated with it. The ID button calls an ASP page that counts the number of records in the file and returns a value to the ID field that represents the automatic next value for the record. Save the code for this page as GetID.asp in your root directory or a subdirectory within the root directory. Make sure that you substitute your own server path for the one listed in the following example:

```
<%
Dim Serv, Conn, RecordView, output, SQL
Serv= "Driver={Microsoft Access Driver (*.mdb)}; _
DBQ=d:\Inetpub\Wwwroot\ASPbase\emailFlash.mdb;"
Set Conn = Server.CreateObject("ADODB.Connection")
Set RecordView = Server.CreateObject("ADODB.Recordset")

Conn.Open Serv
SQL="SELECT * FROM EmailTable"
RecordView.Open SQL, Conn
```

```
Counter=0
Do While Not RecordView.EOF
Counter = Counter +1
RecordView.MoveNext
Loop

output="ID=" & (Counter+1)
Response.Write output

RecordView.Close
Conn.Close
Set RecordView = Nothing
Set Conn = Nothing
%>
```

This script is very much like the initial scripts used in this chapter to examine the contents of the database. However, all it does is cycle through the database, counting how many records are in it, and returns the next ID number to the Flash movie's text field associated with the variable named ID. The ActionScript to launch the script is as follows:

```
on (release) {
    loadVariablesNum
("http://your.URL.com/ASPbase/GetID.asp", 0);
}
```

Substitute your URL for the one listed here.

The script for the Add Record button, which inserts data into the database, must access a file on the NT server. To do that, we used a little HTML that would not interfere either with the ASP page or Flash. Notice that the HTML has no body tag and is nothing more than a way to access an ADO (Active Data Objects) file. The most work is getting the format for the SQL command right, and after that's done, the script follows a familiar path. Save this file in your root directory as AddAccess.asp, substituting your own server's path for the one listed. And remember that Source=d:\Inetpub\Wwwroot.... needs to be changed to your home path (for example, Source=d:\home\hnt1a2345...) provided by your hosting company.

```
<!-- METADATA TYPE="typelib"
FILE="C:\Program Files\Common Files\System\ado\msado15.dll" -->
<HTML>

<%
Dim Conn, Cmd, intNoOfRecords, nID, nName, nEmail, SQL
nID=Request.Form("ID")
nName=Request.Form("Name")
nEmail=Request.Form("Email")
```

```
Conn = "Provider=Microsoft.Jet.OLEDB.4.0;" & "Data _
Source=d:\Inetpub\Wwwroot\ASPbase\emailFlash.mdb;"
Set Cmd = Server.CreateObject("ADODB.Command")
Cmd.ActiveConnection = Conn

SQL= "INSERT INTO EmailTable(Id, Name,Email) VALUES (" & _ nID
& ",'" & nName & "','" & nEmail & "')"
Cmd.CommandText =SQL

Cmd.CommandType = adCmdText
Cmd.Execute intNoOfRecords
Set Cmd = Nothing
%>
</HTML>
```

Once in the VBScript, the variables are dimensioned and then data from Flash are pulled into the page using `Request.Form()`. The variables from Flash are `ID`, `Name`, and `Email`, and they are set in ASP variables of the same name preceded by the small letter *n*. Next the connection protocols establish a link with the database. (If you are using Access 97, substitute 4.0 with 3.1 right after `OLEDB`.)

When using the SQL command `INSERT INTO`, you must list the names of each field, and then insert data into them. After `VALUES`, placing literals into the table would look like the following example:

```
"...VALUES (15, 'Suzy Smith', 'ssmith@lottsaluck.edu')"
```

Because you need to use variables instead of numeric and text literals, the variables must be concatenated into the format recognized by VBScript. Only the variables themselves need not be in quotation marks, and all other text must have single quote marks around it. When copying the SQL contents, be very careful. (Remember that the underscore at the end of the SQL assignment line simply means that the line is extended. In your text editor, you can place it all on one line and leave out the underscore.)

The script associated with the Flash 5 button symbol for adding a record is just a little different from most of the ActionScript in this chapter, as the following example shows:

```
on (release) {
     loadVariablesNum
("http://your.URL.com/ASPbase/AddAccess.asp",
0, "POST");
name="sent to database"
email="sent to database"
}
```

The button script starts off like most of the others in this chapter except that it does POST the variables. After that information is sent, you can change the values of the variables associated with the text fields where data is to be entered. By changing the values, you enable the user to see that something has happened to the data he or she just entered. So after the name and e-mail data are sent, the sent to database message appears and gives the user some feedback.

The ASP page for the Verify Record button simply loads the last record from the database into the page so that the user is certain the data is correctly stored. This is accomplished by going through all the records using an array and loading the last array element. The array is set to 100, but you can make it larger or smaller by changing the array limits in the Dim statement line. Save the file in the root directory as VerifyRecord.asp and make sure that you change the path in the following example to the one that your server is using:

```
<%
Dim Serv, Conn, RecordView, Ename(100), Email(100), output
Serv= "Driver={Microsoft Access Driver (*.mdb)}; _
DBQ=d:\Inetpub\Wwwroot\ASPbase\emailFlash.mdb;"
Set Conn = Server.CreateObject("ADODB.Connection")
Set RecordView = Server.CreateObject("ADODB.Recordset")

Conn.Open Serv
SQL="SELECT * FROM EmailTable"
RecordView.Open SQL, Conn

Counter=0
Do While Not RecordView.EOF
Ename(Counter)=RecordView("Name")
Email(Counter)=RecordView("Email")
Counter=Counter+1
RecordView.MoveNext
Loop
output="verify=" & Ename(Counter-1)& " " & Email(Counter-1)
Response.Write output

RecordView.Close
Conn.Close
Set RecordView = Nothing
Set Conn = Nothing
%>
```

The button script requires no posting of variables because all the information is being pulled out of the database. Set the URL to the one for your server in the following script:

```
on (release) {
    loadVariablesNum
("http://your.URL.com/ASPbase/VerifyRecord.asp", 0);
}
```

Text Fields layer

Create the two dynamic text fields and two input text fields that you need in the Text Fields layer by following these steps:

1. Create the ID text field by using the Text tool and position it to the left of the ID button.

2. In the Text Options panel, select Dynamic Text, mark the Border/Bk check box, and enter **ID** as the variable name.

3. Create the verification field with the Text tool and place it above the Verify Record button.

4. In the Text Options panel, leave Border/Bk unchecked and enter the variable name **Verify.**

5. Create two input text fields, one each for the name and e-mail data to be entered.

6. In the Text Options panel, make sure that you check the Border/Bk check box for each field and enter the variable names **Name** and **Email** respectively.

The data entered into the two input fields is sent along with the value generated in the ID field to the ASP page that sends the data to the appropriate field in the Microsoft Access 2000 database file on the server. Figure 3-18 shows what the user sees after he or she enters data (with the `sent to database` message disabled).

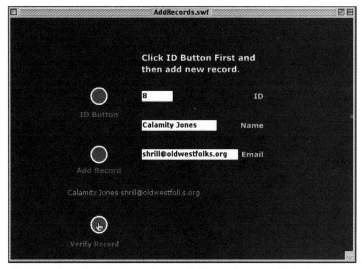

Figure 3-18: Flash can use its capability to host multiple forms and buttons with ActionScripts to effectively organize data in a database such as that of Microsoft Access 2000.

Summary

The introductory materials in this chapter are designed primarily to show how Flash and ASP can work together and with databases. Although this chapter just scratches the surface of what Flash 5, ActionScript, ASP, SQL and Microsoft Access 2000 can do, we hope that you can see the potential in the connection between Flash and server-side scripts and data sources. The most important knowledge you should take away from this chapter is how the linkages between Flash and ASP scripts work. ASP offers far more than we can cover in this chapter, but if you like the way ASP works, we encourage you to look into it further. The easiest part is making the connection between Flash and ASP, especially compared to making the connections between ASP and databases. Delving further into ASP gives you far more tools to complete the tasks that you want to accomplish.

The next chapter provides an alternative to ASP called PHP. In some respects, the two server-side languages are the same, but they have many differences as well. If this is the first time you've examined back-end computers and the use of databases over the Web, you are in a great position to compare different approaches to server-side computing.

✦   ✦   ✦

Using Flash 5 with PHP4 and MySQL

♦ ♦ ♦ ♦

In This Chapter

Learning the basics of the PHP language

Transferring data between PHP and Flash

Integrating MySQL with PHP and Flash

♦ ♦ ♦ ♦

If you like the look and feel of ActionScript and JavaScript, you should find PHP to your liking as well. With PHP, you can launch server-side scripts using Flash as a front end and pass variables back and forth between Flash and the PHP pages. Along with PHP, you can use MySQL as a database to store data and later retrieve it, again using Flash as a database. If you are familiar with structured query language (SQL) commands, you will find a similar set of commands used in a PHP script to issue instructions to a MySQL database. Using Flash as a front end, you can pass data and variables between the MySQL database, PHP, and Flash to enhance your Web page's functionality in managing databases.

The PHP4 Scripting Language

For Flash 5 users, PHP is a good introduction to server-side Web scripting languages. In its fourth incarnation, PHP4 is officially named PHP Hypertext Preprocessor. Developed in 1994 by Rasmus Lerdorf as a server language for his personal home page (hence the name PHP), the language has taken on a life of its own. It is now a program scripting language with many similarities to ActionScript; so you should find it relatively simple to master.

Accessing your PHP files

PHP runs either as a mix of HTML and PHP or PHP alone. In either case, PHP is saved in the Web server's root directory with the php extension. The root directory varies depending on your system setup. If you are using your JTLNet account, put your files into the `public_html` folder and use your domain name as the root. (*Do not,* however, put your PHP files in the `cgi-bin` directory in the Public HTML folder.) For example, my domain is `www.sandlight.com`, and if I save my PHP program in the `public_html` directory, I would enter the following line to call a PHP program:

```
http://www.sandlight.com/myProgram.php
```

Generally, however, I like to leave my root directory uncluttered, so I put in additional directories for my different projects. For learning how to use Flash 5 with PHP, you might want to add a directory in your Web server root directory named `FlashPHP` and put all of your PHP programs there. With the added directory, I would now enter

```
http://www.sandlight.com/FlashPHP/myProgram.php
```

to access my PHP file. The addressing process is identical to HTML files, but you have to keep in mind the file's relative relationship to the Web server's root directory.

If you have installed the Apache server from the CD-ROM on your PC and you are using `localhost` as your Web server, put the PHP files into the `htdocs` directory in your Apache installation directory. You would access PHP files saved in the `htdocs` directory with the following line:

```
http://localhostPHP/myProgram.php
```

But as with files saved on the JTLNet server, I recommend creating a folder within the `htdocs` directory for your PHP files. Just open the `htdocs` directory and create a folder (a directory) for your PHP files. For example, to address a folder named `Flash5PHP` with your PHP programs saved in it on your own computer's Apache server, you would use the following line:

```
http://localhostPHP/Flash5PHP/myProgram.php
```

Using PHP tags

PHP has three options for starting and ending tags to contain a PHP script.

Option 1:

```
<?php
PHP script
?>
```

Option 2:

```
<?
PHP script
?>
```

Option 3:

```
<script language="php">
PHP script
</script>
```

For this book, we use Option 1. We like it because the beginning tag clarifies the fact that the script is PHP without a great deal of extra effort. The other two methods work fine, and you can substitute one of them if you prefer.

Writing and testing PHP script

Use a text editor like Notepad (Windows) or SimpleText (Macintosh) to write your PHP scripts. To get started, write the following script:

```
<?php
phpinfo();
?>
```

Caution If you use Notepad, make sure that Notepad doesn't add a `txt` extension to your `php` extension when you save your file as a text file. Place quotation marks around the name of your file when you save it to prevent Notepad from adding the unwanted `txt` extension.

Save the file as `phpinfo.php` in your server root directory or subdirectory. For this example, we've saved our PHP file in a folder (directory) named `FlashPHP` in our Web server's root directory, `www.sandlight.com`. To launch the program, we would type

```
http://www.sandlight.com/FlashPHP/php.info.php
```

Substitute your domain name for `www.sandlight.com` and your directory name for `FlashPHP`. If you're using `localhost`, you would type in the following line, making the appropriate substitutions for the subdirectory name:

```
http://localhost/FlashPHP/php.info.php
```

Figure 4-1 shows what you should see if everything is in the right place and installed correctly. If you see the page depicted in Figure 4-1 (or one looking close to it), you have correctly accessed PHP in your Web server.

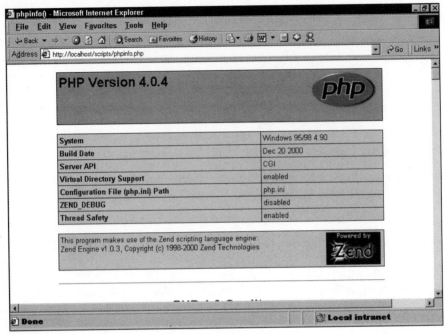

Figure 4-1: A successful test of phpinfo.php.

Understanding basic formats

Throughout this chapter, you will see the echo command in use. The command works something like a print command in Basic. The echo command takes the materials to the right of the command and displays them in a Web page. Generally, the echo command uses this format:

```
echo "Display this message.";
```

You can also use the echo command to display functions, as in the following:

```
echo sqrt(250);
```

The output would show the square root of 250. You will see the echo command used often because it is the workhorse command for displaying information to the user through Web pages. The echo command can also be used, however, to send data back to a Flash SWF file.

Like ActionScript, PHP expects a semi-colon at the end of most lines. But PHP is stricter about semi-colons than ActionScript is. If you leave a semi-colon out of a certain PHP lines, the program will not execute. This simple variable definition, for example, requires that the variable declaration itself have a semi-colon at the end of the line:

```
<?php
$score = 50;
?>
```

The semi-colon is the instructor terminator for statements. But like ActionScript conditional statements, PHP conditional statements never have semi-colons after a curly brace. The following example shows where the semi-colons belong:

```
<?php
if ($topScore => $currentScore) {
$currentScore = $hitScore + 10;
}
?>
```

PHP is very unforgiving when it comes to semi-colons at the end of a command line, so keep an eye out to make sure your script contains the semi-colons it needs. When you debug your script, first check to see whether your semi-colons are where they belong.

Comments

Comments in code help developers remember what they were doing with the code when they were developing it. PHP has several options for flagging comments, but throughout this chapter and elsewhere in the book, we use the same convention as used in ActionScript: the double forward slash (//). The following example shows the correct use of comments in a PHP script:

```
<?php
$item += $item * .07;
//The item must include a 7% sales tax.
echo $item;
?>
```

The comment line is another exception to the semi-colon requirement. You can write anything in a comment line because as soon as the parser sees the two slashes, it ignores the entire line.

Escape characters

Also like ActionScript, PHP uses the backslash as an escape character so that certain characters, such as quotation marks, may be displayed and not parsed as part of the running script. The following script, for example, escapes the quotation marks around the nickname "Speedo."

```
<?php
$move = "They called him \"Speedo,\" but his real name was Mr.
Earl.";
echo $move;
?>
```

When the program is executed, the viewer sees the following on the screen:

```
They called him "Speedo," but his real name was Mr. Earl.
```

Initially, the only character you have to remember to escape is the double quote mark ("). But when preparing data for a MySQL database, other characters need to be escaped, such as the single quote mark (') and the ampersand (&). PHP can handle either character without escaping them, but the database cannot. PHP's addslashes() function helps take care of the problem by adding the needed slashes automatically when the PHP script is used to add data to a MySQL database. Another function, stripslashes(), can then be used to remove the slashes so they won't cause a parsing problem with PHP.

Declaring variables

Declaring a variable in PHP is not unlike doing so in ActionScript except that all variables in PHP are preceded by a dollar sign ($) and they are case-sensitive. The following script shows the three data types, integers, doubles (floating-point numbers), and string literals, entered into PHP variables:

```
<?php
$wholeThing = 6744;
$someFractions=22.95;
$stringBean= "Eat your vegetables!";
echo "<br>$wholeThing";
echo "<br>$someFractions";
echo "<br>$stringBean";
?>
```

The output of this example is as follows:

```
6744
22.95
Eat your vegetables!
```

The `<br>` tag places the output from the `echo` statement on separate lines. For the most part, when dealing with PHP and Flash, you handle the formatting by placing the output in the appropriate variable or movie clip. What is viewed on the screen depends on whether you are placing the output from PHP into a variable associated with a dynamic text field or a movie clip.

Caution

ActionScript is case-*insensitive* and PHP is case-*sensitive*. For ActionScript, the following variables are treated as the same:

```
SalesTax
Salestax
SALESTAX
```

In PHP, however, all of these variables are *different*. So make sure that *all* the ActionScript variables you are using in conjunction with PHP are case-sensitive. In that way, you won't run into a problem because you expect a PHP variable named `$Salestax` to read your ActionScript variable named `SalesTax`. Other than case-sensitivity, other naming conventions in ActionScript and PHP are pretty much the same. The `Hit_Score` variable in ActionScript will be equated with the `$Hit_Score` variable in PHP.

Using operators and conditional statements

Most of the operators in ActionScript and PHP are the same. Table 4-1 shows the operators used in PHP.

	Table 4-1	
	PHP Operators	
Operator	**Use**	**Format example**
=	assignment	$posMX =100;
+	add	$sumNow = $firstVal + $secondVal;
-	subtract	$sumLoss = $firstVal - $secondVal;
*	multiply	$taxCalc = $item * .07;
/	divide	$centLoad = $loadNow / $loadTotal;
. (dot)	concatenation	$fullName = $firstName . $lastName;
%	modulus	$remain = 75 % 4;
==	equal to (compare)	if ($firstTry == $secondTry) ….
===	equal to + data type	if($typeA === $typeB) ….

Continued

Table 4-1 *(continued)*

Operator	Use	Format example
!=	not equal to	if ($better != $worse) ....
>	greater than	if ($most > $more) ....
<	less than	if ($least < $less) ....
>=	greater than or equal to	if ($now >= $then) ....
<=	less than or equal to	if ($fun <= $work) ....
+=	compound assign add	$sum += 6; //Adds 6 to $sum
-=	compound assign subtract	$refund -= $item;
.=	compound concatenation	$firstName .= $lastName
&&	logical AND	if ($a = = $b && $c <= $d) ....
||	logical OR	if ($x = = = $y || $a = = $z)....
++	increment (pre or post)	for ($ct=1; $ct <=34; $ct++)
--	decrement (pre or post)	for ($ls=50; $ls >=12; $ls--)

One key difference between ActionScript and PHP4 is how each language concatenates strings. In the Flash 5 version of ActionScript, strings are concatenated with the plus (+) operator; PHP4 uses the dot (.) operator. PHP4 also includes a "triple =" operator. The triple = looks to see if the values and the data type are the same in a comparison. Otherwise, most of the operators will be familiar to Flash 5 ActionScript users. Remember also that PHP4 was not written with Flash in mind while ActionScript very much was. (In other words, don't expect to find a `gotoAndPlay()` statement in PHP.)

Conditionals

The conditional statements in PHP4 are very similar, but not identical, to those in ActionScript. PHP4 supports three different statements for branching a script.

The if statement

PHP4 uses the `if` statement in the same way as ActionScript does. When the condition in parentheses is met, the program executes the next line. If the condition is not met, the code in the next line is ignored. For example, the following code triggers the `echo` line:

```php
<?php
$apples=10;
$oranges=20;
```

```
if ($apples != $oranges) {
echo "I didn't think so.";
}
?>
```

The else statement

When you have an alternative to the conditional statement using `else`, the `else` clause is initiated automatically when the `if` condition is *not* met. The following script shows how this statement works:

```
<?php
$suzy="smart";
$ralph="strong";
if ($suzy=="smart" && $ralph=="smart") {
echo "Off to gifted class";
} else {
echo "To each his or her own.";
}
?>
```

Note in the preceding script how the logical AND (&&) operator is used in the script. Both PHP4 and Flash 5 use logical operators in the same way.

The elseif statement

The formatting of `elseif` in PHP4 and Flash 5 ActionScript is slightly different. PHP4 uses the single term `elseif` while ActionScript uses `else if` as two words. The rest of the formatting, however, is similar. The following example illustrates how an `elseif` statement is set up in PHP4:

```
<?php
$suzy="smart";
$ralph="strong";
if ($suzy=="smart" && $ralph=="smart") {
echo "Off to gifted class";
} elseif ($suzy=="smart" || $ralph=="smart") {
echo "At least one is bright";
}else {
echo "That means you'll have to be a computer programmer";
}
?>
```

Like the operators in PHP4 and ActionScript, very few differences exist between ActionScript and PHP conditional statements. Conditional statements are important for server-side scripts because such statements are the decision-makers. On dynamic sites, the data from the Flash 5 front end often has to be analyzed in a PHP script, so noting the similarities and differences between formatting conditional statements in ActionScript and in PHP is important.

Loops

PHP has three types of loops, and they are structured very similar to ActionScript loops.

The while loop

At the beginning of the `while` loop, a statement specifies the conditions under which the loop terminates. All loop actions take place between the curly braces and include a variable that increments or decrements a counter variable.

```php
<?php
$counter=32;
while ($counter >1) {
    echo $data[$counter];
}
?>
```

The do...while loop

The `do...while` loop works like the `while` loop, but the counter is at the bottom of the loop rather than the top. Because the counter is at the bottom, the loop must be processed at least once.

```php
<?php
$counter=$totalData;
do {
echo $data[$counter];
$counter -= 1;
} while ($counter >1);
?>
```

The for loop

A beginning value, a termination condition, and the counter (index) control the `for` loop. Increments and decrements in the index counter can be before or after the index variable. If the increments or decrements are before the index variable, the change occurs before the counter is employed; increments and decrements after the index variable generate change after the loop has been gone through at least once.

```php
<?php
for ($counter=0; $counter <80; ++$counter) {
  echo $data[$counter];
}
?>
```

Arrays

The concept of arrays is identical in both ActionScript and PHP, and the differences
are minor. Arrays are especially important in PHP for organizing database information. PHP has a number of different ways to create an array. First, you can just use
an array name and assign literal values to each element in the array. For example,
the following is a simple array in PHP:

```php
<?php
$item[0] = "monitor";
$item[1] = "keyboard";
$item[2] = "motherboard";
$item[3] = "mouse";
?>
```

Like arrays in other scripting and programming languages, the initial element is the
zero (0) element, not one (1). If you list array elements with only the brackets and
no numbers, PHP will automatically assign each element's identifier based on the
order of assignment beginning with zero (0).

You can also use the array constructor to build an array. It works very much like
ActionScript's constructor. For example, the following is an array of flowers:

```php
<?php
$blooms = array ("rose", "daisy", "buttercup", "zinnia",
"sunflower");
?>
```

The first value in the array is a rose and is assigned an element identifier of 0. The
others are assigned element numbers sequentially, so sunflower would be element
four (4). The following script would echo a rose and a buttercup:

```php
<?php
echo $blooms[0];
echo $blooms[2];
?>
```

A nice array feature of PHP is the ability to set the index. A special array operator,
=>, sets the sequence. For example, if you wanted your $blooms array to begin with
1 instead of 0, you could write the following:

```php
<?php
$blooms = array (1 => "rose", "daisy", "buttercup", "zinnia",
"sun flower");
?>
```

With these changes, the array elements are now rose=1, daisy=2, buttercup=3, and so forth. In addition to renumbering, you can use the => operator to create string-indexed arrays. The following code, for example, uses abbreviations for car models to index an array of those models:

```
<?php
$RollsRoyce = array ("SG" => "Silver Ghost", "PH" => "Phantom",
"SC" => "Silver Cloud", "SS" => "Silver Shadow", "SSpur" =>
"Silver Spur");
echo $RollsRoyce[SC];
?>
```

In the example, the echo statement returns Silver Cloud because the string index SC has been associated with the string literal Silver Cloud in the array. Note in the script that the index in the echo statement was not surrounded by quotation marks ($RollsRoyce[SC] instead of $RollsRoyce["SC"]).

Looping through arrays

In most computer languages, when you set up an array, pulling out elements is a matter of looping through the array until the element you're seeking matches a condition. The same is true of PHP. For example, the following script places values in five elements and then looks for one using a loop:

```
<?php
$city=array("London" ,"Paris" ,"New York" ,"Tokyo",
"Bloomfield");
while ($search != "New York") {
$search = $city[$i];
$i += 1;
}
echo $search;
?>
```

When you organize databases, keep in mind that at some point data needs to be entered and retrieved, and using arrays in PHP can aid this process. Note how the preceding loop took advantage of the index beginning with 0. Initially, $i is 0 (undefined), so the first time through the loop, the index picks up the first element in the array and keeps on going until the search condition is met.

Functions

Like ActionScript, PHP has both built-in functions and user functions. For example, the phpinfo() function, used previously in this chapter, is built into PHP4. A number of other functions are built into PHP as well, but we discuss only a small subset of these in this book as they are used with Flash 5. (See the PHP manual at www.php.net for a full listing of functions in PHP4 along with detailed explanations.) User functions in both ActionScript and PHP are similar in structure and application. A user function is defined with a word using optional arguments and then a list of statements. For example, a function to add tax and shipping to an item could be written as follows:

```php
<?php
function taxShip ($item) {
return   $item + ($item *.07) +4.95;
}
echo taxShip(19.95);
?>
```

The trick is, of course, to get the input from Flash 5 and use the data to do something. Eventually, you want to be able to use PHP to take the Flash 5 data and put it into a data file. You also want to be able to pull data out of a file and output it in a Flash 5 movie.

Moving Data Between Flash 5 and PHP

Passing data between a server-side script, PHP, and Flash 5 is relatively simple. The variable names generated in Flash 5 are recognized by the same variable names in PHP, with the exception that PHP variable names are preceded by a dollar sign ($). Therefore, the variable named $item in PHP is recognized as the item variable in Flash. The opposite is true as well. When a variable named score in Flash is passed to PHP, PHP recognizes the variable named $score. How are these variables passed back and forth? The following sections show you the process.

Sending data from PHP to Flash 5

Flash 5 uses the loadVariablesNum() action to bring in data from remote sources. The action expects a URL containing the data source and a level to load the data. The target can be a text file in the same directory as the Flash movie or a remote target. The following ActionScript, for example, targets a PHP file at a URL that happens to belong to one of the authors:

```
loadVariablesNum ("http://www.sandlight.com/PHP/data.php", 0);
```

The variable names are created in the external source. The format for external variables in a text field loaded using loadVariablesNum() is

```
VariableName=Data in the variable.&NewVariable=More data.
```

No spaces are allowed between the variable name, the equal sign (=), and the variable's contents. New variables are separated by an ampersand (&) and follow the same rules as the initial variable, and no spaces are allowed between the end of the first variable's data and the ampersand.

Note Optionally, you can place an ampersand (&) before the initial variable name. Some developers like to place the ampersand before the first variable so that identifying all of the variables is easier because they all contain a leading ampersand.

In PHP scripts, all of the variables are placed between quotation marks. The PHP `echo` command sends the text block to Flash. The following script, for example, places a variable named `myHotVariable` into Flash when the `loadVariablesNum()` action targets the PHP file.

```
<?php
echo "myHotVariable=This message is from a server-side script."
;
?>
```

This next Flash movie shows the steps involved in pulling data from a PHP script and displaying it in Flash 5. The movie contains the following layers:

✦ Text Field

✦ Button

✦ Background

Save the movie as `LoadPHP1.fla`.

Color palette

All color palettes are from a set of color combinations that complement one another and help improve the general appearance of the movie. You add each color by first using the values (hexadecimal) for each color in the Mixer panel and then selecting Add Swatch from the pop-up menu in the Mixer panel's upper-right corner. Table 4-2 shows the color palette for `LoadPHP1.fla`.

Table 4-2 Color Palette for LoadPHP1.fla			
Color	**R Value**	**G Value**	**B Value**
A	EE	19	00
B	00	17	D7
C	8A	B0	D7
D	EE	F3	E6
E	00	00	00

Background layer

The background layer is made up of a red (Color A) rectangle on top of the movie's background color (Color D). Select Modify, Movie and choose Color D from the movie's color palette. Then use the Align panel to center the rectangle to the stage's center. Lock the layer when you are finished. Figure 4-2 shows how the background looks on the stage.

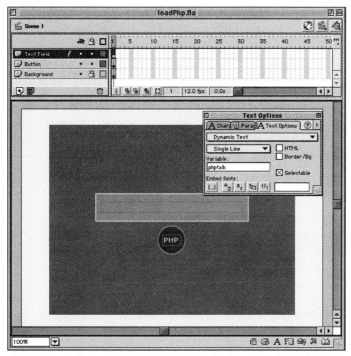

Figure 4-2: The stage area contains a single text field and a button for the ActionScript.

Text Field layer

The text fields in Flash can act as input and output windows, and both dynamic and input text fields can be associated with a variable name in the Text Object panel. Note in Figure 4-2 how `phptalk` is used as the variable name associated with the dynamic text field. Set up the Text Field layer with the following steps:

1. Draw a backdrop for the text field with the Rectangle tool; use Color B for the fill and Color C for the stroke. Look at Figure 4-2 as a guide.

2. Use the Text tool to create a text field.

3. Select the text field and open the Text Options panel by clicking the text icon on the launcher bar and then clicking the Text Options tab. Select Dynamic Text from the top pop-up menu in the Text Options panel.

4. In the Variable box, type **phptalk** to associate this variable name with the text field.

Button layer

The button holds the ActionScript that loads the variables from PHP. This next set of steps shows how to set it up:

1. Use the Oval tool to draw a circle and use Color B for the fill and Color C for the stroke. Using the Text tool, type **PHP** on top of the button.

2. Select the circle and text and press the F8 key to open the Symbol Properties dialog box. Select Button for the Behavior, and in the Name window, type **phpbutton.** Click OK to create a button symbol.

3. Select the button instance and click the Action panel icon (arrow) on the launcher bar to open the Objects Action panel. Enter the following script, substituting the URL with the one you use as your root directory and subdirectory in your root directory:

```
on (release) {
    loadVariablesNum ("http://www.sandlight.com/
PHP/data.php", 0);
}
```

4. When you enter the ActionScript in Normal mode, place the parameter values as shown in Figure 4-3. Use the default Level value of 0, and type in the URL in the URL window. You do not want to send any variable to PHP so leave the Variables pop-up menu in the default state of Don't send.

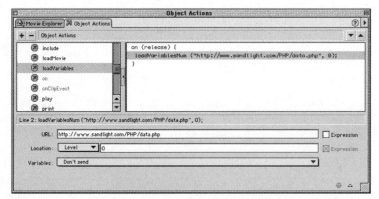

Figure 4-3: In the Normal mode, the parameter values are placed at the bottom of the ActionScript editor.

That concludes the Flash portion of the project.

The PHP variable

This first PHP script does one thing: It passes a variable to Flash. As noted previously, the format is fairly straightforward. The variable format consists of an ampersand followed by the variable name, an equal sign, and the contents of the variable. After you write the script, save it in the root directory or a subdirectory of the root directory under the name `data.php`:

```php
<?php
echo "phptalk=Hello from the server." ;
?>
```

Figure 4-4 shows the output in Flash.

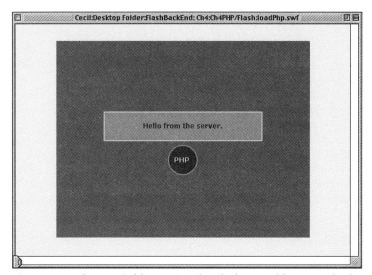

Figure 4-4: The text field associated with the variable name displays the contents from the server-side script.

Sending data from Flash to PHP

To send data from Flash to PHP, you need to have some way of directing the data out of Flash and making it go somewhere else. Like HTML, Flash provides two methods of sending data: GET and POST. The GET method has proved to be the best cross-platform method, so it is used throughout this book. The general format for sending data from Flash to a server script is

```
loadVariablesNum ("http://www.sandlight.com/PHP/grand.php", 0, "GET");
```

The format looks identical to the format for loading variables into Flash, except that GET is added after the level value. Which variables are sent from Flash? All of them. To catch the Flash variables, PHP adds a dollar sign ($) to the name of each Flash variable. For example, a Flash variable named MyGreatVariable is caught in PHP by a variable named $MyGreatVariable.

Suppose you send a variable named spud from Flash. The following PHP script would take that variable and do something with it and return it to Flash as a variable named display. But instead of simply using the echo command to send the variable back to Flash, the code first places the variable inside a PHP variable and then returns it to Flash with echo command:

```php
<?php
$spud .= " are destined for a fast food joint.";
$show= "display=$spud";
echo $show ;
?>
```

This next Flash movie demonstrates how a variable in Flash is sent to a PHP script, concatenated with a PHP literal, and sent back to Flash. The purpose of sending the variable back to Flash is to show that it is actually the value that came from Flash in the first place. By adding a bit of material, you can begin to see how data in the server-side script can interact with the data sent from Flash. Save the movie as LoadPHP2.fla. The movie contains the following layers:

✦ Input

✦ Output

✦ Button

Color palette

Use the color palette in Table 4-3 for the movie. Use Color B for the background color.

<table>
<tr><td colspan="4">Table 4-3
Color Palette for LoadPHP2.fla</td></tr>
<tr><td>*Color*</td><td>*R Value*</td><td>*G Value*</td><td>*B Value*</td></tr>
<tr><td>A</td><td>00</td><td>73</td><td>CC</td></tr>
<tr><td>B</td><td>00</td><td>FF</td><td>A6</td></tr>
<tr><td>C</td><td>E6</td><td>CC</td><td>00</td></tr>
<tr><td>D</td><td>FF</td><td>4C</td><td>00</td></tr>
</table>

Input layer

In this movie, both an input and output layer are required. Figure 4-5 shows an overview of the movie with the text field used for input at the top of the stage.

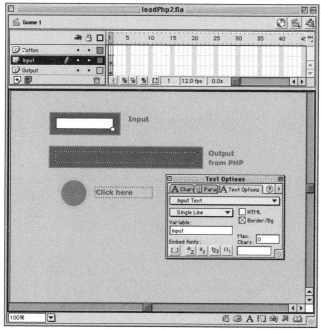

Figure 4-5: Two text fields provide an entry portal to PHP (input) and a return data window from PHP (output); a button contains the ActionScript necessary to launch the process.

This next set of steps covers the process for creating the Input text field:

1. Use the Rectangle tool to draw a background for the text field. Use Color A as the fill color and Color D as the stroke color.

2. Select the Text tool and draw a rectangular text field over the background rectangle as shown in Figure 4-5. Open the Text Options panel and select Input Text from the top pop-up menu.

3. In the Variable box on the Text Options panel, type **input** for the variable name to be associated with the text field.

Output layer

The Output text field goes directly below the Input text field, as shown in Figure 4-5. Follow the steps for the Input layer except select Dynamic Text from the pop-up menu in the Text Options panel and type **output** for the variable name to associate with the text field.

Button layer

The button holds the ActionScript that loads the variables from PHP. This next set of steps shows how to set it up:

1. Use the Oval tool to draw a circle, using Color D for the fill and Color C for the stroke.

2. Select the circle and press the F8 key to open the Symbol Properties dialog box. Select Button for the Behavior, and in the Name box, type **postbutton**. Click OK to create a button symbol.

3. Select the button instance and click the Action panel icon (arrow) on the launcher bar to open the Objects Action panel. Enter the following script, substituting your own path:

```
on (release) {
    loadVariablesNum
("http://www.sandlight.com/PHP/data2.php", 0, "GET");
}
```

While entering the ActionScript in the Normal mode, place the parameter values as shown in Figure 4-6. Use the default Level value of 0, and type in the URL in the URL box. In the Variables pop-up window, select Send using GET. That completes the Flash side of the equation.

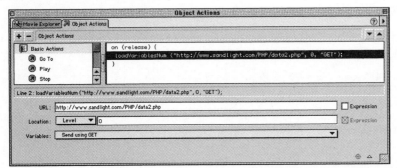

Figure 4-6: All variables in the Flash movie are sent using Send using GET.

PHP mirror variables

The data sent to PHP is the contents of the text field associated with the `input` variable. Therefore, you want a mirror variable named `$input` in the PHP script to store the data sent from Flash. If you had 10 or 100 variables in the Flash movie, PHP could handle them all as long as you included a PHP mirror variable to hold the contents passed from Flash. The following script takes the data entered into the input text field and stores it in $input. Then you can do with it what you want. In this case, the contents of the variable are concatenated with the phrase from PHP with a space between the first quotation mark and the first word. Otherwise, the data would run together.

To send the data back to Flash with the new phrase, use the output variable associated with the second text field. A PHP variable, $output, is defined to contain the necessary data for Flash. The new contents of $input are defined in the variable to be sent back to Flash. The echo command then sends the variable $output back to Flash. Save the following script under the name data2.php in your root directory or the subdirectory in the root directory:

```php
<?php
$input .= " from php";
$output= "output=$input";
echo $output ;
?>
```

Run your SWF file and enter some text in the input text field. As shown in Figure 4-7, whatever you enter in Flash bounces back from PHP with the concatenated message.

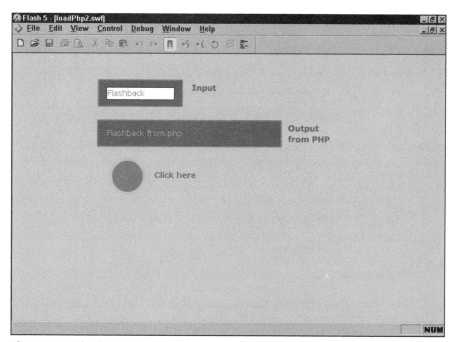

Figure 4-7: The input from Flash is modified in PHP and returned as output in Flash.

Using Flash data and PHP calculations

The next step is to see how data gathered in a Flash front end can be used in calculations generated by PHP. Even though most calculations could be accomplished by client-side scripts in ActionScript, seeing how to pass calculated data from a PHP script with data originating in Flash is the first step in using wholly PHP-generated data for output in Flash.

This next Flash movie is similar to the previous one, but it takes the data sent from Flash, performs a calculation, and then returns the calculated results back to Flash. In this movie, you can begin to see the benefits of PHP. Several different Flash movies could use the same PHP script, and if values need to be changed (tax rates or shipping costs, for example), a single change in the PHP script would suffice to change the output in all the Flash movies that need the same data calculated. This movie has the same three layers as the previous movie:

✦ Button

✦ Input

✦ Output

Save the movie as LoadPHP3.fla.

Color palette

Use the color palette in Table 4-4 for the movie. Use Color B (deep red/brown) for the background color.

Table 4-4 Color Palette for LoadPHP3.fla			
Color	R Value	G Value	B Value
A	FF	BD	33
B	99	00	19
C	B3	FF	CC
D (Black)			
E (White)			

Input layer

Like the last movie, the input field is used to provide data associated with a variable that is sent to the PHP script on the server. This next set of steps covers the process for creating the input text field:

1. Select the Text tool and draw a rectangular text field near the top of the stage, as shown in Figure 4-8. Open the Text Options panel and select Input Text from the top pop-up menu. In the Variable box on the Text Options panel, type **input** for the variable name to be associated with the text field.

2. In the Character panel, select Verdana as the type and black for the text color.

3. Using Color C and a bold Verdana 12-point font, type in **Enter item price:** as shown in Figure 4-8.

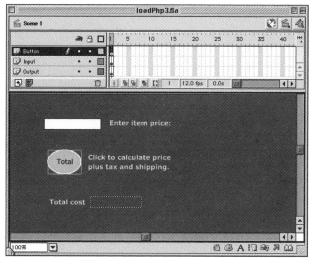

Figure 4-8: The first text field is used to input data that is sent to the PHP script, calculated, and then returned to Flash in the output window.

Button layer

The ActionScript in the button sends data to the PHP script, but it does no calculation itself. The script is almost identical to the script in the previous Flash movie, but the button is a little different:

1. Use the Oval tool to draw an oval, using Color A for the fill and white for the stroke. Type **Total** on top of the oval.

2. Select the oval and text on the oval and press the F8 key to open the Symbol Properties dialog box. Select Button for the Behavior, and in the Name box, type **calcToPHP**. Click OK to create a button symbol.

3. Select the button instance and click the Action panel icon (arrow) on the launcher bar to open the Objects Action panel. Enter the following script, substituting your own path:

```
on (release) {
    loadVariablesNum
("http://www.sandlight.com/PHP/data3.php", 0, "GET");
}
```

4. Use the default Level value of 0, and type in the URL in the URL window. In the Variables pop-up window, select Send using GET.

Output layer

The output text field goes below the button as shown in Figure 4-8. Follow the steps for the Input layer except select Dynamic Text from the pop-up menu in the Text Options panel and type **output** for the variable name to associate with the field. Also, enter **Total cost** as the label for the field.

PHP calculations

This next PHP script does the relatively mundane chore of adding tax and shipping costs to a value. Like the script in the previous movie, this script wraps the result into a variable and sends it back to Flash with the echo command:

```
<?php
$input += $input * .07;
$input = $input +5.99;
$output= "output=$input";
echo $output ;
?>
```

Save the PHP file as data3.php and place it in your root directory or the subdirectory in the root directory. When you launch your Flash SWF file, the value you enter into the input text field is put into the calculations of the PHP script. Because the text field is associated with the input variable in Flash ActionScript, the data is passed to the $input variable in PHP. The calculations are carried out and the results are returned to the output variable in Flash. Because the second text field is associated with the output variable, the results appear in the text field window.

Passing data generated in PHP functions

Using PHP functions to pass data to Flash requires arranging your PHP code so that the function contains everything required to organize and send the data to Flash.

The function definition must contain everything for doing calculations and formatting data for Flash; it also must have an `echo` command to send the results scurrying back to Flash. The generic format looks like this:

```php
<?php
function funcName ($arguments) {
//calculations and formatting stored in $variable
$backToFlash="FlashVariable=$variable"
echo $backToFlash;
}
funcName($valueFromFlash);
?>
```

The function name and arguments are standard, as are the calculations and formatting statements. But once all of the formatting is completed and stored in PHP variables, the Flash variables have to be formatted to read the PHP variables while they are within the function's curly braces. The `echo` command replaces the `return` statement in the function, but the format is almost identical to the previous functions section. The following function, for example, is another tax and shipping one; but the Flash formatting has been added to this function. When the function is called from Flash, it returns the input value from Flash with the tax and shipping added.

```php
<?php
function taxShip ($item) {
$total=$item + ($item *.06) +4.95;
$output="output=$total";
echo $output;
}
taxShip($input);
?>
```

Save this the PHP file as `taxShipFunction.php` in your root directory on the server. Then, using the movie from the previous example (`LoadPHP3.fla`), change the button script to read as follows:

```
on (release) {
    loadVariablesNum
    ("http://www.sandlight.com/PHP/taxShipFunction.php", 0,
    "GET");
}
```

Try out the movie by pressing Ctrl+Enter (Windows) or Cmd+Return (Macintosh). When the SWF file appears, type in a value and click the button. You should see the value you entered returned with tax and shipping costs added, as shown in Figure 4-9.

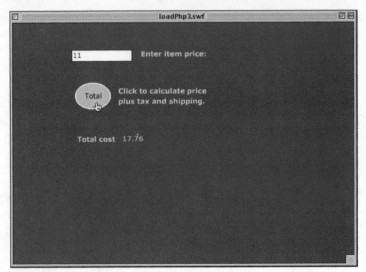

Figure 4-9: The data in the Total cost field was generated through calculations in a PHP script and returned to Flash for output.

Passing array data between Flash and PHP

The process of passing array elements between Flash 5 and PHP is important to understand because you can place data from a database into an array for transfer to and from Flash and PHP. Arrays are treated no differently from variables. The great advantage of an array, though, is that you can use a series of numbers to access the array. By understanding how to use array elements and associated values, you can establish a better way to organize and pass data between Flash and PHP.

On the Flash side, you can associate the arrays with text fields to display any or all elements of the array. On the PHP side, you can coordinate the array elements to the text fields. In this way, whatever value is passed from Flash to PHP can be used to coordinate PHP data and Flash output. This next movie contains five text fields and five buttons associated with the text fields. Each of the text fields is an element in an array, and each button contains a script that sends information to a PHP script that uses its own array to verify that a button has been clicked. This movie uses the following three layers:

✦ Background

✦ Buttons

✦ Text Fields

Figure 4-10 provides an overview of the movie and its major components. Save the movie as `ArrayData2.fla`.

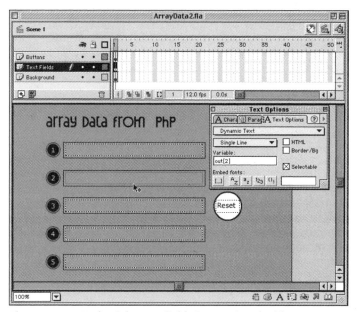

Figure 4-10: Each of the text fields is associated with an array element.

Color palette

The movie uses a simple gray, purple, black, and white color scheme whose values are shown in Table 4-5.

	Table 4-5		
	Color Palette for ArrayData2.fla		
Color	**R Value**	**G Value**	**B Value**
A	A6	99	E6
B	A6	A6	A6
C (Black)			
D (White)			

Background layer

Begin by using the purple (Color A) to color the background; choose Modify ⇨ Movie and then select the palette's purple color. In the Background layer, draw gray rectangles with black strokes to serve as backdrops to the text fields as shown in Figure 4-10. Use the Info panel to set the rectangle dimensions to W=259 and H=28. After you complete the first rectangle, select it and then choose Modify ⇨ Group so that the stroke and fill are grouped. Then make four identical copies of the rectangle and line them up vertically using the Align panel to space and align them.

Buttons layer

Create five buttons and label them from 1 to 5 as shown in Figure 4-10. Then create a sixth button and label it Reset.

Array buttons

The buttons adjacent to the text fields contain scripts that send (POST) data to the PHP script and fire the PHP script. The value of the `myData` variable is the array element value of the text field adjacent to the button. The PHP script shows how that value is used to return the correct message when the button is clicked. Substitute your URL for the one provided.

```
on (release) {
    myData = 1;
    loadVariablesNum
("http://www.sandlight.com/PHP/arrayData2.php", 0, "POST");
}
```

Reset button

The Reset button launches a PHP script that places a space in each of the five text fields, effectively resetting them all.

```
on (release) {
    loadVariablesNum
("http://www.sandlight.com/PHP/arrayClear.php", 0);
}
```

Text Fields layer

The text fields are all associated with the same array – `out[n]`. Use the following steps to set them up:

1. Lock the Background layer so that you don't select the background rectangles. In the Character panel, set the font to Verdana, selecting black for the color and 12 for the font size.

2. Create the first text field adjacent to the button numbered 1 over the text field background (rectangle). Using the Info panel, make sure that the width (W:) is 250. Center the text field over the background rectangle (this action requires that you temporarily unlock the Background layer) by using the Align panel.

3. With the text field selected, open the Text Options panel and select Dynamic Text from the pop-up window. In the Variable box, type in **out[1]**. That variable (array element) is now associated with the text field.

4. Repeat steps 1 through 3 for four more text fields. In the Variable box in the Text Options panel, use the array element names **out[2]** through **out[5]**.

Tip You can save some time by selecting the first text field and then using Alt+drag (Windows) or Option+drag (Macintosh) to make copies of the text field. Then all you need to do is to align the new fields and rename the elements in the Text Options panel.

PHP scripts

Two PHP scripts are required for the movie. The first script generates an array and then, depending on the button clicked in the Flash movie, sends an array element back to Flash in a text field associated with the output array (out[n]). The important part of the script is where the $output variable uses the value of $myData, which was sent as myData from Flash. Each numbered button's script sends a value in myData consistent with the text field's element number next to the button. The value is also linked to a value in the array in the PHP script. Thus, the button numbered 3 sends a value of 3 in the myData variable. In the PHP script, $item[3] states "You clicked the third button" and appears in the text field associated with out[3] in the Flash movie. All of these elements are placed in the $output variable by concatenating the array element out[$myData] with the equal sign (=) and with the PHP array element $item[$myData]. Then the whole thing is echoed back to Flash. Save the script in the server's root directory or in a subdirectory in the root directory under the name arrayData2.php.

```php
<?php
//Create a simple array.
$item[1] = "You clicked the first button.";
$item[2] = "You clicked the second button.";
$item[3] = "You clicked the third button.";
$item[4] = "You clicked the fourth button.";
$item[5] = "You clicked the fifth button.";

//Concatenate the output in Flash 5 format.
//Use the dot for concatenation and $myData (myData)
//sent from the ActionScript in the Flash buttons.

$output = "out[$myData]" . "=" . $item[$myData];
echo $output;
?>
```

The second PHP script clears out all of the text fields by placing a space in the field. In the following script, be sure to put a space between the equal sign (=) and the ampersand (&). Save the script in the server's root directory or in a subdirectory in the root directory under the name arrayClear.php.

```php
<?php
echo "out[1]= &out[2]= &out[3]= &out[4]= &out[5]= ";
?>
```

Figure 4-11 shows the SWF file where three of the buttons have been clicked.

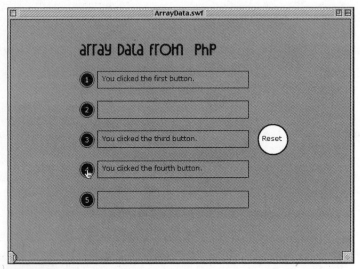

Figure 4-11: Arrays written in PHP can connect with an array in ActionScript.

Communications Among Flash, PHP, and MySQL

Information storage and retrieval is the domain of databases. This section examines how to use Flash 5 as a front end for databases housed on the Web. Most readers are likely to be familiar with using databases such as Microsoft Access, FileMaker, or even Microsoft Excel. More powerful databases called relational database management systems (RDBMS) store data in tables that are connected (related) to one another through common fields. The tables are organized into rows and columns, with each column representing a *field* and each row representing a *record*.

As a front end, Flash 5 serves to provide a portal to data access and storage. Using ActionScript, Flash 5 sends data to PHP, which in turn retrieves or stores the data in the database by translating the request into a language the RDBMS can understand. If a request for data is made, PHP sends the query on to the RDBMS, which sends the information back to PHP, which translates it for Flash 5. Like PHP and ActionScript, RDBMS have their own languages, so all of the languages have to be coordinated. Think of PHP as a translator who speaks both ActionScript and RDBMS.

One of the most popular RDBMS used on the Web is MySQL. MySQL can be downloaded and used for professional database development. Although you can use it without charge for learning and most personal uses, a small fee is required for commercial uses. Like PHP, MySQL is Open Source Software, so can you modify it to best suit your needs. Versions of MySQL are available for Windows, MacOS X Server (PowerPC), Unix, and Linux. At this writing, the latest version is 3.23.29a-gamma; by the time you read this book, a later version will no doubt be available. Check out www.mysql.com for the newest version and full support of this language.

The focal point of this section involves a three-language link. MySQL has its own database language (SQL is an acronym for *Structured Query Language*), including a whole set of commands for creating databases and tables and entering and retrieving data. PHP has a special subset of functions dedicated to MySQL, and all of this data has to be handed off to ActionScript. The major work is getting a good clear communication link between PHP and MySQL, and PHP provides several MySQL functions to make that job relatively easy. Figure 4-12 shows the relationship between Flash, PHP, and MySQL.

Figure 4-12: PHP is the translator between Flash 5's ActionScript and MySQL.

Using MySQL commands

This section explains how to use MySQL commands to create databases and tables and store and retrieve data in the tables. If you are using your computer as both client and server, you will need the MySQL server running along with the Apache server. If you are using your JTLNet account or some other hosting service, you can assume the Apache server and MySQL are working once you set the necessary parameters. Working on a remote host is far less troublesome, and if you have a Macintosh, you should begin using the remote host from the start. (See the section "Creating a MySQL database and user on the hosting service" later in this chapter.)

Use the following steps if you're running everything on your Windows PC for the initial setup:

1. Choose Start ➪ Programs ➪ Accessories ➪ MS-DOS Prompt and then select the DOS icon to open a DOS window.

2. In the DOS window, type **cd c:\mysql\bin** and press Enter. You will see the DOS window with white type and a black background.

3. Type **mysqld -- standalone** and press Enter. (Be sure you have a space between **mysqld** and --.) After a momentary delay, you will see the DOS prompt again.

4. Enter the MySQL monitor by typing **mysql** and pressing Enter. If you've successfully entered the monitor, you will see a mysql> prompt. Note that all commands in the MySQL monitor must be terminated with a semi-colon.

5. To create a new database user, type in this code:

```
mysql> use mysql
Database changed

mysql> INSERT INTO user
    -> (host, user, password)
    -> VALUES(
    -> 'localhost',
    -> 'willie',
    -> password('yourOwnPW')
    -> );
```

The MySQL monitor should respond as follows:

```
Query OK, 1 row affected (0.05 sec)

mysql>
```

6. Exit the MySQL monitor by typing **exit**. You should see the C:\mysql\bin> cursor.

7. Type **mysqladmin flush-privileges** and press Enter. That command allows the user, willie, to access the databases with the password yourOwnPW.

8. To establish the current user, re-enter the MySQL monitor using the following command sequence (shown with MySQL responses):

```
C:\mysql\bin>mysql -h localhost -u willie -p
Enter password: *******
Welcome to the MySQL monitor. Commands end with ; or \g.
Your MySQL connection id is 15 to server version: 3.23.29a-
gamma-debug

Type 'help;' or '\h' for help. Type '\c' to clear the buffer

mysql>
```

Setting up MySQL usually isn't so onerous after you have established a user host and password. Usually, you start the MySQL monitor by using steps 1 through 3 and 8 only.

Creating databases and tables

Once you are in the MySQL monitor, you should be able to create databases and tables and add records to the tables. To create a database, type the following code. (Note that the convention in MySQL is to type all of the commands in uppercase and type the tables and database names in lowercase.)

```
mysql> CREATE DATABASE flashbase;
```

The name of the database you just created is flashbase; you can see it by issuing a SHOW DATABASES command:

```
mysql> SHOW DATABASES;
```

MySQL responds to this command with something similar to the following display:

```
+-----------+
| Database  |
+-----------+
| flashbase |
| flashtab  |
| mysql     |
| test      |
+-----------+
4 rows in set (0.00 sec)
```

The command displays all the established databases. The databases named mysql and test are established by default. The flashbase database is the one just created, and flashtab is an additional user-defined database. As you can see, creating a new database is straightforward and simple.

To add a table to the database, first issue a USE flashbase; command to select the desired database. The next step is to create a table to show the e-mail addresses of a list of people stored in a database. Each field in the table must include a name, a data type, and the length of the field. Table 4-6 lists a sample of the main data types.

	Table 4-6 MySQL Data Types	
Data type	**Description**
INT	Integer number
FLOAT	Floating-point number (single precision)
DOUBLE/REAL	Floating-point number (double precision)
DECIMAL	Float stored as string
DATE	Any date
TIME	Any time
YEAR	Any year (from 1900 to 2155)
CHAR	Fixed-length string from 0 to 255
VARCHAR	Variable length string from 0 to 255
TEXT	Text field from 0 to 65535 bytes

To create a table, use the following format:

```
mysql> CREATE TABLE tablename (field1 DATATYPE(N), field2 DATATYPE(N), etc.);
```

For the example in this chapter, the table has only two columns (fields). One holds an individual's name and the other holds an e-mail address. The name field (ename) uses a fixed-length string of 30 characters, and the e-mail field (email) uses a fixed-length string of 40 characters.

Note Whenever you press the Enter key without a semi-colon when in the MySQL monitor, the next line is indicated by a -> symbol where you can add more code to the command line or statement. As soon as the semi-colon is in place, the command line is terminated, and the command is issued.

To create a table in the flashbase database, make sure that the database is still selected and then enter the following code:

```
mysql> CREATE TABLE emailflash (
    -> ename CHAR(30),
    -> email CHAR(40)
    -> );
```

The MySQL monitor should display the following:

```
Query OK, 0 rows affected (0.11 sec)
```

After issuing the CREATE TABLE command, you can check to make sure the table is in the current database by using the SHOW TABLES command:

```
mysql> SHOW TABLES;
+---------------------+
| Tables_in_flashbase |
+---------------------+
| emailflash          |
+---------------------+
1 row in set (0.00 sec)
```

Entering and retrieving records

After you have created a database and table, you need a way to enter and retrieve records in order to put the database to good use. To insert records into a table, first be sure the correct database is selected and then use the following format:

```
mysql> INSERT INTO tablename VALUES('field1', 'field2');
```

The data that makes up field1 and field2 comes from the Flash front end that you develop later in this chapter. So, in addition to entering the data as literals, you can use variables passed from Flash 5 to PHP to MySQL to enter data into MySQL. Passing Flash variables is much easier than using the MySQL monitor. The following code shows the correct procedure for entering a record:

```
mysql> INSERT INTO emailflash VALUES(
    -> 'Pewee Goliath',
    -> 'little_giant@anomaly.com')
    -> ;
```

The MySQL monitor provides this feedback:

```
Query OK, 1 row affected (0.00 sec)
```

To make sure that the records are indeed in the database, you can use MySQL's SELECT statement with a wildcard character (*) to reveal all of the records in the table. The following shows both the correct statements and the results:

```
mysql> SELECT * FROM emailflash;
+------------------+----------------------------+
| ename            | email                      |
+------------------+----------------------------+
| Bill Sanders     | bill@sandlight.com         |
| Mark Winstanley  | winstanley@carumba.org     |
| George Lincoln   | greatpres@whitehouse.gov   |
| Betty Boop       | popopeedo@speakeasy.net    |
| Nancy Smith      | nsmith@schoolyard.edu      |
| Karl Schultz     | kbone@doghouse.com         |
| Pewee Goliath    | little_giant@anomaly.com   |
+------------------+----------------------------+
7 rows in set (0.00 sec)
```

For more specific selections, MySQL requires more information. For example, to select information about a specific person in the `emailflash` table, you must specify the field name(s) and the name of the person you're trying to find.

```
mysql> select ename, email from emailflash where ename="Bill
Sanders";
+---------------+-----------------------+
| ename         | email                 |
+---------------+-----------------------+
| Bill Sanders  | bill@sandlight.com    |
+---------------+-----------------------+
1 row in set (0.05 sec)

mysql>
```

Practice with the basic MySQL commands. Enter records into a table and select records from a table to get the feel of the commands. In the next section, you will see how to link PHP with MySQL and get information from a MySQL database using PHP. Once the data has been passed to PHP, getting it into Flash is relatively easy. Likewise, sending data from Flash to MySQL involves simply taking data from Flash, sending it to PHP, and then sending it on to MySQL.

Communicating with MySQL and Flash from PHP

Working with MySQL or PHP separately is fairly simple. But when you use your own computer for a server and client with both, you may find that you spend more time dealing with errors resulting from access privileges in MySQL than learning how to make the three-way connection between Flash, PHP, and MySQL. To simplify matters and provide experience working in a real-world developing environment, the examples and explanations in this section use JTLNet's MySQL.

Creating a MySQL database and user on the hosting service

You first need to create both the user and the database using the MySQL utilities provided by JTLNet. Once you learn how to set up the user and database, the rest is simply a matter of creating tables for the database and storing and retrieving data using PHP and Flash.

1. Open your browser and go to your personal control panel. Use the URL to your root directory followed by a slash and `controlpanel`. For example, the control panel for a domain named, "yourDomain" would be `www.yourDomain.com/controlpanel`. You should see the password box shown in Figure 4-13. When you enter your username and password, the information is used to establish the security in the MySQL databases you create and use.

2. In the Control Panel home pages (Cpanel 3), select Advanced Menu, SQL Database to arrive at the MySQL page. Under Sql Account Maintenance, you will see the Databases and Users in [database_name] list. Next to each database name and user a Delete button stands out. Initially, you will see no databases or users, and you must create one of each to get started.

Figure 4-13: The username and password help establish the security parameters for MySQL.

3. In the Db: text box, type the name for a database. Figure 4-14 shows a database to be added named `flashook`. Click the Add Db button to insert the database into your MySQL account.

4. In the UserName text box, type a username you want. In the Password text box, type a password. Figure 4-14 shows `joe` for the username and `coolbeans` for the password. Click the Add User button.

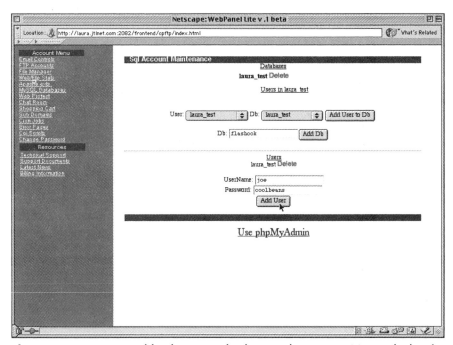

Figure 4-14: You must add at least one database and user to MySQL on the hosting service.

After you have added the database and user, you will find that their names have been altered. Both the database and the username will have your account username attached to the beginning of the names you entered. Your database will now be accountName_username. In the example, the sample account is called sandligh, and so now the database's name is sandligh_flashook. (The appended account name is the hosting service's convention and not a MySQL requirement. Different hosting services may have similar or different requirements.) Likewise, the username for MySQL is sandligh_joe or whatever the name of your account is appended to the username you entered.

Note   Remember the database name and username for each account and user. You need to use the full name of the user and database provided by the hosting service (for example, sandligh_joe, sandligh_flashook) in the PHP scripts you create in this chapter. Also, you must remember the password associated with each user. For simplicity's sake, begin with a single user and database. In the example, you would want to record the username (sandligh_joe), the password (coolbeans), and the database (sandligh_flashook).

5. Finally, you must add a user to a database. In the pop-up menus in the User and Db: windows, select a user and database and click the Add User to Db button.

Once you have established a database and an associated user, you are all set to start writing PHP scripts that access the database in your JTLNet site. (If you have a different hosting service that provides MySQL, check with it to see about setting up your databases.)

Most hosting services do not allow direct access to your MySQL through Telnet but do provide alternatives for examining your MySQL databases. JTLNet provides an online program called phpMyAdmin for administering MySQL databases. If you add your own tables and records from the PHP scripts provided in this book, you do not need to use phpMyAdmin, but you will find it handy for inspecting your MySQL database. You can use the same commands as you do with the MySQL monitor. Figure 4-15 shows one of the screens from phpMyAdmin where a MySQL command is issued. Clicking the Go button issues the command.

This next section introduces several PHP functions specifically for MySQL. Table 4-7 provides an overview and summary of the functions that are used. (For a full list of PHP MySQL functions, see www.php.net/manual/ref.mysql.php.)

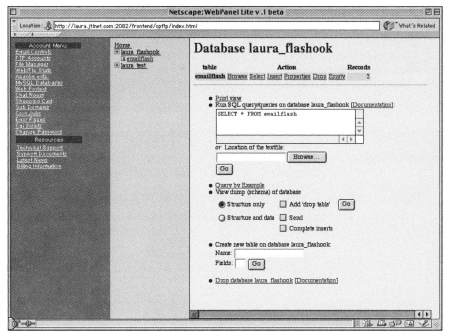

Figure 4-15: From the phpMyAdmin utility, you can write SQL queries similar to those issued in the MySQL monitor.

Table 4-7
PHP MySQL Functions

Function	Result
mysql_connect	Establishes a connection to a MySQL Server
mysql_num_rows	Returns the number of rows in result
mysql_query	Sends a MySQL query
mysql_result	Gets result data
mysql_select_db	Chooses a MySQL database

Establishing a PHP connection to MySQL

One of the several MySQL functions built into PHP is mysql_connect(). Before PHP can do anything with a MySQL file, it must first make a general connection to MySQL. The mysql_connect() function expects three arguments: server, user-name, and password. The password and username provide database security, and although the security features may be troublesome when you are learning how to use PHP and MySQL, they are features you will appreciate when you have data in MySQL files that you do not want others to see. To set up the connection, a good strategy is to set up variables for the connection, and then use those variables in the arguments. If you want to change the server, username, or password, all you have to do is to change the variable names.

The or die (message) is often used to help locate connection problems to the different links that must be made to MySQL. If the connection does not take place, the die() function returns the bad news. You can use the following PHP script to test your connection to the MySQL server:

```php
<?php
//Set up and connect
$server="localhost";          //Server name
$user="sandligh_willie";      //Username
$pass="yourOwnPW";            //Password

//Make the connection
$hookup = mysql_connect($server, $user, $pass) or die ("No joy
Ace.");

if ($hookup) {
$feedback="You're hooked up Ace.";
}
echo "$feedback";
?>
```

Save the script in the root directory of your server or a directory within the root directory as **first_connect.php**. In JTLNet, the root directory would be the public_html directory. We added the scripts subdirectory to store the PHP scripts for MySQL, so for us the URL to launch the script would be

```
http://www.sandlight.com/scripts/first_connect.php
```

The server is named localhost in the JTLNet setup so that the name is used in the connection. One of the users was defined as sandligh_willie with the password yourOwnPW. So if all goes as planned, you will see the good news, "You're hooked up Ace." If you fail to make the connection, you will see a message like the following in your browser:

```
Warning: MySQL Connection Failed: Access denied for user:
'sandligh_willie@localhost' (Using password: YES) in
/home/sandligh/public_html/scripts/first_connect.php on line 8
No joy Ace.
```

If your connection fails, check your script to make sure the server name, username, and password are correct. If they are correct, then you need to make sure that on your hosting service you have established the correct user and databases and have connected the user and database. The greatest number of problems you will encounter are going to be with the security setup of MySQL, but once you have a good connection, the rest is relatively easy.

Selecting a database

The next step is to select the database you plan to use with the PHP function mysql_select_db(databaseName, connection). The database name is the name you have given the database on the host. The connection name is the variable where the mysql_connect() data are stored. In this example, an at sign (@) is placed in front of the mysql_select_db function to suppress the automatic feedback to the Web page. This sign ensures that only the die() function message will be displayed.

```
<?php

//Set up and connect
$server="localhost";                 //Server name
$user="sandligh_willie";             //Username
$pass="yourOwnPW";                   //Password
$flashbase ="sandligh_flash1";       //Database name

//Make the connection
$hookup = mysql_connect($server, $user, $pass);

//Select the database
$debase=@mysql_select_db($flashbase,$hookup) or die ("No luck
with the database Jack");

if ($debase) {
$feedback="Database is selected and ready to go.";
}
echo "$feedback";
?>
```

Once you are able to connect to MySQL and the desired database, the rest is pretty smooth sailing.

Note

We found that far fewer problems occurred when using the hosting service than when attempting to run both the Apache server and MySQL monitor on our own computers. Several security problems kept cropping up with MySQL, and although everything worked great when no security conflicts were detected, the security conflicts kept reoccurring at different times for no apparent reasons.

Inserting tables into the database

After you have all of your connections made and the database selected, you need to insert a table. The previous section entitled "Creating databases and tables" shows how MySQL commands are used to create a table. Those same commands must now be used in a PHP script to create a table for the database. The two-step process involves first creating a string with the MySQL commands. Usually, we prefer to use a variable for the table name so that when a different table needs to be inserted, all we need to do is to substitute table names.

In the first step, the string with the command elements replicates the same statements and arguments that would be used in the MySQL monitor. Other than the variable name substituted for the actual table name, the script between the quotation marks is exactly what would be written in the MySQL monitor when a table is created. Next, the `mysql_query(query,connect)` function is used to send the command to MySQL.

The following script creates a table named `emailflash` in the `sandligh_flash1` database. Substitute your own names for the username, password, database name, and table name. If you are using JTLNet, use the server name in the listing, but otherwise change it to the name that is appropriate to your hosting service.

```php
<?php

//Set up and connect
$server="localhost";          //Server name
$user="sandligh_willie";      //Username
$pass="yourOwnPW";            //Password
$flashbase ="sandligh_flash1";  //Database name
$bilz_table="emailflash";     //Table name

//Make the connection
$hookup = mysql_connect($server, $user, $pass);

//Select the database
$debase=mysql_select_db($flashbase,$hookup);

//Build the query statement
$sql = "CREATE TABLE $bilz_table (ename char(30), email
char(40))";

//Execute the query
$result = @mysql_query($sql,$hookup) or die("Table not
created.");

if ($result) {
echo "Table has been created.";
}
?>
```

Save the script as add_table.php and launch it from your browser. If you get any result other than "Table has been created," check your script and the names of the different connections.

Inserting records into a table using PHP and Flash

At this point, you can begin thinking about using Flash as a front end to enter data into your database. As you have seen in previous sections, you can pass data between Flash and PHP by using the GET method in an ActionScript statement.

The following PHP script gets two variables from Flash. One is name, and the other is email. The two Flash variables become $name and $email in PHP. The $name variable is part of a record that goes into the ename field, and the $email variable goes into the email field in a table named emailflash. The general MySQL statements are loaded into the $sql variable. Then the data is sent into MySQL as a record with the mysql_query function.

```php
<?php

//Set up and connect
$server="localhost";              //Server name
$user="sandligh_willie";          //Username
$pass="yourOwnPW";                //Password
$flashbase ="sandligh_flash1";    //Database name
$bilz_table="emailflash";         //table name

//Make the connection
$hookup = mysql_connect($server, $user, $pass);

//Select the database
mysql_select_db($flashbase,$hookup);

//Variables from Flash become data for MySQL.
$sql="INSERT INTO $bilz_table (ename, email)
VALUES('$name','$email')";

//Use the query function to send record to MySQL.
mysql_query($sql,$hookup);

?>
```

Save the PHP file as flash_in_new_records.php and put it in your root directory or in a folder in the root directory. Flash accesses this file, and the GET method sends variables from Flash to PHP.

Inputting data in Flash

The Flash 5 portion of inputting data is quite simple. The Flash movie requires only two input text fields to collect the data to be sent to PHP and on to MySQL and a button to fire the ActionScript. Figure 4-16 shows the SWF file displaying the two text fields and the button.

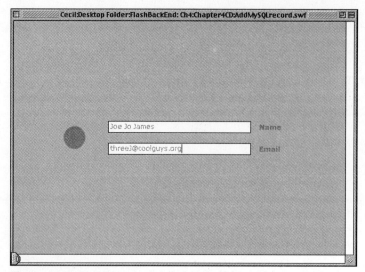

Figure 4-16: An input movie sends information for two fields to the MySQL database.

Use the following layers in developing the movie:

- ✦ Input Fields
- ✦ Button

Save the Flash movie as AddMySQLrecord.fla.

Input Fields layer
Use the following steps to add the input fields:

1. Use the Text tool to create two text fields with widths of 250. The Info panel will help you set the correct width. Arrange the text fields one above the other (see Figure 4-16).

2. Open the Text Options panel and select Input Text from the top pop-up menu. In the Variable box, type **name** for the top text field and **email** for the bottom text field. When these variables are sent to the PHP script, the names will be recognized as $name and $email.

3. Label the top text field **Name** and the bottom one **Email**, as shown in Figure 4-16.

Button layer
The button's sole purpose is to contain a single script to fire the PHP script:

1. Use the Oval tool to draw a circle.

2. Select the circle and press the F8 key to open the Symbol Properties dialog box. Select Button for Behavior and enter **FireInput** as the name. Click OK.

3. Select the button and open the ActionScript editor. Then enter the following script substituting your own domain name or IP address:

```
on (release) {
    loadVariablesNum
("http://www.sandlight.com/scripts/flash_in_new_records.php",
0, "GET");
}
```

Although creating the Flash movie is quite easy, the movie provides a great deal of help in managing the database. Instead of having to use the MySQL commands either in the MySQL monitor or through phpMyAdmin in the hosting service, you can just type a name and e-mail address in Flash and click the button.

Retrieving records from a table with Flash

Getting records from a MySQL database via PHP and sending them to Flash for output requires a little more information. The PHP script first makes the connection and selects the database. Then the script queries the MySQL table with the `SELECT` statement. To better illustrate what happens when you select data from a table, everything on the table in this example is selected through the use of the wildcard asterisk (*) and stored in a variable. After all of the data is obtained, the next set of statements in PHP finds the precise data you need.

Initially, the `SELECT * FROM tablename` pulls out all the information in the table and stores it in a variable named `$result`. Next, the `mysql_result()` function returns the data in one cell from a result set. The result set is broken down into the row and field. For example, the following statement stores the returns of the contents of row 1 of the `ename` field from the result set of the `emailflash` table stored in the `$result` variable:

```
$name=(mysql_result($result,1,"ename"));
```

You can change the row value (1) to anything you want as long as your number is from 0 to the number of rows in your table minus 1. (If you have 6 rows, the top row would be 5 because the first row is 0.)

Because the `ename` field contains a name of someone, the `$name` variable now should contain the name of whomever you put into the second row (row 1) of the table. To pass that name to Flash, you need to translate it into a format that Flash understands. The following line does that:

```
$name ="name=$name";
```

You should have a text field with the `name` variable in your Flash 5 movie so that when the `echo "$name";` statement executes, you can see it on the screen.

A similar translation for the second field, email, has to have an ampersand in front of it because it is a new variable for Flash. In the second translation line, you see an ampersand (&) attached to the beginning of the first email in quotation marks.

```
$email ="&email=$email";
```

Without the ampersand, Flash would treat the data from $email as part of the $name variable and send the output to the variable titled name.

Save the script in Listing 4-1 as select_fields_flash.php and put it into your root directory or a subdirectory in the root directory. After you have successfully run the program with Flash, change the record to something other than 1 in the following lines:

```
$name=(mysql_result($result,1,"ename"));
```

and

```
$email  =(mysql_result($result,1 ,"email"));
```

Make sure that the numbers you change are the same for both lines. Otherwise, the name and e-mail won't match one another.

Listing 4-1: **The select_fields_flash.php File**

```php
<?php

//Set up and connect
$server="localhost"; //Server name
$user="sandligh_willie";       //Username
$pass="yourOwnPW";      //Password
$flashbase ="sandligh_flash1"; //Database name
$bilz_table ="emailflash";  //Table name

//Make the connection
$hookup = mysql_connect($server, $user, $pass the connection

//Select database
mysql_select_db($flashbase,$hookup);

//Query specific table in database
$result = mysql_query("SELECT * FROM $bilz_table",$hookup);

//Select field and record number from query data
$name=(mysql_result($result,1,"ename"));

//Turn it into Flash variable format
```

```
$name ="name=$name";
echo "$name";

//Select a different field from the same record
$email  =(mysql_result($result,1 ,"email"));

//Turn it into a second Flash variable beginning with '&'
$email ="&email=$email";
echo "$email";
?>
```

Displaying the database information in Flash

The Flash 5 movie to launch the PHP script and display the database information requires a single button and two separate fields. It's almost identical to the previous movie except that both of the text fields are output fields. Use Figure 4-16 as a guide to see where the text fields and button go.

Use the following layers in developing the movie:

✦ From Database

✦ Button

From Database layer

Both of the text fields in this layer are Dynamic Text fields with a single line. The top one contains the variable name name, and the bottom one should have the variable name email. To the right of the fields, label the top field **Name** and the bottom one **Email Address**. Each text field is 200 pixels in length.

Button layer

The ActionScript code for the button only receives data from the PHP script, so no GET method is required. After creating a button, select it, open the Object Actions panel, and enter the following code in the ActionScript editor substituting your own domain name or IP address:

```
on (release) {
    loadVariablesNum
("http://www.sandlight.com/scripts/select_fields_flash.php",
0);
}
```

Test the movie by choosing Control ➪ Test Movie from the menu bar. When you click the button, you should see the name and e-mail address for the person you had entered into the MySQL database in the second row (row 1). Change the row number in the PHP script, resave the file, and click the button in Flash again. You should get a different record.

Controlling record retrieval

The next step is to control record retrieval from MySQL using Flash. By making slight variations in the PHP script, you can create a Flash movie that can easily scroll through the records. In Listing 4-2, the variable $rn (for record number) has replaced the literal used for the record indicator in the previous PHP script.

Listing 4-2: **PHP Script for Controlled Record Retrieval**

```php
<?php

//Set up and connect
$server="localhost";                      //Server name
$user="sandligh_willie";                  //Username
$pass="yourOwnPW";                        //Password
$flashbase ="sandligh_flash1"; //Database name

//Make the connection
$hookup = mysql_connect($server, $user, $pass);

//Select database
mysql_select_db($flashbase,$hookup);

//Query specific table in database
$result = mysql_query("SELECT * FROM emailflash",$hookup);

//Flash sends variable data 'rn' to PHP script--$rn
$name=(mysql_result($result,$rn,"ename"));

//Turn it into Flash variable format
$name ="name=$name";
echo "$name";

//Flash variable value remains constant for both fields
$email  =(mysql_result($result,$rn ,"email"));

//Turn it into a second Flash variable beginning with '&'
$email ="&email=$email";
echo "$email";
?>
```

The Flash front end for the PHP script requires both input and output fields. The input sent to the PHP script selects the record number for the two fields. (References to record numbers are the same as references to row numbers in the MySQL table.) Then the PHP script queries the MySQL database and returns the selected records to PHP and then on to output in two Flash windows: one for the name and the other for the e-mail address. The difference is that the user controls which record number is selected. Figure 4-17 shows the SWF file along with the buttons and text fields. The button on the left is green and increments the record number, and the red button on the right decrements the record number, enabling the user to scroll through the records. The movie, called `click_record.fla`, uses the following three layers:

✦ Output from MySQL

✦ Selected Record

✦ Buttons

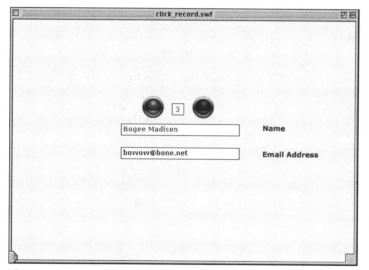

Figure 4-17: Two buttons in Flash control the record to be retrieved from the MySQL database.

Output from MySQL layer

The following steps show how to set up the Output from MySQL layer:

1. Use the Text tool to create two text fields and place one above the other as shown in Figure 4-17. Open the Text Options panel by clicking the Text icon on the launcher bar and then selecting the Text Options tab.

2. Select the top text field and then select Dynamic Text from the top pop-up menu in the Text Options panel. Type the word **name** in the Variable text box. Repeat the process for the bottom text field except type in the word **email** in the Variable text box. Both fields should have the Border/Bg check box checked.

Selected Record layer

The Selected Record layer consists of a single text field. Use the Text tool to draw a single text field and select Input Text from the pop-up menu in the Text Options panel. In the Variable text box, type **rn** as the variable name used to choose the record number from the MySQL file. Center the text field above the bottom two text fields using Figure 4-17 as a guide.

Button layer

The Button layer has two buttons on either side of the text field that displays the record number. One button increments the record number, and the second one decrements it. The following steps show how to set up these buttons:

1. Choose Window ➪ Common Libraries ➪ Buttons from the menu bar. When the Library-Buttons.fla window appears, select the folder titled (circle) LED Button Set. Drag one each of a red button and a green button from the folder and place them on either side of the record display text field.

2. Double-click the green button to enter the Symbol Editing mode. Select the button in the Up frame and change its size to W=35, H=35 using the Info panel. Repeat the process in the Over frame. In the Down frame, change the dimensions to W=25, H=25. Exit the Symbol Editing mode, and then re-enter the mode by double-clicking the red button. Repeat the same process for the red button. Exit the Symbol Editing mode.

3. Select the green button and open the Object Actions panel and ActionScript editor by clicking the Show Actions icon on the launcher bar. Enter the following ActionScript, substituting your own domain name or IP address for the domain shown:

```
on (release) {
rn +=1;
    loadVariablesNum
("http://www.sandlight.com/scripts/record_browse.php", 0,
"GET");
}
```

4. Select the red button and open the Object Actions panel and ActionScript editor by clicking the Show Actions icon on the launcher bar. Enter the following ActionScript substituting your own domain name or IP address for the domain shown:

```
on (release) {
rn -=1;
    loadVariablesNum
("http://www.sandlight.com/scripts/record_browse.php", 0,
"GET");
}
```

Using Flash as a database search-and-retrieval front end

The purpose of any front-end application is to make it easy for the user to accomplish a task that would not be better achieved by some other method. The task of entering data is far simpler using Flash as a front end than either trying to put the data in the MySQL monitor directly or writing scripts for PHP to enter data into MySQL. (Usually, the easier the task is for the user, the more challenging the programmer's work is.)

In this last PHP script, the goal is to take a string sent from Flash and then open MySQL and see whether a matching string can be found in the database. If a matching string is located, then the e-mail address for that string will be sent back to Flash as output. After making the connection and selecting the database, the script makes the query to the database, as has been done in the previous scripts. Then using the `mysql_num_rows()` function, the script finds the number of rows in the table. One (1) is then subtracted from the number of rows returned because the row numbers begin with 0 instead of 1.

To search for the matching record, a counter variable beginning with 0 is initialized, followed by a loop that goes through all the records until a match is found or the maximum of records is exceeded. The `$search` variable is initiated as `search` in Flash, passing on the name typed in by the user. Once the match is made, the match variable uses the counter minus 1 as the record number. (The counter increments once after the match, so 1 must be subtracted so that the match variable [`$match`] gets the correct data.) If no matches are made, the script defines `$email` as `"Name not found."`

Finally, the data is converted into a format that Flash can read. The `echo` statement then sends it along its way, and the data is displayed as output in Flash. Save the script in Listing 4-3 as `search_record.php` in the root directory or a subdirectory within the root directory.

Listing 4-3: **The search_record.php File**

```php
<?php

//Set up and connect
$server="localhost";              //Server name
$user="sandligh_willie";          //Username
$pass="yourOwnPW";                //Password
$flashbase ="sandligh_flash1";    //Database name
$bilz_table="emailflash";         //Table name

//Make the connection
$hookup = mysql_connect($server, $user, $pass);
```

Continued

Listing 4-3 *(continued)*

```
//Select database
mysql_select_db($flashbase,$hookup);

//Query specific table in database and find the number of rows
in the table
$result = mysql_query("SELECT * FROM $bilz_table",$hookup);
$numrows=mysql_num_rows($result);
$numrows = $numrows-1;

//Search for match
$counter=0;
do  {
$name=(mysql_result($result,$counter,"ename"));
++$counter;
}
while ($search != $name && $counter <= $numrows);

//Define match variable and find the match
$match=$counter-1;
$email = (mysql_result($result,$match,"email"));

//Name is not in database
if($search != $name) {
$email="Name not found.";
}

//Turn the results into a format Flash can read
$email ="email=$email";
echo "$email";

?>
```

The Flash side of the equation requires three elements: an input field, an output field, and a button to launch the ActionScript program that fires the PHP script. To get started, create the following four layers and save the FLA file as `search_record.fla`:

✦ Background

✦ Search Field

✦ From Database

✦ Button

Figure 4-18 shows the initial setup of the movie with all of its layers and components, and Table 4-8 provides the values for the color palette.

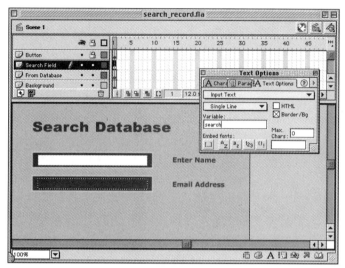

Figure 4-18: The top text field contains a search word sent to the PHP script to locate an e-mail address in the MySQL database.

| Table 4-8 | | | |
| Color Palette for search_record.fla | | | |
Color	*R Value*	*G Value*	*B Value*
A	6B	00	55
B	D1	B8	F8
C	FF	CC	00

Background layer

All of the labels and backdrops for the text fields are placed in this layer. The following steps explain how to set up the layer:

    1. Use Color A from the palette for the labels **Search Database, Enter Name,** and **Email Address**.

2. With the Rectangle tool, draw the rectangle backdrops for the text fields using Color A for the fill and Color C for the stroke. Set the stroke to 3 in the Stroke panel. Each backdrop should have dimensions of W=220, H=28. Use Color B for the background color.

3. Lock the layer when you are finished.

Search Field layer

The Search Field layer contains the text field for the user input:

1. Use the Text tool to draw a text field with the dimensions W=200, H=19. Open the Text Options panel and select Input Text from the top pop-up menu.

2. Type in **search** in the Variable text box in the Text Options panel. The `search` variable is sent to the PHP file to find out whether a match for it exists in the MySQL file.

3. Check the Border/Bg check box in the Text Options panel.

From Database layer

In the From Database layer, you create the field to receive information from the PHP script:

1. Use the Text tool to draw a text field with the dimensions W=200, H=19. Use the Text Options panel to select Input Text from the top pop-up menu.

2. In the Text Options panel's Variable text box, type **email** for the variable name. This variable passes the data from the PHP script back to Flash as output. Deselect Border/Bg for this field.

Button layer

Like the other buttons used in this chapter, this one's primary purpose is to launch the PHP script and send a variable originating in Flash to the PHP script:

1. Using Color A as the stroke and Color C as the fill, work with the Oval tool to draw a circle.

2. Select the circle and Press F8 to open the Symbol Properties dialog box. Select Button for the Behavior, name the button **NowSearch**, and click OK.

3. Select the button and click the Show Actions icon on the launcher bar to open the Actions Panel and ActionScript Editor. In the ActionScript editor, type the following script, substituting your own domain name or IP address:

```
on (release) {
    loadVariablesNum
("http://www.sandlight.com/scripts/search_record.php", 0,
"GET");
}
```

Figure 4-19 shows the Flash movie in action.

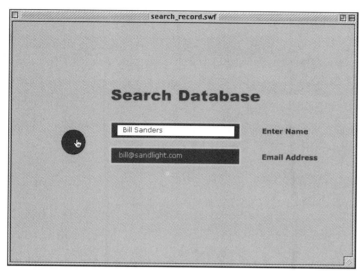

Figure 4-19: The e-mail address in the same record as the search name is returned to an output field.

Summary

As a server-side language, PHP is very easy to use and format for use with Flash. Variables can be passed back and forth between PHP and Flash easily using data from forms in Flash or from calculated data stored in variables to a PHP script. In conjunction with MySQL, PHP can store data from a Flash form in a database. Likewise, Flash can go through a PHP script to access data in a MySQL database and show it on the screen. Also, because Flash is fully cross-browser compatible, you don't have to worry about creating different scripts for the different browsers when it comes to accessing data in forms.

In Chapters 10 and 11, PHP is employed with Flash to create an eBusiness site for potential customers and a Flash administrative tool to process orders online customers make. You will see further uses of PHP with Flash, including a module that automatically sends an email from PHP. Because this book only scratches the surface of what PHP can do, take a look at the many excellent PHP books that are available.

✦   ✦   ✦

Back End Objects and Printing

Reading XML Documents with Flash 5

✦ ✦ ✦ ✦

In This Chapter

Writing a basic XML document

Transferring XML data to Flash

Using Flash to find the XML data you need

✦ ✦ ✦ ✦

Almost any introduction to Extensible Markup Language (XML) in a single chapter may appear either glib or uninformed due to the rich conceptual framework and document object model (DOM) of XML. However, to jump into lots of examples of loading an XML document into Flash 5 without any discussion of XML courts disaster. As you see in this chapter, the ActionScript for gathering up data from XML requires more than intuitively hooking up the ActionScript XML objects to a file written in XML. You can wrestle a good deal with ActionScript only to find that the XML document is not well-formed and all the ActionScript in the world can't help you out. So, although this introduction to XML is hardly more than a brief encounter, it is an important step to take before leaping into a Flash 5 example without a clue of what XML is all about. Far from warning you off using XML with Flash 5, this chapter shows you why you should learn everything you can about XML.

Structuring Data with XML

XML is at its heart a way of organizing and structuring data, and it may well become *the* model for dealing with data on the Web. Unlike HTML, XML has no formatting tags; it has tags only for ordering data. What's more, you provide names for the tags that make sense to you instead of using a predefined set of tags, as is the case with HTML. For example, you can probably figure out what the following XML data structures are by looking at the names of the tags and the elements made up of tag pairs (for example, `<name> </name>`):

```
<?xml version="1.0" ?>
<eFolks>
   <contact>
    <name>Bill Sanders</name>
    </contact>
   <contact>
    <name>Mark Winstanley</name>
    </contact>
</eFolks>
```

You can write this document in your favorite text editor, such as Notepad in Windows or SimpleText on the Macintosh. Save it as `contact1.xml`. (All XML documents can be written and saved as text files.) If you load that document into a browser that reads XML (Internet Explorer 5 or Netscape Navigator 6), you would see the following:

```
Bill Sanders Mark Winstanley
```

XML is for structuring data, and you need something to show that data in a useful way. Most developers use Cascading Style Sheets (CSS). For example, the following CSS script provides formatting in the form of a 14-point bold green font for the data in the XML file:

```
name {display:block; font-size: 14pt; color: #009900;font-weight: bold}
```

By saving the file as an external style sheet named `contact.css`, you can use it to format the elements with the tag label `name`. Now the XML document looks like the following example:

```
<?xml version="1.0" ?>
<?xml-stylesheet type="text/css" href="contact.css" ?>
<eFolks>
   <contact>
    <name>Bill Sanders</name>
    </contact>
   <contact>
    <name>Mark Winstanley</name>
    </contact>
</eFolks>
```

The output is now formatted, as shown in Figure 5-1.

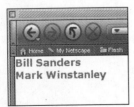

Figure 5-1: XML requires formatting from another source because XML does not have its own formatting tags.

Because XML has no formatting capabilities, Flash 5 can come to the rescue and take care of the data formatting. In previous chapters in this book, you see again and again that Flash 5 can take data out of any database and display it in any way the developer wants. Designers have far more freedom and options using Flash 5 to display data in text fields than they do when using HTML. And now that ActionScript includes XML objects in its source code, using Flash 5 as a front end for XML databases is a far better option than using limited HTML pages.

The rules of writing XML

Although XML is a close cousin of HTML because both share a common ancestry in Standard Generalized Markup Language (SGML), the two languages are very different when it comes to the rules for writing. The following list summarizes the differences:

✦ XML is case-sensitive, and HTML is not. So if you have a `<Name>` tag, do not try to use `<name>` in XML.

✦ XML has no formatting tags of its own.

✦ The user defines the element names. (An opening and a closing tag constitute an element: `<name>` `</name>`.)

✦ XML requires newer browsers than HTML does. Internet Explorer 5 and Netscape Communicator 6 are the earliest browsers that can reliably read XML.

✦ XML is unforgiving for little mistakes, but HTML is very loose and forgiving.

✦ All XML elements must have a closing tag (for example, `<customer>` and `</customer>`); HTML lets you get away with a single opening tag (such as `<br>`).

✦ Well-formed XML requires a Document Type Definition (DTD) or schema for each element.

✦ All elements are self-contained mini-XML documents.

Creating an XML document

To create an XML document, you need to first declare it as an XML document. You do so with the following line:

```
<?xml version="1.0" ?>
```

You can add more information, such as whether the XML document depends on another XML document or is a standalone. It defaults to standalone. You may also select from a number of encoding values. Here is a partial list:

✦ `UTF-8`: Compressed Unicode, to which XML defaults

✦ `UTD-16`: Compressed Universal Character System

✦ ISO-8859-1: Western European Languages

✦ ISO-2022-JP: Japanese

If you want to include encoding values, you would enter the following:

```
<?xml version="1.0" encoding="iso-8859-1" ?>
```

But for most applications that are not linked to another XML file, all you need is the version number in your declaration.

Creating a root element

After you create the XML document declaration, you need a root declaration to create a root element. The *root element* contains everything you put into the XML document. In other words, all the other elements must lie between the tags identifying the beginning and end of your root element. In the XML example we've been using, the root element is `<eFolks>`:

```
<?xml version="1.0" ?>
<eFolks>

all of the other elements

</eFolks>
```

The name `eFolks` can be in all uppercase, all lowercase, or a combination as used in the example. Remember, though, that whatever combination of cases you use, you will be using that same combination throughout the document. Unlike HTML, which is not case-sensitive, XML very much is.

Creating other elements

After you put in the root element, everything that follows is a child of the root element, and the root element is the parent of the elements within its opening and closing set of tags. The terms *parent*, *element*, and *child element* refer to the relationship of XML elements that are part of a set of elements defined within a root element. The following is an example of a set of XML elements with a parent element and child element:

```
<parent>
    <child>Larry</child>
    <child>Curly</child>
    <child>Mo</child>
</parent>
```

The three child elements with the data Larry, Curly, and Mo are siblings because they share a common parent element (`<parent>`). In the Flash 5 ActionScript XML objects, you see methods referring to child, parent, and sibling; these methods address the set of parent and child element references (see Table 5-1).

Table 5-1
Flash 5 XML Objects with Child, Parent, or Sibling References

Methods	Properties
appendChild	firstChild
hasChildNodes	lastChild
	nextSibling
	parentNode
	previousSibling

After you declare your document and root elements, you can declare all the other elements in your XML document:

```
<?xml version="1.0" ?>
<eFolks>
   <contact>
    <name>Bill Sanders</name>
     <email>bill@sandlight.com</email>
    </contact>
   <contact>
    <name>Mark Winstanley</name>
     <email>mark@smoggywood.com</email>
    </contact>
</eFolks>
```

In the preceding example, the XML document now has the following four elements:

✦ eFolks

✦ contact

✦ name

✦ email

The example uses repeated elements. The root element appears only once, but all other elements can repeat as often as needed. For example, the contact, name, and email elements are all employed twice.

Creating document type definitions

Understanding and correctly using document type definitions (DTD) with XML pages can be a bit tricky, and unless you are careful, you can create a poorly formed XML file that doesn't work correctly when you attempt to load data from the file into Flash. Basically, DTD tells the parser what type of data can be expected in the different elements that make up your page. If you do not provide the right information, problems occur. In the simple pages demonstrated so far, we have not bothered to include a DTD, but not doing so severely restricts what can be done with the data. DTD is the connection between the XML processor and the application receiving the data.

DTD and the one-trick pony

To see how to set up and use DTD, take a look at the following example, where the root element is the only element in the document:

```
<?xml version="1.0" ?>
<!DOCTYPE eFolks [
<!ELEMENT eFolks (#PCDATA)>
]>
<eFolks>DTD makes this a well-formed page. </eFolks>
```

Save this document as oneTrick.xml and load it into your browser to make sure that it works correctly. If the document parses correctly, you see the following on-screen message: DTD makes this a well-formed page.

The format for an internal DTD begins with the following lines:

```
<!DOCTYPE rootElement [
<!ELEMENT rootElement (element[s] or dataType) >
]>
```

Because the oneTrick.xml file has only a single element, the root element is described as a data type, #PCDATA (character data), instead of in terms of the elements that it embodies. Usually, the root element consists of one or more other elements, but this simple example shows a minimalist and (almost) bulletproof instance of how to work with DTD.

Note

A developing alternative to DTD is *schema*. Like DTD, schema is a set of validation rules for XML documents, but it is written in XML style and enables you to validate data types such as integer, time, and date. World Wide Web Consortium (W3C) is working on a schema recommendation, and Microsoft Corporation has developed its own schema vocabulary that can be learned and used. To see W3C's progress on its schema draft and Microsoft's schema, visit www.w3.org/TR/xmlschema-1/ and http://msdn.microsoft.com/xml/reference/schema/start.asp.

XML validation

Because both Internet Explorer 5 and Netscape Communicator 6 can parse XML, you would think they could validate the code as well. They cannot. But if you attempt to bring invalid XML into Flash 5, you can run into problems. Before you start thinking about the ActionScript, you need to work with XML and to validate your XML with a validation application. If you make a mistake in your DTD, a validation program makes that fact abundantly clear.

Several applications are available for XML validation, but my favorite is at Brown University. The URL for the Scholarly Technology Group's validation page at Brown is `www.stg.brown.edu/service/xmlvalid/`. The initial page provides a window where you can browse your hard drive for your XML files, as shown in Figure 5-2.

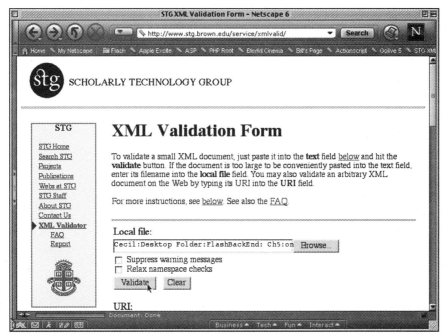

Figure 5-2: An online validation form enables you to check the validity of your XML and DTD.

After you select the file that you want to validate, click the Validate button (refer to Figure 5-2). If your XML file is well-formed, you see a validation message, as shown in Figure 5-3.

If your XML is not well-formed, all your errors are paraded before you (as shown in Figure 5-4), and sometimes you can immediately tell where the problem lies. The significance of a valid DTD is that errors tend to be magnified if an error on one level leads to errors on others. In this case, the sins of the parent nodes are truly visited on the child nodes.

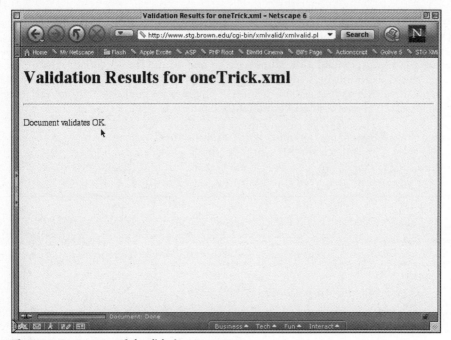

Figure 5-3: A successful validation message.

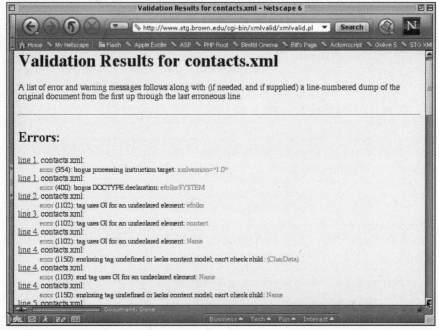

Figure 5-4: If mistakes are encountered in the coding or DTD, the errors are listed.

Data types and well-formed XML

DTD can be formatted as part of the XML document, or it can be placed in an external file. For this first example, the DTD remains in the XML document so that you can see both the DTD format and the document. The code for the file you are creating is in Listing 5-1. The rest of the section explains what this code is doing.

Listing 5-1: **The contacts.xml File**

```
<?xml version="1.0" ?>
<!DOCTYPE eFolks [
<!ELEMENT eFolks (contact+)>
<!ELEMENT contact (name,email)>
<!ELEMENT name (#PCDATA)>
<!ELEMENT email (#PCDATA)>
]>
<eFolks>
    <contact>
        <name>Bill Sanders</name>
        <email>bill@sandlight.com</email>
    </contact>
    <contact>
      <name>Mark Winstanley</name>
        <email>mark@smoggywood.com</email>
    </contact>
    <contact>
        <name>Betty Boop</name>
        <email>ooh@speakez.net</email>
    </contact>
</eFolks>
```

In this example, the first !ELEMENT definition is of the root element, eFolks, which is defined in terms of the contact element. Because the root element contains more than one contact element, the description of the data must include a plus (+) sign after it. So the data type definition for the root element is (contact+).

The next element is contact, and all the contact elements contain one name element and one email element. To order the data in an XML file when defining the data, place a comma (,) between each of the elements in the definition. (If it doesn't matter which order they're in, use the vertical bar (|) or pipe character to separate elements in the definition.) Because we want the person's name to come before the e-mail address, we wrote the definition as (name,email). You may wonder why we didn't place a plus (+) sign after each of the two elements because the document clearly has more than a single element of both. If you look between the <eFolks> and </eFolks> tags, you see more than one <contact> tag. However, if you look between the <contact> and </contact> tags, only a single instance of both the name and email elements appear. All that's left to do is to define the name and `email` elements. Because they contain no other elements, and they do contain character data, both are defined using `(#PCDATA)`.

After you finish, save the document as `contacts.xml` and use a validation program to make certain that the document is well formed. After you validate the `contacts.xml` document, put it in the directory where you create the Flash movies for this book. It serves as the basis for your initial Flash movie that brings in XML.

Continuing with XML

Before going on to the next section where you see how to use XML documents with Flash, we want to emphasize the fact that this introduction to XML only touches on some key features of XML. We left out far more than we included in our discussion. However, we wanted to provide a clear path from basic XML to using XML with Flash 5 instead of focusing on creating XML documents in all their nuances. XML is an elegant solution to storing and retrieving databases and is nowhere near as limited as this short introduction may have made XML appear to be. Elements can have attributes, entities, and far more than simple data or other elements. Likewise, XML documents can contain other languages and functions (for example, JavaScript). So, although we could add further materials about XML documents, we leave that exploration to you and other books on this important language. For now, we need to discuss linking Flash 5 and XML.

 Note

Top on our list of recommended reading is *XML: A Primer* (Second Edition), by Simon St. Laurent (IDG Books Worldwide, Inc.). St. Laurent's book explains why XML is important, what the DOM is, and how to get started in XML. For writing XML, look at *XML: Your Visual Blueprint for Building Expert Web Pages*, by Emily Vander Veer and Rev Mengle (IDG Books Worldwide, Inc.). This book breaks down the process of writing XML into microsteps. Pay close attention to the section on setting up your Document Type Definition (DTD).

Reading XML in Flash

After you create your validated XML document, you are ready to begin exploring what can be done with Flash as a front end to read and present XML on the Web in a Flash movie. As you see in previous chapters, loading data into Flash 5 requires a translation process so that Flash can read the data. The same is true with XML files except that you are not required to use the `variable1=data&variable2=more data` format. You can bring in data directly from the elements in the XML document. But the way in which the data comes in depends on your DTD as well as your ActionScript.

Bringing in data from XML to Flash

The best way to get started is to begin with a simple Flash movie and the `contacts.xml` document. The movie takes the information from the XML document and presents it in a Flash 5 window.

> **Note** Although commenting code is a good habit and one to which we both subscribe, the ActionScript code in the following examples contains no comments. By first showing the script without comments and then discussing each section of code in text, we can better present the flow and structures of the ActionScript and provide more in-depth explanation of the code.

Creating the Flash movie

This Flash movie contains a single script in the first frame to load the data into a text field. But unlike some of the earlier chapters where you are merely required to use `loadVariablesNum()` and decide whether to POST or GET your variables, extracting XML data is a bit more interesting in ActionScript. The first movie should be saved as `FirstContact.fla` using the following three layers:

✦ ActionScript

✦ Text Field

✦ Background

The color scheme is simply a black background, a dark gold backdrop rectangle, and the white from the text field's background. Figure 5-5 shows the initial setup.

Background layer

Follow these steps to create the Background layer:

1. Choose Modify ⇨ Movie and change the background color to black.

2. Draw a dark gold (#FFCC00) rectangle in the middle of the stage with the dimensions W=320, H=205.

3. Above the rectangle, use the Text tool to type **XML Database** and position the text above the rectangle, as shown in Figure 5-5. Use a 16-point bold Verdana text in the same dark gold color as the rectangle.

4. Select the rectangle and then press down the Shift key and press the up arrow key four times and the left arrow key four times to provide the correct offset from the center where the text field is to be positioned.

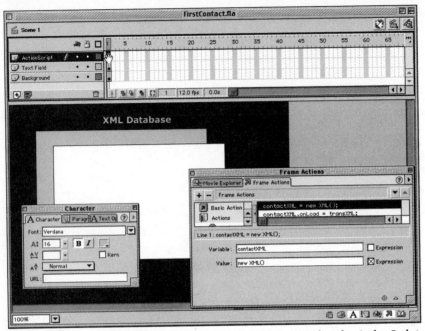

Figure 5-5: Most of the work to set up the movie is in creating the ActionScript.

Text Field layer

Create the Text Field layer with these steps:

1. Using the Text tool, create a dynamic text field with the Border/Bg box checked and the dimensions set to W=320, H=205.

2. In the Text Options panel, type **display** for the variable name.

3. Use the Align panel to set the text field in the vertical and horizontal center of the stages.

ActionScript layer

Now that your movie's structure is established, you're ready to add the ActionScript that brings the XML data into your Flash movie. Click the first frame in the ActionScript layer and right-click the mouse (Cmd+click on the Macintosh) and choose Action. After the Frame Actions panel opens, type the following script in the ActionScript editor. (You're likely to find using the Expert mode for this script easier. Press Ctrl+E/Cmd+E to enter the Expert mode in the Frame Actions window.)

```
contactXML = new XML();
contactXML.onLoad = transXML;
display = "Getting XML.";
contactXML.load("contacts.xml");
function transXML () {
```

```
    if (this.loaded) {
        display = "XML data is up.";
    }
    keyTag = new XML();
    contactList = new Array();
    keyTag = this.lastChild;
    contactList = keyTag.childNodes;
    display = "";
    for (kid=1; kid<=contactList.length; kid += 2) {
        display += contactList[kid];
    }
}
```

After you finish, make sure that you save the Flash file in the same directory or folder as the contacts.xml file. If you get an error message indicating that the movie is having trouble loading the XML file, first check to see where your SWF file is located. If it's in a different directory than your XML document, put them both in the same directory or folder. Test your movie by pressing Ctrl+Enter or Cmd+Return. Figure 5-6 shows what you see if all is working according to plan.

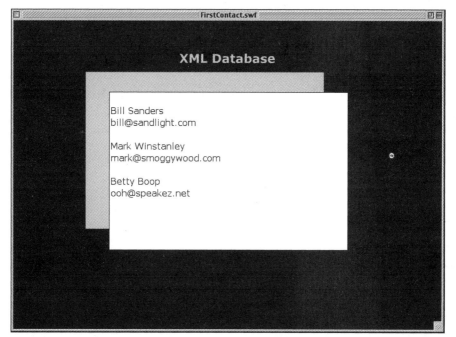

Figure 5-6: The data on-screen reflects the data in the XML document.

Dissecting the code

Now that you have a working program, time to see what happened. The ActionScript used is a very simple application of XML objects, but these objects represent a good starting point. You may want to get out your Flash 5 manual and note the different types of XML objects used.

The constructor object

The first line employs the XML `constructor` object. With the `constructor` object, you provide an object for the XML document you are loading:

```
contactXML = new XML();
```

We used a name for the object that related to the XML data and document rather than using a more generic name.

Loading the data

Most of the work that is done to gather up, parse, and output the XML data occurs inside of a big function. After your establish your XML object in the first step, you can invoke the `onLoad` method and assign the function name to the process, as follows:

```
contactXML.onLoad = transXML;
```

If you have a big XML document, you may want to give the user something to look at while waiting for the data. By assigning a loading message, as in the following example, you let the user know that the job is under way:

```
display = "Getting XML.";
```

Next, you specify the XML file from which you plan to extract the data. The XML `load` method requires only the file's URL. (Because we always put the XML documents in the same folder/directory as the SWF file, we have short URLs.)

```
contactXML.load("contacts.xml");
```

After the loading process begins, you fire the function that is initiated by the `onLoad` method.

The big function

After the loading process begins, your next step is to have a function that handles all the data arriving in your Flash movie. You have already specified the name of the function when you used the `onLoad` method, so make sure that your function uses the same name but add a set of parentheses, as follows:

```
function transXML () {
```

Next, you can employ the XML `loaded` method to check whether all the data are loaded. The self-reference `this` provides the name of whatever is currently being loaded:

```
if (this.loaded) {
    display = "XML data is up.";
}
```

Usually, the viewer doesn't see that message very long because as soon as it arrives, the text field is filled with the XML data. But you can easily create a special text field to place the messages about the loading of the data and have a separate text field for the data itself. With larger files, a message field can serve both for error-checking and giving the viewer something to assure him that the data is loaded.

Two more objects need to be declared: an object for the root node and an array that collects all the data. We used the label `keyTag` for the root node label and `contactList` for the array within the root node, as follows:

```
keyTag = new XML();
contactList = new Array();
```

To find the root node, you just use the last child's node name. The closing tag's element name is the same as the root element's opening tag and so is considered the "last child." (To check this out, comment out the loop by using double slashes in this next section and type **display=keyTag.nodeName;**. The text field displays eFolks, the root node.) Declare the `keyTag` variable as the root directory.

```
keyTag = this.lastChild;
```

Now that you have the root node in a variable, you can define the child nodes of the root node as an array. While you're at it, you may as well clear the display text field:

```
contactList = keyTag.childNodes;
display = "";
```

Finally, you want to get the elements out of the array `contactList`. Use a loop to go through the array. The counter named `kid` is used to remind you that the two elements that make up the `contact` element are its child nodes, as follows:

```
for (kid=1; kid<=contactList.length; kid += 2) {
    display += contactList[kid];
}
}
```

Extending the data fields but not the ActionScript

Suppose that you want to extend the information you have in your XML database. You decide that, in addition to the names and e-mail addresses, you want to store the phone numbers as well. What's more, you want to display the whole thing in Flash. A well-formed XML document can be revised easily, and because the data were organized with the idea that more information categories (fields) may need to be added, the task is a simple one. You must, however, take care to revise the DTD to reflect the new fields.

For purposes of illustration, we are adding only one new field for a telephone number to the contacts document. All you need to do is to declare a phone element in the DTD and include the phone element in the contact declaration. Then, within the contact containers, add the phone elements. The bold text in Listing 5-2 shows where changes are made from the original contacts.xml document. All you need to do is load the contacts.xml document, make the changes, and then save this new XML document as contactPh.xml in the same directory as your Flash movie.

Listing 5-2: **The contactPh.xml File**

```
<?xml version="1.0" encoding="UTF-8"?>
<!DOCTYPE eFolks [
<!ELEMENT eFolks (contact+)>
<!ELEMENT contact (name,email,phone)>
<!ELEMENT name (#PCDATA)>
<!ELEMENT email (#PCDATA)>
<!ELEMENT phone (#PCDATA)>
]>
<eFolks>
   <contact>
      <name>Bill Sanders</name>
      <email>bill@sandlight.com</email>
      <phone>866-555-4321</phone>
   </contact>
   <contact>
      <name>Mark Winstanley</name>
      <email>mark@smoggywood.com</email>
      <phone>916-555-9434</phone>
   </contact>
   <contact>
      <name>Betty Boop</name>
      <email>ooh@speakez.net</email>
      <phone>415-555-1925</phone>
   </contact>
</eFolks>
```

On the Flash side of the equation, the only change you must make is to the name of the XML file that Flash loads. So you need to change the following line:

```
contactXML.load("contacts.xml");
```

You change the preceding line to the following:

```
contactXML.load("contactPh.xml");
```

Choose File ➪ Save As and save the new movie as `contactPh.fla`. Figure 5-7 shows that an entire new field is now added in this movie.

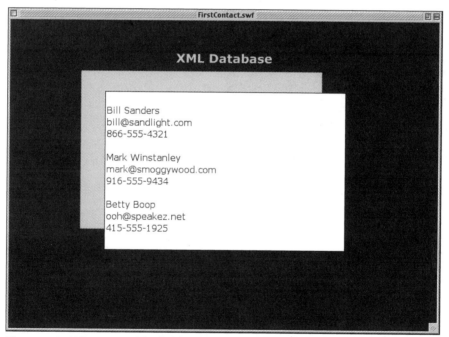

Figure 5-7: When you add a field (new element) to the XML file, the data in the new field can appear in Flash with no new additions to the ActionScript other than changing the name of the XML file to load.

Breaking down the data arrays further

As the data are now organized in the XML document, `contacts.xml`, getting contacts as units of names and e-mail addresses is easy. But what happens when you need to separate the names and e-mail addresses? If, for example, you wanted to do a search on a particular name in a *very large* XML database to find an e-mail address, you would need to scroll through a lot of output in Flash to get what you need. But if you could break up the data into discreet units, you could do a search on a name that would return an e-mail address associated with the search name and nothing else.

To create this new movie, all you need to do is load `FirstContact.fla` and save it as `SecondContact.fla`. Then add the new ActionScript to the first frame and you see a different output when you run the movie.

Creating a new array

Listing 5-3 in this section uses the sample XML file to show how the ActionScript breaks down the root node into the `contact` node's elements: `name` and `email`. First look at the ActionScript and then look at the explanation of the new code added to the initial ActionScript.

Listing 5-3: Extracting Individual Elements from an XML Array

```
contactXML = new XML();
contactXML.onLoad = transXML;
display = "Getting XML.";
contactXML.load("contacts.xml");
function transXML () {
  if (this.loaded) {
      display = "XML data is up.";
  }
  keyTag = new XML();
  nodeID = new XML();
  nameList = new Array();
  contactList = new Array();
  keyTag = this.lastChild;
  contactList = keyTag.childNodes;
  display = "";
  for (kid=0; kid<=contactList.length; kid++) {
    if (contactList[kid].nodeName.toLowerCase() == "contact") {
        nameList = contactList[kid].childNodes;
        for (nl=0; nl<=nameList.length; nl++) {
            nodeID = nameList[nl];
            elementID = nodeID.nodeName.toLowerCase();
            if (elementID == "name") {
                name = nodeID.firstChild.nodeValue;
            }
            if (elementID == "email") {
                email = nodeID.firstChild.nodeValue;
            }
        }
        display += name+" = "+email+newline;
    }
  }
}
```

In the previous section, the loop through the root's first child (`<contact>`) created an array for all the XML data, and because the data were well formed, outputting them to the text field (display) was simple. But to break up the elements that make up the `contact` element requires an array made up of the `contact` element. So the first order of business is to find the `contact` element using a loop through the big array called `contactList`, as follows:

```
for (kid=0; kid<=contactList.length; kid++) {
    if (contactList[kid].nodeName.toLowerCase() == "contact") {
```

As soon as the `contact` node is located, the `nameList` array is defined as the child nodes of the child nodes of the element of the array where the node name was identified. In other words, when an array element is identified, it is an array with its own elements. This can be confusing because XML elements refer to data within a tag container and array elements refer to elements of the array. (Remember from the XML document that the `contact` element is defined in terms of the `name` and `email` elements, so the `contact` element is indeed the parent node of the two child nodes, `name` and `email`, and the array extracts those child nodes of the `contact` element — or *grandchildren* of the root element.)

```
nameList = contactList[kid].childNodes;
```

After the array is identified, the script uses a loop to search the array for the `name` and `email` child nodes. The `nodeID` is an XML object used to capture the XML data. Then `elementID` becomes the variable name for the node name, as follows:

```
for (nl=0; nl<=nameList.length; nl++) {
nodeID = nameList[nl];
elementID = nodeID.nodeName.toLowerCase();
```

Next, the script checks to see whether the element is labeled `"name"` or `"email"`. If it is the former, the data are placed into the `name` variable, and if it is the latter, the data go into the `email` variable:

```
if (elementID == "name") {
name = nodeID.firstChild.nodeValue;
}
if (elementID == "email") {
email = nodeID.firstChild.nodeValue;
}
```

All that's left to do is to put the (now separate) datum into the output window in Flash. In creating your output, use caution in placing it among all of the closing curly braces generated by the multiple loops and the conditional statement, not to mention the big function, as follows:

```
}
display += name+" = "+email+newline;
        }
    }
}
```

Figure 5-8 shows what you now see with the reformatted data from the XML file.

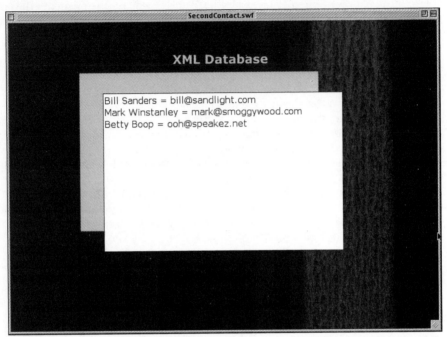

Figure 5-8: After the individual data elements are separated from the XML file, the ActionScript can rearrange their output.

Adding more nodes in the XML file

After you have your data contained in separate variables, you can add more data to your XML files without changing the ActionScript. If you want to add more child nodes to the contact node, all you need to do is to add more conditional statements to identify the new nodes and then add them to your concatenated output. Alternatively, each piece of datum in the file could be placed into its own array. Then you could easily search through the data to link different components of the same record. The next section shows how to do exactly that.

Searching for XML Data Using Flash

The use of Flash for pulling data out of an XML file is greatly enhanced by the ActionScript XML objects and further enhanced by a well-formed XML document. But most uses of databases require some mechanism for searching through data to give viewers what they want. As seen in previous chapters, middleware such as ASP and PHP search MySQL or Access files and then translate findings for Flash. So far, using XML documents as databases has not required any middleware at all, and in this next example, you see that you can create a search function in Flash 5 ActionScript that goes through the database and returns the information you need.

In the previous two projects, the XML elements are put into arrays. First, in the FirstContact.fla movie, the root element is placed into a big array that outputs combined data in the contact element. Second, in the SecondContact.fla movie, the contact element is broken down into an array, and the individual data elements are placed into two variables, name and email. The next step is to place the name and email items into an array instead of variables. By coordinating the element values in the arrays, matching record items is quite simple. You just use the same values in the two different array elements. The search process then becomes a matter of entering the search element in one text field, and using the variable name associated with the text field to search for the associated element in the same record (sibling set). In the Flash 5 movie project for this section, the name element is used to search for the associated email element.

Creating the XML search movie

This movie begins with a new stage and two different text fields and a button to launch a search. Open a new movie and enter the following five layers:

✦ Background

✦ Search Field

✦ Found Field

✦ Button

✦ ActionScript

Save the movie as SearchMe.fla and then add the colors in Table 5-2 to the Swatches panel.

Table 5-2
Color Palette for SearchMe.fla

Color	R Value	G Value	B Value
A	EB	DE	80
B	19	73	B8
C	F0	21	26
D (White)	FF	FF	FF
E (Black)	00	00	00

The movie has short action scripts in the first frame and the button, and the main search script is in the second frame. Figure 5-9 shows the initial setup.

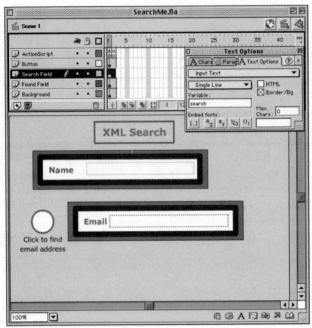

Figure 5-9: One text field provides the search variable and the other provides the match variable.

Background layer

Use the tan from the color palette for the background color and follow this next set of steps for creating the labels and backdrops:

1. Use the Rectangle tool to create a rectangle measuring W=325, H=70. Use the red (Color C) for the stroke and fill colors. Copy the first rectangle and paste it below and to the right of the first one, using Figure 5-9 as a guide.

2. Set the Stroke value to 10 and, with a black stroke and white fill, draw a second set of rectangles on top of the first two, as shown in Figure 5-9. For easier management, select each set of rectangles and group them by first selecting them and then pressing Ctrl+G or Cmd+G.

3. Add a rectangle at the top, using the blue stroke color with no fill, and type the label **XML Search**. Add **Name** and **Email** labels on the rectangle backdrops, as shown in Figure 5-9. Finally, add the **Click to find email address** below where the button is to be placed.

Search Field and Found Field layers

Setting up the two text fields is simple enough, but be careful in following these next two steps and use Figure 5-9 as a guide:

1. Use the Text tool to create a text field over the top backdrop rectangle. In the Text Options panel, create an Input field with Border/Bg selected. Do not select HTML in the panel. If you do, the length of your variable is that of the text field and not the `search` variable! The text field should be W=200, H=21. Use a 14-point Verdana bold font with the red from the movie's palette. Finally, in the Variable window, type **search**.

2. Place a second text field over the bottom backdrop rectangle. Make the second field a dynamic text field in the same dimensions of the first and leave all boxes, including Border/Bg, unselected. Type **found** as the variable name.

Button layer

Use the Oval tool to draw a circle with a white fill and blue stroke. Create a button symbol by selecting the drawing, pressing the F8 key, and choosing Button as the behavior. Save the symbol as **Seek**. Add the following ActionScript:

```
on (release) {
    gotoAndPlay (2);
}
```

All the script does is release the `stop` action in the first frame so that the big script in the second frame can launch.

ActionScript layer

The two action scripts in this layer constitute the heart of the movie. The script in Frame 1 is pretty simple. It focuses the cursor in the top text field and stops the movie. The purpose of focusing the cursor is to immediately guide the user to the correct field.

```
Selection.setFocus("_root.search");
stop ();
```

The next script is placed in the second frame. Notice that the first part of the script is similar to the scripts in the previous two Flash movies that use XML. But more arrays and variables are added so that the code can match one array element with another and output the results in another text field (see Listing 5-4).

Listing 5-4: **ActionScript for Frame 2 of SearchMe.fla**

```
contactXML = new XML();
contactXML.onLoad = transXML;
display = "Getting XML.";
contactXML.load("contacts.xml");
function transXML () {
    if (this.loaded) {
      display = "XML data is up.";
      }
keyTag = new XML();
nodeID = new XML();
nameList = new Array();
contactList = new Array();
name = new Array();
email = new Array();
Nseek = 0;
Eseek = 0;
flag = 0;
keyTag = this.lastChild;
contactList = keyTag.childNodes;
for (kid=0; kid<=contactList.length; kid++) {
if (contactList[kid].nodeName.toLowerCase() == "contact") {
            nameList = contactList[kid].childNodes;
            for (nl=0; nl<=nameList.length; nl++) {
                nodeID = nameList[nl];
                elementID = nodeID.nodeName.toLowerCase();
                if (elementID == "name") {
                  name[Nseek] = nodeID.firstChild.nodeValue;
                      if (name[Nseek] == search) {
                          flag = 1;
                      }
                    Nseek += 1;
                }
                if (elementID == "email") {
                  email[Eseek] = nodeID.firstChild.nodeValue;
                      if (flag == 1) {
                          found = email[Eseek];
                          flag = 0;
                      }
                    Eseek += 1;
                }
            }
        }
    }
}
```

Breaking down the ActionScript

The first part of the ActionScript in the second frame is so close to the previous two movies that this analysis begins where the script begins looking for a match. An array called name is declared in the script; and so when the name element is located, the node value of the element is placed into the name[] array with the counter Nseek. Next, a conditional statement checks to see whether the array element matches the search word made of the variable associated with top text field. Using the variable name search simplifies identifying the purpose of the variable. If the variable does match, a flag variable is set. If no match exists, the counter variable (Nseek) increment by one.

```
if (elementID == "name") {
    name[Nseek] = nodeID.firstChild.nodeValue;
        if (name[Nseek] == search) {
            flag = 1;
                }
                    Nseek += 1;
                }
```

The next segment of the script places the contents of the next node identified as email into the email[] array. (The email [] array is declared near the beginning of the script.) If the name matches the search name, the flag variable is set to a value of 1. So all the script must do is see whether flag is set to 1, and if it is, the script assigns the array element's value to the found variable, which is the variable name associated with the second text field. Then the flag variable is reset to 0 so that the rest of the email array elements don't appear in the text field.

```
if (elementID == "email") {
    email[Eseek] = nodeID.firstChild.nodeValue;
        if (flag == 1) {
                found = email[Eseek];
                    flag = 0;
                    }
                    Eseek += 1;
                }
```

For a larger XML data file, instead of having the flag variable reset to 0 to prevent duplicate output to the text field associated with the found variable, using a While loop or even a Break statement to exit altogether is preferable. Then your script does not waste time as it keeps searching the XML document. With a very large file, where the chances of name duplication increase, you can increase the size (dimensions) of the text field where search matches are to be placed. Figure 5-10 shows what a successful search of your XML document produces.

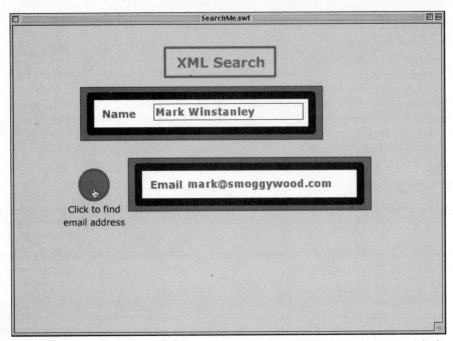

Figure 5-10: If the name you enter matches the name in the XML document, Flash displays the e-mail address associated with the name.

Further Adventures with XML and Flash

At this point in time, XML is still in a rapidly emerging and changing environment. One of the most important developments is the use of schemas that the World Wide Web Consortium (W3C) is still drafting at the time of this writing. After the W3C settles on a standard, XML can be universally verified with schemas as it now can with DTD. As it is now, the Microsoft version of schemas is all that is reliably available. So in the interim, DTD is the only standardized verification process.

Using Flash as a front end for reading XML documents is made possible by Macromedia's insight in including XML objects in Flash 5 ActionScript. But writing to an XML document using Flash as a front end is a far more complex operation because the middleware, ASP or PHP, needs to read and write to a database and configure the data into XML format. A few books on the market have taken steps to explain the integration of ASP with XML, and as you see in Chapter 3, Flash can readily communicate with ASP. Configuring database files into XML, ASP or PHP, or some other middleware enables Flash to use its XML objects rather than relying on the somewhat awkward translation process now required for Flash to communicate with online databases.

Another Flash innovation that is ahead of the curve is the XML Socket objects. Without a stable socket server for these Flash objects, using — and certainly writing about — XML sockets is a bit dicey. Still, XML Socket objects are important innovations. They enable a rapidly changing movie to receive data almost instantaneously through an open socket to a data source. In this way, a game or other Flash application can have rapid and complex interactive objects without needing to load all the data first. New and updated data available over the Internet can readily flow into and out of Flash in real time. So, although Flash can do a good deal with XML documents, far more integration with Flash and XML is on the near horizon.

Summary

This chapter shows that using Flash's XML objects with ActionScript can pull data out of an XML document. What's more, when the XML data is extracted, Flash makes a great front-end for displaying the data. By thinking of XML as a many-tiered array or tree, you can go deep into the rich data formatting capabilities of XML and display them in the equally rich display formatting tools in Flash.

After you pull data out of an XML file, you may want to think about printing it out for hardcopy distribution. Chapter 6 shows how to format and print data using Flash. Although Flash is primarily a tool for displaying data on the Web, it can also be used to send data from Flash to a printer. If you want your XML data handed out at the next board meeting, see the next chapter to find out how to make it look good.

✦　　✦　　✦

Printing Directly from Flash

As much as the Internet has changed the way information is sent back and forth, many people still prefer to hold information in their hands and flip through it or walk into a meeting and spread out their data across a table. Printing with Flash is a great way to transfer data to a place where it can be physically handled. Flash 5 lets you take both textual and visual information that you've stored in your movies and send it to the printer of the person viewing them.

Printing Basics

Before you can learn what ActionScript code to use to target a user's printer for massive paper consumption, you need to review a few basic printing matters, such as fonts and graphic formats.

Fonts in Flash

When creating text fields in Flash, you first use Flash's Text tool to place your text field on the stage. Using the Text Options panel (shown in Figure 6-1), you then configure the field to be Static, Dynamic, or Input. The Dynamic and Input menu options enable you to embed font sets within your Flash movie.

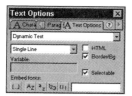

Figure 6-1: You choose fonts for your text fields in the Text Options panel.

By clicking the buttons at the bottom of the panel, you can specify to include either the entire font set or only certain characters of the font you're using when you export your Flash movie. Including the font set enables those people who don't have the font you're using installed on their computer to still be able to view it. This feature is important to keep in mind when you are configuring text content in Flash for the possibility of being printed out. If the text is in a dynamic text field, make sure that you export the font with field. Exporting the font makes the Flash SWF file somewhat larger, but at least people can see your fonts.

When you include Static (nondynamic) text in your Flash movie, do either of the following tasks in order to make sure people can view your chosen fonts correctly:

✦ Break the text all apart using Ctrl+B. This task is very time-consuming and prevents you from going back and editing your text later.

✦ Convert text blocks into Graphic symbols and then place those onto the stage. Flash then exports the text blocks as graphics and not as text in a font that no one can see.

After you've made sure that you have you're fonts configured correctly, you can be assured that anyone viewing your Flash movie will be able to see them and print them as well.

Flash vector graphics

Flash uses primarily vector graphics to ensure small file sizes and easy replication on most anyone's computer. Often times, though, you might like to include bitmaps. As you'll notice in Flash, when you scale a bitmap image that you've imported to a larger size, the image becomes quite pixilated. Printing in Flash often causes objects that are small on the stage to be enlarged to a very large size on the page you're printing them on, revealing a lot of pixilation.

To prevent this pixilation, you can either avoid using bitmaps altogether when you know you'll be printing something from Flash or use a higher quality bitmap image file so that it won't look so pixilated when it scales up to the size of an 8.5 by 11 page. Using high-quality bitmaps will add to the size of your Flash movie just like embedding your fonts will, but it's a good way to ensure higher quality prints, if that's what you're after.

Flash prints vector graphics very smoothly and scales them nicely on a PostScript-enabled printer, and just about every printer sold today has PostScript capability. If by chance someone viewing your printable Flash movie doesn't have a PostScript-enabled printer, he or she will still be able to print your Flash content, but it will be converted to a bitmap image first and then sent to the printer. The resulting output will be at a lower quality than if the viewer were using a PostScript printer. Unfortunately, there's no way to prevent this. If the document must look right everywhere and anywhere it's to be printed and seen, you may want to check the quality of anything you're designating as printable in Flash by printing it on both PostScript and non-PostScript printers.

Note When a PostScript-enabled printer is detected, all the content in Flash that's being printed is first converted to PostScript and then sent to the printer. This conversion can result in a temporary file size that is much larger than what the size of the actual SWF file is and may possibly load down a network of printers or an intranet if the file size happens to be ludicrously huge. You can check this file size by exporting any frames in Flash that you want to print into an EPS format. The total size of these EPS files determines the file size that a viewer's computer will send to the viewer's printer or network.

Printing from Flash

Flash 4 first had the ability to print its content through a special updated version of the Flash 4 plug-in. But developers shied away from implementing the printing feature in their movies because many people didn't have this plug-in. With Flash 5, the printing capability is solidly in the plug-in and a new ActionScript has been added that is devoted solely to printing from Flash.

Advantages to Flash printing

The advantages of printing from Flash are many! Flash has the unique capability to not only print what is viewable on the stage, but also to print frames in a movie clip that is completely hidden. Common uses for Flash printing include the following:

✦ Printing a multipage document from a banner ad that is very small by hiding a movie clip that contains all your printable frames on the stage with its visibility set to 0

✦ Providing security for Flash movie content by specifying which frames are printable and thereby preventing the user from choosing the Print command in the context menu of the plug-in itself and printing frames that you haven't specified

✦ Creating games where players can print out statistics on how well they played after they finish the game. (The game itself can even be related to printing: the object of the game could be to design a unique layout in Flash and print the results when you're done.)

✦ Providing printed hard copy receipts for purchases made by customers on an e-commerce site that uses Flash

✦ Providing scalable graphics, such as maps or blueprints, and letting the user choose how big or small to scale them and print them out

✦ Providing some show-stopping graphics that look so cool that people want to hang them on their walls

You could probably dream up hundreds of uses for letting users print out content from a Flash movie you create. When you see all of the available options, it may spur you to change the way you build your Flash movies and structure them so they are easily printable.

The print action

The ActionScript in Flash 5 that starts the printing process is print. The basic syntax for the print action is

```
print( target , bounding box);
```

The print action can be executed from anywhere in Flash, and the two arguments following it let you specify what timeline, level, or movie clip is to be printed, as well as what frames or portions of those frames are to be included.

Flash can print only individual frames. It prints each frame you've designated as printable as one page on the printer (see Figure 6-2). Although you can control what portions of each frame are printed and how objects in those frames are scaled, there's no way to combine multiple frames into one printed page.

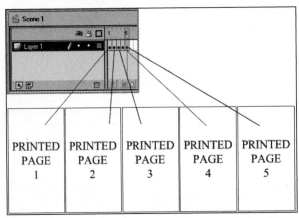

Figure 6-2: If you have five frames you're printing from Flash, you'll have five pages coming out of your printer, with one frame per page.

Normally, you'll execute the print action from a button, but you can also attach it to a frame action or clip event because users will still have to confirm printing options in their computers' normal Print dialog box that pops up. But if users see this dialog box just pop up of out of nowhere, they may be confused, so from a usability standpoint, attaching the print action to a button the user can click is the best way to go.

The target parameter

The target parameter of the `print` action is for you to specify the basic location of the frames you want to print. You can specify a level or a target movie clip. When you reference a level, the action should be `printNum`, and when you reference another target, the action should be just plain `print`.

The target can be a specific movie clip, or you can reference `_root` to designate the main timeline. The target parameter *does not* need quotations around it, although we recommend that you use them. As with most other places in ActionScript, you can dynamically name a target using variables and concatenation.

After you specify a target, Flash prints all the frames in that movie clip or timeline. But suppose you want Flash to print only a few frames. For instance, if you have a movie clip that contains 50 frames and only Frames 10, 12, and 30 contain text or pictures you want to print, you would need to label each of the frames you'd like to print with #P. Of course, adding this label results in duplicate frame labels. Normally, you never want to have duplicate frame labels in your Flash movie because Flash may become confused when trying to use a statement such as `gotoAndPlay(frame label)` to send the Flash playhead to a certain frame. In this case, though, a duplicate frame label is fine to use because we're not labeling any frames #P for any purpose other than designating them as printable.

Caution When you test or export your Flash movie, Flash is going to caution you that you have duplicate frame labels present in your movie. Don't worry about this warning, duplicate frame labels are perfectly okay as long as the duplicates are all #P labels. (This warning is an oversight on the part of Macromedia; it would probably take only a few lines of code in the Flash architecture to make it ignore #P frame labels.)

Flash scans through the timeline specified by the target parameter of the `print` action and extracts only those frames labeled #P for the purpose of sending them off to the printer. When it finds one of these frames, it exports everything visible on the stage in that frame across all timeline layers to the printer. If Flash can't find any frames labeled #P, it will begin at Frame 1 of the target timeline and print each and every frame after that until it reaches the last frame of that timeline.

Note All the testing for #P frame labels and converting the frames to a printable format happens in the background, and users never see anything transpiring visually in the Flash movie. Users do see their usual Print dialog box popping up and asking them to choose their printer and print options. This result is no different than if they had tried to print a page from a word processor, a spreadsheet, or a graphics program.

Another important point to note is that you need to decide in advance which frames in your target movie clips and timelines are the ones that you're going to want to print. Because Flash is depending on frame labels to tell it which frames are printable, and you can't create frame labels dynamically once you've exported your movie, some planning is required when you are creating a movie if you need to specify certain frames as printable.

Tip The #P labels can be attached to keyframes only, so you'll need to account for this if you have tweened sequences in your timeline or movie clips. The best way to deal with this issue is to add a layer on top of all your existing timeline layers that contains only blank keyframes with the #P labels used to designate those frames as printable. Having this layer enables you to print stills from the middle of tweened sequences. Figure 6-3 shows what this layer may look like.

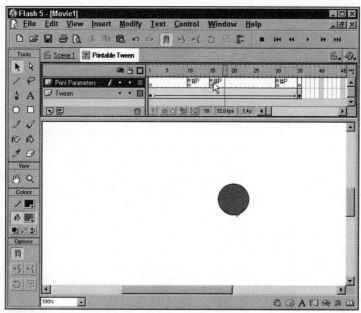

Figure 6-3: A separate layer has been created to designate printable frames in this movie clip, which contains tweened animation. This layer prevents having to add unnecessary keyframes in the middle of your motion tweens.

The bounding box parameter

The second argument that the print action accepts is the bounding box parameter. This parameter provides information on where Flash should create an artificial crop or boundary around your frames and images when it prepares to print them. Macromedia decided to pick some interesting and conflicting words to use when specifying these boundaries, so you may need some time to make sense of it all. The confusion arises from simple logic regarding what each boundary option is referencing. We provide many examples in this section to help you make sense of it all, so warm up your printer!

Whenever you use the print action, you *must* specify a bounding box area. The bounding box parameter accepts one of three different parameters: bmovie, bmax, or bframe. In the following sections, each of these bounding box parameters is presented in detail. Because the variations between these parameters are difficult to distinguish at a glance, we recommend that you go through all the examples in the following sections in the order in which they're presented.

The bmovie parameter

Setting bmovie as the bounding box parameter of the print action tells Flash to use one specific frame of whatever target timeline you've specified as the cropping area for all frames printed from that target timeline. After Flash crops all the frames to this bounding area, it then enlarges the cropped portions to the full size of the printed page!

The way you specify that one specific frame is by labeling it with the #b frame label. Unlike the #P frame label, the #b label can be used on only one frame. If you try to attach the #b label to more than one frame in the target movie clip or timeline, Flash will become confused, and you probably won't get the cropping you desire. Let's take a look at how the bmovie parameter works in a real-world application:

On the CD-ROM

This next example uses the bmovie.fla file found on the CD-ROM. This Flash movie has five frames that contain graphics created by Nate Yarrington of entertainovision.com. Copy this file to your local hard drive and then open it in Flash for the purpose of editing it.

1. Scroll through the five frames in bmovie.fla to get an idea of the pictures they contain. Each frame has a large vector graphic in the center of the stage with smaller scale versions of the same graphic around it.

2. Create a new timeline layer above the existing Graphics layer and name it **Print Parameters**.

3. The new Print Parameters layer should already have a blank keyframe at Frame 1. Create two more blank keyframes at Frames 2 and 5.

4. Give Frames 1, 2, and 5 each the frame label **#P** by using the Frame panel. This step creates duplicate frame labels, but this duplication is okay. You are telling Flash that these are the only frames that it is allowed to print on this timeline.

5. Return to Frame 1 and attach a stop(); frame action to it to keep Flash from playing through all these frames when you test the movie.

6. In Frame 1 of the Print Parameter layer, create a button on the stage or drag one from Window ➪ Common Library ➪ Buttons and place it in the upper left corner of the stage. Use static text next to this button to label it **PRINT**.

7. Attach the following code to the button you just created:

```
on (release) {
    printNum (0, "bmovie");
}
```

Now the movie is set up to print Frames 1, 2, and 5 in Level 0 that you've specified for printing with the frame label #P. You've specified bmovie as your bounding box area parameter, so Flash will look for a frame labeled #b to find out what segment of Frames 1, 2, and 5 to print. The next step is to create this bounding box area:

1. Create a blank keyframe at Frame 10 in the Print Parameters layer and attach the **#b** frame label to it by using the Frame panel.

2. With Frame 10 in the Print Parameters layer selected, use the Rectangle tool with a fill and stroke color of black to create a square in the center of the stage measuring approximately 150 x 150 pixels. The Info panel can assist you in setting this exact size, and the Alignment panel can help you center it to the stage.

3. Use the onion skinning feature in the visual layout of the timeline to view all the frames at once and you'll see that the black 150 by 150 square covers only the center object in each frame. In many cases, the images are slightly bigger than the square, but this size difference is okay, because you'll be seeing how this square will crop these images.

This black square is now the area of the stage that will determine the cropped printing area for any frames marked with #P, because the black square is in a frame that you have designated #b for the bmovie bounding box area. Keep in mind that once Flash extracts the designated area from each of the #P frames, it will then scale the cropped images to fill each printed page. Figure 6-4 shows the final layout of the timeline. (The completed file is available on the CD-ROM as bmovie_complete.fla if you're experiencing any difficulties laying out the timeline.)

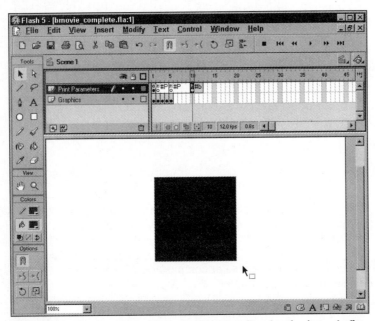

Figure 6-4: The completed layout of the timeline for the bmovie.fla file with Frames 1, 2, and 5 designated for printing and Frame 10 designated as the bounding box area.

Test the movie in Flash or in your Web browser. It should stop on Frame 1 and show a little montage of the universe. Click the button you created, and your computer's Print dialog box should appear. Choose the correct options for your computer and designated printer and then start printing!

Only three pages should come out of your printer, one for each frame specified by your #P labels, which in this case are Frames 1, 2, and 5. Because we used the bmovie bounding parameter in the print action along with the #b frame label on Frame 10 containing the 150 by 150 black square, you should see only that 150 by 150 area from the stage containing the center object in each frame. But after cropping to this 150 by 150 area, Flash then blows up the image to fill the entire printed page, so you'll see a giant flower, house, and tree come out of your printer.

Some of the images might have been cropped too much. Try returning to the Flash movie and changing the size of that 150 by 150 black square in Frame 10 to a bigger size that totally encompasses the center images in Frames 1, 2, and 5. The onion skinning feature on the timeline can assist you with this adjustment. Test your movie and print it again. Notice that the print area for all the frames changes with the size of the black square. Now all those center images should print without any of their sides, tops, or bottoms missing.

Try specifying more or fewer frames as printable by adding or removing #P frame labels. You'll find that the number of pages printed increases or decreases accordingly. Finally, try making more than one black square in Frame 10 or even using multiple circles and complex shapes in a variety of colors. You'll see that the bounding box that surrounds all the elements in Frame 10 is what is used to designate the bounding area for the #P frames.

Note   The elements in the frame you label #b do not create a mask for the printable frames in and of themselves. Instead, the square area that encompasses all the elements in the #b frame is what basically masks the printable frames. A quick way to see this area is to convert any elements in the #b frame into a symbol so that when you select the symbol, a square bounding box appears around it.

Suppose you wanted a more accurate representation of all the objects in every frame you've labeled #P to be printed out. You want to see everything that's on the stage in each of those frames. To accomplish this, change the size of the black square in Frame 10 to 550 by 400 pixels and center it to the stage. Test the movie and view the printout. Every object in every frame labeled #P should print out to each page. If printing every object in every frame is your goal, though, using bmovie makes for extra steps in the process. The bmovie parameter is useful for when you want to print out an area smaller than the area encompassing all the objects in each frame. To print the area encompassing all the objects in each printable frame, use the bmax parameter.

In many of the examples, you'll probably notice that the button that you're clicking to print is showing up in your printouts. To correct this problem, move all the frames containing any images to a frame other than the one containing the button. As long as the frames you want to print are marked with the #P label, Flash will find them and print them. Another solution is to put all the frames you want to print in a separate movie clip and then use the target parameter of the print action to specify that movie clip.

The bmax parameter

The bmax bounding box parameter of the print action is useful for when you want to print all the objects present in each printable frame and you want consistency in the printed pages. When you print using bmax, everything will come out looking much like it does on the stage.

What bmax does is tell Flash to take a look through all the printable frames and look at all the objects present in each of those frames. Then in a sort of behind-the-scenes onion-skinning operation, Flash creates a bounding box area for you of a size that can encompass all the objects in all the printable frames. It then applies this new maximum bounding box area to each frame as it is printed to ensure that every object in every printable frame makes it to the printer.

To see this in action, open the file you created in the previous bmovie section or the version of it on the CD-ROM called bmovie_complete.fla and then follow these steps:

1. Save this file to your hard drive as bmax.fla and open it in Flash. You should see five frames in the Graphics layer; each frame contains a large graphic in the center of the stage surrounded by four smaller version of the same graphic. Frames 1, 2, and 5 are labeled #P to designate them as printable.

2. Frame 10 of the Print Parameters layer is labeled #b and contains a black 150 by 150 square that is used to designate the bounding area of the printable frames when you use the bmovie parameter. Delete Frame 10 from the time-line. You don't need this frame anymore because you're going to now be using bmax in the print action and letting Flash create an automatic bounding area.

3. In Frame 1 of the Print Parameters layer is the button that is used to execute the print action. Change the ActionScript attached to this button to the following:

```
on (release) {
    printNum (0, "bmax");
}
```

The movie is now configured to have Flash create a bounding box print area that can accommodate every object in every frame designated as printable. Test the movie and click the button. (If you encounter any difficulties, the completed file is available on the CD-ROM as bmax_complete.fla.) As each page is printed out for its corresponding frame, every element in that specific frame is viewable on the printed page. Figure 6-5 illustrates the approximate look of your printed pages.

Figure 6-5: The approximate look of three pages printed with the bmax parameter where all the objects in the printable frames are viewable on the printed pages at an accurate relative scale.

Herein lies the power in designating bmax as your bounding box parameter. It is the quickest and simplest way to ensure that every object in every frame you've designated as printable makes it onto the printed page, and every frame that's printed has a relative scale. If you're printing out only one frame in your designated target timeline, bmax is usually the option you'll most often want to choose, unless you need the cropping power of bmovie.

Tip   The bmax bounding box parameter is the best way to get an accurate scale representation across multiple printed frames. Objects inside Flash that look small in one frame, in comparison to objects that look big in another frame, retain these ratios when you use the bmax parameter in your print action.

What if you want to ensure that every object in every frame makes it to the printed page but that all those objects are scaled to fill the printed page on a frame-by-frame basis? Keep this file you've just worked on handy and move on to the final bounding box parameter, bframe, to find the answer.

The bframe parameter

Like the bmax parameter, the bframe bounding box parameter of the print action is used when you want every object in every frame you've designated as printable to make it onto the printed page. But with bframe all frames are scaled to fill the printed page instead of maintaining their relative size as they do with the bmax parameter.

The best way to illustrate bframe is to compare it directly to bmax:

1. Open the file you created in the previous bmax example or use the bmax_complete.fla file on the CD-ROM. Then save the file on your hard drive as bframe.fla and open it in Flash.

2. If you're not familiar with how this movie looks when printed out, test it now and view the printout. Return to Flash and you'll see that the print action on the button in Frame 1 of the Print Parameters layer designates bmax as the bounding box area. Frames 1, 2, and 5 are labeled #P and contain every object in their respective frames at an equal scale when they are printed out.

3. Select Frame 5 in the Graphics layer and move the four small trees toward the center tree until they're as close as you can get them. This stage layout is shown in Figure 6-6.

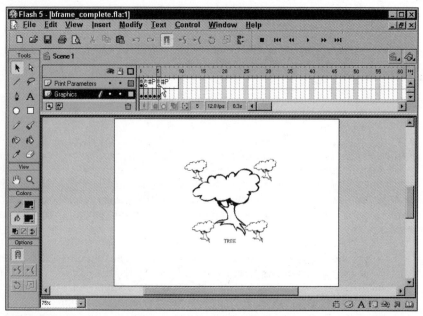

Figure 6-6: The layout of the stage containing the four smaller trees moved in very close next to the center tree.

4. Test the movie and view the printout. You should see that the page printed with the trees on it corresponds in scale to the other two printed pages. In other words, the scale has not changed, you've just changed the position of the smaller trees.

5. Return to Flash and change the ActionScript attached to the Print button in Frame 1 of the Print Parameters layer to the following:

```
on (release) {
    printNum (0, "bframe");
}
```

You have just configured the `print` action to print out all the frames using the `bframe` bounding box parameter.

6. Test the movie and click the Print button to print out the designated frames. (If you encounter any problems, this file is available on the CD-ROM as `bframe_complete.fla`.)

When viewing the printout, look at the page with the trees that you moved in toward the center. You should have a giant set of trees that fills the whole page! This size change occurs because when Flash was exporting to the printer, it went frame by frame through each of the frames designated as printable with #P and looked at the maximum area for each of those frames. Flash then scaled each frame to fit the page. Because the other two frames that were printed (Frames 1 and 2) contained objects spread out over a great distance all the way to the edges of the stage, Flash had to maintain the relative positioning and printed them out much the same as they were printed when Flash was using the `bmax` parameter. When Flash reached the frame containing the trees, it found all the objects tightly grouped in a small area. Flash then had a much smaller bounding box area around all the objects in that frame and scaled up that entire area to fill the printed page.

The `bframe` parameter of the `print` statement is useful when you have multiple frames to print and you want the bounding box for each frame to be determined on a frame-by-frame basis instead of being an average of all the printable frames. So if you have many frames to print that contain different object layouts (some tightly grouped and some spread apart) and you want them to all appear as big as possible on the printed page without any regards to large scaling differences between pages, use the `bframe` parameter.

> **Note**
>
> When using the `bmax` and `bframe` parameters, you do not need to add any special extra frames to the Flash movie. In contrast, you have to add a #b frame label to a frame to designate the bounding box area when using the `bmovie` parameter. In fact, even though the frame containing the #b label and the black 150 by 150 square was removed in one of the examples, this step wasn't necessary. When the `bmax` or `bframe` parameter is used, Flash determines the bounding box area on its own and completely ignores any frame with a #b frame label.

The printAsBitmap action

Up until now you've been printing out very simple vector graphics. You've seen how they scale up and down very nicely with the bounding box parameters. But if the images in the Flash movie frames you want to print are mostly bitmaps or contain alpha effects, transparencies, gradient fills, or otherwise resemble bitmap graphics, Flash is going to have a hard time printing them out using the regular `print` action.

In these situations, ActionScript's `printAsBitmap` comes to the rescue. When Flash starts exporting all the frames to the user's printer, it doesn't try to convert anything into vectors when `printAsBitmap` is used. Flash instead takes a bitmap snapshot of the stage and then sends that image to the printer. The advantage to this action is that complicated images (whether they're vectors or bitmaps or both) export very quickly to the printer. The disadvantage is that scaling some images could introduce pixilization.

All the same bounding box parameters apply when you use `printAsBitmap` as apply when you use regular old `print`. The variation for printing levels instead of targets applies as well: When specifying a level, you'll need to use the syntax `printAsBitmapNum`. The general syntax for `printAsBitmap` looks like

```
printAsBitmap( target , bounding box);
```

Using `printAsBitmap` can be a real time saver when the images you want to print are either bitmaps themselves or have been created in Flash to resemble bitmaps, with lots of transparencies, gradients, points, and color areas. It can take an eternity to print some of these images using the standard `print` action, often times causing Flash or the entire computer to freeze and even crash.

To take a look at a file that can benefit from the help provided by the `printAsBitmap` action, open the `printAsBitmap.fla` file in Flash and proceed with the following steps to modify it:

On the CD-ROM

Locate the file `printAsBitmap.fla` on the CD-ROM and transfer it your local hard drive. This file contains five frames of great color graphics produced by NateYarrington of entertainovision.com.

1. Scroll through the timeline to view the five different pictures presented. They are very complex images containing bitmaps, vectors, and many areas of varied color.

2. Create a new timeline layer above all the existing numbered layers and name it **Print Parameters**.

3. The new Print Parameters layer should already have a blank keyframe at Frame 1. Create two more blank keyframes at Frames 2 and 5.

4. Give Frames 2 and 5 each the frame label **#P** by using the Frame panel. This labeling will result in duplicate frame labels, but such duplication is okay in this case. This step tells Flash that Frames 2 and 5 are the only two frames on this timeline that it can print.

5. Return to Frame 1 and attach a `stop()`; frame action to it to keep Flash from playing through all these frames when you test the movie.

6. In Frame 1 of the Print Parameters layer, create a button on the stage or drag one from Window ➪ Common Library ➪ Buttons and place it in the upper left corner of the stage. Use static text (most likely with the color white) to label this button **PRINT**.

7. Attach the following code to this button:

```
on (release) {
    printAsBitmapNum (0, "bmax");
}
```

8. Save the changes. Test the movie in Flash or in your browser and click the Print button. If you have any problems, the completed file is available on the CD-ROM as `printAsBitmap_complete.fla`.

You should have two pages coming out of your printer corresponding to the two frames you designated with #P: one contains a futuristic-looking ballerina and the other contains an evil pumpkin. Depending on the speed of your computer, it may take a little time for Flash to compile and print these pages. This brief period, however, pales in comparison to the time it would take for Flash to print these frames using the standard `print` action.

Caution

You may be tempted to try and print these two frames (or more) out of `printAsBitmap.fla` using the standard `print` action instead of the `printAsBitmap` action just to see how much longer it takes. If you want to do this comparison, save all your important work and close any other open programs. Your computer may freeze or crash. The difference is worth experiencing, but be prepared to call up whatever command you need to quit a hanging program when and if Flash hangs trying to export these images. Try designating all the frames as printable to really see the difference in speed!

The reason for the delay if you've tried using standard `print` here is that, as mentioned earlier in the chapter, Flash is trying to convert everything into a vectorized PostScript format and there's just too much data to work with. Rather than having Flash trying to perform all that math on the pictures and hanging up a user's computer or network as a result, it's more efficient to just deal with images as bitmaps and sacrifice a little bit of quality in some instances for the speedier printout or just the capability to print the images at all!

The best way to figure out when and if you need `printAsBitmap` is to start with just the standard `print` action and test the effects on your own computer and the computers of some friends you enlist to help you. Always warn them of the possibility of their system hanging, however! If the standard `print` action is speedy and produces the desired quality of output, stick with it. If getting anything to the printer seems like it takes forever, switch to `printAsBitmap` and see whether you can live with the image quality reduction, if any. Many times you'll find that switching to `printAsBitmap` doesn't seem to effect to your image quality at all.

Advanced Printing Options

Flash's printing power is quite a bit more than just printing out some neat-looking pictures that are visible on the main timeline of your Flash movie. Flash also has the power to do the following:

✦ Print individual frames from a tweened sequence that is not even playing, kind of like extracting still frames from a roll of film

✦ Print frames from a movie clip that is completely invisible

✦ Print frames from an SWF movie that has been loaded externally either to a level or a target

✦ Print dynamic text fields that are in a hidden frame or movie clip and have these text fields show data gathered from anywhere in your Flash movie

To demonstrate these amazing features in detail, this section presents two projects. The first project focuses on printing frames from a tweened sequence inside a movie clip that isn't visible. The second project focuses on printing hidden dynamic text fields and printing frames from an SWF file that you've loaded into Flash.

Printing tweened frames

This project details Flash's capability to extract frames from a timeline even when a motion tweened action occurs in those frames. We also explain how to print from a movie clip that cannot be seen. The advantage to the latter is that you can create a Flash movie with a stage size only as big as the button to which you attach the `print` action. The information that is printed out can be as big as you'd like because it will be scaled by the bounding box parameters you choose.

On the CD-ROM   Locate the file `tween.fla` and transfer it to your local hard drive.

Open the `tween.fla` file inside Flash. The only thing present in the initial file is one timeline layer with a button labeled Print in the center of the stage. Notice the extremely small stage size of this movie; it's only 100 by 100 pixels. In addition to the button, the Library contains two graphics symbols: one depicting a flower and one depicting a silhouette. Change this file according to the following instructions:

1. Create a new symbol by using the menu Insert ➪ New Symbol and choosing Movie Clip. Give the clip the name **Moving Images**. You'll immediately be transferred into the editing view for the symbol you've created and you'll see a blank stage in front of you.

2. Rename the existing layer from Layer 1 to Flower. Create a blank keyframe in Frame 2 of this layer and drag the Flower symbol from the Library onto the stage.

3. Using the Info panel, resize the flower to be 125 pixels high by 110 pixels wide. Position it at x-coordinate -210 and y-coordinate 0.

4. Create another keyframe in the Flower layer at Frame 20 by selecting Frame 20 and pressing F6 to create a duplicate of Frame 2. Reposition the flower in Frame 20 at x-coordinate 210 and y-coordinate 0.

5. Select any frame in between Frames 2 and 20 in the Flowers layer and create a motion tween with Insert ➪ Create Motion Tween.

6. Create another layer above the Flower layer in the Moving Images timeline and name this layer **Silhouette**. Create a blank keyframe in Frame 2 of this layer and drag the Silhouette symbol from the Library into Frame 2, resizing it to 150 pixels wide by 125 pixels high. Position it at x-coordinate 0 and y-coordinate -170.

7. Create a keyframe in Frame 20 of the Silhouette layer by pressing F6 and creating a duplicate of Frame 2. Position the Silhouette graphic in Frame 20 at x-coordinate 0 and y-coordinate 170.

8. Select any frame in the Silhouette layer between Frames 2 and 20 and create a motion tween by choosing Insert ➪ Create Motion Tween. Move the Flash playhead along the timeline to get an idea of how the images on the stage move relative to each other.

9. Create another layer in the timeline and label it **Print Parameters**. Create blank keyframes in Frames 2, 14, and 20 of this layer. Label each of these three keyframes with the **#P** frame label.

10. Place a `stop()`; frame action in Frame 1 of the Print Parameters layer. Figure 6-7 shows the complete layout of the timeline for the Moving Images movie clip.

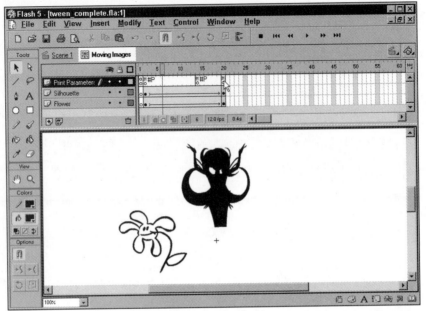

Figure 6-7: The layout of the layers and objects in the timeline of the Moving Images movie clip.

11. Return to the main timeline of the movie where the Print button resides. Create a new layer in this timeline and name it **Target**. Select Frame 1 of the Target layer and drag the Moving Images movie clip symbol from the Library to the stage.

12. Because Frame 1 of the Moving Images clip is blank, you'll see only a small dot on the stage as a place marker for this movie clip. Position it wherever you'd like, and with it selected, give it an instance name of **movingImages** in the Instance panel.

13. Select the Print button in the Button layer and attach this ActionScript:

```
on (release) {
    print ("_root.movingImages", "bmax");
}
```

14. Test the movie in Flash or in your browser and click the Print button. If you encounter any difficulties, the complete file is available on the CD-ROM as `tween_complete.fla`.

Three pages should come out of your printer, each representing a frame in the timeline of the Moving Images movie clip. The first page shows the flower and silhouette graphics at their start positions while the second page shows them just after they cross, and the final page shows the graphics at their ending positions. You have just printed frames pulled from a tweened sequence that was inside a movie clip that was completely invisible to the user!

Notice that Flash used the inside of the `_root.movingImages` movie clip as the reference for where to place the elements on the printed pages. The `bmax` parameter made Flash look at all the frames in that movie clip and created a bounding box area to depict the graphics across the full length of their travels. It didn't matter where on the main timeline you placed the clip, as long as you gave it the same instance name you referenced in the code for the Print button.

Note Try changing the `bmax` parameter on the Print button to `bframe`. You'll see that as the graphic objects move closer together they appear larger on the printed pages. Because the objects are contained in a smaller area when they are closer together, Flash scales them up to fit the page because `bframe` operates on a frame-by-frame bounding box basis.

Even though we created the Moving Images movie clip to have a blank first frame, you could easily delete that first frame. Of course, doing so would make the movie clip completely visible on the main timeline; to make the movie clip invisible, you could add the following clip event ActionScript to it:

```
onClipEvent(load)
    this._visible=0;
}
```

This ActionScript would render the movie clip invisible the moment it loads. However, through the unique power of the `print` action, Flash would still print the frames you designated for printing inside the Moving Images movie clip.

Tip Using the method described here you could easily produce a large brochure printed from a small Flash movie measuring the size of a banner ad or smaller. Create a movie clip whose frames contain all the pages of your brochure and either leave the first frame blank or use the movie clip's `_visible` property to render it unseen. If you name the instance and target it properly in the `print` action (along with the proper bounding box option), a large brochure will magically appear from the user's printer even though the Flash movie he or she is viewing is very small.

Printing an invoice/receipt

Flash's `print` action has a few more surprises left to reveal. In this project, you build an invoice/receipt-generating Flash movie that pulls dynamic data to be printed from a completely different area of the Flash movie than the one being printed. You also explore Flash's capability to load in an external SWF file, fill it with data, and print it out.

Dynamic text field printing

As far as dynamic text fields go, you can place them anywhere in the timeline that you are targeting for printing. As long as the variables exist wherever each dynamic text field's variable parameter is referencing them, their values will be printed out from Flash. This capability enables you to compile data into complex reports and have those reports printed directly from Flash regardless of whether they're visible on the stage. A basic example of this capability is presented in the following steps:

On the CD-ROM Locate the file receipt.fla on the CD-ROM. Copy it to your hard drive and open it in Flash to perform the modifications outlined in this project.

1. Take a look at the initial stage layout of receipt.fla. It consists of a header logo, some static text designators on the left hand side of the stage, and a Create Invoice button at the very bottom of the stage.

2. Create some dynamic input text fields next to each content label that is already on the stage. There are six in all. Use the following table to find the variable name to enter in the Variable text box in the Text Options panel for each text field you create. Make sure the Border/Bg check box is checked for each field you create, and they should all be Single Line, Input Text fields, unless otherwise noted. All text fields for the rest of this project utilize 18-point Times New Roman black.

Stage label	Variable name
Client Name:	clientName
Address: (two lines)	clientAddress
Phone Number:	clientPhone
Mowing Services: $	mowingServices
Other Services: $	otherServices
Raw Materials: $	rawMaterials

3. To create the invoice, create a new movie clip by using Insert ⇨ New Symbol and choosing Movie Clip. Enter the name **Invoice**. You will now be transported to the editing mode for your new Invoice symbol.

4. Add a stop(); action to the one blank keyframe.

5. Create a blank keyframe in Frame 2. Give it the now-familiar **#P** frame label.

6. Using the Rectangle tool with a black 1-point stroke and no fill, create an outline that is 470 pixels wide and 410 pixels high in Frame 2. Use the Info panel to help you. Use the Align panel to center the outline both vertically and horizontally to the stage. This outline is the border in which you put the elements of the receipt.

7. In Frame 2 of the Invoice movie clip, drag the Logo Header symbol from the Library onto the stage and position it inside the border you created, near the top. Use Figure 6-8 to help you lay out the rest of the Invoice movie clip.

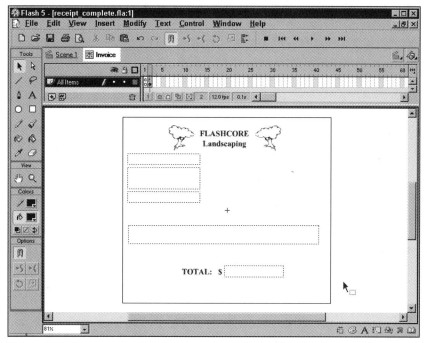

Figure 6-8: The layout of the Invoice movie clip inside of `receipt.fla`.

8. In Frame 2, just inside your border, create a single-line, dynamic text field. Specify `_root.clientName` as the variable and leave the Border/Bg check box unchecked. Position the field near the top left of the layout at approximately x-coordinate -143 and y-coordinate -112. This text field should be about 165 pixels wide and 25 pixels high.

9. Directly below this text field, create two more: one that is a multiline dynamic text field with a variable reference of `_root.clientAddress` and the other a single-line dynamic text field with a variable reference of `_root.clientPhone`. Leave the Border/Bg check box unchecked for both fields.

10. Further down within the border, create a single-line dynamic text field that is approximately 430 pixels wide and 40 pixels high. Give this field the variable reference `_root.message` and position it so that it's centered in the layout.

11. At the very bottom of your virtual invoice, use some static text to place the words **TOTAL: $** on the stage. Next to these words, place a dynamic text field with the variable reference `_root.total` that is approximately 130 pixels wide. Use Figure 6-8 as a guide. (The completed file is available on the CD-ROM as `receipt_complete.fla`.)

12. Return to the main timeline where you originally placed all the input text fields. Add a layer to the timeline and name it **Invisible Invoice**. Select Frame 1 of this layer and drag the Invoice movie clip you just created from the Library and place it on the stage. Because Frame 1 of this clip is empty, you'll see only a little dot on the stage to signify where the clip is located.

13. Place the Invoice movie clip anywhere on the stage you'd like. Select the clip and give it an instance name of **invoice** in the Instance panel.

14. In the Input Area layer, select the Create Invoice button and attach the following ActionScript to it:

```
on (release) {
    total=Number(mowingServices)+Number(otherServices)+
        Number(rawMaterials);
    message="Thank You very much "+clientName+"! Have a
        nice day!";
    print ("_root.invoice", "bmax");
}
```

Test the movie in Flash or inside your browser. Enter any contact information you'd like along with any dollar values for services. Click the Create Invoice button and view the printout. You'll notice that all the values you entered for your contact information have been correctly output in a new layout with a special message to you and the total dollar value of all the values you entered. Again, if you need any help, the completed file is available on the CD-ROM as `receipt_complete.fla`.

How exactly does this invoice work? As you typed data into the input text fields present on the main timeline, the corresponding values were set and stored right there in the _root. The dynamic contact information fields in the `invoice` movie clip then pulled out these values by directly referencing them on the _root. The remaining two variables output in the invoice, `message` and `total`, are created when you click the button to create the invoice.

The `total` variable is just a total of all the dollar values you entered into the input fields on the main timeline (all input data is now treated by Flash as strings, so the values had to be converted with `Number()` first). The `message` variable is just a text message with the `clientName` variable concatenated into the middle. These variables are set and held in the main timeline when you click the Create Invoice button. The text fields in the Invoice movie clip pull these values by referencing them directly on the _root, like with `_root.total` for the total field.

The magic here is the capability to print frames inside an invisible movie clip that contains dynamic text fields. This capability means that you can generate custom invoices, receipts, and reports based on data entered by the user. You can even customize the documents with the user's name or other unique information!

Tip

Leaving the Border/Bg check box unchecked when printing dynamic data is a great way to make the documents you print look fully customized and dynamic. If you leave the backgrounds in, Flash prints them, and they look rather blocky and form-like. People expecting a customized printed document will appreciate the fluid integration and slick look of text without blocks around it!

Loaded SWF printing

Flash can print frames contained inside SWF files that have been loaded in flash through `loadMovie` and `loadMovieNum`! This capability opens up the possibility of having many different loaded-in print layouts that can pull data from another time-line and just present it in a different way. As always in Flash, you can accomplish this task in many different ways, so we present a modification to the last project that illustrates this concept in the simplest light.

In the last project, we showed how printable frames inside a hidden movie clip can print data from the main timeline just by placing the correct path and variable reference in the Text Options panel for those text fields. In this example, we use the same basic file from the last example, but we modify it to load a receipt template from an external SWF file.

On the CD-ROM For this example, you'll need the CD-ROM files `template_receipt.fla` and `receipt_complete.fla` (or use the file you completed in the last example). Transfer both of these files to the same directory on your local hard drive.

Take a look at the file `receipt_complete.fla` if you're unfamiliar with it from the last example. It contains input text fields on the main timeline. A button at the bottom of the stage then prints out a frame from a hidden movie clip on the main timeline that has an instance name of `invoice`. Dynamic text fields inside of the `invoice` movie clip reference the variable values on the main timeline and print out the corresponding data.

Notice that the file `template_receipt.fla` has a very small stage size because the only thing on the stage is a replica of the Invoice movie clip from `receipt_complete.fla` with a few minor changes. Double-click on this movie clip inside of `template_receipt.fla` to see that Frame 1 is empty with a `stop` action and Frame 2 (with its `#P` label) contains a different layout than the Invoice movie clip inside `receipt_complete.fla`.

Next, take a look at the text fields contained in Frame 2 of the Invoice movie clip inside of `template_receipt.fla` and notice that all the text fields reference variable names set by `receipt_complete.fla` except that all the variable names are preceded by `_level0`. This name difference is due to the fact that this alternate template receipt layout is loaded dynamically from `receipt_complete` into Level 1 of the Flash Player, and the dynamic text fields in this Invoice movie clip need to peer back into Level 0 to obtain their values.

Return to the main timeline of `template_receipt.fla` and click on the small dot on the stage representing the Invoice movie clip. With the ActionScript panel open, notice that this code is attached to the movie clip:

```
onClipEvent (load) {
    print (this, "bmax");
}
```

This event accomplishes two purposes. First, it waits until this movie clip has completely loaded until performing any actions, which is great because this whole SWF file is going to be loaded into Level 1. Secondly, once loaded, it tells Flash to print any printable frames contained within itself (by referencing with this). In this case, the only frame marked for printing is Frame 2.

Use the File ➪ Publish option to create an SWF file named template_receipt.swf from the template_receipt.fla file. This SWF file should be in the same directory as receipt_complete.fla. Then return to receipt_complete.fla and test the movie in Flash or in your browser. Enter any values you'd like in the fields and click the Create Invoice button to view what the printout looks like when you use the default Invoice movie clip contained inside this movie. Hold on to this printout to do an A-B comparison with the template you're about to implement.

Return to the Flash authoring environment for receipt_complete.fla to add the code to use the template layout contained in template_receipt.swf to display any printed data. Click the Create Invoice button at the bottom of the stage and change its ActionScript code to the following:

```
on (release) {
    total=Number(mowingServices)+Number(otherServices)+Number(rawMaterials);
    message="Thank You very much "+clientName+"! Have a nice day!";
    loadMovieNum ("template_receipt.swf", 1);
}
```

The first lines of code remain the same as what was already there (these just create some new variables), but the last line, instead of containing a print statement, now contains a loadMovieNum action that loads template_receipt.swf into Level 1.

Now you can test the receipt_complete.fla movie in Flash or your browser, enter some values in the text fields, and view the new print layout. No additional steps are necessary because as soon as the template_receipt.swf file arrives in Level 1, its Invoice movie clip and clipEvent execute the action to print itself out, with its text field variables referencing values from _level0, which is the main timeline of receipt_complete.swf.

Use the page you printed out previously to do a comparison between the two layouts. Figure 6-9 presents a visual representation of the differences between the two printed layouts (without any values filled in).

You've successfully loaded a completely different receipt layout! This capability enables you to create all kinds of dynamic files that you can load in to be printed out that can reference data pulled in from somewhere else in the Flash Player. Alternatively, they might not contain any text fields and might just be great-looking graphics that you want the user to be able to print.

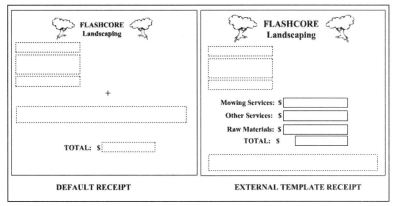

Figure 6-9: The differences between the default receipt/invoice layout contained within `receipt_comlete.fla` and the external one loaded in from `template_receipt.fla`.

There's one stone left unturned here, though. You may be thinking to yourself, "Why even bother loading into `_level` when you can load the `template_receipt.swf` file into the target `_root.invoice` in `_level0`, thereby replacing the default invoice with the new one?" Good question. The answer is because it doesn't work! When you load an SWF file into a target, any dynamic text fields you're trying to print can't properly pull their values from where they need to in time to send them to the printer. All graphic images display properly, however, so feel free to load external SWF files into targets (instead of levels) if all you need to do is print their great-looking graphics.

Tip   Using the `onClipEvent(load)` action is a great way to create a quick and easy preloader for any movie clip, including the ones in this last example. It saves you the trouble of having to manually create a preloader if you have only one (or a few) movie clips that need to exist in the SWF file you're loading into Flash.

Summary

Flash's printing feature is an amazing way to add dynamic interactivity to your Flash movie. Imagine a viewers' surprise when they click a button and images come out of their printers that are nowhere to be seen in the Flash movie! Most people are used to printing out Web pages where what they see is what they get. Flash adds the element of surprise, especially when a very large document can come out of a very tiny Flash movie. Use Flash's printing feature when it's appropriate and Web viewers will delight in returning to your site because you've created a complete interactive experience that bridges the gap between the online and offline worlds.

✦   ✦   ✦

Data Format for Generator Objects

A chart, a radio button, and a table are examples of objects you can make with a Generator template to enhance the looks of your Web site. Generator objects can be understood in two wholly different but related contexts. One context is a static one where data files provide one-time information for an object to be placed in a Flash movie and then on a Web page. Another context for Generator objects is one where data in the Generator templates is changed dynamically so that new data can be sent to the template and the object's appearance and even sound can be changed. For example, a user may want information about his or her stock portfolio, and with online processing of the Generator template, the latest data can be entered into the template, and a unique and updated chart can be presented on the Web page.

What the two contexts have in common is that the data sources and format are similar. Once the format is established, all that needs to be changed in a dynamic context is the data. This chapter examines the process of formatting data for different Generator objects and the tools used to create objects and data formats for storing data used in different objects.

Generator Object Palette and Panel

All of the common Generator objects are contained in the Generator Object palette. You add objects to a Flash movie by dragging them from the palette onto the stage. Once the object is on the stage, you use the Generator panel to set different parameters depending on the object selected. Figure 7-1 shows the common objects that come with Generator and are ready to use.

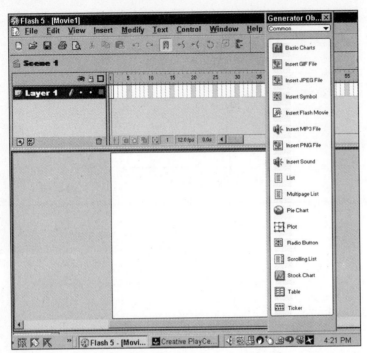

Figure 7-1: The Generator Object palette provides the common set of objects associated with Generator.

To access the Generator Object palette, choose Window ⇨ Generator Objects. If you're working with Generator objects, Flash doesn't require you to open the palette anew each time you work on a movie. Like other palettes and panels, the Generator Object palette will be be on the screen if left there when you close Flash.

Open the Generator panel by choosing Window ⇨ Panels ⇨ Generator. Depending on which object you have selected when you begin using the Generator panel, you will see different displays. Some displays of the panel have several options and parameters while others have relatively few. For example, Figure 7-2 shows the Generator panel that appears when the Basic Charts object is selected.

Most of the work done with Generator involves the use of the Generator Object palette and panel. In addition, you will be using a text editor such as Windows WordPad or Macinosh SimpleText. Generator uses data from the text files to fill the templates you develop when you are using the Generator panel.

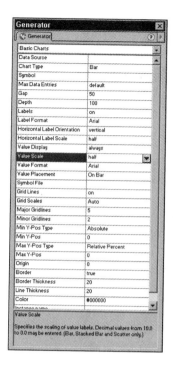

Figure 7-2: The Generator panel that appears when the Basic Charts object is selected shows a wide range of options.

Basic Data Formatting

Generator has two formats for external data for Generator objects. As you will see in the next section, each object requires its own variation of the two formats that are saved as text files. At a minimum, a single column of values is required, but some formats either require or have options for more than a single column. Columns need to be labeled correctly as well. If you want to use a column for color, for example, the column must be labeled *color,* and the entries beneath the label must be in the correct format.

Name-and-value format

The name-and-value format is set up to read variable names and their associated single value from a text file. The left column is for the variable name, and the right column is for the variable's associated value. In the first row, the labels `name` and `value` are both required in the following format:

```
name, value
```

Below the column labels, place the variable name, a comma (,), and the variable's value. Quotation marks are optional except where a comma is part of the value. For example, the following shows a legitimate list of variables and their values:

```
name, value
primate, monkey
whale, "Oh wow, look at that!"
population, 5776
growth, "280,543,321"
China, 1,345,324,198
```

The output from this list of variables would be as follows:

Variable	Output
Primate	monkey
Whale	Oh wow, look at that!
Population	5776
Growth	280,543,321
China	1

The only surprise is China. Because no quotes were placed around China's value, only the number to the left of the second comma in the line appears.

Defining variables in this manner is much different than using the standard URL encoding with ampersands discussed in Chapter 1. Because Generator likes its variables in this format, you cannot just load name/value pairs from a URL-encoded text file without first rearranging the data to conform to the new format outlined here. In fact, you'll notice the complete absence of any URL encoding in dynamic text files containing Generator variable data.

The next step after defining Generator name/value pairs is to use those variables and values inside a Generator template. Normally in ActionScript you would just reference the variable's name in your code, and Flash would insert the value. When creating a Generator template, however, you need to place the variable's name inside of curly braces ({}) to reference it either directly in a text field or in a parameter of the Generator panel.

Throughout this chapter you'll be using the Generator panel to enter parameter values for each Generator object. If you want to reference a variable in an external text file (formatted for Generator) instead of directly specifying that value in Flash, you can just put the variable's name in curly braces. For example, in the previous table the `Population` variable has a value of `5776`. If you wanted Generator to pull this variable from the external text file and use its value as a Generator parameter, you would type **{Population}** into the appropriate parameter field of the Generator panel.

As you've seen throughout the book, another great place to put variable values in your Flash movies is dynamic text fields. Normally when not using a Generator template, you need dynamic text fields to get the values of any variables displayed on the stage. When using a Generator template with external text file variables formatted for Generator, however, you don't need a dynamic text field! All you have to do is place static text on the stage, and anywhere you want Flash to insert the value of a variable, just place the variable's name in curly braces. For example, if you had an external Generator data text file that defines a variable named `coolProgram` to have a value of `Flash`, you could put the following static text on the stage:

```
I really love {coolProgram} !!!
```

Whenever Flash processed the Generator template, the viewer of the final Flash movie would see these words on the stage:

```
I really love Flash !!!
```

This process is known as creating a placeholder for your variables, and later in this chapter, you'll be using placeholders like these to dynamically place externally loaded text on the stage, all without any dynamic text fields!

Column name-and-value format

Use this second format when you have several variables and more than one value for each variable. If you are attempting to compare seasonal sales in four regions, for example, the seasons could be the variables, and the regions could be the different values that the variables contain. Stacked bar, line, and area charts are objects that require more than a single value for a variable. The following shows an example of how data might be organized to show how a company's products sold during the first half of the year and the second:

```
Hardware, Software, Services
250, 340, 440
833, "2,232", "3,121"
```

The optional quotation marks work the same way they do in the name-and-value format. Generally, it's a good habit to place quotation marks around all of the values, and the quotation marks are absolutely necessary when the value contains a comma you want to preserve. As you will see in the following section, all objects require data in one of these two formats.

Data Formatting for Objects' External Data Sources

This section shows how to set up data files for the different objects requiring external data. Each of the 11 objects that require a data source is discussed in turn. Text files showing sample data formatting for each of the objects and a short Flash example provide all the formatting information you need.

The Basic Charts object

The Basic Charts object is actually several different charts in a single object template. We are starting with a simple bar chart, and then we will look at the other types of charts associated with this object. The minimum data requirement is a single value column, but you can optionally include a color column, and we have done so in the example. Use the following steps to set up a basic bar chart and data source:

1. Drag the Basic Charts icon from the Generator Objects palette to the stage. Select the object, and using the Info panel, change the dimensions to W=400, H=300. Save the file as `Chart1.fla`. Figure 7-3 shows what your movie should look like at this point. Note the Info panel values.

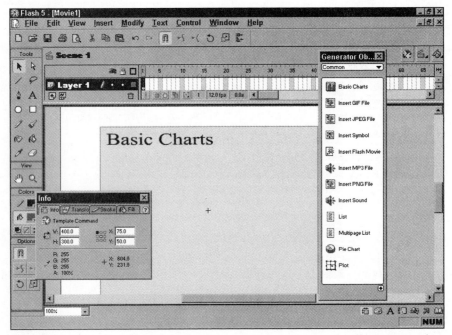

Figure 7-3: Once an object is on the stage, you can resize it using the Info panel.

2. Open a text editor such as Notepad (Windows) or SimpleText (Macintosh) and enter the following code, including the headings:

```
value, color
9,#079933
21,#A6F3C0
```

```
30,#A6A640
43,#803333
12,#FFFF80
29,#999999
```

Save the file as `chart1.txt` in the same folder as the Flash file you just saved.

3. Open the Generator panel by choosing Window ⇨ Panels ⇨ Generator. (You can close the Generator Object palette because you won't need it to complete this movie.) Use the following list as a guide to the settings you will choose. Some of the selections, such as Chart Type, Labels, and Max Y-Pos Type, have pop-up menus. When you click the chart parameter, the pop-up menu appears. When you click Color, a color well appears, and double-clicking the color well causes a color picker to appear.

Basic Charts

Data Source: chart1.txt

Chart Type: Bar

Symbol: leave blank

Max Data Entries: default

Gap: 75

Depth: 100

Labels: on

Label Format: Arial

Horizontal Label Orientation: vertical

Horizontal Label Scale: half

Value Format: Arial

Value Placement: On Bar

Symbol File: leave blank

Grid Lines: on

Grid Scales: Auto

Major Gridlines: 5

Minor Gridlines: 2

Min Y-Pos: 0

Max Y-Pos Type: relative Percent

Max Y-Pos: 0

Origin: 0

Border: true

Border Thickness: 20

Line Thickness: 20

Color: #000000

Instance name: chart1

4. Once all of the values have been inserted, press Ctrl+Enter (Windows) or
   Cmd+return (Macintosh) to test the movie. If all is in order, you will see the
   chart shown in Figure 7-4.

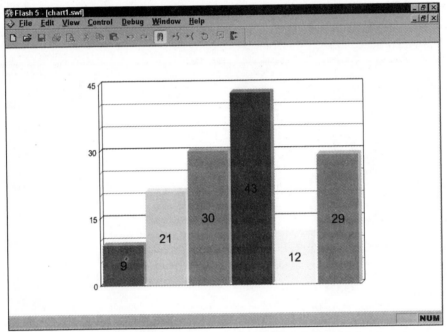

Figure 7-4: The settings listed in step 3 produced this 3-D bar chart.

Stacked charts

Data Source is the most important setting in the Generator panel. If you change the
Chart Type setting from a bar chart to either a line or an area chart, you can use the
same data source, but the other charts available in the Basic Charts object require
different data sets. For example, the following data shows four variables named
after a company's regional markets and a color variable. Each of the variables has
two values that can be shown on a stacked chart that could be used to compare
business in the first and second half of a year. The top row of values appears in the
top portion of the chart and the bottom row in the bottom portion of the chart
bars. Note also that the chart uses a text file in the column name-and-value format
rather than the name-and-value format of the unstacked charts.

```
North, East, South, West, Color
10,15,20,8,#FF260C
20,11,14,22,#B3B399
```

Save this data in a file named `chart2.txt`. Leave all of the parameters in the Generator panel the same except change the Data Source setting to `chart2.txt` and the Chart Type setting to Stacked Bar. Figure 7-5 shows the resulting chart.

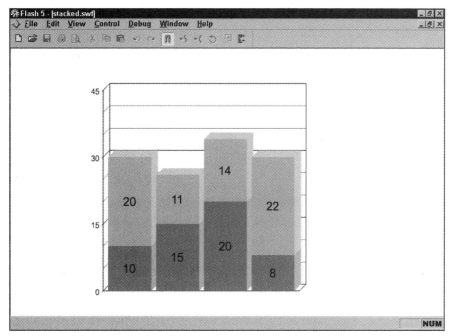

Figure 7-5: Stacked charts require different sets of data and formats than unstacked bar, line, or area charts.

Change the Chart Type setting from Stacked Bar to Stacked Line and Stacked Area and test the results. You can change some of the parameters to experiment with a design that works with the rest of the movie and the site you're preparing the chart for.

Scatter charts

The final basic chart is the scatter chart. Generator provides both scatter and line scatter versions. Scatter charts focus attention on key events and can show trends in specific directions based on several data points. Minimally, the chart requires an X and a Y column. Type the following data into your text editor and save the text file as `chart3.txt`.

```
X,Y
14,30
45,50
70, 40
90, 60
115,90
```

Scatter charts require some different parameter settings and optimally could use a symbol as well. This next set of steps shows how to set up a scatter chart:

1. Use the Oval tool to draw a circle with a green radial fill with the dimensions W=13, H=13. Select the circle and press the F8 key to open the Symbol Properties dialog box, and then select Graphic for Behavior. Type in **greenPlot** for the symbol's name in the Name box. Click OK.

2. If the little ball you just turned into a symbol is still on the stage, delete it from the stage. Generator scatter charts will access the object in the library.

3. In the Generator panel, make the following changes:

> Scatter
>
> Data Source: chart3.txt
>
> Chart Type: Scatter Line
>
> Symbol: greenPlot
>
> Value Placement: Over Bar
>
> Grid Lines: off
>
> Color: #FF0000

Figure 7-6 shows how the final scatter line chart appears in the SWF file.

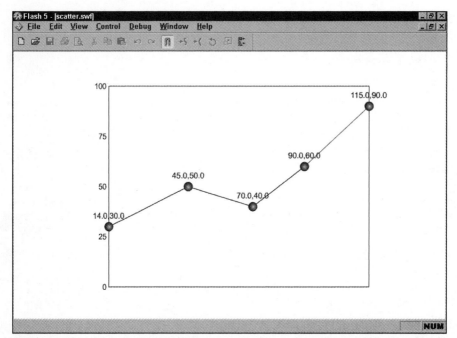

Figure 7-6: Scatter charts focus on the data points, but the line provides trend information as well.

Lists

Generator provides four different types of list objects. Using data from external data sources, the lists generate movie clips selected from the Clip column of the data source along with optional columns for inserted text. Each of the three list types is examined separately.

Standard list

The List object places selected movie clips on the screen along with optional text derived from a data source. Using Generator, you can change the movie clips or other placeholders (such as text) in the list to update their information. For example, a Web design company may want to list its services, but it also wants to be able to change the services or movie clips for those services regularly to keep its site interesting and up-to-date.

This next project uses two different movie clips to generate a list of three services, using one of the movie clips twice and the other one once. Open a new Flash page and create these three layers for the movie:

- ✦ List
- ✦ Labels
- ✦ Title

Save the movie as `List1.fla`. Figure 7-7 shows the initial stage and layout.

Begin by creating a text file and saving as `list1.txt` in the same folder where you saved the Flash movie. Use the following text:

```
Clip, service
flashMe, Engaging Flash
designMe, Cool Designs
flashMe, Backends
```

The first column provides the symbol names of the movie clips. The flashMe movie clip is used twice. The second column is reserved for words that describe the service. In the movie clip, those text blocks showing {service} will have their text replaced by the words in the second column.

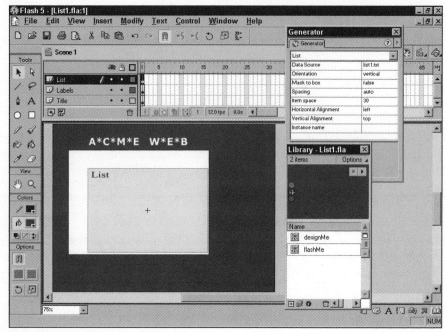

Figure 7-7: The movie clips that make up the list are not placed on the stage, but they are stored in the Library window.

List layer

On this layer, you will place the List object and set the Generator parameters. You will also create the movie clips that the List object will pull up in the SWF file. Use the following steps:

1. Open a new Flash page and drag the List object to the stage. Select the List icon on the page and, using the Info panel, change the dimensions to W=300, H=200. Use Figure 7-7 as a guide for placement.

2. Open the Library window by pressing Ctrl+L or Cmd+L. Near the top of the Library window, press the Options arrow to open the Library Options menu and select New Symbol. When the Symbol Properties dialog box opens, select Movie Clip for Behavior and name the movie clip **designMe**. Click OK.

3. In the Symbol Editing mode, add a layer and name the top layer **Rock** and the bottom layer **Service**. Click Frame 24 in the top layer and drag the mouse down to the bottom layer and press the F5 key to insert frames out to row 24.

4. Click the first frame of the Rock layer, and in the middle of the screen, type in a 32-point bold letter **D** using the Trajan font or another serif font you like. Use the Info panel to center the letter in position X=0, Y=0 relative to the center of the stage.

5. Click Frame 12 and press the F6 key to insert a keyframe. Select the letter, and in the Transform panel, click the Rotate button and type in **45** for the degree angle.

6. Click Frame 24 and press F6 to insert a keyframe. Change the rotation of the letter to 0 using the Transform panel. Figure 7-8 shows the movie clip in the Symbol Editing mode.

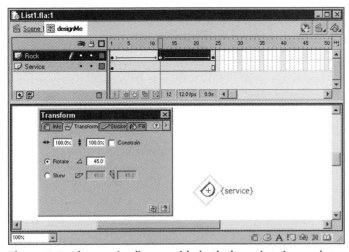

Figure 7-8: The movie clips provide both the animation and placeholders for the variable text used in the list.

7. Click Frame 1 in the Service layer and type in **{service}** in 14-point Verdana font as shown in Figure 7-8. Use the Info panel to set the text block to W=200. Note that the variable text can be much longer than the placeholder variable name ("service" is one of the two columns in the `list1.txt` text file). Choose Edit ➪ Edit Movie from the menu bar to exit the Symbol Editing mode.

8. Repeat steps 2 through 7 and create a second movie clip. Use any animation you want, but keep the scale small enough to serve as an icon in a list, roughly 55 by 55 in dimension. Name the movie clip **flashMe,** and check to make sure that it exists in the Library window. Also be sure to include a {service} placeholder next to the main icon.

9. Fill in the Generator panel cells as shown in the following list:

> List
>
> Data Source: list1.txt
>
> Orientation: vertical
>
> Mask to box: false
>
> Spacing: auto

Item space: 30

Horizontal Alignment: left

Vertical Alignment: top

Instance name: leave blank

Labels layer

Before starting this layer, drop in a dark blue background color (#003399) by choosing Modify ➪ Movie and then selecting the color from the background color well. This layer is where you can place your labels for the list. In this movie, we just put in the title A*C*M*E W*E*B, the name of a little-known and fictitious (as far as we could tell) Web design outfit serving the uninhabited deserts around Gila Bend, Arizona. You can add any other appropriate labels required. Use the Text tool with a 24-point bold Verdana and a cream color (#FFFFCC) to create the label.

Title layer

The Title layer is a backdrop for the List object. You may have noticed that when you put in the background color that the List object placeholder remained white. To provide a background color for the List object, you need a colored image behind it. Use the Rectangle tool to place a rectangle with the dimensions W=350, H=250 behind the List object. Position the layer so that it approximates the screen shown in Figure 7-7. Test the movie and you should see something like Figure 7-9 in your SWF file.

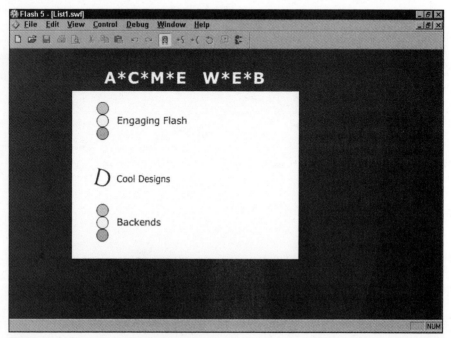

Figure 7-9: The data source provides specific text for the text variables and the order and type of symbols in the list.

Scrolling list

A scrolling list is almost like the standard list except that you can scroll it up and down. The scrolling is accomplished by adding two buttons: one to scroll up and one to scroll down. Also, you must use the Scrolling List object instead of the List object. By making a few changes in the standard list movie from the last section, you can create a scrolling movie.

A scrolling list works by a `play()` action being issued to the Scrolling List object using the instance name of the object. The Scrolling List object is treated as and addressed as a movie clip and the `play()` action initiates the scrolling movement. To reverse the movement, a script must issue a `prevFrame()` action addressed to the instance name of the Scrolling List object. That's really all there is to it. Using the `List1.fla` movie, this next set of steps shows how to make changes to the movie to transform it into a scrolling list:

1. Open the `List1.fla` movie and save it under the name `ScrollMe.fla`. Add a layer and name it **Buttons**. Select the List object and delete it. In its place, drag a Scrolling List object from the Generator Object palette to the stage and resize it to the dimensions W=300, H=200.

2. In a text editor, write and save the following text as `list2.txt`:

```
Clip, service
flashMe, Engaging Flash
designMe, Cool Designs
flashMe, Backends
designMe, Navigation
flashMe, E-business Solutions
designMe, Low Bandwidth
```

3. Open the Generator panel and put in the following values. One important difference to note is that the Mask to box parameter is true. By making it true, you prevent the objects from appearing out of the scrolling list box and in the title. Also, you must have an instance name. In this case, **roll** is used to reference the Scrolling List object. The step size determines the scrolling speed. Higher values increase the scroll speed, and lower values decrease it.

    Scrolling List

    Data Source: List2.txt

    Orientation: vertical

    Mask to box: true

    Step size: 10

    Spacing: auto

    Item space: 25

    Horizontal Alignment: left

    Vertical Alignment: top

    Instance name: roll

4. Click the Button layer and create two arrow buttons, one pointing upward and one downward. For the up arrow, use the following script:

```
on (release) {
_root.roll.play();
}
```

5. Enter the down arrow script to move the movie one frame down for each click:

```
on (release) {
_root.roll.prevFrame();
}
```

Figure 7-10 shows how the revised list movie now appears.

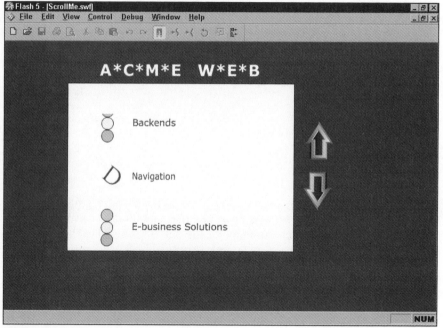

Figure 7-10: By adding scroll buttons and the accompanying ActionScript, a list can be as long as you need it.

Ticker

A Ticker object works like an automatic scrolling list. Using the same data source as the `ScrollMe.fla`, you can quickly center the Flash movie around a Ticker object instead of a scrolling list. The following steps show how:

1. Save the `ScrollMe.fla` movie as `TickerIt.fla`. Delete both buttons and the Scroll List object on the stage. Drag a Ticker object from the bottom of the Generator Object palette to the stage. Adjust the Ticker object size to W=300, W=200.

2. Select the Ticker object and fill out the Generator panel as shown in the following list:

> Ticker
>
> Data Source: List2.txt
>
> Orientation: vertical
>
> Mask to box: true
>
> Step size: 4
>
> Spacing: auto
>
> Item space: 0
>
> Horizontal Alignment: left
>
> Vertical Alignment: top
>
> Instance name: leave blank

That's all there is to it. You don't need an instance name for ActionScript to target because the Ticker object is self-starting and scrolls automatically and continuously.

Multipage list

The final list object is one that depends heavily on symbols and the data source. The Multipage List object is typically the only object on the stage, and a single layer and frame make up the movie. All the work is done in filling out the Generator panel, creating symbols, and arranging the data source. The key to this object is planning.

Our example of a multipage list is a project management one. For tracking purposes, a project is broken down into a number of tasks, and each task in the project is assigned to one or more individuals. As the project grows and changes, the individuals involved and the tasks they assume change, and for very large projects, a multipage list helps keep track of everyone. To add a bit of e-world project management to the list, we assumed that none of the people are in contact except by e-mail. As tasks and individuals are added or removed from the project, their names and duties can be changed in the data source text file. Figure 7-11 shows the initial page of the SWF file with a multipage object.

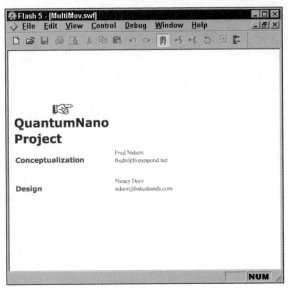

Figure 7-11: The initial page contains a heading from a text symbol and a customized navigation pointer.

Creating the data symbols

The first part of the project involves preparing symbols used in Multipage List objects. These symbols are referenced in both the data source and in the Generator panel. Those referenced in the data source need to be set up first. Only three symbol components are referenced in the data source: heading, project, and contact. The heading symbol appears on the first page only, and the other symbols and their associated data appear on different pages depending on their position in the data file. This next set of steps shows the process for creating the symbols used as placeholders for the data:

1. Drag a Multipage List object icon from the Generator Object palette to the stage. Save the movie as `MultiMov.fla`. In the Generator panel, enter the following data:

   > Multipage List
   >
   > Data Source: ProjMan.txt
   >
   > Items per page: 3
   >
   > Previous Symbol: Back
   >
   > Home Symbol: Home
   >
   > Next Symbol: Next
   >
   > Text Symbol: Contact
   >
   > Symbol spacing: 50

Line spacing: 50

External Symbol File: leave blank

Instance name: leave blank

Note that the Text Symbol, which is named Contact, is a source for the bulk of the text in this movie.

2. Choose Insert ➪ New Symbol from the menu bar. Select Graphic for Behavior and name the symbol **Contact**. Click OK.

3. In the Symbol Editing mode, use the Text tool to create a text box. Use a 12-point Times New Roman font colored dark green. When you type in the following text, use only a single text box for both text placeholders.

```
{name}
{email}
```

4. Create a second graphic symbol and name it **Project**. Using a bold, brick red, 14-point font, type in

```
{name}
```

5. Create a third graphic symbol and name it **Heading**. Instead of using a text placeholder, a single word is used in the same manner as a literal would be instead of a variable. Using a bold, dark blue, 24-point font, type in the following heading, placing a carriage return after QuantumNano:

```
QuantumNano
Project
```

Creating the data source

The data source for a Multipage Object relies on the placeholders in the symbols and the format in the Generator panel. The first column is Text, and because the Contact symbol has been defined in the Generator panel as the Text Symbol, all that is required is to enter the placeholder names in the column. Because both name and email were placed in the Contact symbol, those column headings are all that is required in the column list. They have been placed on the far right side. A second column for Symbol refers to any other symbols you plan to use, whether they have literal text or text placeholders.

Type in the following text in a text editor and save it as projMan.txt in the same folder where you saved the FLA file:

```
Text, Symbol,Project,Name,Email
,Heading,,,,,
,Project,Conceptualization,Fred Nabors,fredn@frozenpond.net
,Project,Design,Nancy Door,ndoor@bakedsands.com
,Project,Front End,Jessica Blink,jblink@openplains.com
,Project,Back End,Leon Jackson,leonj@highmountain.net
,Project,Database,Jared Patel,jaredp@humidityhi.com
,Project,Artwork,Laura Case,laurac@seashorehome.net
```

Creating the navigation symbols

The final step is to create the navigation symbols. These symbols can be any shape you want. We used two pointing fingers for the next and previous symbols and a rune for the home symbol. In the Generator panel, the names for the symbols must match the symbol names used in the actual symbols. In all three cases, use graphic symbols (*not* buttons or movie clips) and name them **next, home,** and **back** so that they match the symbol names in the Generator panel. You can use any names you want as long as they match the names you put into the Generator panel. When you are finished, you should have a total of six symbols in the Library window: the three navigation symbols and the three data symbols. The Multipage List object automatically arranges the navigation buttons, as shown in Figure 7-12.

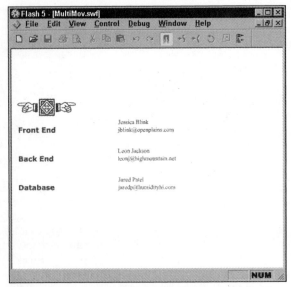

Figure 7-12: The Multipage object automatically arranges the navigation symbols on the page and will navigate to the next, previous or home (first) page in the movie.

Pie chart

Pie charts are used for displaying distribution. If a company is attempting to keep track of expenses, for example, one way to quickly see what organizational units are costing the most is to place all of the unit expenses into a pie chart. In Generator, all of the pie charts show proportional representation based on a given set of values. So although absolute values are displayed on each pie slice, what you are actually seeing is a slice based on the value's proportion to the whole. As a result, you can see both absolute and proportional values simultaneously.

To create a pie chart, you need a two-column data source. One column contains the values to be placed in the slices, and the other column is a color code. In your text editor, type in the following table and save it as `myPie.txt`.

```
Value,Color
56,#EE452B
44,#DECC00
26,#6E5E00
28,#C5660C
54,#FFE673
33,#FFB340
```

Caution   Avoid using black as a color code if your labels are going to be placed on top of the slices because the text color is black.

After you have your data source, look at this next set of steps to find out how to create a pie chart. As you will see, it is one of the easiest charts to create.

1. Open a new Flash page and drag a Pie Chart object icon onto the stage. Using the Info panel, set the dimensions of the icon to W=400, H=400.

2. Select the Pie Chart icon, open the Generator panel, and then enter the following values:

> Pie Chart
>
> Data Source: myPie.txt
>
> Depth: 350
>
> Value Display: Always
>
> Value Format: Arial
>
> Value Placement: Inside
>
> Value Scale: Half
>
> External Symbol File: leave blank
>
> Border: False
>
> Border Thickness: leave blank
>
> Color: leave blank
>
> Instance name: leave blank

The values can be placed inside or outside of the slices. If a slice is too small to contain a value, the value is automatically placed on the outside of the slice. If you select Half on the Value Scale, the values are more likely to be small enough to fit within the slices, and they tend not to overwhelm. Figure 7-13 shows the SWF file with the parameters and data used in this example.

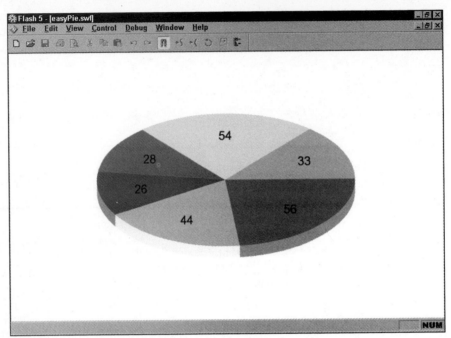

Figure 7-13: Pie charts are used to show distribution quickly and clearly.

Plot

The Plot object relies heavily on movie clips and the data source because the Generator panel itself requires little data other than minimum and maximum parameters. Movie clips can be simple or complex, and depending on how you use the Plot object, you can give it an instance name to be referenced and used with ActionScript.

The basic use of a Plot object, however, is to create a way of displaying data points using one or more movie clips. In this respect, it is not unlike a Scatter object. The main difference lies in the control you have over the clips in the plot. In addition to controlling the x- and y-coordinates, you can control the size (scale) and rotation of the objects.

Suppose you have a client with products in both domestic and international markets. You want to show how well different products are doing in both markets, how profitable the product is, and what the performance is relative to the previous year. In addition, you have new products that you want the same information about, except for the comparison to the previous year. The plot's vertical axis represents sales in international markets, and the horizontal axis represents the domestic market. The size (scale) of the movie clip represents the product's profitability. Established products are represented by triangles that point upward for a better performance than the previous year, downward for poorer performance, and sideways for no change. New products are represented by green circles; the scale of each circle reflects that product's profitability (bigger is more profitable). With this type of information, the plot shows at a glance the three different types of information for each product and, in the plot context, how each product is faring relative to the others.

To set up this project, open a new Flash page and use the following layers:

- ✦ Plot
- ✦ Label

Save the movie as ThickPlot.fla and then start putting the parts together.

Plot layer

Select the Plot layer in the movie and follow these steps to get started:

1. Drag a Plot object from the Generator Object palette to the stage. Select the Plot object and, using the Info panel, set the dimensions to W=400, H=350.

2. The Plot object allows you the option to substitute names for the different columns instead of using the default names such as X and Y or Xscale and Yscale. This example takes advantage of that feature and renames the x-axis **Domestic** and the y-axis **International**. Using such names helps remind you what each is used for when entering the data in the data source. In the Generator panel, enter the following values:

     Plot

     Data Source: myPlot.txt

     Min X-Pos: 0

     Max X-Pos: 100

     Min Y-Pos: 0

     Max Y-Pos: 100

     X Column: Domestic

     Y Column: International

     X-Scale Column: leave blank

     Y-Scale Column: leave blank

     Rotate Column: leave blank

     Symbol Name Column: leave blank

     Instance Column: leave blank

     Border: on

     Border Color: black

     Border Thickness: 20

     Instance name: leave blank

3. Open up a text editor and enter the following text and save it as `myPlot.txt`. Notice that instead of using X and Y columns for the x/y position of the data points, we are able to substitute `Domestic` and `International`.

```
Clip,Domestic,International,Xscale,Yscale,Rotate
NewProd,50,70,0.5,0.5,0
NewProd,20,50,1,1,0
NewProd,70,20,1.5,1.5,0
NewProd,60,80,0.2,0.2,0
Prod, 7,10,0.7,0.7,180
Prod, 45,20,0.2,0.2,90
Prod, 70,70,1.5,1.5,0
Prod, 23,67,0.5,0.5,180
Prod, 92,40,0.3,0.3,0
```

Label layer

In this layer, you need to add labels to the horizontal and vertical axis. This layer would also be a good place to create the movie clips needed to represent the product categories. The following steps outline the process:

1. Use a dark green (#006600), 14-point, bold Verdana font to type the word **International** along the left side of the Plot object icon. After each letter, press Enter/Return to create a vertical label in all caps. With the same font type in all capital letters, type the word **Domestic** directly beneath the Plot object icon on the stage. After each letter, press the space bar to add some breathing room for the label because it's in all capital letters.

2. Press Ctrl+F8 or Cmd+F8 to open Symbol Properties dialog box. Select Movie Clip for Behavior and enter **Prod** for the name. Click OK to enter the Symbol Editing mode. Draw a triangle with a yellow (#FFCC00) fill and black stroke with dimensions of H=40, W=40.

3. Repeat step 2 using the name **NewProd** and drawing a circle with a dark green (#006600) fill with the same dimensions of H=40, W=40 as the other symbol.

After you have completed the movie, test it. Figure 7-14 shows the SWF file you should see. Change the parameters in the data source file to experiment with placement and scale.

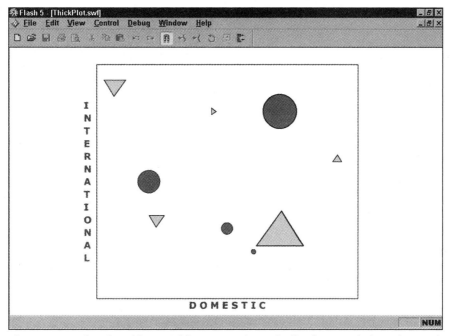

Figure 7-14: The Plot object enables you to dynamically place symbols and control their placement, scale, and rotation properties.

Stock chart

The Stock Chart object is optimized for tracking stocks, but you can use it for other data that have a beginning value, an ending value, and highs and lows in between. Weather values, for example, could be usefully plotted on such a chart. Like the Plot object, the Stock Chart object relies on the information placed into the Generator panel and data source.

The data source for the Stock Chart object requires four column headings: Open, Close, High, and Low. Each value can be expressed as either an integer or a floating-point number. But you cannot put in fractions, such as 10 ⅜. All fractions must be expressed as decimals. For example, type the following text in a text editor and save it as `StockPortfolio.txt` in the same folder as your Flash movie.

```
Open, Close, High, Low
22,25,27.3,21.2
25,27.5,28.3,24.7
27.5,27.8,29.9,26.2
27,25,28.3,22
25,30,31.3,23.7
30,22,33.3,21.2
22,25,27.3,21.2
```

Open a new Flash page and save it as `StockExchange.fla`. Rename the layer **Stock** and most of your work is done. The only other task is to drag a Stock Chart icon from the Generator Object palette, resize it to the dimensions H=400, Y=350, and then enter the following data in the Generator panel. When you're finished, save your file. Figure 7-15 shows the finished Flash movie.

Stock Chart

Data Source: StockPortfolio.txt

Chart Type: Candlesticks

Max Data Entries: default

Start Offset: 0

Gap: 0

Open Column: open

Close Column: close

High Column: high

Low Column: low

Labels: On

Label Format: Arial

Horizontal Label Orientation: vertical

Horizontal Label Scale: .20

Value Format: Arial

Value Display: Always

Value Scale: .20

Value To Display: Close

Value Placement: Over Bar

External Symbol File: leave blank

Grid Lines: on

Grid Scales: Auto

Major Gridlines: 5

Minor Gridlines: 2

Min Y-Pos Type: Absolute

Max Y-Pos :0

Max Y-Pos Type: Relative Percent

Max Y-Pos: 50

Border: true

Border Thickness: 20

Line Thickness: 20

Color: #B38026

Instance name: leave blank

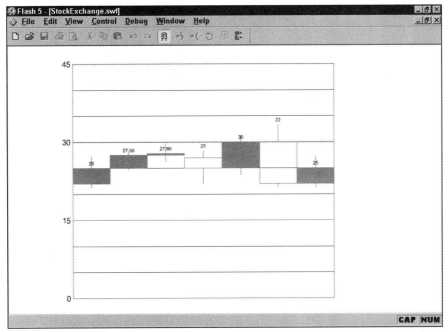

Figure 7-15: Vertical lines in the Candlestick format show the highs and lows; the boxes show the opening and closing values.

Table

The Table object is a bit trickier than it would appear to be. Each element in the table is a symbol, including all the text. The text symbols provide placeholders for the different text material in the table. The data source contains the same number of symbols as the number of cells in the table. Each column positions the material in the corresponding column in the table. To best understand how tables work in Generator, begin with the following text, which constitutes a data source used in the sample table. Enter the data in a text editor and save it as QuickTable.txt. (Note how the data has been grouped in rows of three; that grouping is for purposes of clarification only.)

```
Clip,phone,address

Ambulance,0,0
phone,911,0
address,0,521 E. Arlington

Police,0,0
phone,911,0
address,0,211 Orange Road

Fire,0,0
phone,911,0
address,0,832 Polk Street

Bus, 0,0
phone,555-6843,0
address,0,99 Main Street

Information,0,0
phone,555-INFO,0
address,0,6772 Apricot Lane
```

The first column on top refers to the movie clips used as row headings, and each of the two other column headings are for variables named in the text symbols. The groupings of three rows represent the three columns in each row. For example, the third grouping of data after the column headings begins with Fire. In this project, we used a fire engine symbol to begin the row and followed it with the phone number. In the second row of the grouping, the clip is a text symbol called phone, and because the data for the telephone number goes in the second column, the second column contains the number 911. In the next row, the address clip is used, and the data goes in the third column. Placing a 0 in the second row ensures that the address will not be placed there incorrectly (the address goes in the third column). By using the same name for the variable and the symbol, you can use the intersection of the row and column of the same name to help put data in the correct place. Figure 7-16 shows the Flash movie being prepared with several symbols containing either text or icons for row headings.

The sample movie, Table.fla, uses two layers:

   ✦ Table

   ✦ Labels

The table is set up to use icons to quickly identify essential services. The emergency icons have animated flashing lights and the non-emergency icons are graphic symbols with no animation.

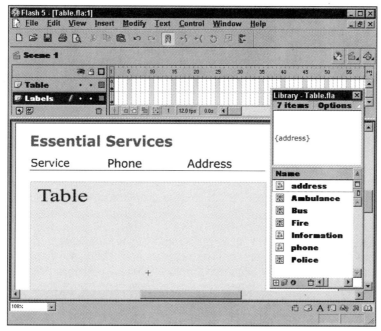

Figure 7-16: Symbols containing placeholders for text are an essential part of Flash movies that use Generator Table objects.

Table layer

To set up the Table layer, drag a copy of the Table object icon from the Generator Object palette to the stage. Resize the Table icon to the dimensions W=400, H=300. The table in the movie has five rows and three columns. Because the cells tend to get in the way of the information in the table, the border has been turned off. The following data shows how to fill out the Generator panel for the Table object:

> Table
>
> Data Source: QuickTable.txt
>
> Rows: 5
>
> Columns: 3
>
> Horizontal Alignment: left
>
> Vertical Alignment: top
>
> Sizing: fixed
>
> Default Symbol: leave blank

Row Labels: leave blank

Column Labels: leave blank

Label Format: Arial

Label Sizing: auto

Symbol File:

Border: off

Border Color:

Border Thickness:

Instance name:

Labels layer

In the Labels layer, the focus is on setting up column labels for the table. You will have to use some trial-and-error to position the labels just where you want them depending on precisely where the columns appear in your table. Because no border or grid is used to separate the data, the labels must be aligned above the correct column. Wait until you have tested your movie with all of the parts working before trying to align the labels. For the time being, use Figures 7-16 and 7-17 as rough guides for where to type in the **Essential Services** title and **Service, Phone,** and **Address** headings. You can make adjustments later.

The heart of Table objects lies in preparing the text symbols and row symbols. Use the following steps as a guide:

1. Prepare the text symbol by choosing Insert ⇨ New Symbol from the menu bar to open the Symbol Properties dialog box. Enter **phone** as the name, Graphic as the Behavior, and then click OK. You are now in the Symbol Editing mode.

2. Select the Text tool and use a 14-point purple type to type {phone}. That creates the phone variable placeholder. Select the text box, and in the Info panel, set the width to W=140. Remember that the text box has to be long enough to hold data that may be longer than the variable name.

3. Repeat steps 1 and 2 to create a second text symbol and use the variable name {address}. Set the width of the text box to W=180.

4. Repeat step 1, except select Movie Clip as the Behavior. In Symbol Editing mode, draw an ambulance and optionally add blinking lights.

5. Repeat step 4 until you have additional movie clips showing a police car, fire truck, bus, and information symbol. You should have five movie clips total. Figure 7-17 shows you what your table will look like when it is completed.

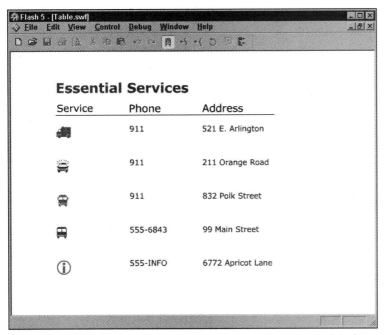

Figure 7-17: If any of the information in a table has to be updated or changed, all you need to do is to change the data source information.

After going through all that work to create a table in Generator, you may conclude that you could do the same thing with less effort using HTML and a Web development tool such as Dreamweaver or GoLive. But if your table data is regularly updated, all you need to change in a Generator table is the data itself and the information can then be sent to all the sites that use the same data source. You don't have to resave a Web page or go into a site to make a new page for data that changed in one of more of the site's pages. Weather tables are especially well suited for the Generator Table object because their data is updated regularly.

Replicate

Those banner ads that appear when you open a Web page in many commercial sites can be anything from informative and effective to annoying. But if you do them right, you can get a lot of information to a lot of people and not be a pest. Using the Replicate object from Generator, you can take any number of symbols and put on a slide show on the Web. What's more, once the banner is in place, you can change it simply by changing the information in the data source.

Setting up an effective Flash movie using the Replicate object requires setting two different Generator panels. Neither panel requires much information, but because more than a single panel must be set, one panel must reference the data source set up in the other. The banner ad in this example is for the fictitious company Acme HiRisk a boiler-room outfit attempting to recruit e-mail solicitors using the Internet and home computers. Four movie clips are repeated in the banner along with text broken down into a key remark, a question, and an answer. Begin by typing in the following data source file and saving it as `rep.txt`. (Added spacing between the lines is for clarity. Each of the five rows has four columns separated by a comma and no carriage returns except at the end of each row block.)

```
Clip,Key,Question,Answer

LittleTree,Your money can grow.,But how?,Acme HiRisk!

BigTree,You need a comfortable place,When can I start?,Now with Acme!

Busy,We know you're busy,Where will I find time?,Little time is required!

Computer,Home Computer Business,How can I learn?,Acme HiRisk will teach you!
```

Creating a Replicate object

After you have the data source file saved, open a new Flash movie and rename the default layer **Replicate**. It is the only layer in the movie on the main timeline. Save the movie as `RepBanner.fla` and use the following steps to get started:

1. Prepare the text symbol by choosing Insert ⇨ New Symbol from the menu bar to open Symbol Properties dialog box. Use **TextBlock** as the name, Graphic as the Behavior, and then click OK. You are now in the Symbol Editing mode.

2. Select the Text tool and click the stage. In 16-point, bold, dark green Verdana font, type {**Key**}. Click below the first text block, and in a new text block using a 14-point, nonbold, dark green Verdana font, type {**Question**}, press Enter or Return, and type {**Answer**}. Use the Align panel to left-align the two text blocks.

3. Return to the main timeline by clicking the Scene 1 icon in the upper-left corner of the window. Select the text graphic symbol TextBlock and drag an instance of it to the stage. Open the Generator panel and select Replicate in the top pop-up menu. You have now created a Replicate object. (You may have noted that the Generator Object palette has no Replicate object icon to drag onto the stage.)

4. With the TextBlock instance selected, make the following entries into the Generator panel:

   Replicate

   Data Source: rep.txt

   Expand Frames: true

Setting up the slide show

Once the Replicate object is set up, you need to work on it in the Symbol Editing mode and put the Insert Symbol object inside the Replicate object. This next set of steps shows how:

1. Double-click the TextBlock on the stage to enter the Symbol Editing mode for the TextBlock symbol.

2. Open the Generator Object palette and drag the Insert Symbol icon onto the stage to the left of the text variable placeholders.

3. With the Insert Symbol icon selected on the stage, open the Generator panel and insert the following information:

   Insert Symbol

   Data Source: {Clip}

   Scale to Fit: true

   Instance name: leave blank

   The information for the Data Source is a variable instead of a specified file. Because the Insert Symbol object is inside a Replicate object, the Insert Symbol object can indirectly reference the Clip variable in the Replicate object's data source, rep.txt. (It essentially references the Clip column in rep.txt.)

4. To space the sequence of the replicated and inserted symbols, click Frame 24 and press the F5 key to insert a frame. At 12 frames per second, that amount of spacing gives each image and message 2 seconds before the next image and message appear. You can make it longer or shorter by adding or subtracting frames. When you're finished, exit the Symbol Editing mode by pressing Ctrl+E or Cmd+E.

All that is left to do is to create four graphic symbols with the images you want to put into the banner. Figure 7-18 shows one image and text message you will see on the stage when the movie runs.

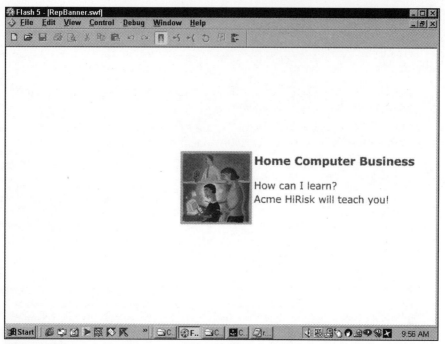

Figure 7-18: Using the Replicate and Insert Symbol objects together, you can create animated banners that can be easily updated by changing the information in an external data file.

Linking to External Data Sources

Flash 5 movies created using Generator objects can use external data sources as well as data sources in the same folder as the SWT/SWF files. In the Data Source parameter of Generator Objects, you can just as easily put in a URL to a remote site. You can also put the data into a server-side script or a more dynamic file such as a SQL or MySQL database to be retrieved by Generator. Any scripts like these must output the data in a format that Generator can understand. Likewise, HTML files that generate text files can serve as a source of external data for Generator objects.

For the most part, though, all you need is a simple text file. You can store that text file in any Web server and access it by typing in the URL in the Data Source row of the Generator panel. You could, for example, create a data file on a Windows PC, store it on a Linux-based server, and then develop the page on a Macintosh. When the file is launched, everything will work fine.

You can specify links to external data sources containing variables and name/value pairs for the main timeline as well as individual movie clips. Press the Generator Environment Variable button at the upper-right corner of the timeline when you're on the main timeline or in the editing mode of a movie clip timeline. A small window pops up asking you to type in the path (relative or absolute) to the text file or server script that is going to send variables back in a Generator-friendly format. There are also buttons to specify whether the data is being delivered in column name-and-value format or name-and-value format for simple variable declarations. Once Generator variables are loaded into the specified timeline, any object in that timeline can use them by just referencing a variable's name and enclosing it in curly braces.

Note   You can't specify an external data source for the timelines of buttons or graphic symbols. You can still press the Generator Environment Variable button and display the pop-up window, but specifying any external data sources in these symbol types has no effect and does not load your data correctly.

One additional feature of the Data Source pop-up window is that you can directly enter your data name/value pairs as you would if they were in an external text file. You just need to place a pound sign (#) as the first character in the first line. So if you wanted to set three Generator name/value variables that reside permanently in the SWT template, you would just pop open the Generator Environment Data Source window and enter code something like the following:

```
#NAME, VALUE
bobAge, 26
steveAge, 32
mikeAge, 19
```

This method works effectively for name/value pairs only. It's useful for setting variables that you need to update only once in a while. You don't want these variables ever hanging around on the server in a text file where someone might take a look at them; they're more secure inside of the SWT template where no one can see them but you.

Using the Generator Server Programs

This section explores the Generator Server programs in detail. Many people are often confused by when to use Generator, what Generator is, what it can do, and how to install it. Generator comes in several different "flavors" and has many unique uses; we'll try to cover many of the common uses as well as the ones that are most easily accessible by the average developer on a typical budget.

Generator demystified

Any Flash content dynamically manufactured by Generator consists of four parts that need to come together before the final output is achieved:

✦ The Generator SWT template created in Flash

✦ The data source, whether internal to the SWT template or loaded from an external text file

✦ Any raw materials, such as images or sounds, that need to be pulled into Generator

✦ The Generator Server program that compiles the template, data source(s), and any raw materials into a final SWF Flash movie file

The last part concerning Generator Server can confuse you if you don't understand what Generator Server consists of and what it is meant to do. Generator Server is not a program in the same way that Flash is. You can't open it up on your desktop and use some handy drop-down menus to configure it and perform tasks such as saving files.

Generator Server is a plug-in system for many of the most popular server types. Once installed, Generator lurks around in the background of the server waiting for someone surfing the Web to stumble upon a Web page containing an SWT template. When this happens, Generator springs to life and looks at the SWT template along with data source and raw materials (if applicable) and compiles a full Flash SWF movie that is delivered to the viewer. The person looking at the final compiled extravaganza never knows that Generator was used at all.

Generator processing happens in the background on the server, and viewers see the final Flash movie as they would see any other nongenerated Flash movie that may have been on the server. Using the Generator Server in this manner is referred to as using *Online Generator* or *Online mode* because the processing happens online and in real time each and every time a viewer looks at a Web page with an SWT template.

You can use the Generator Server in another equally powerful and even more interesting way. This other method is referred to as using Offline Generator or Offline mode, and it means that the Generator Server program is not acting in real-time response to requests for Web content but is being told directly and specifically by you (or by a CGI script you create) to manufacture Flash movies. The power in this method lies in the fact that you can create SWT templates that have prescribed object movements (such as moving a bitmap image around the stage) and then dynamically create a whole army of SWF Flash movies in a matter of seconds that all use identical object movements but have unique and different objects in each SWF file!

Offline mode can generate more than just SWF files. It can create GIFs, JPEGs, PNGs, Quicktime movies, text files, image maps, and both PC and Mac Projector files. Many output file formats can be batched and generated using Offline mode, and although you may be hard-pressed to find a use for some of them, at least you know they exist!

Generator Enterprise Edition

Just like the *Starship Enterprise* on old episodes of *Star Trek*, the Generator Enterprise Edition is the flagship of the Generator product line. It used to cost a measly $30,000, but in April of 2001, Macromedia changed the price to $2,999 per processor. This pricing means that if you have two Web servers, each with a dual processor, you'll need four licenses at $2,999 each. Although Generator Enterprise Edition still isn't cheap, it definitely has the power to supply high-traffic Web sites with real-time generated content each and every time a viewer to that Web site requests a page containing an SWT template.

The Enterprise Edition was designed for business applications, and when used in Online mode, it is capable of processing hundreds of requests per second. Its true power lies in the fact that it can generate real-time content for tens of thousands of Web viewers every day in Online mode. The more processors on the server CPU, the more powerful Enterprise Edition becomes. Unfortunately, the more generating you need it to do, the more it's going cost you. This program can be a hard sell to cost-conscious clients, and it's definitely not going find its way into any mom-and-pop Web sites. Macromedia seems to have almost priced itself out of a market where many more companies would be using Generator and consequently thousands of more developers would take an interest in learning and deploying Generator. Generator's price reduction from $30,000 range is definitely helping this situation to improve.

Enterprise Edition can be used in Offline mode as well and makes short work of whipping up massive batches of Flash movies. It can also employ a unique feature in Online mode called *caching* where it keeps track of the content most often generated; this feature enables Enterprise Edition to work even faster. Speed is the key selling point of the Enterprise Edition, but most common folk would wait a few extra seconds if they could save about $2,000, so Macromedia has created another edition of Generator.

Generator Developer Edition

Generator Developer Edition can do everything that Enterprise Edition can do, except for the caching, and sells for the more reasonable price of about $999. If you're running a high-power Web site with massive amounts of traffic and plan on using Generator in the real-time Online mode, this edition might be too slow for your needs. In many cases, though, you'd be surprised at how admirably Developer Edition performs in comparison to the more robust Enterprise Edition.

In Offline mode, Developer Edition performs the same exact tasks as Enterprise Edition but is somewhat slower in manufacturing Flash files. Offline mode usually means that the content doesn't need to be available on a split-second basis, so a few extra seconds to process the templates doesn't make a difference to most people when they can save thousands of dollars. Developer Edition is targeted more at Web developers and small Web sites, as well as people running small servers on collocated boxes or on a DSL line out of their apartments.

Generator installation

Installing any Generator edition on your computer or Web server is fairly easy because Generator comes with a standard installer utility. Generator can be run on Windows 95/98/2000 with or without a Web server as well as Windows NT, Sun Solaris, or Red Hat Linux. The Offline mode will run fine on any of these systems, although for Online mode you'll need to be running a Web server on your operating system so that means you need Personal Web Server 4.0 for Windows 95/98/2000, IIS for Windows NT, Apache or Netscape for Sun, and Apache for Red Hat Linux. The newest edition of Generator was released in March 2001 and includes support for many other Web servers operating on these platforms. Generator doesn't currently run on any Macintosh platform. For complete details of the system requirements and platforms Generator supports as well as patches and updates, you can visit `www.macromedia.com`.

Both Generator Enterprise Edition and Developer Edition are available for 30-day free trial download from Macromedia's Web site. (A trial version of the Developer Edition is also available on the CD in the back of this book.) In order to work through the examples in the upcoming section, we recommend that you go to the Macromedia Web site and get the correct free trial version for the platform you're using. Don't worry about running a Web server; we'll be talking more about offline generating.

Once you download the trial version, make sure to uncheck the installation option for the Jrun server extensions or any other server package listed if you don't have a Web server running on your machine. Also be sure to fill out your correct e-mail address on the big long form that you submit before you download the trial version to make sure that you'll receive the serial numbers Macromedia will automatically send to you. You can't install any of the Generator software without these serial numbers. When the download is complete, just launch the file that you downloaded, and the automatic installation will start. Choose the correct option regarding running a Web server and then enter the serial number Macromedia e-mailed you.

Caution   On most Windows machines, Generator installs to the directory `C:\Program Files\Macromedia\Generator`, and we recommend that you let it install to this directory because this path is the one most commonly used and referenced when Generator is targeted for the offline generating of files.

The first thing you'll notice if you open up the directory where Generator was installed is a program called `generate.exe`. You would think that clicking this program would make Generator spring to life and perform some miraculous feats, but clicking this file displays a little MS-DOS window that just as quickly disappears, leaving you none the wiser as to how Generator works or what it does. Generator has no GUI (Graphical User Interface) whatsoever; you have to launch and configure it using the archaic commands of the MS-DOS command line.

Note The trial versions of Generator automatically stick the Macromedia logo into all SWF files. It always appears at a different location on the stage, and it always reminds you that you're dealing with a trial version of Generator. With this logo floating around all the time, you'll find it difficult to use the Generator trial version for anything but learning Generator and deciding whether it's the right solution for you.

Online Generator

Online Generator is a very simple way to generate Flash content. If you have one of the supported Web server programs installed on your computer, you can start generating online content immediately. Anytime the server receives a request for an SWT file, Generator springs to life and dynamically delivers the compiled SWF file to the Web browser that requested it. Try placing some SWT templates in your server directories along with any associated data source files and accessing them via a Web browser. You should see the generated SWF files if you installed Generator correctly.

Note The many ins and outs of using and troubleshooting Online Generator are beyond the scope of this book. Because each server type has so many of its own subtleties, a good portion of the money you pay when buying one of the Generator editions is earmarked for tech-support. If you have problems, check Macromedia's Web site for tech notes or give Macromedia a call.

One of the options you have in Online mode is passing variables to the SWT template via a query string much like the methods described at the end of Chapter 1 for doing this with Flash files. The SWT file is embedded in the `<object>` and `<embed>` tags of the HTML page exactly where the Flash SWF file would normally go. All the same options and parameters apply, you just have to specify an SWT file instead of an SWF file. You can pass a query string of URL-encoded variables into the SWT file by just amending it to a query string in either the HTML code or the ASP/PHP/CGI code if you're generating your HTML pages dynamically. For example, the code to place an SWT template named `worldmap.swt` on an HTML page and pass it a variable named `countryName` with a value of `United States` would read as follows:

```
<OBJECT classid="clsid:D27CDB6E-AE6D-11cf-96B8-444553540000"
codebase="http://download.macromedia.com/pub/shockwave/cabs/flash
/swflash.cab#version=5,0,0,0" WIDTH=400 HEIGHT=300>
<PARAM NAME=movie VALUE="worldmap.swt?countryName=United%20States">
<PARAM NAME=quality VALUE=high> <PARAM NAME=bgcolor VALUE=#FFFFFF>
<EMBED src=" worldmap.swt?countryName=United%20States "
```

```
quality=high bgcolor=#FFFFFF WIDTH=400 HEIGHT=300
TYPE="application/x-shockwave-flash"
PLUGINSPAGE="http://www.macromedia.com/shockwave/download
/index.cgi?P1_Prod_Version=ShockwaveFlash"></EMBED>
</OBJECT>
```

Many people reading this book probably don't have a Web server at their immediate disposal where they can install something like Generator. Most hosting companies will not let you install software such as Generator unless you own or collocate your server at that company. Very few companies offer Generator hosting, but they do appear from time to time. But keep in mind that the pricing structure of Generator is such that it is to be sold to the end client and not to be bought and resold by a hosting company.

Offline Generator

You can use Generator in Offline mode if you're running one of the supported operating systems and regardless of whether you have any Web server software installed. The most common application is on Windows 95/98/2000 and Windows NT, so the paths and parameters in this section relate directly to those installations.

Offline Generator allows you to take the SWT templates you create in Flash and use them to output many different file types, including SWF Flash movies. In the following example, you'll create a Generator SWT template with a JPEG image object that performs a motion tween. You'll then use Offline Generator to insert five different JPEG images into the template and create five different SWF files in a matter of seconds. The commands and parameters are sent to Generator via a batch (BAT) file written in a simple text editor and executed by Windows.

Using the MS-DOS command line

New releases of the Windows operating system are still based around the old MS-DOS operating system. In fact, Windows is just a very high-tech disguise for MS-DOS, and after many revisions of Windows, most people have forgotten about MS-DOS altogether. It's still there though, and you can access it by using the Windows Start menu and choosing Start ⇨ Programs ⇨ MS-DOS Prompt. You'll see a little window similar to the one in Figure 7-19.

At the prompt in the MS-DOS Prompt window, enter this code:

```
cd C:\PROGRA~1\MACROM~1\GENERA~1
```

This line is the shorthand way to get you into the directory `C:\Program Files\Macromedia\Generator`. The shorthand way takes the first six letters of any directory name regardless of spaces, capitalizes them, and adds a ~1 to the end. The `cd` is the command to change the directory. Upon entering the complete line of code, you should find yourself in the Generator directory. Although using the MS-DOS prompt program is a time-consuming way to get things done, the MS-DOS window does provide you with a behind-the-scenes look at what the system is doing when you run batch files.

```
MS-DOS Prompt                                                    _ □ ×
T 10 x 16  ▾   ▢ ▣ ▣ ▣  ▣ ▣  A

Microsoft(R) Windows 98
   (C)Copyright Microsoft Corp 1981-1998.

C:\WINDOWS>cd C:\PROGRA~1\MACROM~1\GENERA~1

C:\Program Files\Macromedia\Generator 2>dir/w

 Volume in drive C has no label
 Volume Serial Number is 3D04-6A50
 Directory of C:\Program Files\Macromedia\Generator 2

[.]              [..]            UNINST.ISU      [DEMOS]         GENERATE.EXE
[HELP]           [EXAMPLES]      INSTAL~1.SWT    LICENSE.TXT     README.HTM
[BIN]            SERIAL~1.EXE    [CLASSES]       [JRE]           [LIB]
[LOGS]           [PROPER~1]      [SERVLETS]      [SESSIONS]      [FONTS]
[API_DOCS]       [EXTRAS]
         6 file(s)        700,941 bytes
        16 dir(s)       3,266.98 MB free

C:\Program Files\Macromedia\Generator 2>_
```

Figure 7-19: The MS-DOS window of the Windows operating system.

Note   Backslashes are used in the directory names on your hard drive. They are the opposite of the forward slashes used in your Web browser to navigate through Web directories. When you're mixing the online and offline worlds using Generator, it's easy to forget which paths you're trying to target. As a general rule, local hard drive paths use backslashes (\), and Web directories in your Web browser use forward slashes (/).

Creating batch files

Batch files are like little automated scriptlets that run MS-DOS commands for you without you having to be in that outdated MS-DOS window typing away at your keyboard for wasted minutes and hours. Creating a batch file is as simple as opening your favorite text editor such as Notepad, entering the MS-DOS commands you'd like to be executed, saving the file with a bat extension, and double-clicking it wherever it sits on your desktop or on your hard drive.

To create a simple batch file that jumps to the directory containing Generator, follow these steps:

1. Open a new text file in your favorite Windows text editor.

2. Enter the following code into the first line of the text file:

   cd C:\PROGRA~1\MACROM~1\GENERA~1

3. Save the file as testing123.bat on your desktop.

4. Go to your desktop and double-click on the testing123.bat file.

You should see an MS-DOS output window appear showing the path to the Generator directory similar to what you saw in the MS-DOS command line example. The difference here is that you can't type in the window that just popped up; it's for output only, and it shows you that the commands in your batch file were properly executed. If they weren't executed properly, the window will display the error messages.

In the example in the next section, you'll be creating a similar batch file to make Generator do your bidding. All you'll need to do is add a few simple commands and parameters following the first cd line of code, and you'll be creating lots of generated files in no time.

 Note   If you installed Generator into a directory other than C:\Program Files\ Macromedia\Generator, you'll have to compensate for this by placing the correct path to your Generator installation in the cd line of the batch file.

Generating files with Offline Generator

Generating files with Offline Generator is a great way to create a lot of similar SWF files in a short period of time with a minimum amount of work. Generator can also create numerous other file types including QuickTime movies and image files like JPEGs. Although Generator can be run from the command line of the MS-DOS prompt, this method can be tedious, so we detail the more efficient method of using batch files in this section.

Understanding Generator code syntax and parameters

When you create a batch file to operate Generator, the first line of your file will most always be the change directory (cd) command with the path to the actual Generator program on your hard drive. The lines that follow will then contain the exact commands that Generator needs to process and create the files you want. The basic syntax for these lines is

```
generate filetype outputfilename.xxx templatename.swt
```

No punctuation is required in between the parameters, and no semicolon is needed at the end of the statement. The *filetype* parameter is a special code preceded by a hyphen (-) that tells Generator what kind of file it's going to be creating. Table 7-1 lists some common files that Generator can produce and their *filetype* parameter codes.

Table 7-1
Generator File Types and Codes

File Type to Create	Description	Generator Parameter Code
.SWF	Flash movie	-swf
.JPEG	JPEG image	-jpeg
.GIF	GIF image	-gif
.PNG	PNG image	-png

File Type to Create	Description	Generator Parameter Code
.MOV	QuickTime movie	`-qtm`
.EXE	Windows Projector file	`-xwin32`
.HQX	Macintosh Projector file	`-xmacppc`

The extension on the `outputfilename` parameter in Generator should match the type of file you're creating. For example, if you wanted to use Generator to create a Flash movie named `spaceship.swf` and your Generator template was named `shiptemp.swt`, the code in the batch file would read

```
cd C:\PROGRA~1\MACROM~1\GENERA~1
generate -swf spaceship.swf shiptemp.swt
```

This code would could cause Generator to open up the template `shiptemp.swt` stored on your hard drive, use that template to generate an SWF file, and save the final file as `spaceship.swf` on your hard drive. The tricky part is that even though the names of the output file and template are presented, no path to them is listed. Chances are you're not storing your Generator templates and output files in the same directory as Generator itself because this setup could get very messy. You should place your Generator templates and files in an easy-to-locate directory that you create on your C: drive to house all your Generator documents, such as `C:\gendocs`. The code in the batch file would then need to be

```
cd C:\PROGRA~1\MACROM~1\GENERA~1
generate -swf C:\gendocs\spaceship.swf C:\gendocs\shiptemp.swt
```

Generator now knows to look in the `C:\gendocs` folder for the `shiptemp.swt` template and then save the final file `spaceship.swf` in that directory as well. These two paths do not have to be the same. You could store your templates in one directory and have Generator output all your files to another directory. Using different directories is especially useful if you're running the batch file on a Web server because you can have Generator always place the final files in directories that are immediately accessible via the Web. For example, to place only the final SWF file in a directory named `MyWebFiles` on your C: drive, you would use this code:

```
cd C:\PROGRA~1\MACROM~1\GENERA~1
generate -swf C:\MyWebFiles\spaceship.swf C:\gendocs\shiptemp.swt
```

The next important parameter to understand is `-param`. This parameter lets you directly send values for Generator variables into the SWT template and appears in the batch file at the very end of the `generate` code line following the SWT template declaration. The `-param` parameter is followed by the variable name you'd like to define, a space, and then the variable's value:

```
cd C:\PROGRA~1\MACROM~1\GENERA~1
generate -swf C:\MyWebFiles\spaceship.swf
C:\gendocs\shiptemp.swt -param totalHoops 75
```

This code would set a Generator variable named totalHoops with a value of 75 on the main timeline of the shiptemp.swt template. Note that there is no carriage return or line break in the code, even though it appears as two lines here because of formatting constraints. In your text editor, the generate code line should be continuous. You can also set more than one variable, although you'll need a separate -param designation for each:

```
cd C:\PROGRA~1\MACROM~1\GENERA~1
generate -swf C:\MyWebFiles\spaceship.swf
C:\gendocs\shiptemp.swt -param totalHoops 75
-param totalPenguins 42
```

This code would send an additional Generator variable named totalPenguins with a value of 42 to the main timeline of shiptemp.swt. Keep in mind that these are Generator variables and not ActionScript variables. To make use of the variables you're piping into the SWT template, you'll have to be referencing them somewhere with curly braces (for example, {totalPenguins}) somewhere in a Generator template object parameter or a text field on the stage.

Creating multiple files at once with Offline Generator

In this project, we'll be using Offline Generator to take a series of JPEG image files and place them into a SWT template that quickly motion tweens them and outputs a series of compiled SWF Flash movies.

On the CD-ROM

Locate the files for this chapter on the CD-ROM and you'll see an additional folder named Offline Generator. Open this folder and copy the contents onto your hard drive as described in the first step.

1. Create a new folder on your C: drive named gendocs and copy the five JPEG image files found on the CD-ROM in the Offline Generator folder (flashcore1.jpg through flashcore5.jpg) into the new C:\gendocs folder on your hard drive. Take a look at them in your favorite imaging program to see that they're JPEG images (550 × 400) of print designs for FlashCore.com. All these designs were wonderfully crafted by Maria Tepora of www.flashnique.com. The rest of the files can remain on the CD-ROM and are there for reference if you need them.

2. Create a new Flash movie and save it in your C:\gendocs folder as pictemplate.fla. On the stage of pictemplate.fla, use the Generator Objects panel to drag an instance of the Insert JPEG File object onto the stage in Frame 1 of the existing layer and rename this layer **JPEG Object**.

3. Use the Info panel to resize the JPEG object to 138 pixels wide by 100 pixels high and position it at x-coordinate 80 and y-coordinate 60. The sizing here is exactly one quarter the size of all the JPEG images, and by default Flash and Generator will scale them down to fit this size.

4. With the JPEG object selected, press F8 to turn into a movie clip with a Library name of **Moving Picture**. Double-click this new movie clip symbol to get inside its timeline. Make sure you have the Generator panel open (not the Object panel) and select the JPEG object now inside your movie clip. You should see all the parameters available for this JPEG object in the Generator Panel. For the File Name parameter, enter **{imageName}** because this is the name of the Generator variable you'll be sending into this file from the batch file. (Note that the Scale To Fit parameter is `true` by default to automatically scale the images to the smaller size.)

5. Return to the main timeline where the movie clip exists and create another keyframe at Frame 15 in the same layer by selecting Frame 15 and pressing F6. In Frame 15, select the movie clip containing the JPEG object and use the Info panel to reposition it at x-coordinate 275 and y-coordinate-200.

6. Create another keyframe at Frame 30 in the same layer by selecting Frame 30 and pressing F6. Select the movie clip containing the JPEG object now in Frame 30 and use the Info panel to resize it to 550 pixels wide by 400 pixels high, filling the whole stage.

7. Select any frame on the timeline between Frame 1 and Frame 15 and create a motion tween. Select any frame on the timeline between Frame 15 and Frame 30 and create another motion tween.

8. Select Frame 45 on the timeline and press F5 to extend some standard frames out to Frame 45. If you press Enter to test your movie, you should now have a movie clip containing your Generator JPEG object that moves to the center of the stage and scales to completely fill it.

9. Create a new layer on the main timeline above the JPEG Object Layer. Name this new layer **Text Variable**.

10. Use the Text tool and some static text in the layer to place the text **Created from {imageName}** on the stage. Try using 20-point bold Times New Roman in a hot pink color like #FF3366. Position this text in the lower-left corner of the stage at x-coordinate140 and y-coordinate 380. Make sure to use the Text tool to leave some extra space at the end of the last curly brace. This static text, even though it's not configured as dynamic text, will display the value of the Generator variable `imageName` on the stage in each generated Flash movie. Because you've enclosed `imageName` in curly braces, Generator recognizes this spot as a place to show a variable value.

11. Save the changes to your Flash file and then choose File⇨Publish Settings and select *only* Generator Template. Click Publish to publish the file `pictemplate.swt` to your `C:\gendocs` folder. Don't worry if Flash returns an error when doing this because it's just looking for that `{imageName}` variable and it currently can't find it because you'll only be sending it in later by way of a batch file. The template should still publish correctly here, even with the reported error. Figure 7-20 shows the layout of the stage and the timeline for `pictemplate.fla`. The file is also available on the CD-ROM for reference.

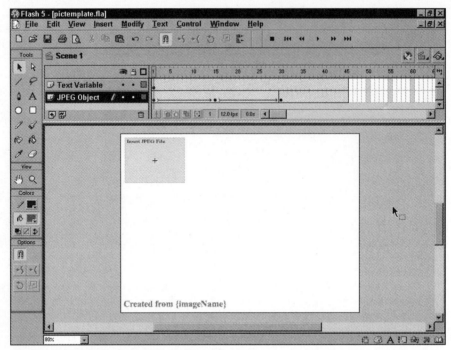

Figure 7-20: The layout of the stage and timeline for pictemplate.fla.

12. Create a new file your favorite text editor (preferably Notepad) and save it as `makemovies.bat` inside your `C:\gendocs` folder. Add the following code lines to the file and then save your changes:

```
cd C:\PROGRA~1\MACROM~1\GENERA~1
generate -swf C:\gendocs\myMovie1.swf
C:\gendocs\pictemplate.swt  -param imageName flashcore1.jpg
generate -swf C:\gendocs\myMovie2.swf
C:\gendocs\pictemplate.swt  -param imageName flashcore2.jpg
generate -swf C:\gendocs\myMovie3.swf
C:\gendocs\pictemplate.swt  -param imageName flashcore3.jpg
generate -swf C:\gendocs\myMovie4.swf
C:\gendocs\pictemplate.swt  -param imageName flashcore4.jpg
generate -swf C:\gendocs\myMovie5.swf
C:\gendocs\pictemplate.swt  -param imageName flashcore5.jpg
```

Please note that although the text as viewed here has several lines, the only carriage retruns that should be present are after the very first line and then after every JPG file declaration. This `makemovies.bat` file is available on the CD-ROM for reference.

13. Navigate to `C:\gendocs` folder using Windows and then double-click your `makemovies.bat` file to put Generator to work creating five unique Flash movies that each use one of the JPEG images you put in the folder.

The MS-DOS output window should spring to life and show that Generator is creating each file. After it's done, you should have five new files in your `C:\gendocs` directory sequentially named `myMovie1.swf` through `myMovie5.swf`. Double-click any one of these files to launch them and see how Generator plugged each unique JPEG image into the template and performed the scaling and motion tweening. You'll also notice that Generator plugs in the value for the `imageName` variable in the lower-left corner of the stage. If you're using the trial version of Generator, you'll also get the great Macromedia logo randomly strewn about all the movies. Figure 7-21 shows the approximate output for one of the movies.

Figure 7-21: Generator has used the SWT template and one of the JPEG images to create an entire Flash movie.

Let's take a closer look at the code in the batch file to go over some of the finer points of the generation process. The first line contains the change directory `cd` command to tell Windows where to look for the Generator program installed on your hard drive. The rest of the lines use the `generate` command and are all identical except for their sequential numbering of JPEG images and output files. We used `-swf` to tell Generator to make a Flash movie and then place it in the `C:\gendocs` directory with a name of `myMovie1.swf`. Immediately following that is the path to and name of the template for Generator to use which is `C:\gendocs\pictemplate.swt`. Finally, the `imageName` variable that the SWT template needs to find the right JPEG image and also fill in the text field on the stage is defined in the batch file. Notice that the only thing separating the variable name `imageName` from its value `flashcore1.jpg` is a simple space:

```
generate -swf C:\gendocs\myMovie1.swf
C:\gendocs\pictemplate.swt  -param imageName flashcore1.jpg
```

Notice that in each `generate` code line the numbers following `myMovie1` and `flashcore1` are incremented by one to tell Generator to use a different JPEG image and then create a new and unique SWF file.

> **Tip** As long you're connected to the Internet while running Generator, you can specify an `http://` reference for an image name in either the SWT template, Generator data text file, or `-param` section of a batch file. For instance, in the previous example, you could easily replace `flashcore1.jpg` with something like `http://www.mydomain.com/anyimage.jpg`.

You can use Offline Generator to create many different types of files. In the previous sample project, try changing the `-swf` reference in the batch file to `-xwin32` instead. This reference will create Flash Projector files to run in Windows. Just remember to also change the `swf` file extensions to `exe` after each `myMovie` reference in the batch file as well.

The one possible drawback to creating lots and lots of files with a Generator batch file is the large amount of code you'd have to enter in the BAT file. You can save time by having any scripting language, including ActionScript, create your batch files for you. As a side project, try creating a simple admin system in Flash that takes input data from a variety of text fields and and then outputting all the lines of properly formatted batch code into a single dynamic text field by using some `if/then/for` loops. You can just cut and paste from the Flash text field into a new batch file in Notepad, save it, and then run it from Windows to have Generator create 50 or 100 different files.

Using ASP with Offline Generator

Offline Generator can be triggered by not only a batch file or MS-DOS command line code, but also by a server language such as ASP. In the specific case of ASP, you need to install a COM object such as ASPExec, which is available at `www.serverobjects.com` and is completely free. Once it is installed on the same NT server as Generator, you can call out to Generator to create any kind of file on the fly. This is great for using complex dynamic code to create what amounts to a dynamic batch file. With ASPExec, the code you would need to place in your ASP page would look something like the following code. (Note that extra carriage returns were placed in the code so that you could see the code lines better.)

```
Set Executor = Server.CreateObject("ASPExec.Execute")

Executor.Application = "cmd /c c:\Program files
\Macromedia\Generator\generator.exe"

Executor.Parameters = "generate -swf C:\gendocs\myMovie1.swf
 C:\gendocs\pictemplate.swt  -param imageName flashcore1.jpg"
```

```
pageOutput = Executor.ExecuteDosApp
Response.Write "<pre>" & pageOutput & "</pre>"
```

Using ASP in this manner is very powerful because you could easily specify file-names, templates, or Generator variables via ASP and even include information from a database in your instructions to Generator. ASPExec can also listen for responses from MS-DOS, and you can have ASP wait until Generator is finished to proceed to some other task.

Cross-
Reference

For more information about using ASP with Flash, be sure to read Chapter 3.

Alternatives to Generator

Using Generator has its drawbacks. One is the obvious expense of buying the software license for your particular application, but there are a few other drawbacks you need to be aware of as well. Generator is a dynamic tool and, therefore, when you are using it in Online mode, there can sometimes be a delay on the server while Generator creates the SWF file.

Imagine if the page the SWT template sits on as well as the data source for that template are generated by ASP. That would be three times that the server has to be called upon to create content: one time for the initial page, a second time to have Generator come to life and process the SWT template, and a third when that template calls for a data source dynamically generated by another ASP file. Finally, the server has to deliver the final Flash movie to the viewer's Web browser. Although servers are usually pretty fast, a process as intricate as this one can induce some lag. Every Web server and CPU is different though, so you always want to test your Web project under a variety of possible conditions to see if there is a possibility of a slowdown anywhere and make appropriate adjustments to your content or strategy.

A few small development companies have built products to compete with Generator that do basically the same types of things on the server side. You still use the same objects in Flash to build your SWT templates, but you then use these other 'generators' to serve up the content in an online or offline capacity. One of the most popular is Swift Generator, which you can find online for a fairly low price. In fact, it's completely free for noncommercial use. Other developers have built products in Perl and even PHP in some cases. These products are good to play around with, but if you need to generate dynamic content in a mission-critical environment, it's best to stick with Macromedia Generator and take advantage of the great tech support that accompanies the purchase of the full version of Generator.

Summary

Macromedia Generator is a unique and powerful tool with an even more unique price tag. It definitely has uses for large Web projects that need constantly updated dynamic Flash content. Once a Generator system is built for a client, that client can create new Flash movies by doing nothing more than changing some simple files in a Web directory. Even when complex Generator data files are needed, they can be created via ASP, PHP, and/or Perl with an admin system to make data entry easy. Offline Generator can be a big time-saver as well for repeatedly creating massive amounts of Flash movies, even for a small Web site.

The Generator 2 Developer Edition might be a great investment for even a small to midsize project to save time and energy, especially if many of the artists and developers working on the project have a limited knowledge of Flash and/or Generator. Finally, with a really cool GUI interface featuring lots of pre-scripted features and a slimmer price tag, it's our belief that Generator could be a dominating force in Web development, with a much wider user base than exists today. Even in it's current state it's definitely worth downloading the trial version and checking it out with the examples in this chapter!

✦   ✦   ✦

The Dynamics of Gaming

Dynamic Game Development: The Essentials

CHAPTER

8

♦ ♦ ♦ ♦

In This Chapter

Uncovering the power of the `for/in` statement

Tracking collisions with `hitTest`

Making games more interesting with multiple hit tests

♦ ♦ ♦ ♦

Flash is undoubtedly the best tool for quickly creating dynamic games that the widest possible Internet audience can play. Although other platforms for delivering interactive gaming are available, the small size of the Flash plug-in coupled with its compact vector graphics ensures that your games can look good, load fast, and be highly interactive!

Although this chapter is titled "Dynamic Game Development," it presents some valuable concepts that can enhance just about any Flash movie. As soon as you create a Flash movie where the user can manipulate objects or where your objects act according to certain rules and boundaries, you are in essence creating a game, even if that is not your intention. Many companies choose Flash so that they can express their message in an entertaining and engaging atmosphere.

You may already be familiar with some concepts in this chapter; others will be new for you. All of the concepts deal with object manipulation and the most efficient ways to track multiple objects. (Although basic principles of movement will be covered, the concepts behind creating 3-D engines and emulating the gravity of the planet Jupiter are best left for a book on physics.) This chapter will change the way you think about building interactive Flash movies, especially ones using object tracking and collision detection.

A new ActionScript command has unbelievable interactive power; it can change the way you build interactive Flash movies by enabling you to find movie clips and operate on them without having ever given them an instance name. Rather than save it for the end, we present this command first, because it is the foundation on which we'll be building many of the later examples.

The For/In Statement

In attempting to create highly interactive experiences using Flash, you may have often found that you need to track the existence of multiple objects (usually movie clips) and had to deal with the chore of naming your instances in a certain way or building multiple arrays to keep track of your objects and variables for you.

Wouldn't it be nice if Flash could just take a look at the stage and figure out what was there all by itself? For example, it could know that ten aliens are on the screen and test whether the lasers firing from the spaceship are hitting each alien, and when a new alien appears, it could test the lasers against that one, too.

Suppose you had a shoebox with a few marbles in it. If someone asked you to roll all the marbles down to one end of the shoebox, you wouldn't have to explain that you don't know their instance names. You would just look in the box, see how many marbles there were, and roll them all down to the end of the shoebox. If someone added a marble to the box and asked you to now roll all the marbles to the other side, you wouldn't have to say that you can't because the new marble hadn't been added to an array tracking the existence of all current marbles. You would just look inside the shoebox again and move them all to other side, the new one included.

You're capable of performing these actions because you can see with your eyes what's going on in that shoebox. Flash can see now, too, in very much the same way with the new and largely undocumented For/In statement.

Using the For/In statement

Unless you scoured the ActionScript manual cover to cover, you'd probably miss the For/In statement, and even if you found it, its power isn't truly apparent from its bland explanation. The For/In statement is capable of evaluating an almost unlimited number of objects anywhere inside of Flash, figuring out how many there are and what type of objects they are and performing any sort of action upon each object or all of them together. When we say objects, we mean movie clips, variables, arrays, functions, and user-defined objects. Flash knows how many it has inside itself at any given moment and can report back to you their names (even if you didn't name them) and whereabouts as well as perform any comparison or action upon them that it normally would. This is powerful stuff!

To see this statement in action, let's create a simple Flash movie that illustrates the box of marbles example mentioned previously.

1. Create a new Flash file and save it to your hard drive as marbles.fla.

2. Use the Oval tool with a stroke color of black and fill color of red to create a circle on the stage. Use the Scale tool and the Info panel to make the circle a size of about 35 by 35. Place this red circle somewhere in the upper left-hand corner of the stage.

3. Select the entire red circle and press F8 to turn it into a movie clip with the symbol name of **Button**.

4. Use the Oval tool with a stroke color of black and fill color of blue to create a circle on the stage. Use the scale tool and the Info panel to make the circle a size of about 20 by 20. This circle is the marble.

5. Select the entire blue circle and press F8 to turn it into a movie clip with the symbol name of **Marble**.

6. Do not give the blue circle an instance name on the stage. Instead, select it and duplicate it five times to give you a total of six marbles on the stage, *all without instance names*.

7. Place the marbles somewhat close together at the center of the top of the stage. Using the Rectangle tool with a black stroke and *no* fill color, draw a vertical rectangle around the marbles (to represent the shoebox) with these dimensions: W=140, H=320.

8. Select this rectangular outline along with all the marbles and press F8 to turn them all into a movie clip with a symbol name of **Shoebox**. You should now have a main timeline stage containing a red button along with a movie clip of the shoebox that has six Marble movie clips nested inside it. Figure 8-1 depicts what this stage should look like.

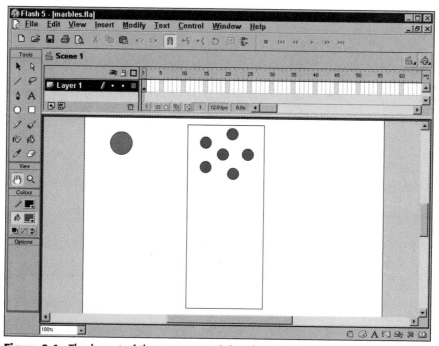

Figure 8-1: The layout of the stage containing the Shoebox movie clip with six nested Marble movie clips inside it.

9. Give the Shoebox movie clip an instance name of **shoebox**. The shoebox needs an instance name so that you can tell Flash where to look for the marbles.

10. Select the red button and attach this ActionScript to it:

```
on(press){
    for(eachMarble in _root.shoebox){
        _root.shoebox[eachMarble]._y+=10;
    }
}
```

Test the movie in Flash or your browser and click the red button. Each time you click it you should see all the blue Marble movie clips inside the Shoebox movie clip moving down to the opposite end of the stage. If you don't, make sure you completed all of the preceding steps or open the marbles.fla file on the CD-ROM for reference.

What's happening in this movie is quite interesting. Flash takes a look inside the shoebox and sees six Marble movie clips. It then increases each one's y-coordinate by 10 pixels. The amazing thing is that you never name any of the marble instances! You don't have to track their names in an array or figure out how many there are. Try editing the Shoebox movie clip and placing more Marble movie clips inside or deleting some. The result is always the same. Flash knows how many movie clips are inside the Shoebox movie clip through the power of the For/In ActionScript statement.

Note   Before we dissect the For/In statement, you must realize that when you didn't name those Marble movie clip instances, Flash named them for you. Every movie clip on every timeline must be assigned a name. Usually you will name the movie clip with the Instance panel, but if you don't, Flash names them for you with names such as Instance1 or Instance35 where the digit at the end of the name is incremented for each movie clip Flash finds on each timeline. This naming system made little difference before Flash 5 because you couldn't target the instance names without knowing what they were. Now with the For/In action you can!

Understanding the For/In syntax

The generic syntax for the For/In statement is as follows:

```
for(variableReference in Object){
    //Perform an action
}
```

In this syntax, the variableReference parameter is replaced with a variable name that you create to represent each object inside the targeted movie clip as it is found by Flash. In the previous example with the marbles, we used the name eachMarble. You could easily replace this name with eachAnything or bananaStuff. It doesn't matter what you pick, as long as you reference it in the action part of the statement so that you can operate upon what Flash finds.

Replace the `Object` parameter with the path to an object that you want Flash to peer inside of and determine what other objects are inside. In the previous example, we wanted Flash to take a look inside the Shoebox movie clip, so we used `_root.shoebox` as the Object parameter in the `For/In` statement. Take a look at the statement in that button action again:

```
for(eachMarble in _root.shoebox){
    _root.shoebox[eachMarble]._y+=10;
}
```

The action part of the statement gets a little tricky. As Flash finds each Marble movie clip inside the Shoebox movie clip, it plugs that marble's instance name into the `eachMarble` variable. The problem is that it plugs in only the name itself, and not a path with it. (As mentioned earlier, Flash automatically names all unnamed instances on export even though you didn't name the instances.) So if Flash looked at the first marble and found it had an instance name of `Instance1`, the `eachMarble` variable would now have the string value `Instance1`. Another way to look at it is that the `For/In` statement references the `_name` property of each movie clip it finds and makes that the value of the variable reference parameter, in this case `eachMarble`.

To target the movie clip named `Instance1` from the button's ActionScript inside of the for/in statement, you couldn't use

```
eachMarble._y+=10;
// (incorrect)
```

because the button executing the for/in action sits on the main timeline and there aren't any movie clips there except for the one with the instance name of `shoebox`. In order to make it work correctly you have to attach the path back on to the variable containing the instance name that Flash found with this code:

```
_root.shoebox[eachMarble]._y+=10;
```

The brackets are used to perform an evaluation. Flash is dynamically joining the instance name contained in `eachMarble` with the path `_root.shoebox` to make a final path/object combination. For example, if there were four movie clips in `_root.shoebox` sequentially named `Instance1` through `Instance4` Flash would be in essence executing the following actions behind the scenes:

```
_root.shoebox.Instance1.y+=10;
_root.shoebox.Instance2.y+=10;
_root.shoebox.Instance3.y+=10;
_root.shoebox.Instance4.y+=10;
```

If you're not familiar with using the bracket method of evaluation, just realize that you omit the dot before the opening bracket and place a dot after it to amend statements. A common mistake would be to put a dot after `shoebox`:

```
_root.shoebox.[eachMarble]._y+=10;
// (incorrect)
```

```
_root.shoebox[eachMarble]._y+=10;
// (correct)
```

Putting a dot before that first bracket will return an error. If you're still confused as to what the brackets are doing and you're familiar with Flash 4, you could use the `eval` statement from Flash 4 instead:

```
eval("_root.shoebox."+eachMarble)._y+=10;
```

Regardless of whether you choose to use the bracket method of evaluation or the `eval` action, you must always remember to include the path again inside the `For/In` statement. Later in this chapter and the next, we'll explain some shortcuts to ease your typing chores if you have extremely long paths to the objects you're targeting with the `For/In` statement. Looking at the correct initial syntax once again:

```
for(eachMarble in _root.shoebox){
    _root.shoebox[eachMarble]._y+=10;
}
```

it performs the duty of targeting each movie clip inside of `shoebox` and then increasing its y-coordinate by 10 pixels. When Flash finds the last object inside of `_root.shoebox`, it stops executing the `For/In` statement.

Targeting objects and their properties

The `For/In` statement finds the name of each movie clip instance and the names of any variables, arrays, objects, or functions as well. As Flash finds all these neat things inside of the path you specified, it not only knows their names, but also their types. Although you could sort out the movie clips from the functions from the variables if you wanted to, you don't need to sort by type when you are dealing with movie clip properties because non-movie clip object types don't have any movie clip properties. For example, Flash can't change a function's `_y` property, because a function has none. Flash just ignores that particular object and moves on to the next one.

We mentioned that Flash finds the name of each object while using the `For/In` statement and places that object's name as the value of the variable reference you specify. The following set of steps demonstrates this action:

On the CD-ROM   Either use the marbles.fla file you created in the previous example or copy it from the CD-ROM onto your hard drive and open it inside Flash for modifications.

1. Just to the right of the Shoebox movie clip, create a vertical dynamic text field of about the size 160 pixels wide by 240 pixels high. In the Text Options panel, enter **output** in the Variable box. Make sure the Border/Bg check box is checked.

2. Change the code on the red circular button to the following:

```
on(press){
        output="";
        for(eachObj in _root.shoebox){
            output+=eachObj+newline;
        }
}
```

3. Test the movie in Flash or in your browser and click the red button.

Notice that the output text field shows instance names for each of the blue Marble movie clips, most likely with names of Instance1 through Instance6 as in the following:

```
instance6
instance5
instance4
instance3
instance2
instance1
```

This result comes from the fact that Flash auto-named all the instances upon export and then the For/In statement loaded each one's name into the eachObj (meaning each object) variable and added it to the output text field.

Try giving each marble an instance name. Pick any names you'd like. Test the movie again and notice that names appear in a seemingly random order in the output text field. This order is actually their stacking order on the timeline of the Shoebox movie clip. Go back to the marbles, and with one marble selected, choose Modify ⇨ Arrange ⇨ Send To Back. You'll notice upon testing the movie again that the name of the movie clip you sent to the bottom of the stacking order appears last in the dynamic text field. Movie clips at the top of the stacking order are the ones Flash finds first.

Try adding some other kinds of objects into the same file:

1. Select the Shoebox movie clip on the main timeline. Add the following ActionScript to it:

```
onClipEvent(load){
        someWord="FlashCore";
        someDigits=12345;
        prettyColors=new Array("red","green","blue");
        function doNothing(){
            //Just for fun
        }
        emptyContainer=new Object;
}
```

2. Preview the movie again and click the red button to see that Flash has found all the objects you defined, as well as the movie clips.

3. To have Flash figure out the types of all the objects inside the Shoebox movie clip, change the red button code to the following:

```
on(press){
    output="";
    for(eachObj in _root.shoebox){
        output+=eachObj+"-
"+typeof(_root.shoebox[eachObj])+newline;
    }
}
```

4. Save the new file you've created as `object_types.fla`; you'll use it later. (It's also available on the CD-ROM if you have any difficulties.)

When you test the movie and click the red button, Flash not only shows the name of each object it found in the shoebox, but the type of that object as well. This result is accomplished via the `typeof` ActionScript, which returns a string specifying that the object in question is either a `movieclip`, `function`, `object`, or in the case of a variable, a `number` or a `string`. Figure 8-2 shows an example of this output.

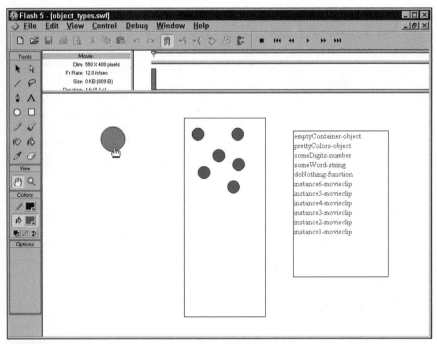

Figure 8-2: Flash has found many movie clips as well as other objects inside the Shoebox movie clip and has returned their correct type.

What does this have to do with shooting aliens with laser guns? Quite a bit actually, and we'll get to all that in a moment. First you have to make a clean, reusable version of the For/In code that you can plug into any dynamic Flash movie.

Associating objects and variables

To create reusable code from the For/In ActionScript statement, start by associating some variable names directly to the objects you want to operate on. So if you're looking to use For/In to operate on objects in a nested movie clip like _root.city. zoo.cage.animals, you first should place that entire path into a variable named masterObj that is much easier to plug into the For/In statement. This set of steps illustrates this process:

On the CD-ROM

Use the object_types.fla file that you created in the last example or copy the object_types.fla file from the CD-ROM to your hard drive for modification.

1. Open the object_types.fla file in Flash. You should see the shoebox full of marbles. An onClipEvent action in the Shoebox movie clip sets additional variables and functions.

2. Change the ActionScript on the red button to the following:

```
on(press){
    output="";
    //Enter the path to your master 'container' object next
    masterObj=_root.shoebox;
    for(eachObj in masterObj){
        finalObj=masterObj[eachObj];
        //finalObj represents each object found by Flash
        //Reference finalObj in actions below
        finalObj._y+=10;
        output+=eachObj+"-"+typeof(finalObj)+newline;
    }
}
```

3. Save the new file as for_in_compact_code.fla and test it in Flash or in your browser.

This code works the same as the code in the object_types.fla file except that it's very clean. All you have to do to attach this action to any movie clip, button, or frame is change the path designated by masterObj to any path to an object that you're trying to reference that has other objects inside it. As Flash finds each nested object, you can operate on that object by just using the pseudo-object name finalObj and then whatever code you'd like. Here we've used finalObj to move all the movie clips 10 pixels south (Flash ignored any non-movie clips), and we added the name of each object found into the output list by using typeof(finalObj). The initial on(press) line can obviously be ignored. The core of the code you need is as follows:

```
masterObj=//Insert target container object here//;
for(eachObj in masterObj){
    finalObj=masterObj[eachObj];
    //finalObj represents each object found by Flash
    //Reference finalObj in actions below
    }
```

Again, there's nothing to change here. You only need to add the path to the object you want Flash to look inside of (usually a movie clip somewhere) and then add any actions to the very end of the code that you want Flash to perform for each unique object it finds. To operate on each of those objects, you just append statements to the end of the code using `finalObj`, as in

```
finalObj.gotoAndPlay("explode");
```

or

```
if(typeof(finalObj) eq "movieclip"){
    finalObj._visible=0;
}
```

The last statement would take any movie clips that Flash found inside the specified `masterObj` object and set their `_visible` property to 0, making them invisible.

Note   You can also specify a timeline as the path by using `_root`, `this`, or a level number. This kind of specification can get messy, though, because Flash can start to look at the very movie clips or objects that are executing the `For/In` statement. Therefore, we recommend choosing a path that is different from the path that the `For/In` statement is being executed from. In this case, it's being executed from a button on the `_root`, so you wouldn't want to specify a `masterObj` of `_root` or you might find some confusing things happening. Additional `if` statements that filter unwanted objects with `typeof` can often solve this problem though.

Checking for Collisions with hitTest

Flash 5 gave developers the great capability to detect collisions between multiple movie clip objects. This capability has opened the door to producing a wide array of not only games, but total interactive scenarios as well!

The `hitTest` action comes in a variety of flavors with certain uses for each. The two most common uses for `hitTest` in gaming are to blow up something or to prevent an object from moving past another, as in the case of an obstacle. When you combine `For/In`, `hitTest`, and `globalToLocal` (as outlined later), all the elements to build some great games and dynamic Flash movies are right at your fingertips!

Bounding box hitTest

The basic `hitTest` statement tests the bounding box of one object to see if it is within the confines of another. This statement is great for most applications where you're not dealing with very weird and complex shapes that let small objects pass around them or through them.

The `hitTest` statement is always contained within an `if` statement and is preceded by one of the movie clips being hit-tested. The basic syntax for the bounding box style of `hitTest` is as follows:

```
movieclip1.hitTest(movieclip2)
```

You replace `movieclip1` and `movieclip2` with the paths to the movie clips you're testing.

These examples show `hitTest` with the `if` statement:

```
if(this.hitTest(_root.fire)){
    this.gotoAndPlay("burned");
}

if(_root.laser.hitTest(_root.spaceship.alien)){
    score+=100;
      _root.spaceship.alien.gotoAndPlay("vaporized");
}

if(_root.key.hitTest(_root.lock)){
    _root.door.gotoAndStop("open");
}
```

You can see that the basic premise behind `hitTest` is usually to check whether two movie clips happen to be touching and then if they are touching, to perform an action on one of the objects. You can make anything happen as the result of `hitTest` though, as in the third `if` statement that utilizes a key and a lock.

Use these steps to start building some basic games:

1. Create a new file in Flash with a standard stage size but with a frame rate of 25. Higher frame rates mean faster collision checking.

2. Use the Oval tool to draw a red circle on the right side of the stage at a size of about 50 by 50. (If at any time all the circles bore you, feel free to substitute any of the mind-blowing graphics you may possess.)

3. With this red circle selected, press F8 to turn it into a movie clip symbol named **Red Circle**. Give this new movie clip an instance name of **redCircle** in the Instance panel.

4. On the left side of the stage, draw a blue circle at a size of about 50 by 50 and press F8 to turn it into a button symbol named **Drag Button**. Attach the following ActionScript to this symbol:

```
on(press){
        this.startDrag(true);
}
on(release){
        stopDrag();
}
```

5. With this button still selected, press F8 again to pop it into a movie clip with a symbol name of **Draggable MC**. The blue button inside this movie clip will allow you drag the movie clip around when you click the button.

6. Select the instance of Draggable MC that is on the main timeline and give it an instance name of **blueCircle**. Then add the following ActionScript to it:

```
onClipEvent(enterFrame){
     if(this.hitTest(_root.redCircle)){
          _root.redCircle._visible=0;
     }
}
```

Using the `onclipEvent(enterFrame)` ActionScript means that Flash will execute these statements over and over at the current frame rate of the movie.

7. Test the movie in Flash or in your browser and click the blue circle to start dragging it around. As soon as it touches the red circle, the red circle will disappear as is about to happen in Figure 8-3. The completed file is available on the CD-ROM as `basic_collision.fla` if you experience any difficulties.

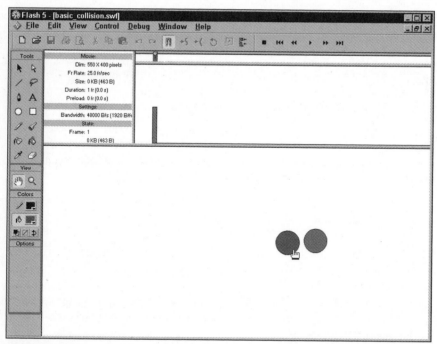

Figure 8-3: When the blue circle being dragged touches the red circle, the red circle will disappear.

The ActionScript behind this movie is fairly straightforward. Using the `onClipEvent(enterFrame)` statement attached to itself, the Draggable MC movie clip that contains the blue button repeatedly checks to see whether it has touched `_root.redCircle`. If the touching occurs, the ActionScript sets the visibility of `_root.redCircle` to 0 and makes it disappear.

> **Note** The self-reference object `this` is used in this example because the ActionScript testing for the collision is on one of the objects being tested. You can easily replace `this` with `_root.blueCircle` in the code and test for the collision from anywhere in the entire Flash movie. Many times, though, using `this` is easier because you'll be putting hit testing onto duplicated movie clips whose names may be difficult to keep track of.

This example shows `hitTest` at its most basic level, with only two movie clips and one clip doing the hit testing. Try adding the following code to the Red Circle movie clip:

```
onClipEvent(enterFrame){
    if(this.hitTest(_root.blueCircle)){
        _root.blueCircle._visible=0;
    }
}
```

Now you have both clips testing to see whether they've hit each other. When you test the movie, you'll see that they both disappear! The ActionScript on each clip affects the other one.

Try different actions with the movie clips. Instead of making the circles invisible, set the `_alpha` to a different setting or change the height and width of the circles. You can add multiple statements inside the `hitTest` action, so you could have code that keeps score or tells another movie clip to stop or play. Experiment by putting all kinds of actions inside the bounds of the `hitTest` action.

For/In and hitTest together

This section takes a big leap by adding the power of the `For/In` statement to the `hitTest` action. Keep working with the file you've created or open the `basic_collision.fla` file on the CD-ROM. Note that the timeline contains two movie clips, one with an instance name of `blueCircle` and the other one with an instance name of `redCircle`. An `onClipEvent` on the blue circle (a self-draggable movie clip) tests for a collision with the red circle, and if they collide, the red circle's visibility is set to 0.

Now you're ready to make some cool modifications to this file:

1. Select Frame 1 on the main timeline and add the following frame actions:

```
for(i=1; i<=10; i++){
    _root.redCircle.duplicateMovieClip("redCircle"+i,i);
    _root["redCircle"+i]._x=Math.random()*500;
    _root["redCircle"+i]._y=Math.random()*400;
}
_root.redCircle._visible=0;
//Set the original circle to be invisible
```

This type of statement is one of the basic Flash actions for duplicating movie clips. The loop runs 10 times, creating 10 duplications of the redCircle instance. Each instance is then placed in a random location on the stage as it is created. Notice the use of the brackets with the _root reference to target each incremented instance name as it is created to randomly place it on the stage. The last line then sets the original redCircle clip to be hidden from view.

2. Test the movie in Flash. You should see 10 randomly placed red circles. A neat shortcut is to just keep pressing Ctrl+Enter (Cmd+Enter on the Mac) to restart the movie and see the random patterns evolve.

3. Add the scripting to test whether the blue circle is colliding with any of the 10 red circles. You could use 10 OR statements or an array that tracks them, but the quickest way is to use the For/In action. Select the blue circle and delete the basic hitTest action in its onClipEvent statement. Replace it with the following:

```
onClipEvent(enterFrame){
    masterObj=_root;
    for(eachObj in masterObj){
        finalObj=masterObj[eachObj];
        if(this.hitTest(finalObj)){
            finalObj.removeMovieClip();
        }
    }

}
```

4. Test the movie in Flash or in your browser. Click the blue circle and move it toward any of the duplicated red circles. You'll see that they immediately disappear. The completed file is available on the CD-ROM as collision_for_in.fla

The red circles aren't just disappearing from Flash because of a change in visibility, they're being removed altogether! The code added in step 3 should be familiar from the sections detailing hitTest and For/In. The only difference is that these actions are combined to make the blue circle test over and over again if it has contacted any of the objects in the root by using `this.hitTest`. When the blue circle contacts one of the objects, it removes that object.

Caution   Notice that the target path is set to `_root` in the example. Although this statement effectively tests collisions against all the duplicated clips, it is also evaluating to true for the blue circle itself! Because the blue circle happens to be on the main timeline with everything else, Flash sees it as an object and tests it against itself everytime through the loop. Flash tries to remove the blue circle using `removeMovieClip`, but it can't because the blue circle is not a duplicated clip.

Note that blue circle is being hit tested against itself, which evaluates to true because the blue circle is indeed "touching itself" all the time. It then tries to remove itself but it can't, because it's a master instance and not a duplicate clip. To see this occurrence in action, change the `finalObj.removeMovieClip();` line in the `onClipEvent` of the blue circle to

```
finalObj._alpha=50;
```

Upon testing the movie, you'll see the blue circle immediately change its alpha to 50 percent. As you drag the blue circle over each red circle, it turns to 50 percent alpha as well. What's happening is that the blue circle hit tests true to itself as soon as the movie starts and changes its own alpha. This occurrence is important to keep in mind when using `For/In`; generally you should check for objects nested in a completely different timeline if you're going to use `For/In` for collision detection. When you were previously using the `removeMovieClip` code you didn't notice any effect on the blue circle because it was an original clip and couldn't be removed. Now that you're changing `_alpha`, the code is effecting every object in the designated path including the blue circle. Figure 8-4 illustrates the changing of the alpha for the hit-tested movie clips.

Here it's okay because the original goal was to remove the duplicate clips. The original red circle is made invisible as soon as all the duplicates are done in the frame action `_root.redCircle._visible=0;` because otherwise the circle would never be removed, because it, like the blue circle, also is a master instance and not a duplicate clip. Instead of making it invisible, you could also place it off to the side of the stage where it would never be seen in the final exported file.

We're getting closer to building a real game. For example, imagine that instead of dragging that blue circle around, you were operating it with your keyboard arrow keys. Or suppose that blue circle represents just one of many small objects that represent laser blasts from a canon, and each time one of these laser blasts hits its target, the target disappears! Feel free as you work through the examples to substitute any of your own graphics for the simple shapes presented here.

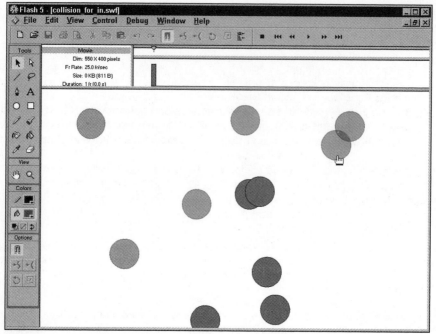

Figure 8-4: As the blue circles contact the red circles, their alpha is changed to 50 percent.

Handling Multiple Hit Tests

In the realm of multiple hit testing, many objects are constantly checking to see if they've hit other objects and are constantly affecting each other. This section begins with the tried-and-true blue and red circles. (As mentioned previously, feel free to import your own cool gaming graphics.)

Creating the basic game layout

This example expands on the file you created in the last example where you can drag the blue circle around to make the duplicated red circles disappear. You'll make some changes to add keyboard control to the blue circle and also give it a cannonball weapon to destroy the evil red circles!

On the CD-ROM

Use the file you created from the last example or open the `collision_for_in.fla` file on the CD-ROM.

1. On the main timeline, delete all the frame actions from Frame 1. You'll no longer be duplicating the red circles from here.

2. Select the red circle on the main timeline; it should have an instance name of `redCircle`. Press F8 to wrap another movie clip around it. Name this new movie clip symbol **Multiple Circles** and give it an instance name on the main timeline of **multipleCircles**.

3. Double-click the `multipleCircles` movie clip instance on the main timeline to get into its editing mode. The `redCircle` instance should be the only thing inside it. On Frame 1 of the Multiple Circles timeline, add this frame action:

```
for(i=1; i<=10; i++){
    redCircle.duplicateMovieClip("redCircle"+i,i);
    this["redCircle"+i]._x=Math.random()*500;
    this["redCircle"+i]._y=Math.random()*200;
}
redCircle._visible=0;
```

This action duplicates the red circles on the Multiple Circles timeline, and all the duplicates become objects nested inside the Multiple Circles timeline. The path to access one of them would be something like `_root.multipleCircles.redCircle7`.

4. Return to the main timeline and test the movie. You should see the circles duplicated, but they are probably off in one corner because Flash is randomly placing them in relationship to the center of the `multipleCircles` movie clip and not the main timeline. To correct for this problem, place the `multipleCircles` instance on the main timeline at an x-coordinate and y-coordinate of 0 by using the Info panel. When you test the movie again, the duplicated red circles appear randomly across the top of the stage.

5. To make a cannonball to be fired at the red circles, choose Insert ➪ New Symbol and choose movie clip. Then enter **Cannonball** for the name of the movie clip. You should now be inside the Cannonball movie clip with a blank stage in front of you.

6. Using the Oval tool with a stroke color of black and a fill color of green, place a circle on the stage where the x- and y-coordinates are equal to 0. Use the Info panel to change the circle's dimensions to 15 by 15. Select this entire circle and press F8 to turn it into a graphic named **Ball**.

7. Within the Cannonball movie clip, select Frame 10 on the timeline and press F6 to create another keyframe. In this Frame 10 keyframe, adjust the coordinates of the green ball graphic you created to be X:0 and Y: -100. These coordinates should place the green ball higher than the center of the clip by 100 pixels.

8. Select any frame between Frame 1 and Frame 10 and create a motion tween with Insert ➪ Motion Tween.

9. Select Frame 11 now and press F7 to place a blank keyframe in this frame. Add the frame action: `stop();` to this keyframe. The timeline of the Cannonball movie clip is now complete. Figure 8-5 shows the layout of the Cannonball movie clip.

10. Press Enter on your keyboard to observe the cannonball flying forward 70 pixels ready to eradicate the enemy.

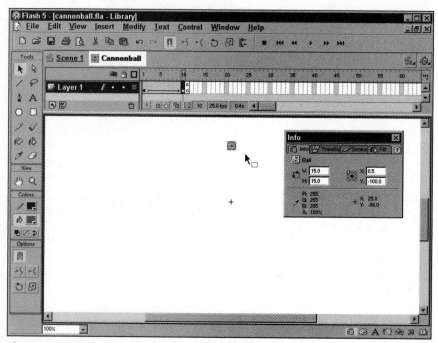

Figure 8-5: The layout of the timeline inside the Cannonball movie clip.

11. Return to the main timeline and drag an instance of the completed Cannonball movie clip to the stage. Position the movie clip somewhere off to the left of the main portion of the stage, with a negative x-coordinate in the Info panel. This setting hides the initial cannonball from the viewers. Select the movie clip and give it an instance name of **ball**.

12. Position the blue circle anywhere in the lower half of the stage. Save this file to your hard drive as `cannonball.fla`. Figure 8-6 shows the stage layout at this point.

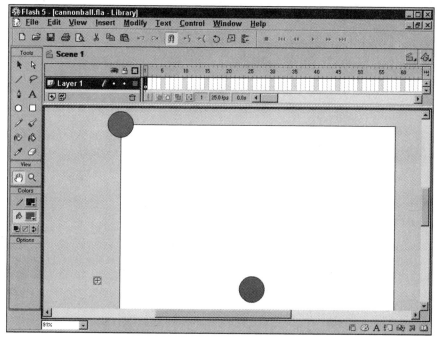

Figure 8-6: The layout of the timeline inside the cannonball.fla file.

Adding ActionScript to the game

Now that the basic assemblies and layouts are complete, it's time to add the ActionScript that powers this game. The first ActionScript makes the blue circle movable via the keyboard. Because the movie clip for the blue circle still contains a button for dragging, you will be able to use the mouse as well. Select the movie clip for the blue circle on the main timeline and delete any `onClipEvent` actions attached to it. Then add these new clip actions:

```
onClipEvent(enterFrame){
    dist=5;
    if (Key.isDown(Key.UP)) {
        _y-=dist;
    }
    if (Key.isDown(Key.DOWN)) {
        _y+=dist;
    }
    if (Key.isDown(Key.RIGHT)) {
        _x+=dist;
    }
    if (Key.isDown(Key.LEFT)) {
        _x-=dist;
    }
}
```

Test the movie and you'll see that you can move the blue circle around by using the arrow keys on your keyboard. Each time you press an arrow key, the _x or _y property of the blueCircle movie clip is changed by the amount specified in the dist variable, which is set to 5 here. You can change this amount to suit your need for speed; increasing the distance increases the speed of the blue circle's movements.

The ActionScript on this clip is using simple if statements and the key action to check whether one of the arrow keys on your keyboard is pressed. Each key action, such as Key.isDown(Key.UP), refers to a specific key on your keyboard, such as the up arrow key in this example. A complete listing of all the possible key codes and combinations is included in the ActionScript reference that comes with Flash.

You now need to add one more key action to fire a cannonball (seemingly) from the blue circle toward the enemy red circles when you press the spacebar. Select the blueCircle movie clip instance and double-click it to edit its master symbol instance Draggable MC. Inside this clip is the Drag Button button that has the drag actions on it. Add the following extra on action to this button:

```
on (keyPress "<Space>") {
        count+=1;
        _root.ball.duplicateMovieClip("ball"+count,count);
        _root["ball"+count]._x=this._x;
        _root["ball"+count]._y=this._y;
}
```

Test the movie and use your arrow keys to move the blue circle around. Press the spacebar at any time to launch a cannonball. No hit testing is occurring yet, so all the red circles stay put, but you see the effect. This effect is the result of attaching a keyPress action to the button inside the blue circle. Each time you press the spacebar, a new Cannonball movie clip is generated on the main timeline and is positioned on the current stage location of the blue circle. The last two lines of code reference the circle's _x and _y properties to pinpoint the correct position.

This code places the Cannonball movie clip in the exact center of the blue circle. But if you wanted the Cannonball clip more at the blue circle's "vertical top," you could change the last line of code to the following:

```
_root["ball"+count]._y=(this._y-(this._height/2));
```

This line of code would place the cannonball duplicates at the vertical top of the blue circle clip by figuring out the circle's height property and adjusting the _y position for the cannonball accordingly.

We didn't have to attach this section of code to the button inside the blue circle. It could easily have been placed on any button anywhere in the movie. The only difference would be that you'd need to specify blueCircle as the clip for the cannonball to "snap to" by naming it specifically:

```
_root["ball"+count]._x=_root.blueCircle._x;
    _root["ball"+count]._y=_root.blueCircle._y;
```

You may also be wondering why we didn't just attach this whole section of code to the cannonball instance `ball` itself using an `if (Key.isDown(Key.SPACE))` code block right after the `if` statements for the arrow keys. We could do that, but because the `onClipEvent(enterFrame)` actions execute over and over as fast as the movie frame rate, you would get a constant barrage of cannonballs flying out when the spacebar is held down. If you want this effect, feel free to use the clip duplication and positioning actions in this manner.

Setting up the hit testing for the game

To make the game complete, you need set up the hit testing. The only thing you have to do is to hook up the Cannonball movie clip so that when it contacts one of the red circles, it "destroys" it. All these actions are part of the `ball` instance itself. Select the green cannonball instance `ball` on the main timeline and add the following clip action to it:

```
onClipEvent(enterFrame){
    masterObj=_root.multipleCircles;
    for(eachObj in masterObj){
        finalObj=masterObj[eachObj];
        if(this.hitTest(finalObj)){
            finalObj.removeMovieClip();
        }
    }
}
```

Save your file, test the movie, and fire away! You should be able to destroy all the red circles on the stage by launching your cannonballs with the spacebar. Try using your mouse to click and drag the blue circle around while firing as well. If you encounter any problems, the completed file is available on the CD-ROM as `cannonball.fla`.

The code you added to the cannonball should be very familiar. The only piece of it that needed to be altered from the standard template for the For/In and `hitTest` code was the path to `_root.multipleCircles`, which is the container movie clip for all the duplicated circles.

Tip

As you play, you may notice that Flash starts to slow down after more and more cannonballs have been fired. This slowing down is because all those duplicated cannonball movie clips are still laying around on the stage, even though they've stopped at their blank keyframe in Frame 11 of the Cannonball movie clip. The way to fix this is to select Frame 11 inside of the Cannonball movie clip, add the line of code `this.removeMoveClip();` below the `stop()` action, and save your file again. You'll now have full speed at all times, because Flash will be removing each duplicate cannonball as soon as it reaches the end of its range.

Modifying the game with advanced multiple hit testing

Because the Cannonball movie clip has a blank keyframe and `stop()` action at Frame 11 of its timeline, it seems to disappear and therefore have range. You could change the tweening to make it move faster or slower and change its position to make it move shorter or longer. As long as the last keyframe of the movie clip is blank and contains a `stop()` action followed by `this.removeMovieClip()`, it will disappear and not slow down Flash. You can even make curvy cannonballs by attaching the Ball graphic symbol in the Cannonball timeline to a motion path! The CD-ROM file `cannonball_curvy.fla` contains an example of this modification.

To make the game in `cannonball.fla` more interesting, you can add a high score and do some additional hit testing (adding some cool graphics wouldn't hurt either). The rest of this section describes these changes and other modifications you can make to the game.

On the CD-ROM

To make these modifications, either use the file you created in the previous example or copy the file cannonball.fla from the CD-ROM to your hard drive and open it in Flash for modifications.

Changing the firing pattern and adding penalties

To add some randomness to the firing pattern of the cannonball, select the green Cannonball movie clip instance `ball` and add the following ActionScript after the closing bracket of the `onClipEvent(enterFrame)`:

```
onClipEvent(load){
    _rotation=Math.random()*360;
}
```

Test the movie and notice that the cannonballs are now firing in all directions, which adds a degree of difficulty. You may also want to increase the value of the `dist` variable on the `blueCircle` movie clip action to 10 to make it move faster.

To penalize the player for having the blue circle touch any of the red circles, add some code that slowly fades out the blue circle each time it contacts one of the red circles. To keep the code clean, you can add this clip action after the one that is already there. This addition means that the code will have two `onClipEvent(enterFrame)` actions, but that's okay. Select the `blueCircle` movie clip on the main timeline and add this clip action code:

```
onClipEvent(enterFrame){
    masterObj=_root.multipleCircles;
    for(eachObj in masterObj){
        finalObj=masterObj[eachObj];
        if(this.hitTest(finalObj)){
            this._alpha-=1;
        }
    }
}
```

Test the movie to see that anytime the blue circle touches any of the red circles it slowly begins to fade out. You could easily replace the line of code with _alpha to make anything happen to the blue circle that you want.

Keeping score

To implement a scoring system, follow these steps:

1. The one layer on the timeline is getting mighty crowded, so create a layer above the existing one and name this layer **Scoreboard**.

2. In the Scoreboard layer, create a dynamic text field in the upper right corner of the stage and enter **score** in the Variable text box in in the Text Options panel. Make sure that the Border/Bg check box is checked so that you can see the score better.

3. Change the onClipEvent(enterFrame) code block on the ball instance of the Cannonball movie clip on the stage to have one extra line of code:

```
onClipEvent(enterFrame){
    masterObj=_root.multipleCircles;
    for(eachObj in masterObj){
        finalObj=masterObj[eachObj];
        if(this.hitTest(finalObj)){
            finalObj.removeMovieClip();
            _root.score+=100;
        }
    }
}
```

4. Test the movie and note that you can now keep score! Every time you blast one of the red circles, your score will increase by 100.

Making the targets move randomly

What else can we do to liven up this game? How about moving targets?

1. Open the Library and double-click Red Circle Target to get into its editing mode. The red circle inside should be the raw circle you drew with the Oval tool. Select this circle and press F8 to turn it into a graphic symbol with the name **Red circle graphic**.

2. Still in the editing mode of the Red Circle Target movie clip, select Frame 10 and press F6 to create a keyframe there. Do the same for Frame 20.

3. Back in Frame 10, move the circle outward from the center in any direction about 50 to 100 pixels. Create two motion tweens: one between Frames 1 and 10 and another between Frames 10 and 20.

4. Test the movie and you'll see all the circles moving in the same direction, which is not much fun.

5. To make the circles' movements more interesting, double-click the Multiple Circles movie clip in the Library to get into the movie clip's editing mode. You'll see one instance of `redCircle` on the stage.

6. In Frame 1 of this timeline is the code for generating all of the circles. Change this frame action to the following (new lines are in bold):

```
for(i=1; i<=10; i++){
    redCircle.duplicateMovieClip("redCircle"+i,i);
    this["redCircle"+i]._x=Math.random()*500;
    this["redCircle"+i]._y=Math.random()*200;
    this["redCircle"+i]._rotation=Math.random()*360;
    myScale=Math.random()*100;
    this["redCircle"+i]._xscale=myScale;
    this["redCircle"+i]._yscale=myScale;
}
redCircle._visible=0;
```

7. Test the movie again and wow! You have all kinds of circles of different sizes and rotations moving in different directions. Figure 8-7 shows the effect on the stage of the SWF movie. The only problem with the circles' movements now is that the circles all begin and end their cycles at the same time. To fix this problem, you need to add a randomized play statement to the `redCircle` clip inside the Multiple Circles movie clip.

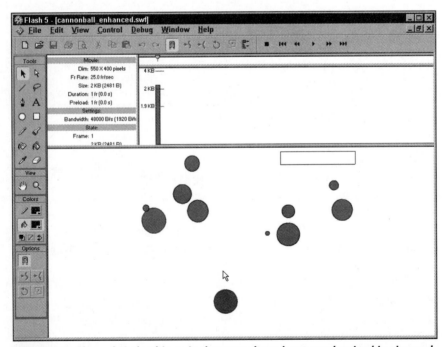

Figure 8-7: The red circle objects in the game have been randomized in size and direction of movement.

8. From the Library, double-click the Multiple Circles movie clip to get into its editing mode. Select the instance of redCircle movie clip you see there and attach this clip action to it:

```
onClipEvent(load){
    rnd=Math.floor(Math.random()*20);
    gotoAndPlay(rnd);
}
```

9. Save your movie as cannonball_enhanced.fla (it's also on the CD-ROM). Test the movie once again and you'll see that you have a very random game.

The more random a game becomes the less predictable it is and the more fun it is to play. Each red circle starts its movement cycle on a different frame thanks to the rnd variable that is used in the gotoAndPlay statement. If the Math.floor statement is confusing, it's just the new Flash 5 way to do what in Flash 4 looked like

```
rnd=int(random(20));
```

which looks a lot cleaner than that Math.floor statement. Unfortunately, both the rnd action and the random action have been deprecated in Flash 5, so we all need to start using the Math object with its methods and properties.

Caution You may be wondering why you have to add the playhead randomizer actions as an onClipEvent and not just stick them in the Frame 1 action of the Multiple Circles movie clip where all the circles are duplicated and their sizes are adjusted. The problem is that in order to control the playhead in a movie clip, you need to instantiate the movie clip, which means it must exist first. Until Flash's entire playback mechanism moves another frame beyond where it duplicates the movie clip, the clip doesn't exist yet and, therefore, any actions specifying a timeline control like gotoAndPlay need to be put somewhere other than the code block where you duplicate those movie clips. This is an anomaly for sure, but it's one you should be aware of.

Creating new targets

As one final modification to the cannonball game, you can make it so that every time one of the red circles is destroyed, another one pops up to take its place. This way, the game can continue, until perhaps a certain score is reached.

On the CD-ROM Use the cannonball_enhanced.fla file you saved from your last example or copy it from the CD-ROM to your local hard drive and open it in Flash for modification.

1. Double-click the mulitipleCircles instance on the main timeline (the one with the redCircle clip inside it). On Frame 1 of the of Multiple Circles timeline, you'll notice the actions that duplicate the movie clips. Delete all these actions. You'll be putting these actions outside the clip using a clip action and a function.

2. Select the `mulitipleCircles` instance on the main timeline. Attach the following clip actions to it:

```
onClipEvent(load){
    function makeOneCircle(){
        i+=1;
        redCircle.duplicateMovieClip("redCircle"+i,i);
        this["redCircle"+i]._visible=true;
        this["redCircle"+i]._x=Math.random()*500;
        this["redCircle"+i]._y=Math.random()*200;
        this["redCircle"+i]._rotation=Math.random()*360;
        myScale=Math.random()*100;
        this["redCircle"+i]._xscale=myScale;
        this["redCircle"+i]._yscale=myScale;
    }
    for(z=1;z<=10;z++){
        makeOneCircle();
    }
    this.redCircle._visible=false;
}
```

The bold formatting highlights the more important points of the code. Most of it you're probably familiar with, but now we've put the capability to duplicate and randomly size and place a `redCircle` movie clip into a function named `makeOneCircle()`. The `for` statement that follows the function executes the function 10 times to generate the initial 10 clips that you want placed on the stage. It then sets the initial clip's visibility to `false` so that it can't be seen.

The problem now though is that when Flash goes to make extra circles, they also will be invisible. This problem is overcome by using the statement following the `duplicateMovieClip` action to set the visibility of the newly created clip to `true`.

To modify the hit testing of the cannonball so that it makes a new red circle appear each time one is destroyed, select the `ball` instance of the green cannonball from the main timeline. Add the one line of code in bold to the existing clip actions:

```
onClipEvent(enterFrame){
    masterObj=_root.multipleCircles;
    for(eachObj in masterObj){
        finalObj=masterObj[eachObj];
        if(this.hitTest(finalObj)){
            finalObj.removeMovieClip();
            _root.score+=100;
            masterObj.makeOneCircle();
        }
    }
}
onClipEvent(load){
    _rotation=Math.random()*360;
}
```

Because we specified the `masterObj` here to be `_root.multipleCircles`, we're calling the `makeOneCircle()` function inside of it that as we know, creates another red circle. Test the movie and you'll see that every time you shoot down one of the circles another pops up to replace it.

Try moving your blue circle up to where the upper left-hand corner of the stage would be, where that original red circle is placed in the authoring environment. You probably notice your blue circle fading out. This occurs because even though the original red circle's visibility has been set to false, the circle is still there. To fix this problem, first remember that in the `For/In/hitTest` combinations we've used the `eachObj` variable to represent the instance name of each movie clip Flash encounters. Because you know that the original `redCircle` movie clip contains a name that is nine letters long and all the duplicated clip names are longer because they have a digit tacked on them, you just make sure that `eachObj` has more than nine letters. To do this, find the statements on both the cannonballs and the blue circle that read

```
if(this.hitTest(finalObj)){
```

and change them to read

```
if(this.hitTest(finalObj) && eachObj.length>9){
```

Now the hit testing will work only if the instance of the red circle that Flash finds has a name longer than nine characters, meaning that it cannot be the original hidden red circle.

All of the project modifications in this section and the following section are available in the file cannonball_enhanced2.fla on the CD-ROM.

Ending the game

To end the game after a certain score is reached, create a large box-shaped movie clip the size of the stage in any color you want with some text to the effect of **GAME OVER**. Place it on the main timeline in a new topmost layer covering up everything else and attach the following clip actions to it:

```
onClipEvent(load){
     this._visible=false;
}
onClipEvent(enterFrame){
     if(_root.score>2000){
          this._visible=true;
     }
}
```

Whenever the score reaches over 2000, the game will be over because the black square will obscure everything except the cannonballs that have been duplicated to higher levels. For a quick workaround for situations like this, keep in mind that Flash has 16,000 levels to duplicate movie clips to (0 to 15,999), and you can use the higher levels to place objects above all the other objects in a timeline, even duplicate ones. In this example, you would change your code on your GAME OVER movie clip to the following:

```
onClipEvent(load){
    this._visible=false;
}
onClipEvent(enterFrame){
    if(_root.score>2000){
        this._visible=true;
        this.duplicateMovieClip(this,15999);
    }
}
```

If you're getting the picture that building an involved game requires a lot of planning, you're 110 percent correct! Each time you need to add an element, you need to adjust for other elements. As your game building progresses, you'll get better at planning out all the elements.

Summary

Many of the core basics of building an interactive game are presented in this chapter. Assuming you've worked with Flash for a while now, you know that there are typically 25 ways to accomplish the same thing. ActionScript is very much a creative tool, and programmers have unique artistic styles. Just because certain actions were placed in certain places in this chapter (on a button versus a frame versus a clip action) doesn't mean that you must always put them there. These actions were placed where they work well in this chapter's game, but you can apply the core pieces of the code examples wherever they best fit into your game schema. Happy gaming!

✦   ✦   ✦

Advanced Gaming Concepts

In This Chapter

Making objects move realistically

Restricting object movement with obstacles

Detecting collisions with complex shapes

Keeping your objects on track

◆   ◆   ◆   ◆

A number of advanced concepts are important to gaming and dynamic development. In the last chapter, you saw how basic collision detection combined with object position tracking and the For/In statement could build a basic game. In this chapter, we cover the creation of obstacles, advanced movement, and collision detection for complex object shapes.

Obstacles

Obstacles are objects that you want to prevent another object from passing through. Obstacles are probably one of the most important concepts to master in gaming because without any obstacles, objects in your game are always free to go wherever they please. It does no good to build a maze game if your character can walk right over the walls of a maze as if they weren't there to begin with! You can use obstacles to build walls and traps and other places that you want to keep the objects in your game from touching.

You can also use obstacles to confine an object to an area. For example, the old arcade game Sprint involved racing a car around a racetrack, and the car could move only if it was on the racetrack road surface. The second you approached the edge of the track, the game would let your car drive no further. In this section of the chapter, you create some objects that can move around in free space and then place obstacles in that space to make it less free.

Establishing freedom of movement

Objects in your game need to be free to move in any direction the user chooses to be somewhat realistic. For example, when you walk around a room, you can turn in any direction that you want and not just increments of 45 of 90 degrees. In this project, you create a character that walks around a room in much the same way.

Copy the file `man.fla` from the CD-ROM to your hard drive and open it in Flash for editing.

The file `man.fla` on the CD-ROM contains an overhead view of a character created by Nate Yarrington of entertainovision.com. The character is a movie clip of a little man that contains 11 frames of what is known as a *walk cycle*. Test the movie in Flash and you see that, as the movie clip plays, the man goes through the cycle of walking with his hands swinging at his sides and his little feet moving back and forth. Our goal in this project is to give this little man the capability to walk forward and backward as well as turn in any of 360 degrees. The real trick, though, is that after he's turned facing a certain direction, he moves in that direction instead of just increments of 45 or 90 degrees.

The first thing to do is create an object that can spin in any degree of 360 degrees and then move in the direction it's facing in the same way that your car moves in the direction it's facing no matter how many degrees you turn the wheel. After you complete the movement ActionScript, you could easily replace the graphics in the movie clip with those of a racecar, a boat, an animal, or anything else you can dream up. In the Flash authoring environment for `man.fla`, start the process by selecting the Man movie clip on the stage and adding the clip actions in Listing 9-1.

Listing 9-1: Setting Walk and Rotation Speed

```
onClipEvent (enterFrame) {
    //Set walk speed
    if (Key.isDown(Key.UP)) {
        speed = 5;
        this.Play();
    }
    else if (Key.isDown(Key.DOWN)) {
        speed = -5;
        this.Play();
    }
    else {
        speed = 0;
        gotoAndStop (4);
    }
```

```
//Set rotation speed
if (Key.isDown(Key.RIGHT)) {
    angleChange = 10;
} else if (Key.isDown(Key.LEFT)) {
    angleChange = -10;
} else {
    angleChange = 0;
}
}
```

The statements in Listing 9-1 are nested within an `onClipEvent` statement, which means that they constantly execute as long as the movie clip of the little man exists on the stage. The first set of `if` statements deals with setting a walk speed. The speed is set in pixels in a variable named `speed`. This movie also has a frame rate of 25 frames per second (fps), which is critical for smooth movement. A frame rate of 12 fps does not look as good.

The `if(Key.isDown)` statements look to see whether a key is pressed. If the up arrow key, `(Key.UP)`, is pressed, the speed is set at 5 pixels. If the down arrow key, `(Key.DOWN)`, is pressed, the speed is set at -5 pixels to enable backward movement. Notice that following each of the speed settings is a statement telling this movie clip to `play()` so that the man moves his legs and does not just float across the screen.

The last `else` statement in the `//Set walk speed` code block tells Flash that, if neither the up arrow or down arrow keys is pressed, the man is to stand still. (His `speed` is set at 0.) The `gotoAndStop(4)` statement in this section of code stops the playhead in this movie clip at Frame 4. Frame 4 of the man's walk cycle is the one where he most looks as though he's standing still.

The set of `if` statements in the `//Set rotation speed` code block check to see whether the right- or left-arrow key is pressed. If one of these keys is pressed, a variable named `angleChange` is either set to 10 for clockwise movement or -10 for counter-clockwise movement. Basically, this code sets the variable that denotes how fast the angle changes as you press the right- or left-arrow keys. You add the code to actually rotate the man next.

Test the movie. The only thing that works right now is that, after you press either the up-arrow or down-arrow key on your keyboard, the man moves through his walk cycle. If no arrow key is pressed, the man stands perfectly still.

Now you can add the rest of the code to get this little guy moving. Still within the same `onClipEvent` statement that you created with Listing 9-1, add the code in Listing 9-2 right after the closing curly brace of the `angleChange=0` statement. Save the file as `man_walking.fla`.

Listing 9-2: **Making the Man Move**

```
//Create the new Angle
   myAngle = myAngle+angleChange;

//Keep myAngle between 0 and 360
   if (myAngle<0) {
       myAngle += 360;
   }
   else if (myAngle>360) {
       myAngle -= 360;
   }

//Calculate the distance to move x and y
   xchange = (xmove*-1)+(speed*Math.sin(Math.PI/180*myAngle));
   ychange = (ymove*-1)-(speed*Math.cos(Math.PI/180*myAngle));
   xmove +=xchange;
   ymove +=ychange;

//Move the little man
   this._y+=ymove;
   this._x+=xmove;
   this._rotation=myAngle;
```

The first line of code in Listing 9-2 adds myAngle to any possible angleChange put forth by the arrow keys. If you look at the very last line in Listing 9-2, you see that the code eventually gets around to setting the little man's rotation to equal myAngle. Before that happens, though, the angle is constrained by the block of code following //Keep myAngle between 0 and 360. This code constantly checks to see whether the angle or rotation you're setting is less than 0 or greater than 360. If either of those occurrences is true, the myAngle variable is adjusted by +/- 360 degrees to keep you from ending up with angles such as 1,243 degrees.

The next segment of code, beginning with //Calculate the distance to move x and y, uses some physics and geometry and introduces the xchange, ychange, xmove, and ymove variables. The first time through the loop, before any arrow keys are pressed, the variables' values are 0. But as soon as a positive or negative speed number is detected, it is combined with whatever angle is set in myAngle to create new coordinate values that are then added to the previous coordinate values in these statements:

```
xmove +=xchange;
ymove +=ychange;
```

Explaining all the geometry and trigonometry involved in this code is beyond the scope of this book, but basically what is happening is that all the variables being set with the arrow keys are being evaluated and worked into some x- and y-coordinate changes that you can use to move the little man.

In the last block of code, which begins with `//Move the little man`, the movie clip's x-position and y-position are updated to reflect changes. Because the man can move in any direction, the values for the `xmove` and `ymove` variables can easily be negative numbers. You can take a look at all the variable values by enabling the debugger and testing the movie. The very last line of code sets the visual rotation of the movie clip to equal the angle set in the `myAngle` variable.

Test the movie in Flash or your browser. By pressing the up- or down-arrow keys, you can move the man forward and backward. If the arrow keys aren't having any effect, use your mouse pointer to first click anywhere on the stage of the Flash movie. Pressing and holding the down-arrow key makes the man do a little "Moon Walk" dance move across the stage. Pressing the right- or left-arrow key spins him around. You also can use arrow-key combinations to get neat angular movement effects. You're probably beginning to see how you could adapt this code to use with a boat or racecar. If you're experiencing any problems with the file you just created, make sure that you recheck your steps and reference the completed `man_walking.fla` file on the CD-ROM.

Note

> If you're testing the movie in a browser, you may notice that none of your arrow keys are having any effect at first. For the arrow keys to work, the Flash movie in the Web page you're looking at must be the *focus*. You achieve this focus by clicking anywhere in the Flash movie using your mouse. If you develop games, you should always include a Start the Game button to make sure that the user clicked somewhere in the Flash movie and switched the focus of the Web browser to the Flash movie so that it can then accept keyboard input.

Limiting movement with obstacles

Obstacles are a great way to place boundaries in your games or dynamic Flash movies beyond which objects cannot pass. Creating the graphic for an obstacle is quite easy because you can make it look any way that you want. The hard part is testing to see whether an object that is moving has hit the obstacle and, if it has, constraining that object's movement to prevent it from getting around the obstacle.

The basic concept we're using here to make the obstacle work is simple. In the last chapter, you saw how collision detection worked. The example in this chapter also tests for a collision if an object moves. If a collision with an obstacle is detected, the object that has moved is moved back to where it was because it cannot be allowed to pass the obstacle. You may be asking yourself, "How is that going to look, with objects moving back and forth all the time?" The answer is that it's going to look just fine, because when Flash executes ActionScript code contained in a button, frame, or movie clip, Flash doesn't update the screen until it's done working through all the code.

So if you move some objects around in the middle of an ActionScript code sequence, those objects are moved virtually in Flash's processing memory. You can then set variables based on the positions of those objects and test those variables to see whether they fall within certain guidelines. If the guidelines are not met (say, for example, that an object hits an obstacle or is standing right on top of it), you can just use some ActionScript to move it back. As long as the ActionScript moving the object back to where it was occurs farther down in the code list than the original movement code, Flash leaves the object alone. Alternatively, you could move the object someplace new, and Flash puts it there instead.

The key thing to remember is that, for each frame cycle, Flash computes all the ActionScript code first, and only after it's done does it update the screen with the *final* results. This is great news! Now you can move objects in a virtual manner all across the screen, see if they're near or touching other objects, and then put them all back where they were if you need to without the person viewing the Flash movie even seeing that you've done anything!

Copy the file man_walking.fla to your hard drive and open it in Flash for modification. You can also use the version of this file that you created in the last example if you still have it open.

To use obstacles to limit movement, just follow these steps:

1. Open the Library and locate the movie clip named Obstacle Block. Drag an instance of this movie clip onto the stage and place it anywhere you'd like.

2. Select the Man movie clip and give it an instance name of **man**.

3. With the Man movie clip still selected on the stage and with the Actions panel open, view all the code that was created and explained in the preceding section, "Establishing freedom of movement." Inside that onClipEvent action and *after* the last existing block of code where you moved the little man, add the following ActionScript:

```
//If the man contacts an obstacle,
    //move him back to where he was
    masterObj=_root;
    for(eachObj in masterObj){
        finalObj=masterObj[eachObj];
        if(this.hitTest(finalObj) && eachObj.length>3){
            this._y-=ymove;
            this._x-=xmove;
        }
    }
```

You should recognize this code as the versatile For/In statement from the last chapter. It's modified a bit here, though. The only change is that we added a logical AND (&&) to ensure that the object we're looking at has a name longer than three characters, as follows:

```
if(this.hitTest(finalObj) && eachObj.length>3){
```

Immediately following this line are the following two lines that change the x-position and y-position of this movie clip to counteract the movement in the //Move the little man block of code:

```
this._y-=ymove;
this._x-=xmove;
```

We use _root as the masterObj master object in this example for the sake of simplicity. What this final block of code is doing is going through the entire _root and checking to see whether the Man movie clip has hit anything else. It excludes itself by checking to make sure that every object it checks has a name that is longer than three characters. (The movie clip itself has a three-letter name of Man.) Remember from the last chapter that, if you fail to name an instance (such as the obstacle block), Flash automatically gives it a name of *Instance* and then a number. This name is immediately longer than three characters, so you know the collision must be with something other than the Man movie clip.

If a collision is detected with anything else on the _root level of the stage, Flash moves the little man back to where he was before the collision. Because this activity all occurs in the same piece of ActionScript before Flash updates the screen, the person viewing the Flash movie is never even aware that an object has been virtually moved and then moved back. The entire block of code is in Listing 9-3.

Listing 9-3: **The Entire onClipEvent Code**

```
onClipEvent (enterFrame) {
    //Set walk speed
    if (Key.isDown(Key.UP)) {
        speed = 5;
        this.Play();
    }
    else if (Key.isDown(Key.DOWN)) {
        speed = -5;
        this.Play();
    }
    else {
        speed = 0;
        gotoAndStop (4);
    }

    //Set rotation speed
    if (Key.isDown(Key.RIGHT)) {
        angleChange = 10;
    } else if (Key.isDown(Key.LEFT)) {
        angleChange = -10;
    } else {
        angleChange = 0;
    }

    //Create the new Angle
    myAngle = myAngle+angleChange;
```

Continued

Listing 9-3 *(continued)*

```
//Keep myAngle between 0 and 360
if (myAngle<0) {
    myAngle += 360;
}
else if (myAngle>360) {
    myAngle -= 360;
}

//Calculate the distance to move x and y
xchange = (xmove*-1)+(speed*Math.sin(Math.PI/180*myAngle));
ychange = (ymove*-1)-(speed*Math.cos(Math.PI/180*myAngle));
xmove +=xchange;
ymove +=ychange;

//Move the little man
this._y+=ymove;
this._x+=xmove;
this._rotation=myAngle;

//If the man contacts an obstacle, move him back to where he
was
    masterObj=_root;
    for(eachObj in masterObj){
        finalObj=masterObj[eachObj];
        if(this.hitTest(finalObj) && eachObj.length>3){
            this._y-=ymove;
            this._x-=xmove;
        }
    }

}
```

Test the movie in Flash and you see that, try as you may to move the little man through or over the obstacle block, you simply cannot do so! No matter what side and at what angle you attack the block from, you cannot walk over it and must go around it. If you have any trouble with the code, recheck your steps or open the completed file available on the CD-ROM as man_walking_obstacles.fla. **Figure 9-1 shows the little man trying to get around the block.**

There's not much point in using the For/In statement if you're just going to have one obstacle block. Return to the Flash authoring environment and duplicate the obstacle block that's on the stage as many times as you'd like. Change the scale, height, and width for all the blocks if you'd like. If you have graphics of your own obstacles, you can throw them in, too. Just make sure that they're movie clips. Because you're using For/In, you don't need to name anything at all. A possible layout of the stage is shown in Figure 9-2.

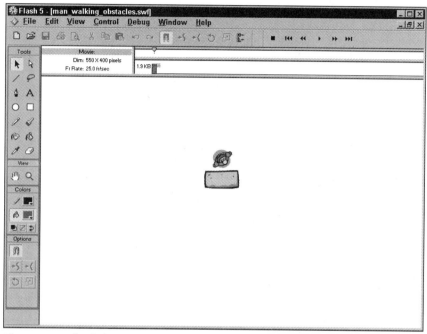

Figure 9-1: The little Man movie clip cannot get through the obstacle you placed for him.

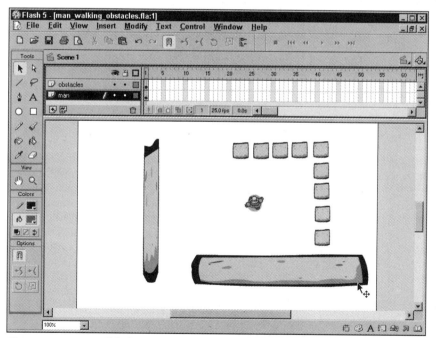

Figure 9-2: A possible layout for the stage after creating lots of obstacles and resizing them.

Try testing the movie again with all the blocks you place all around the stage and you see that you can confine the man to an area of the stage. Using obstacles, you can easily create a maze for the man to walk through. You can also resize the man or change his rate of movement by adjusting the `speed` variable in the code or change his rate of rotation by adjusting the `angleChange` variable. You can also replace the man's graphic with any that you'd like to use.

Caution

Although obstacle collision detection is darn good, it's not completely foolproof. Don't create an obstacle-driven game where the winning prize is a million dollars or anything really valuable. You may have noticed that the little man occasionally gets stuck on an obstacle, although 99 percent of the time he can get free by spinning around. Some of this sticking has to do with his shadow and his arms. Changing his rate of movement can also affect the obstacle "bounce-back." A high rate of speed could catapult him right over the obstacle. Choosing a lower rate of speed works better and also enables the man to get closer to the obstacle before his movements are limited.

Collisions Based on Shape

All collision detection we've done on objects up until this point has been through what's known as *bounding box detection*. That's where the bounding box of one object is tested against the bounding box of another object. The word *box* suggests that these areas are square, so if one of the objects you're testing happens to be a circle, the area being tested includes areas outside the circle.

More complex shapes may have nooks and crannies or open spaces where you don't want collision detection to occur. You can view an object's bounding box by just selecting it on the stage in the Flash authoring environment. Take a look at the movie clip object in Figure 9-3 and you see that the bounding box surrounding it encompasses areas that are completely blank and have nothing to do with its complex shape. Despite having a nonsquare shape, the object is collision-detected as if it were just a big rectangle if you use the `hitTest` methods we've shown up to this point.

The way around this is to use Flash's *shape-testing* method of `hitTest` collision detection. Just testing the shape of one object against the shape of another would be nice, but unfortunately it's not that simple. If using shape-test collision detection, you can test the shape of one object only against a single point on the stage. This limitation means that you can't test two complex shapes to see whether one "fits inside" another in some creative way. The best that can be achieved is to check the shape of a complex object against the center point of another object. (It doesn't necessarily need to be the center point, but that point is the most common one to use.)

The `hitTest` action still performs the collision testing, but the parameters that you provide it are different. The syntax is as follows:

```
someObject.hitTest( xpoint , ypoint , shapeBoolean);
```

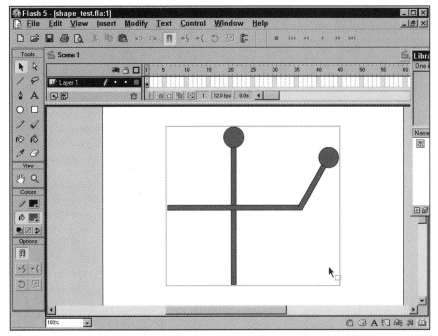

Figure 9-3: Even a complex object has a bounding box that is a simple rectangle.

Obviously, someObject is the name of the object you're testing for hits and should usually be the one that's *more complex in shape*, like the one shown in Figure 9-3. The xpoint and ypoint parameters need to be replaced with numbers or variables containing an x-coordinate and a y-coordinate on the stage. The shapeBoolean parameter needs be replaced with either true or false. Specifying true tells Flash that you want it to use the true shape of the object specified in someObject and test to see whether the point you specify falls anywhere on the shape. The shape in this case refers to the actual graphic, not the bounding box surrounding the graphic. If the point you're testing falls in a blank area of that object, the hitTest is false.

You can also specify false for the shapeBoolean parameter, in which case Flash uses the entire bounding box of someObject and not just its accurate shape to decide whether a collision occurs. As with everything else in Flash, you have lots of ways to accomplish what looks like almost the same thing here.

To see the shape-testing method of hitTest in action, copy the shape_test.fla file from the CD-ROM onto your hard drive and open it in Flash for modification. This file contains one movie clip symbol named Odd Shape, and an instance of it appears on the stage. This shape is the same one that is shown in Figure 9-3. Follow these steps:

1. Create a circle on the stage with the Oval tool that has a fill color of red and a black stroke. Use the Info panel to resize this circle to 20 by 20 pixels.

2. Select the red circle you created and press F6 to turn it into a button object with a name of **Red Circle Button**.

3. With the Red Circle Button still selected on the stage, press F6 again to turn it into a movie clip symbol with the name **Draggable Circle**. Double-click this movie clip to get into its editing mode and back to the button inside it that you created. Attach the following ActionScript to the button:

```
on(press){
    this.startDrag();
}
on(release){
    stopDrag();
}
```

This code makes the Draggable Circle movie clip draggable after you click the button inside it.

4. Return to the stage and select the instance of the Odd Shape movie clip that is there. Give it an instance name of **oddShape** in the Instance panel.

5. Select the Draggable Circle movie clip and attach the following clip actions to it:

```
onClipEvent(enterFrame){
    if(_root.oddShape.hitTest(this._x,this._y,true)){
        _root.output=true;
    }
    else{
        _root.output=false;
    }
}
```

6. Using the Text tool, create a dynamic text field on the main timeline and enter **output** in the Variable text box in the Text Options panel. Make sure that the Border/Bg check box is checked. Place the field anywhere that looks convenient.

7. Use the Character panel to choose a black text color and a font size of 16 for the text field.

Test the movie in Flash or in your browser and click the red button to start dragging it around the stage. As you approach the odd-shaped object, the output dynamic text field you created shows a value of false. Only if the center point of the red circle touches any part of the graphic of the odd shape does the output field display true. Figure 9-4 shows the shape hitTest statement finally evaluate to true.

On the CD-ROM   The completed file is available on the CD-ROM as shape_test_complete.fla if you have any problems.

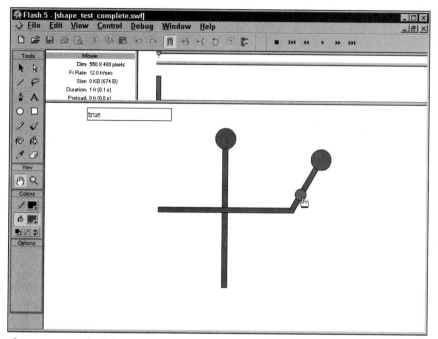

Figure 9-4: Only if the center of the circle crosses a part of the graphic does the hitTest evaluate to true.

In the following example, we choose `this._x` and `this._y` on the Draggable Circle movie clip as the two points to check for in the `hitTest` statement and specify `true` for the `shapeBoolean` parameter:

```
if(_root.oddShape.hitTest(this._x,this._y,true)){
```

To see what the difference is if bounding box detection is used instead of shape detection, just change the value `true` at the end of the `hitTest` statement on the Draggable Circle movie clip so that it is `false`, as follows:

```
if(_root.oddShape.hitTest(this._x,this._y,false)){
```

Test the movie again and you see that, anytime the center point of the circle crosses into the rectangular bounding box area surrounding the odd shape, the `output` text field shows `true`. Figure 9-5 shows this new movie in action.

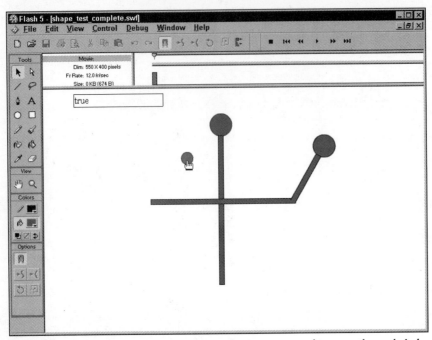

Figure 9-5: The hitTest statement now evaluates to true whenever the red circle center point falls within the bounding box of the odd shape.

Now that you've seen the concept behind using `hitTest` for an actual shape versus just a bounding box, you may be pondering the possible applications for such a `hitTest` action. The next section explores a few of these applications.

Shape Testing Applications

At the most basic level, shape testing with `hitTest` can enable you to streamline certain tasks in Flash. You can turn oddly shaped movie clips into clickable buttons using nothing but ActionScript as well as constrain objects to an area of a certain shape if you're building a game.

Turning movie clips into buttons

In the example in the last section, you first created a circle button and then encapsulated it inside a movie clip. You then had to go back into the movie clip and add `on(press)` and `on(release)` events to the button to get the movie clip to become draggable. Using the shape `hitTest` with an `onClipEvent` can save you the step of ever creating such a button at all!

On the CD-ROM

Open the `shape_test_complete.fla` file on the CD-ROM or use the file you created in the last example if you still have it open.

Follow these steps:

1. Select the Odd Shape movie clip and add the following `onClipEvent` actions to it:

```
onClipEvent (mouseDown) {
    if(this.hitTest(_root._xmouse,_root._ymouse, true)){
        this.startDrag();
    }
}
onClipEvent (mouseUp) {
    this.stopDrag();
}
```

2. Test the movie in Flash or in your Web browser. Place your mouse anywhere over the blue graphics contained within the Odd Shape movie clip and press and hold your mouse button to start dragging the clip around!

Notice that you did not turn this movie clip into a button or put a button inside it. You basically just used `hitTest` to figure out whether the mouse pointer was anywhere over the graphical shape of the Odd Shape movie clip when you clicked the mouse button. If it was, you could drag the clip around. If you clicked in the blank area in between the spokes of the Odd Shape movie clip, no dragging would occur because the mouse pointer was not touching the shape.

You can very easily change the scripting, though, so that you could click anywhere within the bounding box of the Odd Shape movie clip and start dragging it around. Just return to the Flash authoring environment and change the Boolean parameter in the `hitTest` code in the `onClipEvent` for the Odd Shape movie clip to `false`, as follows:

```
if(this.hitTest(_root._xmouse,_root._ymouse, false)){
```

Test the movie again and place your mouse any place in the blank areas between the spokes of the oddly shaped clip. Hold down your mouse button and you can immediately begin dragging the clip around. Figure 9-6 shows this happening.

This whole method of initiating drags is more convenient because you don't need to create an extra button (or invisible button) to stick inside of the movie clips that you want to be draggable. And whenever you do put a button inside of a movie clip symbol to initiate dragging, that button is present and active across all the instances of that clip you place on the stage. Because in this example we used an `onClipEvent` action that is unique to each instance, you can configure different instances of the same symbol to be draggable or not draggable on a per instance basis.

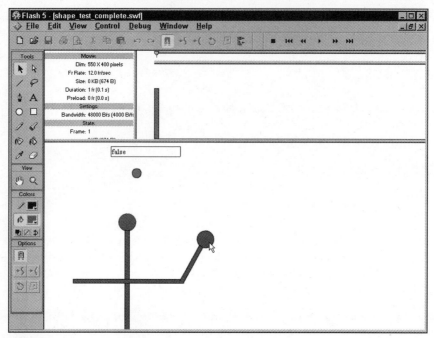

Figure 9-6: By using hitTest with the shape parameters, you can drag movie clips around without using a button.

Tip   Another advantage of using hitTest with an onClipEvent is that, when you're checking to see whether the user is clicking the particular movie clip you attached the code to, the user doesn't see the hand symbol appear the way it would normally in Flash if the user were hovering over a button. This mimics the more traditional operating-system click-and-drag capability of Windows or a Mac operating system. (If you go to drag a folder around your desktop, a silly hand doesn't appear as you roll over it.) You can now create the same kind of environment inside Flash.

Constraining an object to an irregularly shaped area

You can use the shape-testing capability of the hitTest action to keep an object within a certain area (for example, making sure that a racecar stays on the racetrack and doesn't go veering off into the bushes somewhere. In this section, you test a movie clip of a little man to see whether he's on a circular track. If the hitTest action determines that the man is not on the track shape, then he is not allowed to move. The neat thing you find as you work through this example is that the physical shape of a movie clip is determined by every graphical object inside it, including draggable movie clips that can be repositioned to change the shape testing in real time!

Copy the file man_on_circletrack.fla from the CD-ROM to your hard drive and open it in Flash for modification. This file contains the Man Walking movie clip used in the examples at the beginning of this chapter, along with a second movie clip that is in the shape of a circular track. The goal here is to enable the man to walk only within the confines of the track. Figure 9-7 shows the basic stage layout.

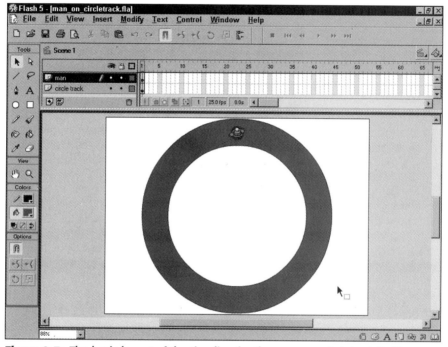

Figure 9-7: The basic layout of the timeline for the man_on_circletrack.fla file.

Now follow these steps:

1. Select the instance of the blue circular track on the stage and, in the Instance panel, give it an instance name of **circleTrack**.

2. Select the instance of the little man on the stage and open the Actions panel to view the onClipEvent(enterFrame) actions attached to him. (If you are not familiar with this set of actions, please reference the beginning sections of this chapter on "Establishing freedom of movement.") The actions are identical to that of the man walking around in the earlier examples of this chapter except that the angleChange variable is changed to reflect a value of 5 instead of 10 so that the little man can't turn as fast on the tight circular track.

3. Test the movie and use the four arrow keys on your keyboard to walk the little man around the screen. Notice that he currently has free reign to run amok all over everything and is blatantly ignoring the circle track he's supposed to be confined to.

4. Return to the Flash authoring environment and select the little man. View his clip actions in the Actions panel and notice that the bottom section of the code where we were doing obstacle collision detections earlier in this chapter is now just the following commented code:

```
//If the man is not within the circle
//track, move him back to where he was
//
```

5. Change this block of code to the following:

```
//If the man is not within the circle
//track, move him back to where he was
if(!_root.circleTrack.hitTest(this._x,this._y,true)){
        this._y-=ymove;
        this._x-=xmove;
    }
```

6. Test the movie in Flash again and use your four arrow keys to move the little man around the track. You see that he is now confined to the circle track and cannot venture beyond its bounds! The completed file is available on the CD-ROM as `man_on_circletrack_complete.fla`.

To understand what these steps are doing, look at the code you added containing the `if` and `hitTest` statement. The key to the whole statement is the exclamation point (!), which stands for the logical operator NOT, at the very beginning of the `if` evaluation. What we're saying in this statement is that we *do* want the man to be touching the shape of the circle track. If by chance he's *not* touching the track after ActionScript moves him somewhere, he's out-of-bounds and needs to be sent back to where he was. This statement tests the little man's x- and y-coordinates to see whether they reside anywhere inside the graphical shape of the circle track.

This example is really just obstacle detection in reverse. In the earlier examples in this chapter, the goal is to keep the little man *away* from any objects on the stage, and if he happens to move to a position where he is touching one of them, the ActionScript sends him right back to where he was before the screen had a chance to update. In the current example, the goal is to keep the little man on top of another object (in this case, the circle track. If ActionScript figures out that he's not touching the shape of the track after making a movement, he gets sent back to where he was, which is someplace still touching the track.

To take this example one step farther, suppose that you were creating a game where an object needed to remain on a path and breaks or gaps that needed to be bridged somehow were in that path. The following steps create a break in the circle track, along with a bridge that can be dragged over the gap to make it passable.

Copy the file `man_on_circletrack_complete.fla` to your hard drive and open it in Flash for modification. You may also use the file you created in the last example if you still have it available.

Follow these steps:

1. Open the Library and double-click the Circle Track movie clip symbol to open its editing view.

2. The blue circle track isn't even a graphic symbol; it's just a raw circle created with the Flash Oval tool. Use the Arrow tool to select one half of this circle, splitting it vertically. Use your right-arrow key to move the right half of the circle away from the left half by about 70 pixels, creating a gap between the pieces. Figure 9-8 illustrates what this looks like.

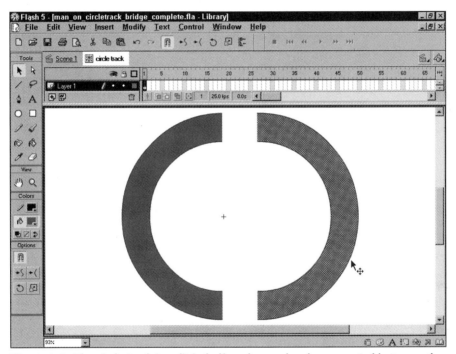

Figure 9-8: The circle track is split in half, and a gap has been created between the sections.

3. Still inside the editing mode of the Circle Track movie clip, use the Rectangle tool with a fill and stroke color of black to draw a rectangle somewhere on the stage.

4. Select this rectangle and use the Info panel to resize it to approximately 95 pixels wide by 52 pixels high. With the rectangle still selected, press F6 to turn it into a movie clip with a symbol name of **Bridge**. You use this bridge to close the gap between the sections of the track.

5. While still inside the editing mode for the Circle Track movie clip that now contains the bridge, select the bridge and add the following clip action to it:

```
onClipEvent (mouseDown) {
    if(this.hitTest(_root._xmouse,_root._ymouse, true)){
        this.startDrag();
    }
}
onClipEvent (mouseUp) {
    this.stopDrag();
}
```

This code should be very familiar from a few pages back, in the section "Turning movie clips into buttons." What we've done here is make this Bridge movie clip draggable whenever someone clicks and drags on it.

6. Position the Bridge movie clip somewhere in the white area of the stage so that it's not touching the blue track.

7. Return to the main timeline and position the little man movie clip so that he is touching and well inside one of the two track sections. Test your movie in Flash or in your browser.

As you move the little man around by using the arrow keys on your keyboard, you see that he stops whenever he reaches the white area separating the pieces of the track. To save the day and let the little man cross over, just move your mouse pointer over the black "bridge" movie clip and click it to drag it into position over the gap in the track. As soon as you do so, you should be able to use your arrow keys to let the little man cross over the bridge to the other side of the track. Figure 9-9 shows the little man happily making his way across the bridge.

On the CD-ROM This file is available on the CD-ROM with the extremely long filename `man_on_circletrack_bridge_complete.fla`.

The little man can do this because the code attached to his movie clip with an `onClipEvent` is checking to make sure that he is always touching the Circle Track movie clip. That means that any graphic object inside the Circle Track clip (including other movie clips such as the bridge) is fair game to be considered as part of the shape of the track.

The code presented in this section is transferable to any application you may need to use it for. You should be able to see by now where you need to make modifications, such as making sure that you always place the correct instance name right before your `hitTest` statement. The applications for this kind of code in gaming are endless. Try creating your own track in a wild-and-crazy shape. You also could create bridges that move in and out by themselves. You are limited only by your imagination.

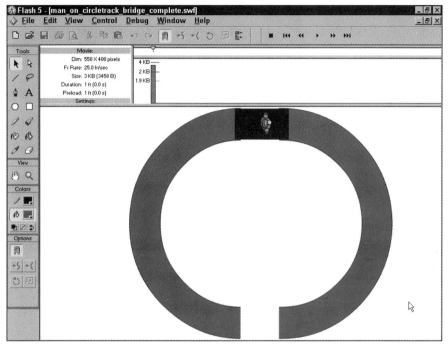

Figure 9-9: The little man crosses over the bridge that was dragged into place to fill the gap in the track.

Summary

Collision detection combined with movement of an object is a great way to create obstacles for gaming or dynamic development projects. As you saw in the last section, collision detection can be applied in unique ways to turn movie clips into buttons or to constrain an object to the shape of a certain unique graphic area. Most of the code and examples in this chapter and the last are easily adaptable to your gaming projects. These concepts and code pieces can help to fill in the missing links in the games you've been creating and plan to create as well as help you think about your game construction and organization in new and unique ways. Happy gaming!

✦　　✦　　✦

The Two Sides of an eBusiness

Setting Up a Flash Front End for an eBusiness Site

If ever a case existed to measure twice and cut once, it is the case of planning an eBusiness Web site. With Flash as a front end, you need to first plan what customers see after they come to the site, what kinds of products or services to offer, and how viewers navigate to find what they want. (Of course, a really great site lures the viewer through a company's wares and services to help the viewer purchase what the company is selling.)

Planning an eBusiness Site

After you have your site planned for navigation and general appearance, you must think about the other task of a Flash 5 front end for an eBusiness site: working with the back end. Although navigation and appearance are not matters for the back end, after an e-customer clicks a button to make a purchase, something on the back end must occur. You need a way to check the inventory (in the database), change the inventory (reduce it by the number of purchases), record the transaction, and let the buyer know that he or she has been billed and the order is being processed. In addition, you need a billing system to charge the customer for the purchase.

All the back-end scripts are built in Chapter 11, but the bridges to those back-end scripts must be created in ActionScript in this chapter. Therefore, the planning process includes deciding what back-end modules are required so that the bridges to those modules and front-end display forms (text fields) are built where required.

Note   This chapter and the next use or link to PHP and MySQL. Because some readers may not have Microsoft Access, we decided that using the freely available MySQL database would ensure that all readers could follow the project in this chapter and Chapter 11. But translating the scripts into ASP requires only minor adjustments in the PHP scripts and connection protocols. So if you prefer using ASP and NT Servers, you find, with a few exceptions, that the front ends in this chapter are perfectly applicable to eBusiness projects that use ASP. Substituting VBScript for PHP in the next chapter requires some changes, but the structures are essentially the same, and you can change the variable names by removing the dollar signs ($) that identify variables in PHP. Chapters 10 and 11 also use the JTLNet protocol for establishing MySQL databases. By doing so, we hope to provide further consistency in a real-world setting. If you are using your own computer for a server and client by installing and running Apache server and the MySQL server, use the same table and database names as used in the JTLNet examples. To get the same real-world consistency with an NT Server, use HosTek.

Using the value bubble

One of the early conceptual paths that has come from research in e-commerce and eBusiness has been the *value bubble*. (Kierzkowski, A., S. McQuade, R. Waitman and M. Zeisser, 1996: "Marketing to the Digital Consumer." *McKinsey Quarterly*, 2, 180–183.) The bubble consists of the following five elements in a successful eBusiness site:

✦ Attract

✦ Engage

✦ Relate

✦ Learn

✦ Retain

eBusiness sites that had these elements were found to be more successful and survived at a far higher rate than those sites that did not. By considering each of these elements, we have a clear goal in mind when deciding what needs to be included in the Flash movie and site.

Attract

Attraction means that the viewer is captivated by what you place on the Web page. In large part, the process of attraction depends on the customer's interest. Younger audiences may be interested in action-adventure computer software, while older audiences may seek out stock portfolio software. Therefore, the first rule of attraction is to consider your audience. Begin with what your target audience finds interesting and go from there.

One of Flash's best qualities is its capability to provide eye-catching animation with sound to add interest to a site's product's and services. But animation also can annoy the viewer, so you must be very judicious in your choice of animated objects and sound. The following are some different types of animation and sound that you can render in Flash:

✦ **The big show:** Some sites provide lots of graphics and sound that is very exciting the first time it is viewed. The strong point of this kind of attractive movie is that people often tell their friends, "You gotta see this URL!" The big show can, however, detract from your product or service, and after being viewed once or twice, it becomes more of a hindrance than an attraction. To successfully have a big show attraction, provide a "skip intro" option or even consider planting a cookie after the viewer has seen it once so that he or she doesn't need to see it again. Make sure that you don't lead the viewer back to the big show in your links.

✦ **Little animations and surprises:** To add fun, whimsy, and excitement to a site, you can attract viewers with little animations that surprise the viewer and perform a function as well. The simplest example of this approach is the *rollover* — a Flash object that changes as the mouse passes over it. By putting in a few unexpected twists and turns in the basic rollover, you can add more interest to the site. For example, one developer's site included an invitation to launch a page from the developer's portfolio. After the viewer clicked the Launch button, a little rocket icon took off to the background sound of a NASA countdown. This rollover provided a little fun, didn't get in the way, and gave the viewer something to grin about while the page was launching.

✦ **New Age float:** For some products or services, a less dramatic but very effective way to use movement to get the viewer's attention is to use slow fade-ins and fade-outs to float different images on-screen. Accompanied by soothing New Age music, such pages promise peace of mind with a product or service.

✦ **Jump the facts:** A final way to attract viewers is to have a key product or service featured. An immediate presentation that is animated and then stops draws attention to the elements that piqued the viewer's interest in visiting the site in the first place.

Engage

To engage viewers, give them something to do. Often in real estate sites, the viewer is provided with a calculator to calculate monthly payments based on interest rates and the purchase price of the house. When using the calculator, the site visitor is subtly encouraged to look at other properties and make similar calculations. Little quizzes, puzzles, or other engaging elements on a Web site that provide an activity for viewers can be important in keeping them at the site.

Relate

Relating to an audience, like attracting an audience, requires that you know your audience. By providing information and special tools, perhaps an online newsletter, you can better make a connection between your business and your customers.

E-mail is another good way to relate to customers. Usually you can add an e-mail feature with a contact form. A contact form is simple to make with PHP and is a good tool to have on your site.

Learn

You can gather information from your site's viewers in many ways. Along with contact forms, survey forms can prove invaluable. Surveys should be relatively short and focused on what your company can provide in services and products. You may discover needed services that you never thought about by using a survey.

Another tool for learning about your customers is to track the buttons and links on your site. Whenever the visitor clicks a button, you can include a little ActionScript to fire off a PHP script that increments a MySQL database to record the click. In this way, you can learn what visitors do and do not do when they visit your site. Such feedback helps you better understand and serve your customers.

Retain

The final important element of the value bubble is retention. Your site should have mechanisms that make your customers want to come back. A cookie placed on the visitor's computer can be turned into a greeting with the visitor's name. Automatic e-mails, online calendars announcing new products or services, news about your company, and message boards or online chat rooms with dialogue between customers provide ways to retain customers.

Planning based on product or service

Your site needs to be designed around your customer and the products or services you have. Some products must be shipped to the customer, such as toys and books. Other products, such as software, can be downloaded, and some products provide access to information on the Web.

Products

The basic distinction between products is whether they must be shipped. Very different front-end and back-end decisions must be made depending on what has to be done with a product to get it to the customer.

Shipped

Shipped products imply some finite inventory and a location for shipment. As products are ordered, the orders can be attached to a database that keeps track of the inventory of the product. After an order ships, the inventory database should be decremented by the number of ordered items. Similarly, a shipping address is required, so the site designer needs to consider having information for both a billing and a shipping address.

Online

Life would be so much simpler for the designer and the client if all products could be dealt with online. Products that can be downloaded save the expense of shipping and having both a billing and shipping address. But downloaded products can be sent to a different e-mail address than the e-mail address from which the product is ordered; therefore, you should consider having an alternative e-mail address for the online products that can be downloaded.

A second type of online product is access to information. Usually if the product is a general type of information, such as expertise on investments or an online magazine, the product is standardized even though the user can select from a variety of choices. No shipping is required, but the designer still needs to include forms for user information for billing purposes.

Services

One of the most ubiquitous services provided over the Internet is *support service*. Usually, this kind of service is packaged as part of another service. Both JTLNet and HosTek, whose hosting services are provided on a trial basis with this book, include extensive support service modules. Both FAQs (Frequently Asked Questions) and e-mail contact with responses to specific questions are provided.

Online

When information is gathered to meet a specific online request, as opposed to being provided as an existing general information product, such as an online magazine, the information is considered a service because the information must be generated uniquely for a request. All the service requirements can be handled online in such situations, so the site developer must include clear e-mail contact with the client as well as phone or FAX numbers.

Face-to-face

Both Dell and Gateway provide maintenance contracts with their computers, and any computer repair must be done on-site. If such on-site service is part of a contract, a site may need three addresses: the ship-to address (when the computer is originally purchased), the bill-to address, and the repair-site address. For example, a company with a central-receiving office may order a product from one location, have it shipped to central receiving, and then send it to a satellite office where the product is used.

Billing

Any billing involving a credit card transaction requires a special module. We don't provide a module for credit card payment in the project in this chapter because we were concerned that someone would set it up and attempt to do online credit card business without the special security required. Several companies, many of which are associated with hosting services, provide online credit card modules that you can seamlessly include in your Flash site. Early on in developing your eBusiness site, contact your hosting service or one of the secure credit card processing companies, such as CyberCash (www.cybercash.com) or LinkPoint (www.linkpoint.com). See what modules they provide for payment. If the module cannot be integrated into Flash, you can link to an HTML page for the credit card information and then come back to the Flash module.

For subscription products and services, the designer needs to include a start date and an ending date that can be stored and checked daily on a database. Other information can be based on a "pay-per-view" system for users who need the information only occasionally, and the billing for this type of site works the same as any one-time product site.

Developing an eBusiness Design Shop Site

To illustrate how Flash can be used with an e-commerce site, we chose to develop a fictitious Web design business using a not-so-fictitious business name and site that one of the authors maintains. (Considering the litigious nature of business, we thought it wise not to risk a fictitious name we did not use ourselves.) The site provides different elements that can be involved in an eBusiness site. Different types of products and services are offered, including shipped, downloaded, and contracted services. The front end also has two different back-end modules to PHP programs. In the next chapter, we discuss using the PHP programs, but in this chapter we set up only minimal scripts for the back-end for testing purposes.

The sample eBusiness movie, DesignShop.fla, is organized into the following six layers:

- ✦ Check out
- ✦ Floating Calculator
- ✦ Label Buttons
- ✦ Menus
- ✦ Shopping Stops
- ✦ Background

Most of the work is done on the Shopping Stops layer, where the viewer selects different options from drop-down menu movie clips. Initially, the site is very simple; it's organized around four drop-down menus, a movable Cart Recorder that keeps track of the amount of purchases, and a Check-out button. A black bottom border and a subdued company sign make up the rest of the initial view, as shown in Figure 10-1.

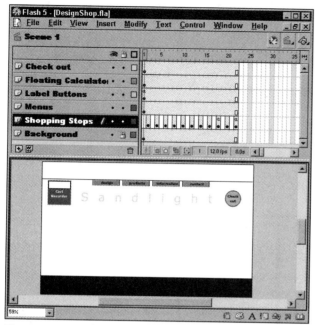

Figure 10-1: A clean and simple frame is the initial view of the site.

The stage is reset to 650 by 400 pixels in the Movie Properties dialog box. (Choose Modify ➪ Movie to access.) The color palette is a calm one using muted greens, gray, black, and white (see Table 10-1). The colors are selected to provide a comfortable environment for the viewer, and although they do not leap out at the viewer, they are effective for attracting attention without distracting from the site.

Table 10-1
Color Palette for DesignShop.fla

Colors	R Value	G Value	B Value
A	99	CC	66
B	66	66	66
C	00	99	33
D	99	99	66
E (White)	FF	FF	FF
F (Black)	00	00	00

The Background layer

At the base of the project is a simple line of text with a line above it and a thick black bar along the bottom. The text is a graphic with the Alpha reduced to 15 percent. It was created with a 35-point Verdana font in black with the AV set to 30. The bar at the bottom has the dimensions of W=650, H=57, and the line above the text is a black line with a stroke of 1.

After you complete the Background layer, lock it. The next step is to create the drop-down menus on two layers: the Label Buttons layer and the Menus layer.

The Label Buttons layer

Each of the menus has a button on top of the drop-down menus. Use the following steps to create four buttons:

1. Using a 10-point bold Verdana font, type the word **design**.

2. Select the text and press the F8 key to open the Symbol Properties dialog box. Choose Button as the Behavior, and name it **Design**. Click OK.

3. Double-click the button and, in the Symbol Editing mode, place a keyframe in each of the three frames with no keyframe.

4. Click the Hit frame and then use the Rectangle tool to place a rectangle with the dimensions of W=79, H=16 over the word design. This step broadens the hit area to the width of the menu bar of the drop-down windows.

5. Repeat steps 1 through 4 using the words **products**, **information**, and **contact**.

6. Drag an instance of each of the four buttons to the stage and, in the Object Actions panel, add the following ActionScripts to the indicated buttons. Each script fires off a movie clip to drop one menu and close the others.

Design button:

```
on (rollOver) {
    _root.dropD.gotoAndPlay(1);
    _root.dropP.gotoAndStop(1);
    _root.dropI.gotoAndStop(1);
    _root.dropC.gotoAndStop(1);
}
```

Products button:

```
on (rollOver) {
    _root.dropP.gotoAndPlay(1);
    _root.dropD.gotoAndStop(1);
    _root.dropI.gotoAndStop(1);
    _root.dropC.gotoAndStop(1);
}
```

Information button:

```
on (rollOver) {
    _root.dropI.gotoAndPlay(1);
    _root.dropP.gotoAndStop(1);
    _root.dropD.gotoAndStop(1);
    _root.dropC.gotoAndStop(1);
}
```

Contact button:

```
on (rollOver) {
    _root.dropC.gotoAndPlay(1);
    _root.dropP.gotoAndStop(1);
    _root.dropI.gotoAndStop(1);
    _root.dropD.gotoAndStop(1);
}
```

After you finish with the buttons, put them aside on the stage. In the next set of procedures, you place them on the menus.

The Menus layer

The primary navigation occurs in the four drop-down menus. Each menu is a movie clip with two or more buttons within the movie clip. As the menus drop down, they reveal the buttons within each menu category. All the menus are constructed using similar parts and techniques, so we go through the steps in making one menu and point out the steps for the others. All the buttons in the menu contain ActionScript to play different parts of the main movie. Just follow these steps:

1. Using Color D from the movie palette, draw a rectangle with the dimensions W=81, H=16. Select it and press the F8 key to open the Symbol Properties dialog box. Select Graphic for the Behavior, enter **open** in the Name box, and click OK.

2. Using Color A from the movie palette, create a rectangle with the dimensions W=80, H=95. Select it and press the F8 key to open the Symbol Properties dialog box. Select Graphic for the Behavior, enter **bg** (for background) for the Name, and click OK.

3. Choose Insert ➪ New Symbol from the menu bar. Select Movie Clip for the Behavior in the Symbol Properties dialog box. Enter **drop** for the Name.

4. While still in the Symbol Editing mode, add three layers to the existing layer for a total of four layers. Use the names **buttons, fill, sides,** and **bar** from top to bottom.

5. Click column 10 and drag the mouse downward to select all four layers. Press the F5 key to add frames out to the tenth column. In the first frame of the Fill layer, place a `stop();` action using the Frame Actions panel. Likewise, put a `stop();` action in the last frame of the Side layer.

6. While still editing the Drop movie clip instance, select the Fill layer and drag an instance of the Bg symbol onto the stage. Select the Bar layer and place an Open instance over the top of the Bg instance. (Because the Open instance is on a lower layer than the Bg instance, it will appear under the Bg instance.) Select the Bg instance and, in the Info panel, change the H value to 1. Draw two lines along either side of the Open instance in the Sides layer. Figure 10-2 shows the position of the line in a 400 percent enlargement of the stage.

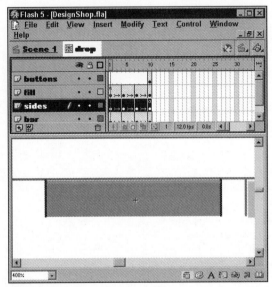

Figure 10-2: The lines on either side of the Open instance (400 percent magnification) show the details of the menu in the closed position.

7. Add keyframes in the Fill, Sides, and Bar layers in Frames 4, 7, and 10. Select all the keyframes in the Fill and Bar layers and, using the Frame panel, add Motion Tweens. Select all the keyframes in the Side layer and add Shape Tweens.

8. Add a keyframe in Frame 10 of the Buttons layer.

9. To achieve a "bounce" effect of the menu dropping and then popping up momentarily and then down again, you must change the dimensions of the Bg instance several times. Click Frame 4 in the Fill layer and then change the dimensions of the Bg instance to W=80, H=95. Click Frame 7 of the Fill layer and change the Bg instance to the dimensions W=80, H=64. Click Frame 10 of the Fill layer and change the dimensions of the Bg instance to W=80, H=80.

10. Along with the Bg instance, you also must move the Open instance. Click the Bar layer and, with a starting Y position of -9, click Frame 4 and move the vertical position to Y=87 using the Info panel. On Frame 7, move the vertical position of the Open instance to 56. On Frame 10, move the Y position of the Open instance to 72.

11. Click the Side layer. In the Info panel, you should see that H=16 for both lines. Click Frame 4 and change the H value to 110 for both lines and then align them vertically with the top and bottom of the Bg and Open instances. Repeat the process in Frame 7, changing the H value to equal 80. In Frame 10, change the H value to equal 95.

At this point, your menu should move up and down with a drop-and-bounce effect. Move the playhead left and right to make sure that all the menu parts coordinate. Figure 10-3 shows how the menu looks with the onion skin enabled in the FLA file.

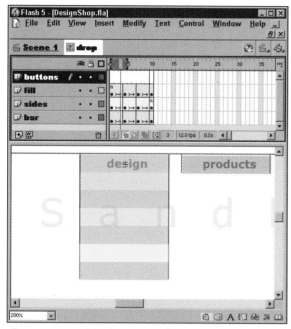

Figure 10-3: After the menu object is complete, it should drop down, bounce, and settle in the extended position.

The final thing that you must do is to provide an instance name to the Drop movie clip. Click Scene 1 to go to the main timeline, select the Drop movie clip, and in the Name box of the Instance panel, type the instance name **dropD**. Each of the other three menu movie clips have instance names of **dropP, dropI,** and **dropC**. The capital letter at the end of the instance names reflects the Design, Products, Information, and Contact names of the menus. After you complete the first Drop movie clip, create three more identical movie clips with the names identical to the instance names: **dropP, dropI,** and **dropC.**

Buttons in the menus

Each of the four menu movie clips (drop, dropP, dropI, and dropC) contain submenus made up of buttons that are text objects that were selected and made into button symbols. Figure 10-4 shows how the submenu heads appear within the Drop instance in the Symbol Editing mode.

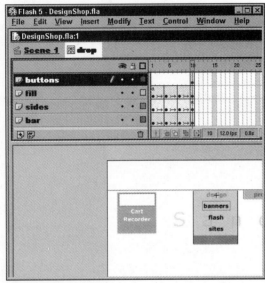

Figure 10-4: Place the submenu buttons on the extended menus in the Symbol Editing mode of the Drop movie clips.

Each menu button contains ActionScript. The buttons on the Design menu contain the following code:

Banners:

```
on (release) {
    _root.gotoAndStop(2);
    this.gotoAndStop(1);
}
```

Flash:

```
on (release) {
    _root.gotoAndStop(4);
    this.gotoAndStop(1);
}
```

Sites:

```
on (release) {
    _root.gotoAndStop(6);
    this.gotoAndStop(1);
}
```

The Action Script for the buttons on the Products menu is as follows:

Downloads:

```
on (release) {
    _root.gotoAndStop(8);
    this.gotoAndStop(1);
}
```

Books:

```
on (release) {
    _root.gotoAndStop(10);
    this.gotoAndStop(1);
}
```

The Information menu has two buttons with the following code:

FAQ:

```
on (release) {
    _root.gotoAndStop(12);
    this.gotoAndStop(1);
}
```

About us:

```
on (release) {
    _root.gotoAndStop(16);
    this.gotoAndStop(1);
}
```

The code for the two buttons on the Contact menu is as follows:

Contact form:

```
on (release) {
    _root.gotoAndStop(14);
    this.gotoAndStop(1);
}
```

Email:

```
on (release) {
    getURL ("mailto:yourEmail@isp.com");
    this.gotoAndStop(1);
}
```

After you create the submenu buttons, place them in the Symbol Editing mode of the appropriate Drop menu movie clip. Select the button layer, move the playhead to the last frame, and then drag each of the submenu buttons to the open frame, as you can see in Figure 10-4.

Shopping Stops layer

The Shopping Stops layer is a series of alternating keyframes and blank keyframes. Each keyframe is the target of one of the submenu selections. (The blank keyframes provide a less crowded layer, making selecting the substantive keyframes while you are editing easier.) Place keyframes in Frames 2, 4, 6, 8, 10, 12, 14, 16, 18, 20, and 22 and place blank keyframes in Frames 3, 5, 7, 9, 11, 13, 15, 17, 19, and 21.

Create two button symbols named **add** and **subtract**. These buttons should have these dimensions: H=17, W=17. To create the buttons, draw a black circle with a green (Color C) stroke. Use the Line tool to draw a white plus sign on one button and a minus sign on the other. Don't use the Text tool to do this because the border from the text box makes the object awkward to adjust.

Banner frame

The first stop at Frame 2 is the banner. An animated Banner movie clip moves text and a ball over a gray rectangle. Below the banner are two labels for services and their costs, as shown in Figure 10-5.

At the heart of the movie are buttons that keep track of what a customer purchases. A floating Cart Recorder with the text field variable name `total` keeps an ongoing record of what the customer selects. The buttons in the different frames in the Shopping Stops layer contain the variables that record what is selected and what is deselected. All the subtract buttons require a conditional statement to make sure that the user does not move the total below zero. The variables ending in *T* are totals for each product or service. Here is the code:

Single Animated Scene Add:

```
on (release) {
    banA = 500;
    banAT += banA;
    sum += banA;
    _root.calc.total = sum;
}
```

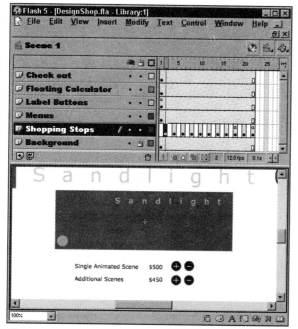

Figure 10-5: An animated banner provides an example of the service product, and a set of four buttons enables the customer to add the service to the floating Cart Recorder.

Single Animated Scene Subtract:

```
on (release) {
    banA = 500;
    banAT -= BanA;
    if (banAT<0) {
        banAT = 0;
    }
    sum -= banA;
    if (sum<0) {
        sum = 0;
    }
    _root.calc.total = sum;
}
```

Additional Scenes Add:

```
on (release) {
    banB = 450;
    banBT += banB;
    sum += banB;
    _root.calc.total = sum;
}
```

Additional Scenes Subtract:

```
on (release) {
    banB = 450;
    banBT -= banB;
    if (banBT<0) {
        banBT = 0;
    }
    sum -= banB;
    if (sum<0) {
        sum = 0;
    }
    _root.calc.total = sum;
}
```

Flash frame

Frame 4 contains a movie clip that appears in parts in a two-second clip. Figure 10-6 shows the Flash Page movie clip in the Symbol Editing mode. Little sound spots emphasize the three nonfunctional buttons that appear along the top of the movie clip. Finally, a separate movie clip made up of a spinning snowflake continues after the Flash Page movie clip stops.

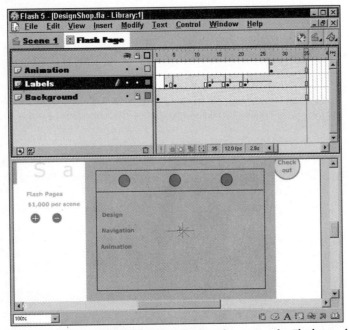

Figure 10-6: A movie clip puts together the parts of a Flash movie before the viewer's eyes.

The following code shows how the Add and Subtract buttons keep track of the selections on the page:

Flash Page Add:

```
on (release) {
    flpg = 1000;
    flashT += flpg;
    sum += flpg;
    _root.calc.total = sum;
}
```

Flash Page Subtract:

```
on (release) {
    flpg = 1000;
    flashT -= flpg;
    if (flashT1<0) {
        flashT1 = 0;
    }
    sum -= flpg;
    if (sum<0) {
        sum = 0;
    }
    _root.calc.total = sum;
}
```

Site frame

Frame 6 is similar to the Flash frame movie. A movie clip quickly presents a growing series of rectangles to represent the elements in a Web site and stops. Sound effects from the Sound Library (which you access by choosing Window ⇨ Common Libraries ⇨ Sounds) provide additional interest. Figure 10-7 shows the movie in the Symbol Editing mode:

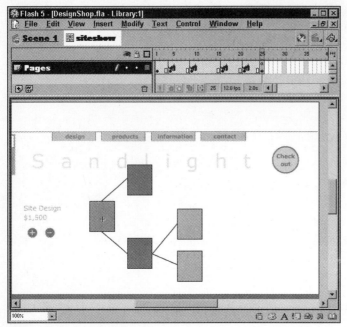

Figure 10-7: This movie clip assembles the parts of a Flash movie in front of the viewer.

The Add and Subtract buttons use the following code to keep track of a user's selections and deletions:

Site Design Add:

```
on (release) {
    siteDev = 1500;
    siteT += siteDev;
    sum += siteDev;
    _root.calc.total = sum;
}
```

Site Design Subtract:

```
on (release) {
    siteDev = 1500;
    sum -= siteDev;
    if (sum<0) {
        sum = 0;
    }
    siteT -= siteDev;
    if (siteT<0) {
        siteT = 0;
    }
    _root.calc.total = sum;
}
```

Downloads frame

Frame 8 represents a departure from the other frames in that no movie clips are used and both products are free. And because downloads can be reproduced infinitely, you don't need to subtract from an inventory or user selection. The Cart Recorder shows `No Charge`, but the ongoing total is not affected because the total has been recorded in the `sum` variable.

In eBusiness, downloads play an important role of attracting customers who may visit the site often just to get the free downloads. If they do want to make a purchase of products or services, the goodwill built up leads the customer to the site. (That's the theory anyway.) Figure 10-8 shows the simple features presented in the Downloads frame.

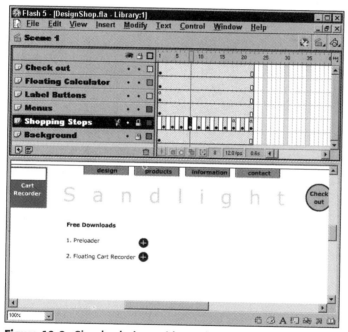

Figure 10-8: Simple choices with no charge make the Downloads frame a popular one.

The buttons use the `getURL()` action to connect the user to the downloads. One of the features on the site is included as a download.

Preloader Add:

```
on (release) {
    _root.calc.total = "No Charge";
    getURL ("http://www.yourDomain.com/downloads/preload.fla");
}
```

396 Part IV ✦ The Two Sides of an eBusiness

Floating Add:

```
on (release) {
    _root.calc.total = "No Charge";
    getURL
("http://www.yourDomain.com/downloads/floatcart.fla");
}
```

Books frame

Frame 10 illustrates a situation where the product incurs shipping charges and requires inventory tracking. The frame itself is quite simple, as shown in Figure 10-9, but the buttons have a bit more ActionScript than what has previously been shown.

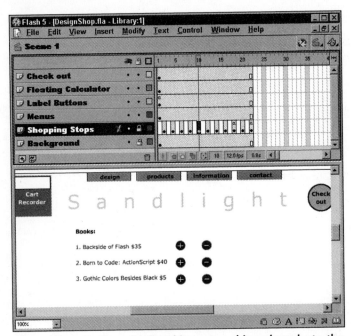

Figure 10-9: Because the listed items are shipped products, the ActionScript in the buttons requires a bit more code.

Backside Add:

```
on (release) {
    bof = 35;
    bofInv += 1;
    ns += 1;
    bofT += bof;
    sum += bof;
    _root.calc.total = sum;
}
```

Backside Subtract:

```
on (release) {
    bof = 35;
    bofInv -= 1;
    bofT -= bof;
    ns -= 1;
    bocT -= boc;
    if (bofT<0) {
        bofT = 0;
    }
    sum -= bof;
    _root.calc.total = sum;
}
```

Born Add:

```
on (release) {
    boc = 40;
    bocInv += 1;
    ns += 1;
    bocT += boc;
    sum += boc;
    _root.calc.total = sum;
}
```

Born Subtract:

```
on (release) {
    boc = 40;
    bocInv -= 1;
    bocT -= boc;
    ns -= 1;
    if (bocT<0) {
        bocT = 0;
    }
    sum -= boc;
    _root.calc.total = sum;
}
```

Gothic Add:

```
on (release) {
    gcbb = 5;
    gcbbInv += 1;
    ns += 1;
    gcbbT += gcbb;
    sum += gcbb;
    _root.calc.total = sum;
}
```

Gothic Subtract:

```
on (release) {
    gcbb = 5;
    gcbbInv -= 1;
    gcbbT -= gcbb;
    ns -= 1;
    if (gcbbT<0) {
        gcbbT = 0;
    }
    sum -= gcbb;
    _root.calc.total = sum;
}
```

In the buttons' ActionScript, both a shipping variable (ns) and inventory variables (xxxInv) are added. The shipping variable is the same for all the products because a standard shipping cost is established for each item. The inventory variables, though, must be unique for each of the three items. If we had more item selections, array variables would be more efficient to use.

FAQ frame

In any eBusiness, a FAQ page saves time, money, and aggravation. Actual questions from customers and anticipated questions that may arise in site testing should be included. Make the questions concise and the answers clear so that the reader can quickly see the focus of the question and the solution in the answer. Think of FAQ pages as customer service pages. All you need to do is to place a blank keyframe in Frame 11 and a regular keyframe in Frame 12 and then put your FAQs in a static text field. Figure 10-10 shows an example of what a FAQ page looks like.

Contact frame

Frame 14 has a contact form that viewers can fill out even if they don't want to purchase anything. From such contact forms, a business both engages viewers and learns from them. Site visitors who use the contact form should receive an automatic e-mail response from a server-side script. If the comments require specific information, you can use a follow-up e-mail.

The Contact frame is made up of several input text fields and a button to initiate a PHP script and send the variables from Flash to the script. Table 10-2 shows the several input text fields and their associated variable names. The input fields are arranged as shown in Figure 10-11.

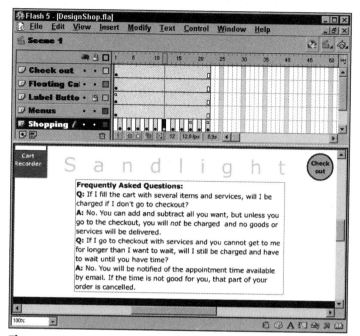

Figure 10-10: FAQ pages should be clear, concise, and informative in an eBusiness site.

Table 10-2 Contact Form	
Text field label	**Variable name**
First Name	fname
Last Name	lname
Address	address
City	city
State	state
Zip	zip
Email	email
Area Code	phoneAC
Phone	phone
Comments	comments

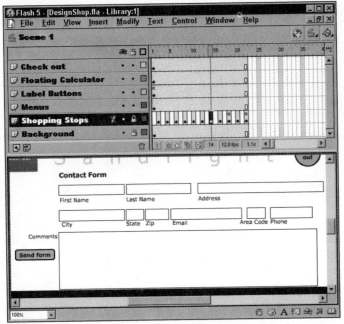

Figure 10-11: Comment forms help engage customers and establish a relationship between the company and the customer.

To send the information in the form, you need some kind of event and event handler. A simple Send Form button works well. Create the button by using the image shown in Figure 10-11 and add the following ActionScript, substituting your own URL or IP address:

```
on (release) {
    loadVariablesNum ("http://www.yourDomain.com/PHP/contact.php", 0, "GET");
}
```

Tip

The GET method seems to work best with Flash and PHP. If you are using ASP, we suggest using the POST method.

About Us frame

People like to know something about the company they're doing business with, and a short "About Us" notice helps them feel more comfortable with an eBusiness. Many e-commerce sites, such as Barnes and Noble Bookstores, were brick-and-mortar businesses for years before the advent of the Internet, so they were well-known when they launched their online bookstores. Other companies, such as Amazon.com, were eBusinesses from the beginning, and they had to tell people more about themselves so that customers could get used to the idea of shopping from an online entity without a storefront counterpart. Figure 10-12 shows how the About Us feature was added to the site.

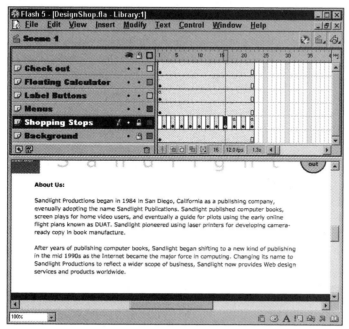

Figure 10-12: The About Us page helps customers get to know the business they are dealing with over the Internet.

Check Out frame

After the viewer clicks the Check Out button, he or she is sent to the first of two Check Out frames. The first one, on Frame 20, asks for the viewer's identity and method of payment. Use Table 10-2 for the information about the identity of the purchaser and Figure 10-13 for the layout.

The Visa and MasterCard buttons are generic examples of selecting a credit card. As each button is clicked, an *x* appears in the adjacent text field to identify the card of choice. The buttons are instances of simple button symbols. Open the Text Options panel and create two small dynamic text fields next to the Visa and MasterCard buttons. In the Variable box of the Text Options panel, enter **visa** as the variable name for the text field next to the Visa button and **mc** for the variable name next to the MasterCard button. Use the following scripts:

Visa button:

```
on (release) {
    visa = "x";
    mc = "";
}
```

MasterCard button:

```
on (release) {
    visa = "";
    mc = "x";
}
```

The only other button on the page is one that jumps to the final Check Out frame. Because the final check out is a necessary sequence, the button was placed on the scene rather than on one of the menus. (Notice that the frame goes *back* to Frame 18 rather than forward.)

Proceed to final check out button:

```
on (release) {
    _root.gotoAndStop(18);
}
```

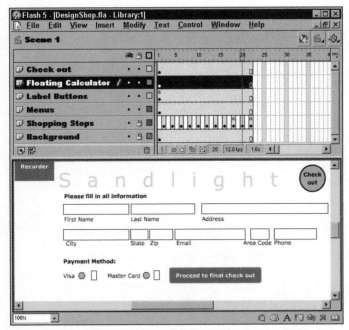

Figure 10-13: The first part of check out obtains the billing/shipping information.

Final Check Out frame

The last step the customer takes is to review his or her purchases and decide whether to confirm the order. The floating Cart Recorder zooms into place next to labeled text fields associated with the total amount for each purchase. Tax and Shipping are automatically computed, and a grand total appears next to the Confirm order button.

To get started, create 10 dynamic text fields using Table 10-3 as a guide to variable names and Figure 10-14 as a guide for placing the fields on the stage. All the fields *except* Grand total have the Border/Bg check box checked.

Table 10-3	
Final Check Out Form	
Text field label	*Variable name*
Banner (top)	banAT
Banner (bottom)	banBT
Flash	flashT
Site Design	siteT
Back of Flash	bofT
Born to Code	bocT
Gothic Colors	gcbbT
Tax	tax
Shipping	shipping
Grand Total	grandTotalS

To move the floating Cart Recorder movie clip to the middle of the text fields, Frame 18 contains the following script:

```
_root.calc._x=280;
_root.calc._y=215;
```

The instance name of the Cart Recorder movie clip is calc, so moving the object requires no more than specifying the desired coordinates by changing the _x and _y properties.

The button is an instance of a button symbol with the name **Confirm order** and the following script:

```
on (release) {
    _root.calc._x = 40;
    _root.calc._y = 60;
    loadVariablesNum
("http://www.yourDomain.com/PHP/confirm.php", 0, "GET");
    gotoAndStop (22);
}
```

The script hooks up with the PHP script that takes care of the back-end work with the order and then goes to and stops at the final frame for the order. The script also puts the floating calculator into the upper right hand corner of the stage to get it out of the way. Figure 10-14 shows the general layout of the stage.

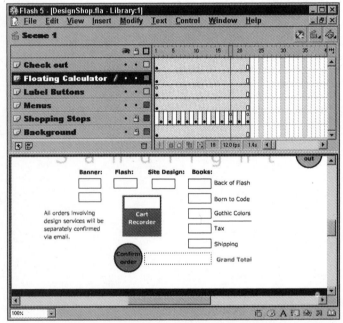

Figure 10-14: The final checkout process presents the customer with information about purchases and a chance to confirm the order.

Order Confirmation frame

The last frame in the movie, Frame 22, contains a script that gathers information collected in the floating Cart Recorder and displays it for the customer. An order confirmation notice is sent from the PHP script to a text field associated with the `confirm` variable name. After the customer clicks the Confirm order button in the Final Check Out frame, the button fires a PHP script that sends the text `confirmed` back to the customer in this frame (see Figure 10-15).

The large dynamic text field in the center of the stage is associated with the
endDisplay variable name. The following script in the frame generates its contents:

```
fullName = fname+" "+lname+newline;
place = city+", "+state+" "+zip+newline;
if (visa="x") {
    card = "Visa";
} else {
    card = "Master Card";
}
payment = "Your "+card+" will be charged "+grandTotal;
endDisplay = fullname+address+newline+place+payment;
stop();
```

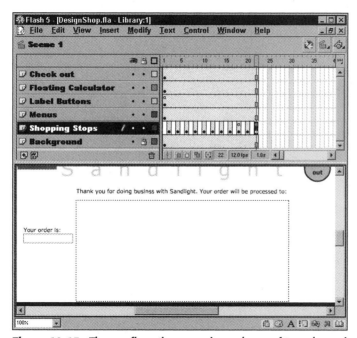

Figure 10-15: The confirmation page is made up of two dynamic
text fields. The smaller one delivers a confirmation signal, and the
larger one displays the information generated by the ActionScript
in the frame.

Floating Calculator layer

The Floating Calculator layer contains a movie clip used to display the total amount a customer is spending as services and products are added and subtracted from the shopping cart. The name Cart Recorder suggests the dual nature of the object: It's a shopping cart as well as a calculator that records the current amount in the shopping cart. The following steps show how to create the Cart Recorder:

1. Create a new symbol by choosing Insert ⇨ New Symbol from the menu bar. Select Movie Clip for the Behavior and type **Calculator** for the Name.

2. In the Symbol Editing mode, create two layers, named **text field** (top) and **Calculator and label** (bottom).

3. Click the bottom layer and use the Rectangle tool to draw a gray (Color B on the movie's palette) rectangle with the dimensions W=72, H=73.

4. Using a 10-point white Verdana font in a Static text field, type **Cart Recorder** and place the text in the horizontal and vertical center of the rectangle. Lock the bottom layer.

5. In the top layer, create a dynamic text field and place it in the horizontal center of the gray rectangle above the Cart Recorder label. (See Figure 10-16.) In the Text Options panel, type the name **total** in the Variable box.

6. Click Scene 1 to return to the main timeline. Select the Calculator movie clip and, in the Instance panel, type the name **calc**. With the Calculator movie clip still selected, enter the following ActionScript in the Frames Actions panel. This script enables the user to drag the object anywhere on the stage.

```
onClipEvent (mouseDown) {
    startDrag (this);
}
onClipEvent (mouseUp) {
    stopDrag ();
}
```

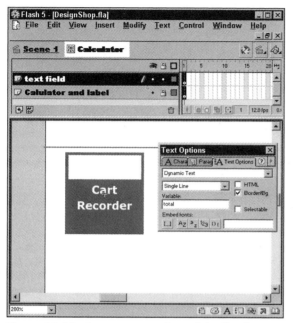

Figure 10-16: A 200 percent view of the floating calculator shows it to be a movie clip with a dynamic text field associated with the total variable name.

Check Out layer

The final object in the movie is a button in the Check Out layer. The button does two things. First, it goes to the first stop on the check out path, calculates tax and shipping costs, and adds up everything to calculate a grand total. But it also serves as a drop-down menu closer. If any of the menus are left open, a rollover on the button closes them.

Create a circle with the dimensions W=47, H=47 using Color A from the palette (lighter shade of green) for the fill and black for the 2-point stroke color. Create a button symbol from the circle. Change the fill color to the darker green (Color C) with the playhead in the Over frame in the Symbol Editing mode of the button. Label the button **Check out**, as shown in Figure 10-17, and enter the following script:

```
on (release) {
    _root.gotoAndStop(20);
    tax = (_root.calc.total)*.08;
    shipping = ns*1.25;
    grandTotal = _root.calc.total+tax+shipping;
    grandTotalS = "$"+grandTotal;
}
```

```
on (rollOver) {
    _root.dropD.gotoAndStop(1);
    _root.dropP.gotoAndStop(1);
    _root.dropI.gotoAndStop(1);
    _root.dropC.gotoAndStop(1);
}
```

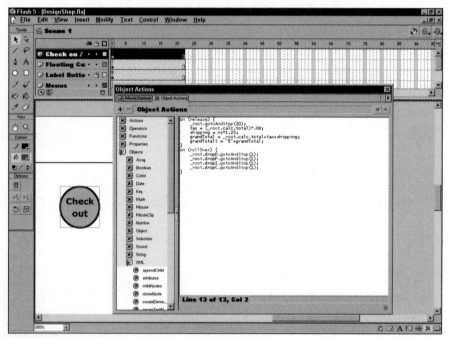

Figure 10-17: A 200 percent view of the button and its associated script.

Summary

In developing the DesignShop.fla movie, we wanted to provide a generic eBusiness site that could be customized to suit different objects a designer or developer may have when creating a site for a client. Modifying the site is a matter of changing it to suit your own needs. Adding buttons and additional submenus along with text fields to hold information should do the trick for simple sites. For sites with a large number of products, use arrays instead of variables and remember to plan, plan, and plan.

✦   ✦   ✦

Establishing the Back End of an eBusiness Site

Establishing goals for a server-side script may appear to be obvious because the goals are pretty well defined by the Flash front end you developed in Chapter 10. But by writing down your goals before you start writing your MySQL databases and PHP scripts, you can better see exactly what you need to do and save time in the long run. Before going any further, review the goals that the server-side scripts need to accomplish:

- ◆ Record and recover customer information
- ◆ Record orders and links to customers
- ◆ Record addresses of customers
- ◆ Display order information for billing and shipping departments
- ◆ Record and respond to contact information
- ◆ Record product inventory
- ◆ Record and respond to service orders

Now that you've clarified the goals for the server-side scripts, you can start building the back end for the eBusiness site you started working on in Chapter 10.

Creating a MySQL Database and Tables

Creating a giant table for all of the information coming from the front-end Flash movie is quite possible in a MySQL database, but a more practical way to handle the information is to use MySQL's relational database capabilities and make relational tables. For this project, three tables should do the trick: one table for basic customer information, a second table for location, and a third table for service and product orders. By using the customer ID as a primary key that automatically increments the ID number, you should be able to use the relational features of the database as long as you have the same ID number on the other two tables.

Using the phpMyAdmin on JTLNet

The initial setup uses the sample hosting service for PHP, JTLNet. Use your JTLNet account to set up your database and tables with the following steps:

1. Go to the JTLNet support page for your account. For example, if your domain name is `www.yourDomain.com`, you would type in `http://www.yourDomain.com/controlpanel`. After entering your username and password, you would be at the main menu of Cpanel 3.

2. Choose Advanced Menu ⇨ SQL Database to enter the mySQL page. In the Db box, type in **designShop** and click the Add Db button. Now you have a database with the name `username_designShop`. (JTLNet adds the username to all databases for security reasons.)

3. When you have your new database, click on phpMyAdmin link near the bottom of the page. (You may have to scroll down to see it.)

4. The left column contains your database name. Click the database name to display a page with the database name on top (for example, `yourDomain_designShop`). Scroll to the bottom of the page where you will see `Create new table on database username_databaseName`.

5. In the Name text box, type in **customer**. Enter **4** in the Fields text box below the Name text box.

6. Table 11-1 shows the values you should enter into the category. (The table also has Index and Unique columns not used in this project.)

7. In the Table comments text box, type **Basic customer info**. Then click the Save button to finish the table.

Table 11-1
Data for the Customer Table in the designShop Database

Field	Type	Length/Set	Attributes	Null	Default	Extra	Primary
cusID	INt	10	UNSIGNED			auto_increment	(checked)
fName	char	15					
lName	char	15					
email	char	30					

Figures 11-1 and 11-2 show how the entries should appear in the phpMyAdmin table.

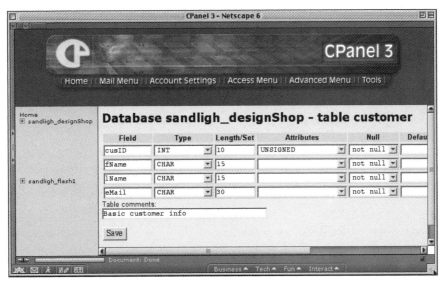

Figure 11-1: The table creation utility provides the same column type options used in the MySQL server.

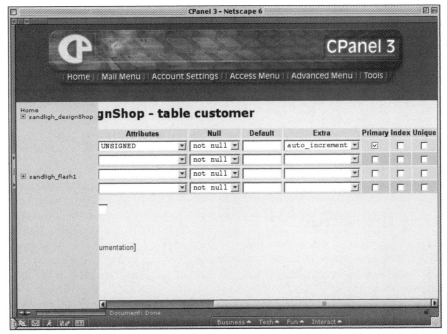

Figure 11-2: On the right side of the table utility, you can enter additional options into the table.

The table creation utility in phpMyAdmin essentially does all of the query work you would do in the MySQL server. After you have finished entering your data and have saved your new table, you can see the MySQL code written in a dump of the table. In the left column of the phpMyAdmin utility, click the Customer table under the username_designShop database to open the table's page. Then scroll down to the View Dump (schema) of Table option and click the Go button. If you entered every- thing correctly, you will see output similar to that in Figure 11-3.

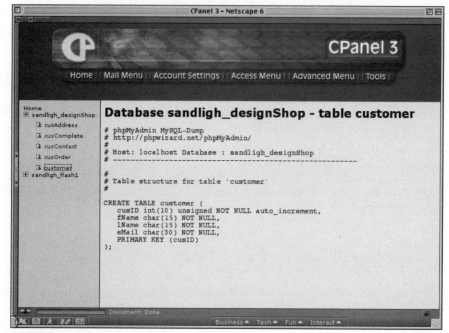

Figure 11-3: The table dump shows the MySQL query code that creates the table.

A total of six MySQL tables are required for the complete designShop database. In the next section, use the values in the MySQL commands to create the remaining tables either in the phpMySQL utility or the MySQL server.

Using the MySQL server

If you prefer, you can set up your database and tables directly in the MySQL server. (Take a look at Chapter 4 for information on setting up your system with MySQL.) Open your MySQL server, and from the C:\mysql\bin prompt, type in the following and press Enter:

```
mysqladmin create designShop
```

You should get the following response:

```
Database "designShop" created.
```

Type in **mysql** and press Enter. You are now in the MySQL mode for issuing database queries. Create the following tables using the indicated code: (You may have already created the first table in phpMyAdmin in JTLNet. If you have, just skip to the next table and enter them either in the MySQL server or in the phpMyAdmin utility on JTLNet.)

The customer table

```
CREATE TABLE customer (
    cusID int(10) unsigned NOT NULL AUTO_INCREMENT,
    fName char(15) NOT NULL,
    lName char(15) NOT NULL,
    eMail char(30) NOT NULL,
    PRIMARY KEY (cusID)
);
```

The cusAddress table

```
CREATE TABLE cusAddress (
    cusID int(10) unsigned NOT NULL AUTO_INCREMENT,
    street char(25) NOT NULL,
    city char(25) NOT NULL,
    state char(2) NOT NULL,
    zip int(6) DEFAULT '0' NOT NULL,
    acPhone int(3) DEFAULT '0' NOT NULL,
    phone char(8) NOT NULL,
    PRIMARY KEY (cusID)
);
```

The custOrder table

```
CREATE TABLE cusOrder (
    cusID int(10) unsigned NOT NULL auto_increment,
    bannerA float DEFAULT '0' NOT NULL,
    bannerB float DEFAULT '0' NOT NULL,
    flash float DEFAULT '0' NOT NULL,
    site float DEFAULT '0' NOT NULL,
    bof float DEFAULT '0' NOT NULL,
    btc float DEFAULT '0' NOT NULL,
    gcbb float DEFAULT '0' NOT NULL,
    tax tinyint(9) DEFAULT '0' NOT NULL,
    shipping float DEFAULT '0' NOT NULL,
    grandTotal float DEFAULT '0' NOT NULL,
    PRIMARY KEY (cusID)
);
```

The cusComplete table

```
CREATE TABLE cusComplete (
    cusID int(10) NOT NULL auto_increment,
    complete char(1) DEFAULT 'N' NOT NULL,
    inventory tinyint(1) DEFAULT '0' NOT NULL,
    PRIMARY KEY (cusID)
);
```

The cusContact table

```
CREATE TABLE cusContact (
    first varchar(15) NOT NULL,
    last varchar(15) NOT NULL,
    addr varchar(25) NOT NULL,
    town varchar(20) NOT NULL,
    st char(2) NOT NULL,
    zcode varchar(5) NOT NULL,
    email varchar(35) NOT NULL,
    ac char(3) NOT NULL,
    pnum varchar(8) NOT NULL,
    comment mediumtext NOT NULL
);
```

The inventory table

```
CREATE TABLE inventory (
    bof int(6) DEFAULT '0' NOT NULL,
    btc int(6) DEFAULT '0' NOT NULL,
    gcbb int(6) DEFAULT '0' NOT NULL
);
```

Creating PHP Scripts to Store Client Data

The only time you should be entering data into the database directly is to test it or repair an error. The data should go from the customer directly to the appropriate table in your designShop database. The data from comments is in one PHP file (contact.php) and the data from the confirmed order goes into another file (confirm.php). All of the data from in the contact.php script goes into a single table, cusContact, in the MySQL database. In contrast, the confirm.php table script must send data to four different tables. Therefore, its PHP script has to be a little more robust, but not very difficult.

Passing and storing the contact data

The plan for the `contact.php` file is to take the contact data sent by Flash to the PHP file, sort it out, and send it to the appropriate record field in the MySQL database. Another nice touch is to send an e-mail message to the person who made the contact. Using PHP, you can do this automatically. (An excellent follow-up would be to read the customer's comments and send an individualized e-mail.)

Cross-Reference   At this point, you may want to review Chapter 4, which lays out both PHP and MySQL commands in greater detail.

The script in Listing 11-1 takes the variables sent from Flash and places their values into the appropriate fields in the cusContact table of the designShop database. It also sends an e-mail to the contact to let that person know that his or her form has been received. The \n characters are new lines or carriage returns to format the e-mail that is sent.

Listing 11-1: **The contact.php Script**

```php
<?php

//Set up and connect
$server="localhost";                        //Server name
$user="domainNm_bill";                      //Username
$pass="yourPassword";                       //Password
$flashbase ="domainNm_designShop";          //Database name
$contact_table="cusContact";                //Table name

//Make the connection
$hookup = mysql_connect($server, $user, $pass);

//Select the database
mysql_select_db($flashbase,$hookup);

//Variables from Flash become data for MySQL
$sql="INSERT INTO $contact_table
(first,last,addr,town,st,zcode,email,ac,pnum,comment)
VALUES('$fname','$lname','$address','$city','$state','$zip',
'$email','$phoneAc','$phone','$comments')";

//Use the query function to send record to MySQL
mysql_query($sql,$hookup);

//Let the user know that the comments are received
echo "contactr=Comments received.";

//Send an e-mail message back to the contact
$sendTo=$email;
```

Continued

Listing 11-1 *(continued)*

```
$subject="Thanks for contacting Sandlight.";
$greet="Hi " . $fname . ",\n\n";
$greet .= "Your comments are important to us, and as soon as we
get a chance to read them, we will get back to you.\n\n";
$greet .= "Sincerely, \nEasy Jones, Public Relations";
mail($sendTo,$subject,$greet);

?>
```

Caution

You have to attend to details when working with PHP and contacting the MySQL database. Be sure that you establish your username and password correctly before putting them into the PHP file. You can have more than one username and accompanying password, so double-check to see that they are correct. If you forget your password, just delete the username and then re-enter it with a password that you can use in your script.

Passing and storing the order data

The trick with PHP files is to be organized. Because the PHP scripts used in this book have organized the contact information into variables, all you need to do is to add a few variables for the new tables and SQL queries, and you're all set to add data from a single source to several different tables. The PHP script in Listing 11-2 pulls together all of the parts in the "confirm order" message and places the data where it belongs.

Listing 11-2: The confirm.php Script

```
<?php

//Set up and connect
$server="localhost";                        //Server name
$user="domainNm_bill";                      //Username
$pass="yourPassword";                       //Password
$flashbase ="domainNm_designShop";          //Database name
$cus_table="customer";                      //Customer table
$cus_add="cusAddress";                      //Customer address
$cus_order="cusOrder";                      //Customer order
$cus_comp="cusComplete";                    //Completed order

//Make the connection
$hookup = mysql_connect($server, $user, $pass);

//Select the database
```

```
//All the tables are in the same database
mysql_select_db($flashbase,$hookup);

//Customer table
$sql="INSERT INTO $cus_table (fName,lName,eMail)
VALUES('$fname','$lname','$email')";

//Use the query function to send records to MySQL
mysql_query($sql,$hookup);

//Repeat process for other tables

//Customer address table
$sql="INSERT INTO $cus_add
(street,city,state,zip,acPhone,phone)
VALUES('$address','$city','$state','$zip','$phoneAc','$phone')"
;
mysql_query($sql,$hookup);

//Customer order table
$sql="INSERT INTO $cus_order
(bannerA,bannerB,flash,site,bof,btc,gcbb,tax,shipping,
grandTotal)
VALUES('$banAT','$banBT','$flashT','$siteT','$bofT','$bocT',
'$gcbbT','$tax','$shipping','$grandTotal')";
mysql_query($sql,$hookup);

//Customer inventory control
$sql="INSERT INTO $cus_comp (bofI,btcI,gcbbI)
VALUES('$bofInv','$bocInv','$gcbbInv')";
mysql_query($sql,$hookup);

echo "confirm=Order Received.";
?>
```

Each of the four tables is treated uniquely using the same query command (for example, `mysql_query($sql,$hookup);`). The only thing you have to change is the `$sql` variable prior to the query command. You can then issue the command repeatedly because changing the `$sql` variable changes the command's contents.

Note   You may have noticed that no customer ID field was used in setting up the several tables that contain such a field. Because the cusID field is an automatically incremented one, it does not need to be listed. As long as the value list is congruent with the list of fields shown in the SQL command, the data goes where it is supposed to go.

Building Administrative Controls

Once you have created a system to gather information from users in the form of orders and customer access, you need a way to use the data. Filling orders is of primary importance, so one module needs to find the orders that have not been filled. The process is not difficult because the default condition of one of the fields is that the order has not been filled. Then the program has to display shipping information for unfilled orders so that they can be shipped or, in the case of service requests, scheduled. Finally, the processed orders need to adjust inventory and clear the completed requests so that they are not sent more than once.

Developing the PHP scripts and Flash movie

For this project, we first worked out PHP scripts to take information from Flash and then used that data to provide output for what is requested. The PHP scripts can be treated as modules that fit with other modules in Flash. The initial stage, shown in Figure 11-4, consists of three buttons. When clicked, the buttons send the movie to a designated frame. The user then chooses different options from within the frame.

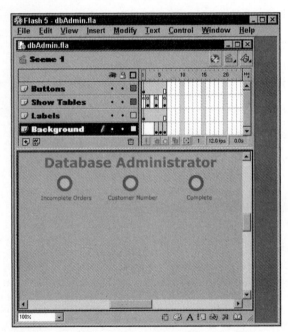

Figure 11-4: The starting stage for the Database Administrator provides three buttons.

The color palette for this Flash movie, dbAdmin.fla, is markedly different from designShop.fla, but the colors are a relaxing collection to use to coast through the administrative record keeping in the database. Table 11-2 shows the colors used for this project.

Table 11-2 Color Palette for dbAdmin.fla			
Color	R Value	G Value	B Value
A	CC	00	33
B	FF	C0	33
C	59	73	C0
D	99	CC	99
E	FF	F3	CC
F (Black)	00	00	00

The movie has four layers:

✦ Buttons

✦ Show Tables

✦ Labels

✦ Background

Open a new movie file in Flash 5, insert these four layers, and save the movie as dbAdmin.fla to get started. Now you can begin working on the administrative side of eBusiness.

The Background and Labels layers

Set up the back ground and labels by using the following steps:

1. Use Color D (light green) for the background color. Then, in the Background layer, insert keyframes in Frames 4 and 6.

2. On the Labels layer, use a 24-point bold Verdana text using Color C (blue) and type in the text **Database Administrator**, centering it horizontally on the stage.

3. On the Labels layer, use a 10-point normal Verdana font in Color A (red) to type in three labels: **Incomplete Orders**, **Customer Number**, and **Complete**. Using Figure 11-4 as a guide, evenly space the labels beneath the Database Administrator heading, leaving room for the buttons.

4. Lock the Labels layer.

The Buttons layer

To create the Buttons layer, follow these steps:

1. On the Buttons layer, use the Oval tool to draw a circle with Color A (red) for the stroke color and Color C (blue) for the fill. Set the stroke to 2.75. Within the first circle, draw a second circle with the dimensions W=18, H=18 and using Color B (gold).

2. Select the circle and press the F8 key to open the Symbol Properties dialog box. Choose Button for the behavior and name it **GenButton**.

3. In the Symbol Editing mode, insert keyframes in the Over, Down, and Hit frames. Move the playhead to the Over frame and change the outside stroke to black, the inside ring to Color E (cream), and the center to Color A (red). Click Scene 1 to exit the Symbol Editing mode. Instances of GenButton are used for all buttons in the movie.

4. Drag two more instances of the button to the stage on the Buttons layer and place one above each of the three labels.

5. Attach ActionScript to each of the buttons. Use this code for the Incomplete Orders button:

```
on (release) {
    gotoAndStop (2);
}
```

Use this code for the Customer Number button:

```
on (release) {
    gotoAndStop (4);
}
```

Use this code for the Complete button:

```
on (release) {
    gotoAndStop (6);
}
```

6. Lock the Buttons layer.

The Show Tables layer

Now that the basics are taken care of, the key parts of the movie must be built. Because the movie is heavily dependent on PHP scripts, we will show the scripts that are called by ActionScript. Each of the following subsections describes the steps involved in creating the movie and the PHP scripts.

Find unfilled orders

First, the Database Administrator must check for unfilled orders. To do this, the Flash movie needs a dynamic text field to display unfilled orders and a PHP script that finds the unfilled orders. Figure 11-5 shows how the stage appears when the playhead moves to Frame 2.

1. In the Show Tables layer, insert a `stop()`; script in Frame 1.

2. Insert a keyframe in Frame 2, and then add a dynamic text field with a long narrow shape, as shown in Figure 11-5. Select the text field, and in the Text Options panel, type **outUnfill** in the Variable text box.

3. Select Frame 2, open the Frame Actions panel, and enter the following ActionScript. Make sure that you substitute your own URL for the one shown:

```
loadVariablesNum
("http://www.yourDomain.com/PHP/getUnFilled.php", 0);
stop();
```

4. In a text editor, enter the PHP script shown in Listing 11-3. Save the script as **getUnFilled.php**. Place the script in the root directory or subdirectory within the root directory used in the URL reference in step 3.

5. Insert a blank keyframe into Frame 3 by selecting the frame and pressing the F7 key.

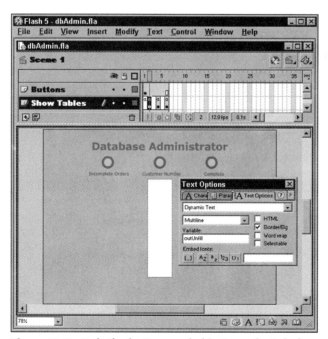

Figure 11-5: Only the buttons and objects on the Labels layer are shown at the outset, but the second frame reveals a text field where unfilled customer numbers appear.

Listing 11-3: **The getUnFilled.php Script**

```php
<?php
//Set up and connect
$server="localhost";                    //Server name
$user="domainNm_bill";                  //Username
$pass="yourPassword";                   //Password
$flashbase ="domainNm_designShop";      //Database name
$cus_comp="cusComplete";                //Completed order

//Make the connection
$hookup = mysql_connect($server, $user, $pass);

//Select the database
mysql_select_db($flashbase,$hookup);

//Customer inventory and fullfillment control
$result=mysql_query("SELECT * FROM $cus_comp", $hookup);
$numrows=mysql_num_rows($result);
$numrows-=1;

//Find customer numbers of unfilled orders
$search="N";
$counter=0;
$newline=chr(13);
do {
   $findKey=(mysql_result($result,$counter,"complete"));
   if ($findKey==$search) {
   $findNum=(mysql_result($result,$counter,"cusID"));
   $finder .= $findNum . $newline;
   }
   $counter++;
   }
while($counter <=$numrows);

$unfilled="outUnfill=$finder";
echo "$unfilled";
?>
```

The getUnFilled.php script searches for the default N in the customer ID section of the cusComplete table. All unfilled orders have the N, so the customer ID numbers of all unfilled orders have the necessary match and are concatenated into a variable named $finder. After all of the tables have been searched, the variable is translated into Flash format and then echoed back to Flash.

Display the order

This next section of the movie uses two text fields. One text field is an input one to select the customer number you want to view the order for, and the other is a dynamic text field to display the order of the selected customer. A button calls up the PHP script to get the data from the database and show it in the text field. Figure 11-6 shows how the frame looks on the stage.

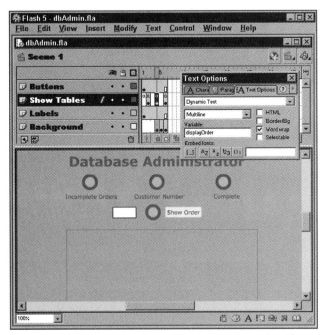

Figure 11-6: The button fires a PHP script that takes the customer number from the input field and returns information from the database.

With Figure 11-6 as a guide, use the following steps to complete this next section:

1. Insert a keyframe in Frame 4 of the Show Tables layer and put in a `stop()` script.

2. Use the Text tool to make a small input text field (use the dimensions W=42, H=19). Select the text field, and in the Text Options panel, type in **orderNum** in the Variable text box.

3. Drag a button onto the stage and position it next to the text field. Enter the following ActionScript, substituting your own URL:

```
on (release) {
    loadVariablesNum
("http://www.yourDomain.com/PHP/ShowOrder.php", 0, "GET");
}
```

4. On the Background layer, click Keyframe 4 and draw a rectangle with the dimensions W=64, H=16. Use Color E (cream) for the fill and stroke. Lock the Background layer.

5. On the Show Tables layer in Frame 4, type in **Show Order** using the Text tool and Color A (red) in a 10-point Verdana type.

6. Use the Text tool to draw a dynamic text field with the dimensions W=348, H=185. Center the field on the table beneath the input text field, button, and label as shown in Figure 11-6. In the Variable box in the Text Options panel, type in **displayOrder**.

7. Use a text editor to enter the PHP file shown in Listing 11-4. Then place the file in the root directory or subdirectory in the root directory that corresponds to the URL in step 3.

Listing 11-4: **The ShowOrder.php Script**

```php
<?php
//Set up and connect
$server="localhost";                    //Server name
$user="domainNm_bill";                  //Username
$pass="yourPassword";                   //Password
$flashbase ="domainNm_designShop";      //Database name
$cus_order="cusOrder";                  //Customer order table

//Make the connection
$hookup = mysql_connect($server, $user, $pass);

//Select the database
mysql_select_db($flashbase,$hookup);
$orderNum -=1;
//Customer Order
$result=mysql_query("SELECT * FROM $cus_order", $hookup);

//Set up array for table
$cOrder= array ("Cus ID", "Banner",
"Added Banner Object", "Flash Page", "Site Design",
"Backend of Flash", "Born to Code",
"Gothic Colors Besides Black", "Tax", "Shipping",
"Grand Total");

//Look at the whole row
$counter=0;
for ($x=0;$x <=$orderNum; $x++) {
$row=mysql_fetch_row($result);
}
for ($y=0;$y<=10; $y++) {
$fullOrder .= $cOrder[$y] . "=" . $row[$y] . chr(13);
}

$orderUp="displayOrder=$fullOrder";
echo "$orderUp";
?>
```

Although the preceding PHP code may appear daunting, most of the work is formatting. After the MySQL query, the script sets up a big array to be used as labels to describe the contents of the table. Next, a loop examines the rows in the table until it terminates with the row corresponding with the order number (the cusID number is used). Then a second loop (*not* nested) goes through the $row array. When the script uses the MySQL query mysql_fetch_row(), the entire row is placed into an array with the first element in the array being the first field in the row. In the cusOrder table, the first field is the customer ID, the second field is a service order for a banner ad, and so on until the grand total owed for the purchase, which is the last field. Because the fields in the $cOrder array correspond to the fields in the $row array, the second loop simply concatenates the two arrays and places a carriage return (chr(13)) at the end so that each field will appear on a separate row in the Flash display text field (displayOrder).

Display address information and complete the order

This last section of the movie displays all the contact information from the customer and shows the inventory of the books. In addition, it records a completed transaction between the customer and the eBusiness. Three separate PHP scripts are fired by the buttons. One script sends the address, phone, and e-mail information to the screen. Another script decrements the inventory and displays it, and a third PHP script changes the customer's order from unfilled to filled. Figure 11-7 shows the stage.

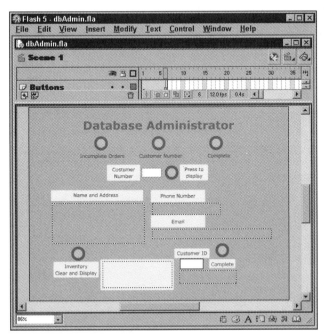

Figure 11-7: Seven text fields and three buttons provide contact information, adjust the inventory, and record completed orders.

Examine Figure 11-7 carefully prior to beginning work on this segment of the movie. Use the following steps to complete the movie:

1. Insert a blank keyframe in Frame 5.

2. Place a keyframe in Frame 6 and enter a `stop( )`action in the Frame Actions panel.

3. On the Background layer, click the keyframe in Frame 6 and unlock the layer if it is locked. Using the Rectangle tool and Color E for the fill and stroke colors, draw nine backdrops for the text labels. One backdrop at the bottom has a dynamic text field on it, but the others are label backdrops. Use Figure 11-7 as a guide. Lock the Background layer when you are finished.

4. Using Color A, the Text tool, and a 10-point red (Color A) Verdana font, place labels on the backdrops as shown in Figure 11-7.

5. To the right of Customer Number label, place an input text field. In the Text Options panel, make sure the Border/Bg check box is checked and enter **cusNum** in the Variable text box.

6. Place another input text field below the Customer ID label. In the Text Options panel, make sure the Border/Bg check box is checked and enter **cusID** in the Variable text box.

7. Create the two multiline, dynamic text fields with none of the options checked in the Text Options panel. Use the dimensions W=194, H=83 for the dynamic field below the Name and Address label and enter the variable name **displayCus**. Place the second multiline dynamic field over the rectangle backdrop next to the Inventory Clear and Display label. Use the variable name **inventory** and the dimensions W=147, H=54 for this text field.

8. Create the final three text fields, which are all single line and have no options checked in the Text Options panel. Below the Phone Number label, place a field with the dimensions W=145, H=23 and the variable name **phone**. Below the Email label, place a field with the dimensions W=252, H=19 and the associated variable name **email**. Below the Complete label, place a dynamic text field, H=120, W=26, with the associated variable name **saleComplete.**

9. Drag three instances of the button symbol to the stage. Place the first one between the Press to display label and the input text field. Insert the following script, making appropriate changes for your own URL:

```
on (release) {
    loadVariablesNum
("http://www.yourDomain.com/PHP/showCusAdd.php", 0, "GET");
}
```

Place the second button centered over Inventory Clear and Display and enter the following script in the Object Actions panel:

```
on (release) {
    loadVariablesNum
("http://www.yourDomain.com/PHP/inventory.php", 0);
}
```

The third button goes directly over the Complete label and uses the following ActionScript:

```
on (release) {
    saleComplete = " ";
    loadVariablesNum
("http://www.yourDomain.com/PHP/complete.php", 0, "GET");
}
```

10. Use a text editor to enter the PHP script in Listing 11-5, Listing 11-6, and Listing 11-7. Place the PHP scripts in the root directory or subdirectory in the root directory of your host. (The examples use the subdirectory named, "PHP.")

11. Publish your Flash pages and put the SWF file and HTML file in the same directory as your PHP files.

The script shown in Listing 11-5 divides the data into three different groups, one each for address, phone, and e-mail address. The customer number is used to find the row with the needed information; the same number is used to open two different tables. The name and e-mail address come out of the customer table, and the rest comes from the address table. Using the row array element values, new variables help sort out the information. Then the information is set up for output to three different text fields in Flash.

Listing 11-5: **The showCusAd.php Script**

```php
<?php
//Set up and connect
$server="localhost";                    //Server name
$user="domainNm_bill";                  //Username
$pass="yourPassword";                   //Password
$flashbase ="domainNm_designShop"; //Database name
$cus_table="customer";                  //Customer table
$cus_add="cusAddress";                  //Customer address table

//Make the connection
$hookup = mysql_connect($server, $user, $pass);

//Select the database
mysql_select_db($flashbase,$hookup);
$cusNum -=1;
$newln=chr(13);

//Customer name
$result=mysql_query("SELECT * FROM $cus_table", $hookup);

//Look at the customer row
$counter=0;
```

Continued

Listing 11-5 *(continued)*

```
for ($x=0;$x <=$cusNum; $x++) {
$row=mysql_fetch_row($result);
}

//Put the name together and get the e-mail address
$fullCus = $row[1] . " " . $row[2];
$email = $row[3];

//Look at the Customer address row
$resultAd=mysql_query("SELECT * FROM $cus_add", $hookup);
$counter=0;
for ($x=0;$x <=$cusNum; $x++) {
$rowAd=mysql_fetch_row($resultAd);
}

//Get the mailing address
$street=$rowAd[1];
$city=$rowAd[2];
$state=$rowAd[3];
$zip=$rowAd[4];

//Get the phone number
$areaCode=$rowAd[5];
$phone=$rowAd[6];
$phone= $areaCode . " " . $phone;

$address=$street . $newln . $city . ", " . $state . $newln .
 $zip;
$fullCus .= $newln . $address;

$customerUp="&displayCus=$fullCus&phone=$phone&email=$email";
echo "$customerUp";
?>
```

The second PHP script (shown in Listing 11-6) handles the inventory and clears product orders. The script uses the MySQL UPDATE command to globally update the table. That means it changes all records in the table. The advantage of using global updates is that you can change all the records (rows) in a table with a single command. (That's also the danger of using global updates!) The first UPDATE query subtracts the total number of books sold from the inventory table to provide an accurate count of products on hand. The second UPDATE query replaces the number of books in the inventory counter in the cusComplete table with zeros so that the same products will not be counted more than once.

Listing 11-6: **The inventory.php Script**

```php
<?php
//Set up and connect
$server="localhost";                    //Server name
$user="domainNm_bill";                  //Username
$pass="yourPassword";                   //Password
$flashbase ="domainNm_designShop";  //Database name
$cus_comp="cusComplete";            //Completed order table
$inven="inventory";                 //Inventory table

//Make the connection
$hookup = mysql_connect($server, $user, $pass);

//Select the database
mysql_select_db($flashbase,$hookup);

//Customer inventory and fullfillment control
$result=mysql_query("SELECT * FROM $cus_comp", $hookup);
$numrows=mysql_num_rows($result);

//Look at all the rows and the number of sales
for ($x=0;$x <=$numrows-1; $x++) {
$row=mysql_fetch_row($result);
$bof += $row[2];
$btc += $row[3];
$gcbb += $row[4];
}

//Change the inventory totals
$sql=mysql_query("UPDATE $inven SET bof=bof-$bof,
 btc= btc-$btc, gcbb=gcbb-$gcbb", $hookup);

//Change the completed inventory fields to 0
$sql=mysql_query("UPDATE $cus_comp SET
 bofI=0,btcI=0,gcbbI=0",$hookup);

$result=mysql_query("SELECT * FROM $inven", $hookup);
$inrow=mysql_fetch_row($result);
$newline=chr(13);
$inven="BackEnd of Flash:" . $inrow[0] . $newline .
 "Born to Code:" . $inrow[1] . $newline . "Gothic Colors:"
 . $inrow[2];
$inventoryNow="inventory=$inven";
echo "$inventoryNow";
?>
```

The final PHP script (shown in Listing 11-7) marks the transaction as complete. In the cus_comp table, a default N for "Not filled" is changed to a Y for "Yes, it's filled." The UPDATE query in this script, though, is not global. It targets a single record identified by the unique customer ID. To target a particular record, the UPDATE query includes a WHERE condition that is identified by the customer number entered in the Flash input text field.

Listing 11-7: **The complete.php Script**

```php
<?php
//Set up and connect
$server="localhost";                    //Server name
$user="domainNm_bill";                  //Username
$pass="yourPassword";                    //Password
$flashbase ="domainNm_designShop";      //Database name
$cus_comp="cusComplete";                //Completed order table

//Make the connection
$hookup = mysql_connect($server, $user, $pass);

//Select the database
mysql_select_db($flashbase,$hookup);

//Mark the transaction as complete
$sql=mysql_query("UPDATE $cus_comp SET complete='Y'
 WHERE cusID=$cusID", $hookup);

echo "saleComplete=Completed";
?>
```

What you should see

To test your movie, first make sure that you have entered some orders using the Design Shop movie from Chapter 10. Then test the Database Administrator movie. When you look at the unfilled orders, you should see a list of customer numbers. However, when you look at a customer order or the address, inventory, and completion information, you will see much more, all of it sent from the database. Figure 11-8 shows how an order will appear, and Figure 11-9 shows the customer and inventory information.

The financial accounting component

As noted earlier, the eBusiness movie and associated PHP scripts and MySQL databases are not set up to deal with the actual transfer of funds. This omission is intentional because you should not create unsecure financial modules in eBusiness. An accounting module would not be difficult to create because all of the financial information is available in the database. All transactions involving money should be done with a secure credit card module from any one of the many vendors available (Chapter 10 mentions some of these).

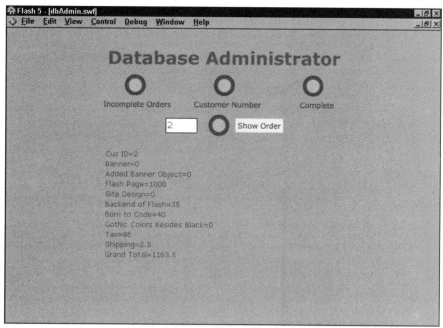

Figure 11-8: The order information shows how much the customer has spent on each of the services or products.

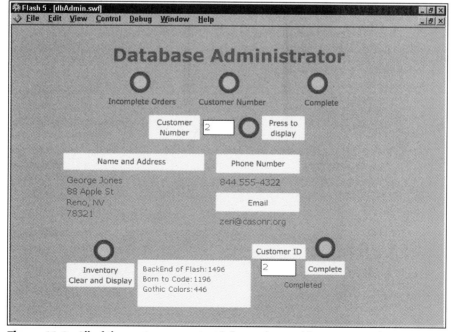

Figure 11-9: All of the customer contact information and inventory totals appear on the last frame of the movie when the buttons are clicked.

When you have a secure credit card fund transfer, the amounts can be put into an accounting module that is accessible only to the account administrator through a secure site. The user should never see the movie developed in this chapter, only the one from Chapter 10. When you add an accounting module, all of the purchases, returns, and payments can be recorded using a Flash 5 front end and PHP, MySQL and an Apache server on the back end. If you prefer, you could translate the scripts in this chapter into VBScript in order to create ASP pages that use an Access database to accomplish the same goals as PHP and MySQL achieve in this chapter.

Summary

When thinking of an eBusiness site using Flash, you need to consider a front end for *both* the customer and the business person who must administer the orders and payments for the site. By considering both front ends in relationship to a back end written in PHP, ASP or Perl, you can simplify and streamline the eBusiness process making it far more effective and efficient for both customer and owner. Perhaps the most important lesson to learn besides the dual coordination of client and administrator modules is using the data entered by the customer most effectively. When an order is placed for a product that reduces an inventory, the data entered by the customer is the same data that will decrement the inventory — you should not have to re-enter it on the administrative side of the equation. Mundane calculations like adding tax and shipping should be automated so that the server or client script can use client data to make all the necessary computations. More complex transactions require more complex coding, but in the long run, the time you spend creating good customer and administrator pages and sites pays off in effective and efficient order processing and customer satisfaction.

✦   ✦   ✦

What's on the CD-ROM?

This appendix provides you with information on the contents of the CD-ROM that accompanies this book. (For the latest and greatest information, please refer to the ReadMe file located at the root of the CD-ROM.) Here is what you'll find in this appendix:

♦ System requirments

♦ What's on the CD

♦ Troubleshooting

System Requirements

Make sure that your computer meets the minimum system requirements listed in this section. If your computer doesn't match up to most of these requirements, you may have a problem using the contents of the CD.

Windows

Macromedia recommends the following minimum requirements for running Flash 5 on a Windows system:

♦ Intel Pentium processor, 133 MHz or equivalent (200 recommended) processor

♦ Windows 95/98, ME, Windows 2000, NT 4.0 or later

♦ 32MB of available RAM (64MB recommended)

♦ 40MB of available disk space

♦ Color monitor capable of 800 × 600 resolution

♦ CD-ROM drive

Macintosh

Macromedia recommends the following minimum requirements for running Flash 5 on a Macintosh:

- ✦ Power Macintosh PowerPC (G3 or higher recommended)
- ✦ MacOS 8.5 or later
- ✦ 32MB of available RAM
- ✦ 40MB of available disk space
- ✦ Color monitor capable of 800×600 resolution
- ✦ CD-ROM drive

Note These are the minimum requirements. As with all graphics-based design tools, more capability is definitely better for using Flash 5, especially in terms of memory and processor speed.

What's on the CD

The CD-ROM contains scripts and FLA files for the examples used in the book, along with trial versions of a number of applications. The following sections provide a summary of the contents of the CD-ROM, arranged by category.

Source code

Every program file with a listing in the book is on the CD-ROM in a folder named after the chapter associated with the file. Source code for Flash 5 files is designated with the FLA extension, and all source files for Flash must be loaded into Flash 5. Files written for different server-side applications are formatted and saved as text files. These files may be opened with any text editor, such as Notepad or WordPad in Windows, or SimpleText on the Macintosh. Sometimes Notepad shows dark blocks where carriage returns should go in the text files with the source code. Either remove the blocks or use another text editor such as WordPad. The source code listings in the book show where carriage returns are required in Notepad.

Applications

Trial, demo, or *evaluation versions* of programs are usually limited either by time or functionality, such as not allowing you to save projects. The CD-ROM provides trial versions of the following programs:

- ✦ Macromedia Fireworks (30-day trial version): Fireworks is a graphics-editing program designed especially for Web applications.

✦ Macromedia Dreamweaver (30-day trial version): A Web site development tool, Dreamweaver can be used with Flash SWF files.

✦ Macromedia Generator 2, Developers Edition (30-day trial version): Generator is an extension of Flash 5 that can be used to create dynamic Flash 5 content for the Web.

✦ Macromedia Flash 5 (30-day trial version): Flash 5 is the most recent version of Flash and must be used with the ActionScript shown in this book.

Freeware programs are free, copyrighted games, applications, and utilities. You can copy them to as many PCs as you like for free, but they have no technical support. The CD-ROM contains the following freeware programs:

✦ Apache Server (Windows freeware): An OSS (Open Source Software) server on which PHP and MySQL run.

✦ PHP 4 (Windows freeware): The most recent version of a cross-platform, HTML-embedded, server-side scripting language.

✦ PHP 4 (Unix freeware)

GNU software is governed by its own license, which is included inside the folder of the GNU software. The distribution of this software is not restricted at all. See the GNU license for more details or visit www.gnu.org. The CD-ROM contains one GNU software program:

✦ MySQL 3.22 (Windows GNU software): An OSS database management system, MySQL is a powerful Structured Query Language for storing data on the Web.

Installing PHP, Apache Server, and MySQL on your own hard drive is fairly simple. By following the prompts, you shouldn't encounter any problems with installation. Configuring your software so that it runs reliably, however, depends on the version of the operating system you are using and the related software on your system. Rather than providing configuration information for the various versions of Windows, Linux, and Unix, we suggest that you start out by using PHP and MySQL on the free trial Web hosting services provided on the CD. Your scripts and databases may work smoothly when you run them on a remote host, but you may run into problems when you use your own system as both host and server. The problems you're likely to encounter depend to a great extent on the type of system you're running, and those variations are too lengthy to cover here. For help on configuring your system to act as both client and server, pick up a book dedicated to the specific software you want to use.

How to access the 30-day free Web hosting

If you want to take advantage of the Web hosting offers provided by JTLNet and HosTek, you can find detailed instructions for accessing these services on the CD. The following steps, however, give you a general idea of how this offer works:

To access JTLNet:

1. Click the JTLNet HTML file provided on the CD to go to the Web page for this special trial hosting offer.

2. Complete the forms that request your name, e-mail address, and so on.

3. When you reach the section of the form requesting credit card information, a message box appears to assure you that your credit card information is used solely for verification purposes. No charges are billed to it during the 30-day free trial period.

4. When you have completed the required information on the forms, click Submit. You receive an e-mail confirmation stating that your order will be processed within 24 hours, and then your username and password are sent to you via e-mail.

You don't have to take any action to cancel the Web hosting service at the end of the 30-day free trial period. You receive an e-mail stating this, and all your credit card information is discarded. This final e-mail includes a link that you can click if you want to continue the hosting service for a fee.

To access HosTek:

1. To access the order page, point your browser to this address:

   `https://www.hostek.net/order.shtml`

2. When you see the question "How Did You Hear About Us?" displayed near the top of the page, click the option for Other and type **HMSSF01** in the box.

3. Fill in the required information, including your credit card data, and click the Submit Form/Read Contract button.

4. Read the Terms of Service and, if you agree to them, click the Accept button.

You must have a domain name to use the service. If you don't have one, HosTek can register a domain (.com/.net/.org) for you for $10 per year. Details about this process are provided in the Domain Name section. This offer is good for NT servers only. Be sure to also choose a hosting plan, even if you use the HosTek service for only the free 30-day trial period.

Note: Your first 30 days are free. You can cancel the service any time before the 30th day and owe absolutely nothing. If you continue past the 30th day, your credit card is charged according to the hosting plan you selected. To cancel your trial account, send an e-mail to: **cancel@hostek.com**, and include your Customer ID and password.

Troubleshooting

If you have difficulty installing or using the CD-ROM, try the following solutions:

✦ **Turn off any antivirus software that you may have running.** Installers some-times mimic virus activity and can make your computer incorrectly believe that it is being infected by a virus. (Be sure to turn the antivirus software back on later.)

✦ **Close all running programs.** The more programs you're running, the less memory is available to other programs. Installers also typically update files and programs; if you keep other programs running, installation may not work properly.

✦ **Reference the ReadMe.txt.** Please refer to the ReadMe file located at the root of the CD-ROM for the latest product information at the time of publication.

If you still have trouble with the CD, please call the Hungry Minds Customer Service phone number: (800) 762-2974. Outside the United States, call (317) 572-3993. You can also contact Hungry Minds Customer Service by e-mail at techsupdum@ hungryminds.com. Hungry Minds provides technical support only for installation and other general quality control items; for technical support on the applications themselves, consult the program's vendor or author.

✦   ✦   ✦

Index

Symbols & Numbers
+= statement, 79
. = statement, 79

A
`<a href>` tags, 46–47
absolute paths, 24–25
`Access2Flash.fla`, 144–146
Action Script Viewer, 23
ActionScript
    case sensitivity, 69
    concatenation of strings, 168
    disguising and protecting code, 22–23
    saving in external files, 45–46
ActionScript editor, 230
    parameter values, 124
Active Data Objects (ADO) file, accessing, 156
Active Server Pages (ASP), 107
    addressing, 108
    array data, passing to Flash, 135–139
    arrays, 118–120
    beginning and ending tags, 108–109
    for calculations, 131–134
    comments in, 110
    conditional statements, 114–116
    data display, 109–110
    data types, 111–113
    `Dim` keyword, 110
    format of, 108–109
    functions, 120–121
    with Generator, 320–321
    HTML and VBScript on, 108
    launching, 109
    line breaks in, 111
    loop structures, 117–118
    mirror variables, 129–130
    moving data to Flash, 121–125
    operators, 113–114
    output, formatting, 111
    receiving data from Flash, 125–130
    `Request.Form()` function, 126

    `Response.write` command, 109–110
    `TypeName()` function, 113
    variables, catching, 129–130
    variables, creating, 125
    variables, declaring, 110
    variables, naming, 121
    `VarType()` function, 111–113
Active Server Pages (ASP) functions, passing data to Flash with, 134–135
Active Server Pages (ASP) programs, calling, 108
Active Server Pages (ASP) scripts
    for arrays, generating, 138–139
    connecting to database file, 142
    for database fields, writing to, 153, 156–158
    for database records, checking on, 153, 158
    for numbers, incrementing, 153, 155–156
    for text fields, clearing, 139
    variable names, 121–122
Active Server Pages Bible (Smith), 108
Active Server Pages For Dummies (Hatfield), 108
`AddAcess.asp`, 156–158
`AddMySQLrecord.fla`, 204
`AddRecords.fla`, 154–156
`addslashes()` function, 166
`add_table.php`, 203
`allPostData` variable, 72
ampersands (&)
    between multiple variable declarations, 10
    URL-encoded equivalent, 4–5, 10–11
    for variable declarations, 9
AND operator
    in conditional statements, 115
    in PHP, 169
angle brackets, preceding filenames with, 93–94
`angleChange` variable, 355
    `myAngle` variable, 356
animation, 379

Continued

Continued

HOSTEK.COM

All Web Hosting Plans Include:

Microsoft FrontPage 2000 & 98

Microsoft 2000/NT Web Hosting

MS Access 2000 Database Support

ASP, Perl, CGI-BIN, Java

PHP4, mySQL

FREE Shared SSL

Unlimited Email Addresses and Forwarding

See for yourself: http://hostek.com/plans.shtml

Sign up TODAY for your 30-Day FREE Trial!
https://www.hostek.net/order.shtml

Step 1: Fill out the order form completely.

Step 2: In the section labeled "How Did You Hear About Us?" make sure you click "Other" and enter the following code (HMSSF01)

Questions?: Email us at sales@hostek.com

*Please note that this offer is not valid for Unix.

Hungry Minds, Inc.
End-User License Agreement

READ THIS. You should carefully read these terms and conditions before opening the software packet(s) included with this book ("Book"). This is a license agreement ("Agreement") between you and Hungry Minds, Inc. ("HMI"). By opening the accompanying software packet(s), you acknowledge that you have read and accept the following terms and conditions. If you do not agree and do not want to be bound by such terms and conditions, promptly return the Book and the unopened software packet(s) to the place you obtained them for a full refund.

1. **License Grant.** HMI grants to you (either an individual or entity) a nonexclusive license to use one copy of the enclosed software program(s) (collectively, the "Software") solely for your own personal or business purposes on a single computer (whether a standard computer or a workstation component of a multiuser network). The Software is in use on a computer when it is loaded into temporary memory (RAM) or installed into permanent memory (hard disk, CD-ROM, or other storage device). HMI reserves all rights not expressly granted herein.

2. **Ownership.** HMI is the owner of all right, title, and interest, including copyright, in and to the compilation of the Software recorded on the disk(s) or CD-ROM ("Software Media"). Copyright to the individual programs recorded on the Software Media is owned by the author or other authorized copyright owner of each program. Ownership of the Software and all proprietary rights relating thereto remain with HMI and its licensers.

3. **Restrictions On Use and Transfer.**

   (a) You may only (i) make one copy of the Software for backup or archival purposes, or (ii) transfer the Software to a single hard disk, provided that you keep the original for backup or archival purposes. You may not (i) rent or lease the Software, (ii) copy or reproduce the Software through a LAN or other network system or through any computer subscriber system or bulletin-board system, or (iii) modify, adapt, or create derivative works based on the Software.

   (b) You may not reverse engineer, decompile, or disassemble the Software. You may transfer the Software and user documentation on a permanent basis, provided that the transferee agrees to accept the terms and conditions of this Agreement and you retain no copies. If the Software is an update or has been updated, any transfer must include the most recent update and all prior versions.

4. **Restrictions on Use of Individual Programs.** You must follow the individual requirements and restrictions detailed for each individual program in the "What's on the CD-ROM?" appendix of this Book. These limitations are also contained in the individual license agreements recorded on the Software Media. These limitations may include a requirement that after using the program for a specified period of time, the user must pay a registration fee or discontinue use. By opening the Software packet(s), you will be agreeing to abide by the licenses and restrictions for these individual programs that are detailed in the "What's on the CD-ROM?" appendix and on the Software Media. None of the material on this Software Media or listed in this Book may ever be redistributed, in original or modified form, for commercial purposes.

5. **Limited Warranty.**

    (a) HMI warrants that the Software and Software Media are free from defects in materials and workmanship under normal use for a period of sixty (60) days from the date of purchase of this Book. If HMI receives notification within the warranty period of defects in materials or workmanship, HMI will replace the defective Software Media.

    (b) **HMI AND THE AUTHOR OF THE BOOK DISCLAIM ALL OTHER WARRANTIES, EXPRESS OR IMPLIED, INCLUDING WITHOUT LIMITATION IMPLIED WARRANTIES OF MERCHANTABILITY AND FITNESS FOR A PARTICULAR PURPOSE, WITH RESPECT TO THE SOFTWARE, THE PROGRAMS, THE SOURCE CODE CONTAINED THEREIN, AND/OR THE TECHNIQUES DESCRIBED IN THIS BOOK. HMI DOES NOT WARRANT THAT THE FUNCTIONS CONTAINED IN THE SOFTWARE WILL MEET YOUR REQUIREMENTS OR THAT THE OPERATION OF THE SOFTWARE WILL BE ERROR FREE.**

    (c) This limited warranty gives you specific legal rights, and you may have other rights that vary from jurisdiction to jurisdiction.

6. **Remedies.**

    (a) HMI's entire liability and your exclusive remedy for defects in materials and workmanship shall be limited to replacement of the Software Media, which may be returned to HMI with a copy of your receipt at the following address: Software Media Fulfillment Department, Attn.: *Server-Side Flash: Scripts, Databases, and Dynamic Development*, Hungry Minds, Inc., 10475 Crosspoint Blvd., Indianapolis, IN 46256, or call 1-800-762-2974. Please allow four to six weeks for delivery. This Limited Warranty is void if failure of the Software Media has resulted from accident, abuse, or misapplication. Any replacement Software Media will be warranted for the remainder of the original warranty period or thirty (30) days, whichever is longer.

(b) In no event shall HMI or the author be liable for any damages whatsoever (including without limitation damages for loss of business profits, business interruption, loss of business information, or any other pecuniary loss) arising from the use of or inability to use the Book or the Software, even if HMI has been advised of the possibility of such damages.

(c) Because some jurisdictions do not allow the exclusion or limitation of liability for consequential or incidental damages, the above limitation or exclusion may not apply to you.

7. **U.S. Government Restricted Rights.** Use, duplication, or disclosure of the Software for or on behalf of the United States of America, its agencies and/or instrumentalities (the "U.S. Government") is subject to restrictions as stated in paragraph (c)(1)(ii) of the Rights in Technical Data and Computer Software clause of DFARS 252.227-7013, or subparagraphs (c) (1) and (2) of the Commercial Computer Software - Restricted Rights clause at FAR 52.227-19, and in similar clauses in the NASA FAR supplement, as applicable.

8. **General.** This Agreement constitutes the entire understanding of the parties and revokes and supersedes all prior agreements, oral or written, between them and may not be modified or amended except in a writing signed by both parties hereto that specifically refers to this Agreement. This Agreement shall take precedence over any other documents that may be in conflict herewith. If any one or more provisions contained in this Agreement are held by any court or tribunal to be invalid, illegal, or otherwise unenforceable, each and every other provision shall remain in full force and effect.

✦   ✦   ✦

GNU GENERAL PUBLIC LICENSE

Version 2, June 1991

Preamble

The licenses for most software are designed to take away your freedom to share and change it. By contrast, the GNU General Public License is intended to guarantee your freedom to share and change free software — to make sure the software is free for all its users. This General Public License applies to most of the Free Software Foundation's software and to any other program whose authors commit to using it. (Some other Free Software Foundation software is covered by the GNU Library General Public License instead.) You can apply it to your programs, too.

When we speak of free software, we are referring to freedom, not price. Our General Public Licenses are designed to make sure that you have the freedom to distribute copies of free software (and charge for this service if you wish), that you receive source code or can get it if you want it, that you can change the software or use pieces of it in new free programs; and that you know you can do these things.

To protect your rights, we need to make restrictions that forbid anyone to deny you these rights or to ask you to surrender the rights. These restrictions translate to certain responsibilities for you if you distribute copies of the software, or if you modify it.

For example, if you distribute copies of such a program, whether gratis or for a fee, you must give the recipients all the rights that you have. You must make sure that they, too, receive or can get the source code. And you must show them these terms so they know their rights.

We protect your rights with two steps: (1) copyright the software, and (2) offer you this license which gives you legal permission to copy, distribute and/or modify the software.

Also, for each author's protection and ours, we want to make certain that everyone understands that there is no warranty for this free software. If the software is modified by someone else and passed on, we want its recipients to know that what they have is not the original, so that any problems introduced by others will not reflect on the original authors' reputations.

Finally, any free program is threatened constantly by software patents. We wish to avoid the danger that redistributors of a free program will individually obtain patent licenses, in effect making the program proprietary. To prevent this, we have made it clear that any patent must be licensed for everyone's free use or not licensed at all.

The precise terms and conditions for copying, distribution and modification follow.

Terms and Conditions for Copying, Distribution, and Modification

0. This License applies to any program or other work which contains a notice placed by the copyright holder saying it may be distributed under the terms of this General Public License. The "Program", below, refers to any such program or work, and a "work based on the Program" means either the Program or any derivative work under copyright law: that is to say, a work containing the Program or a portion of it, either verbatim or with modifications and/or translated into another language. (Hereinafter, translation is included without limitation in the term "modification".) Each licensee is addressed as "you".

Activities other than copying, distribution and modification are not covered by this License; they are outside its scope. The act of running the Program is not restricted, and the output from the Program is covered only if its contents constitute a work based on the Program (independent of having been made by running the Program). Whether that is true depends on what the Program does.

1. You may copy and distribute verbatim copies of the Program's source code as you receive it, in any medium, provided that you conspicuously and appropriately publish on each copy an appropriate copyright notice and disclaimer of warranty; keep intact all the notices that refer to this License and to the absence of any warranty; and give any other recipients of the Program a copy of this License along with the Program.

You may charge a fee for the physical act of transferring a copy, and you may at your option offer warranty protection in exchange for a fee.

2. You may modify your copy or copies of the Program or any portion of it, thus forming a work based on the Program, and copy and distribute such modifications or work under the terms of Section 1 above, provided that you also meet all of these conditions:

a) You must cause the modified files to carry prominent notices stating that you changed the files and the date of any change.

b) You must cause any work that you distribute or publish, that in whole or in part contains or is derived from the Program or any part thereof, to be licensed as a whole at no charge to all third parties under the terms of this License.

c) If the modified program normally reads commands interactively when run, you must cause it, when started running for such interactive use in the most ordinary way, to print or display an announcement including an appropriate copyright notice and a notice that there is no warranty (or else, saying that you provide a warranty) and that users may redistribute the program under these conditions, and telling the user how to view a copy of this License. (Exception: if the Program itself is interactive but does not normally print such an announcement, your work based on the Program is not required to print an announcement.)

These requirements apply to the modified work as a whole. If identifiable sections of that work are not derived from the Program, and can be reasonably considered independent and separate works in themselves, then this License, and its terms, do not apply to those sections when you distribute them as separate works. But when you distribute the same sections as part of a whole which is a work based on the Program, the distribution of the whole must be on the terms of this License, whose permissions for other licensees extend to the entire whole, and thus to each and every part regardless of who wrote it.

Thus, it is not the intent of this section to claim rights or contest your rights to work written entirely by you; rather, the intent is to exercise the right to control the distribution of derivative or collective works based on the Program.

In addition, mere aggregation of another work not based on the Program with the Program (or with a work based on the Program) on a volume of a storage or distribution medium does not bring the other work under the scope of this License.

3. You may copy and distribute the Program (or a work based on it, under Section 2) in object code or executable form under the terms of Sections 1 and 2 above provided that you also do one of the following:

   a) Accompany it with the complete corresponding machine-readable source code, which must be distributed under the terms of Sections 1 and 2 above on a medium customarily used for software interchange; or,

   b) Accompany it with a written offer, valid for at least three years, to give any third party, for a charge no more than your cost of physically performing source distribution, a complete machine-readable copy of the corresponding source code, to be distributed under the terms of Sections 1 and 2 above on a medium customarily used for software interchange; or,

   c) Accompany it with the information you received as to the offer to distribute corresponding source code. (This alternative is allowed only for noncommercial distribution and only if you received the program in object code or executable form with such an offer, in accord with Subsection b above.)

The source code for a work means the preferred form of the work for making modifications to it. For an executable work, complete source code means all the source code for all modules it contains, plus any associated interface definition files, plus the scripts used to control compilation and installation of the executable. However, as a special exception, the source code distributed need not include anything that is normally distributed (in either source or binary form) with the major components (compiler, kernel, and so on) of the operating system on which the executable runs, unless that component itself accompanies the executable.

If distribution of executable or object code is made by offering access to copy from a designated place, then offering equivalent access to copy the source code from the same place counts as distribution of the source code, even though third parties are not compelled to copy the source along with the object code.

4. You may not copy, modify, sublicense, or distribute the Program except as expressly provided under this License. Any attempt otherwise to copy, modify, sublicense or distribute the Program is void, and will automatically terminate your rights under this License. However, parties who have received copies, or rights, from you under this License will not have their licenses terminated so long as such parties remain in full compliance.

5. You are not required to accept this License, since you have not signed it. However, nothing else grants you permission to modify or distribute the Program or its derivative works. These actions are prohibited by law if you do not accept this License. Therefore, by modifying or distributing the Program (or any work based on the Program), you indicate your acceptance of this License to do so, and all its terms and conditions for copying, distributing or modifying the Program or works based on it.

6. Each time you redistribute the Program (or any work based on the Program), the recipient automatically receives a license from the original licensor to copy, distribute or modify the Program subject to these terms and conditions. You may not impose any further restrictions on the recipients' exercise of the rights granted herein. You are not responsible for enforcing compliance by third parties to this License.

7. If, as a consequence of a court judgment or allegation of patent infringement or for any other reason (not limited to patent issues), conditions are imposed on you (whether by court order, agreement or otherwise) that contradict the conditions of this License, they do not excuse you from the conditions of this License. If you cannot distribute so as to satisfy simultaneously your obligations under this License and any other pertinent obligations, then as a consequence you may not distribute the Program at all. For example, if a patent license would not permit royalty-free redistribution of the Program by all those who receive copies directly or indirectly through you, then the only way you could satisfy both it and this License would be to refrain entirely from distribution of the Program.

   If any portion of this section is held invalid or unenforceable under any particular circumstance, the balance of the section is intended to apply and the section as a whole is intended to apply in other circumstances.

It is not the purpose of this section to induce you to infringe any patents or other property right claims or to contest validity of any such claims; this section has the sole purpose of protecting the integrity of the free software distribution system, which is implemented by public license practices. Many people have made generous contributions to the wide range of software distributed through that system in reliance on consistent application of that system; it is up to the author/donor to decide if he or she is willing to distribute software through any other system and a licensee cannot impose that choice.

This section is intended to make thoroughly clear what is believed to be a consequence of the rest of this License.

8. If the distribution and/or use of the Program is restricted in certain countries either by patents or by copyrighted interfaces, the original copyright holder who places the Program under this License may add an explicit geographical distribution limitation excluding those countries, so that distribution is permitted only in or among countries not thus excluded. In such case, this License incorporates the limitation as if written in the body of this License.

9. The Free Software Foundation may publish revised and/or new versions of the General Public License from time to time. Such new versions will be similar in spirit to the present version, but may differ in detail to address new problems or concerns.

Each version is given a distinguishing version number. If the Program specifies a version number of this License which applies to it and "any later version", you have the option of following the terms and conditions either of that version or of any later version published by the Free Software Foundation. If the Program does not specify a version number of this License, you may choose any version ever published by the Free Software Foundation.

10. If you wish to incorporate parts of the Program into other free programs whose distribution conditions are different, write to the author to ask for permission. For software which is copyrighted by the Free Software Foundation, write to the Free Software Foundation; we sometimes make exceptions for this. Our decision will be guided by the two goals of preserving the free status of all derivatives of our free software and of promoting the sharing and reuse of software generally.

No Warranty

11. BECAUSE THE PROGRAM IS LICENSED FREE OF CHARGE, THERE IS NO WARRANTY FOR THE PROGRAM, TO THE EXTENT PERMITTED BY APPLICABLE LAW. EXCEPT WHEN OTHERWISE STATED IN WRITING THE COPYRIGHT HOLDERS AND/OR OTHER PARTIES PROVIDE THE PROGRAM "AS IS" WITHOUT WARRANTY OF ANY KIND, EITHER EXPRESSED OR IMPLIED, INCLUDING, BUT NOT LIMITED TO, THE IMPLIED WARRANTIES OF MERCHANTABILITY AND FITNESS FOR A PARTICULAR PURPOSE. THE ENTIRE RISK AS TO THE QUALITY AND PERFORMANCE OF THE PROGRAM IS WITH YOU. SHOULD THE PROGRAM PROVE DEFECTIVE, YOU ASSUME THE COST OF ALL NECESSARY SERVICING, REPAIR OR CORRECTION.

12. IN NO EVENT UNLESS REQUIRED BY APPLICABLE LAW OR AGREED TO IN WRITING WILL ANY COPYRIGHT HOLDER, OR ANY OTHER PARTY WHO MAY MODIFY AND/OR REDISTRIBUTE THE PROGRAM AS PERMITTED ABOVE, BE LIABLE TO YOU FOR DAMAGES, INCLUDING ANY GENERAL, SPECIAL, INCIDENTAL OR CONSEQUENTIAL DAMAGES ARISING OUT OF THE USE OR INABILITY TO USE THE PROGRAM (INCLUDING BUT NOT LIMITED TO LOSS OF DATA OR DATA BEING RENDERED INACCURATE OR LOSSES SUSTAINED BY YOU OR THIRD PARTIES OR A FAILURE OF THE PROGRAM TO OPERATE WITH ANY OTHER PROGRAMS), EVEN IF SUCH HOLDER OR OTHER PARTY HAS BEEN ADVISED OF THE POSSIBILITY OF SUCH DAMAGES.

CD-ROM Installation Instructions

The *Server-Side Flash: Scripts, Databases, and Dynamic Development* CD-ROM contains a trial version of Flash, along with a number of other helpful programs.

Using the CD with Microsoft Windows

To install the items from the CD to your hard drive, follow these steps:

1. Insert the CD into your computer's CD-ROM drive.
2. A window appears with the following options:

   Install: Lets you install the software and author-created files from the CD

   Explore: Lets you view the contents of the CD in its directory structure.

   Exit: Closes the AutoRun window.

   Note: If you don't have AutoRun enabled, or if the AutoRun window doesn't appear, follow these steps to access the CD:

   1. Click Start ⇨ Run.
   2. In the dialog box that appears, type **d:\setup.exe**, where *d* is the letter of your CD-ROM drive. This opens the AutoRun window described in Step 2 above.
   3. Choose Install, Explore, or Exit from the menu.

Using the CD with the Macintosh OS

To install the items from the CD to your hard drive, follow these steps:

1. Insert the CD-ROM in the CD drive.
2. Double-click the CD icon that appears on the desktop.
3. Double-click any icons with Install indicated (for example, Install MySQL).
4. Follow the prompts for installation.
5. To view the source code for the chapters, drag the chapter folders to the desktop or another directory.
6. If your FLA files do not open in Flash when you double-click them, open Flash and then choose File ⇨ Open. In the Open dialog box, select All Files (*not* All Formats) from the List Files of Type pop-up menu at the bottom of the dialog box. Now you can open the files on your Macintosh. Use Save As to overwrite the original Flash files from the CD-ROM residing on your desktop.